Patrick Francis Moran

Historical Sketch of the Persecutions Suffered by the Catholics of Ireland

Under the Rule of Cromwell and the Puritans

Patrick Francis Moran

Historical Sketch of the Persecutions Suffered by the Catholics of Ireland
Under the Rule of Cromwell and the Puritans

ISBN/EAN: 9783744659536

Printed in Europe, USA, Canada, Australia, Japan

Cover: Foto ©ninafisch / pixelio.de

More available books at **www.hansebooks.com**

HISTORICAL SKETCH

OF THE

Persecutions suffered by the Catholics

OF

IRELAND

UNDER THE RULE OF

CROMWELL AND THE PURITANS

HISTORICAL SKETCH

OF THE

Persecutions suffered by the Catholics

OF

IRELAND

UNDER THE RULE OF

CROMWELL AND THE PURITANS

BY THE

MOST REV. PATRICK FRANCIS MORAN, D.D.

ARCHBISHOP OF SYDNEY.

DUBLIN
M. H. GILL AND SON
50 UPPER SACKVILLE STREET
1884

INTRODUCTION.

Our Divine Redeemer repeatedly forewarned his disciples that they would have to suffer trials and persecutions in this world, and to drink the bitter cup of affliction to the dregs. "You shall lament and weep," said He to them, "but the world shall rejoice; and you shall be made sorrowful, but your sorrow shall be changed into joy" (John, xvi. 20). "I send you as sheep in the midst of wolves. Beware of men. For they will deliver you up in councils, and they will scourge you in their synagogues" (Matt. x. 16). "And they will put you out of their synagogues: yea, the hour cometh, that whosoever killeth you will think that he doth a service to God" (John, xvi. 2).

What our Lord foretold was accomplished to the letter. The disciples and apostles whom he sent to overthrow idolatry and superstition, and to purify the earth from the corruption with which it was infected, instead of being welcomed as benefactors, were everywhere opposed by the perversity and malice of man;

and every human effort was made to impede the success of the heavenly mission in which they were engaged. Edicts were published prohibiting their teaching; their doctrines and practices were proscribed; and when they persevered in their work of charity and religion, they were cast into prison, or sent into exile, or condemned to suffer tortures and death. All the apostles merited the crown of martyrdom; and all sealed their testimony to the faith by shedding their blood in its defence, with the exception of St. John, who, having merited the honours of a martyr when thrown into a cauldron of boiling oil in Rome, was providentially preserved, in order to prevent the spread of errors which sprung up against the divinity of our Lord.

The immediate successors of the apostles, and the inheritors of their authority, together with innumerable multitudes of other Christians, had to undergo the same persecutions and afflictions as their masters in the faith, and to be made like unto the Author of our holy religion, who, for our salvation, became the reproach and outcast of the people, and satisfied for our sins by His agony on the cross.

The blood of the first Christians was shed in torrents in every country where the doctrines of their Divine Master was preached, and His Church established. They were reviled, calumniated, and excluded from the pale of society; they were proclaimed the enemies of the human race, and charged with crimes which they abhorred; they were sent into exile, condemned to work in the mines, subjected to unheard-of torments, and condemned to cruel deaths. But, like sheep among wolves, bearing everything for Christ's sake with patience and resignation, they edified the world by their virtues and good works; and their blood became the seed of new and fervent Christian congregations. The more they were cut down, the more did Christians increase; and, in the course of three centuries, by their prayers, their patience, and virtues, they conquered the whole Roman empire; the cross was raised triumphant on the Capitol and Pantheon, and the proudest monuments of Greece and Rome were consecrated to the worship of the true God.

What happened in the first centuries was repeated in the following ages: the Church was always a prey to persecution; but, notwithstanding all the efforts of her enemies, she increased and prospered; and the fertile vine, planted on Mount Calvary, and watered by the blood of our Redeemer, spread its branches to the remotest regions of the earth, affording protection and refreshment to those who had been languishing in darkness and error.

As nothing could be more edifying than the cons'ancy of Christians in professing their faith, and in protesting against the perverse doctrines and practices of idolatry —so it cannot be a matter of surprise that great care was taken to preserve the names of the martyrs, and to record the sufferings and circumstances of their death: the acts of those heroes of the cross were drawn up by faithful hands; their answers to the tyrants declaring how they adhered to the doctrines of Christ, and detested the worship of idols and false gods, were accurately reported; and their constancy and courage in encountering torments and death were minutely described. Even at the present day, through the simple narratives that have been preserved, everyone is familiar with the sufferings of a Laurence, a Vincent, a Sebastian, and an Ignatius, and with the superhuman courage of the Agneses, the Agathas, the Catherines, and other virgins, in whom we admire the triumph of that faith which raised them above the weakness of their age and sex.

To cherish the remembrance of those who shed their blood for the truth, and to obtain their prayers and protection at the throne of mercy, festivals were established on the day of their victory, pilgrimages were instituted to the spot where they suffered, their sacred remains were preserved with the greatest respect and veneration, and some of the noblest temples of the universe were erected to their memory.

This same anxiety to do honour to the heroes who laid down their lives in her defence, and to propose their glorious deeds to her children for their encouragement and instruction, has been manifested in every age by the Church. It is also in this spirit that our present venerable Pontiff, Pius IX.—who has himself suffered so much from the enemies of religion, and whose courage and constancy in defending the rights of the Holy See, have merited for him the admiration of mankind—determined to canonise several martyrs of Japan, proposing their heroic virtues to the imitation of the faithful in those times of irreligion and indifference, and securing new patrons for the Church in the period of trouble and confusion in which we live. The writers of a wicked and unbelieving press may scoff and sneer at the pious anxiety of the Church to extol the faith and courage of her children; they may call the glorious martyrs of Japan traitors and rebels to the government under which they lived, but all faithful Christians will receive with gratitude the decisions of the Pontiff, and avail themselves of the patronage and intercession of the Christain heroes whom he has placed on our altars.

Whilst it was ever the anxious desire of all Christians—and especially of the supreme pastors of the fold of Christ—to preserve the acts and the memories of the martyrs, it would be strange if the Catholic Church of Ireland were careless about her children who suffered for the faith, or allowed their memory to be forgotten. Far from her the charge of such neglect; she encouraged her children to fight a good fight, and to finish their course with honour; she preserved their memories with veneration, and repeated with gratitude and thankfulness the names of many who shed their blood in order to preserve the faith of St. Patrick pure and uncontaminated, and to transmit to posterity the blessings of true religion which they now enjoy.

Unfortunately, however, we have no regular acts of our martyrs, nor special histories of the unexampled sufferings which they had to undergo during the three centuries of persecution and penal laws through which our country has passed. Our forefathers acted like true soldiers of Christ, and preserved the faith, covering their country and religion with glory, and securing for themselves an imperishable crown; but the circumstances of the country were so deplorable, and war was carried on so actively against religion, that few written records could be kept, and the glorious achievements of so many Christian heroes were preserved only in the memory of the faithful. As an instance of the difficulty of preserving written documents, it may be mentioned that the martyred archbishop of Armagh, Dr. Plunket, in a letter to Rome, states that on a certain emergency, when an outburst of persecution was feared in Armagh, he had to burn all his foreign letters, even the brief of his consecration. "This happened," he adds, "last June twelvemonths (1670), on the vigil of St. John, when it was circulated by the Presbyterians that the Catholics had conspired to murder, on that night, all the Protestants."*

Under such circumstances it were vain to seek for a complete and consecutive history of the persecutions of our forefathers; and hence, although we have, on every side, proofs the most authentic of the fearful persecutions of the Irish Church, yet it is only in private letters and documents, referring but casually to such matters, that the sufferings of individuals are described. When all the materials of this kind shall have been examined and published, it is to be hoped that a history of the martyrs of the Irish Church may be written.

With a view of contributing to this desirable result, the following Historical Sketch of the Sufferings of the Catholics during the Puritan sway in Ireland has been compiled. In it are collected many extracts from unpublished contemporary writings, and from printed works rarely to be met with. The greater part of it was written as an introduction to the "Memoirs of Dr. Plunket," but it now appears in an enlarged form, and contains many new documents. It is hoped that it will aid the future historian in describing the virtues and

---

* See "Memoirs of Dr. Plunket" by Dr. Moran, p. 190.

constancy of Irish Catholics at a time when, because they were unanimous in defending their country, their king, and their religion,* they were sacrificed in thousands by sanguinary hordes of fanatical Puritans, and other furious enemies of the Catholic religion, who pretended to be lovers of liberty, but in reality were enemies of all rights, human and divine.

Though the practice of the Catholic Church and the experience of the past ages show that great edification is derived from the history of those who suffered for the truth—and the faithful are encouraged to constancy and patience in the time of trial, by remembering the sacrifices made by others in its defence—yet, there are some who seem to think otherwise, and who will not fail to condemn the historical sketch now presented to the public. Why, they say, do you occupy yourself with penal laws, and the confiscation of property, why record the massacre of so many Catholics? Such unpleasant recollections ought not to be preserved. It is the tendency of the present age to repair the wrongs of past times, and to heal the wounds then inflicted—why put yourself in opposition to so praiseworthy a spirit?—why not let past grievances be forgotten?

In reply, perhaps, it would not be out of place to examine whether the present age is so liberal as it pretends, or whether the Catholic religion, and the Catholic people in general—and the poor especially—have been treated in Ireland with such generosity as to make them forget all past grievances. It might also be asked whether

---

* The motto of the Council of Kilkenny was—" Pro Deo, Rege et Patria, Hibernia unanimis." V. Hibernia Dom., p. 876.

the spirit of former times is not still active, and still tending to obtain, by indirect and occult means, the same ends which were so long sought for by open persecution. But passing over such questions, we may be allowed to observe that motives of prudence or feelings of delicacy did not prevent the early Christian writers from recording innumerable deeds of pagan cruelty, and describing the noble constancy and courage of their persecuted brethren. Every Christian felt that the propagation or preservation of his religion in the midst of trials and sufferings, was a proof of the truth of Christ's promise to be with his Church in all ages, and the fear of displeasing pagans, or of exciting the feelings of the sufferers against their oppressors, was not considered a sufficient ground for passing over in silence great historical facts, both useful and edifying.

Why should not we act in the same way? for, do not the sufferings of past times supply us with new illustrations of the power of Christian faith, and with motives of thankfulness and gratitude to God for having preserved our religion? The struggle in which our predecessors in the faith were engaged was a very unequal one: they were so weak that, humanly speaking, they could not have resisted the powers that were brought to bear on them for their destruction; yet, through the mercy of God, their poverty was more powerful than the wealth of others, and in their weakness they preserved the most precious of all treasures, their faith, and transmitted it to their posterity, in whom it is now producing an abundance of fruit in their virtues and good works, and in the institutions with which they are covering the land. And here may we not say, with the apostle :—" The foolish things of the world hath God chosen that he may confound the wise, and the weak things of the world hath God chosen that he may confound the strong. . . . That no flesh should glory in his sight." (1 Cor. i.)

Nor is it to be supposed that the memory of past grievances always excites feelings of hatred and rancour. Where the sufferings of true Christians are related, a contrary effect is produced. Their patience and resignation to the holy will of God, the prayers they poured out, like our Divine Redeemer on the cross, for their persecutors, serve to make us patient and obedient, and to act in a spirit of charity and forbearance, even towards those who afflict and persecute us.

Besides, the condition of Ireland is quite unintelligible, unless we keep before us the history of the past. Irish Catholics are frequently taunted with the want of a Catholic literature, and with the rags and poverty of their country. We are even told that our ignorance and our poverty are proofs of the demoralizing effects of our holy religion. Look to the condition of Protestants and Presbyterians : they are rich and flourishing ; they have numerous schools and colleges richly endowed; travelling through the country you cannot but observe the superior wealth and comfort of the Protestant or Presbyterian occupier of the soil—all this difference is a proof of the advantages of Protestantism.

Statements of this kind are made every day : they are repeated in almost all the little anti-Catholic tracts so widely circulated at present. To answer such charges it is necessary to go back to the penal laws, and to past persecutions which fully explain the cause of the anomalous position of Ireland. If Catholics were behind others in education and intellectual acquirements—if they had not so many colleges or literary institutions—the reason was, that Catholic education was prohibited in the country, and all Catholic schools and places of instruction were confiscated and handed over to Protestants. A Catholic was not allowed to teach or to keep school at home, and laws were enacted to prevent him from sending his children to be educated abroad. As all this was done by the Protestant parliaments of England and Ireland, is it meet that the evils thus produced should be charged to Catholics, the sufferers in the case? But though education was so strictly prohibited, the Catholics still preserved a thirst for knowledge, they sought for it in foreign lands; and, since the relaxation of the penal laws, they have covered the country with schools, colleges, and other educational establishments. Thus, a reference to past times shows who were the real friends, and who the enemies of progress and knowledge.

In regard to the poverty of the Catholic portion of the Irish people, it is very easy to explain its origin. The Catholics were persecuted for their religion, and rather than consent to renounce their God and their faith, they submitted to the confiscation of their property, to exile, and death. A great part of Ireland was confiscated several times; the property and the estates of Catholics were handed over to Protestants; the rich lands, the fertile plains, and all places of commerce, were reserved for those who had been found ready to apostatize at the bidding of the ruling powers. Adventurers from England, oftentimes of the lowest class and most degraded character, and covenanters and followers of John Knox, from Scotland, were enriched with the property of the old inhabitants of the country who had remained faithful to the religion of their fathers. Special privileges were granted to the towns and seaports occupied by Protestants and Presbyterians; their trade and manufactories, especially in Ulster, were encouraged, and everything was done to promote their interests, whilst the worst arts were employed to ruin the industry or to occasion the beggary or total extermination of the original inhabitants. Indeed, it was considered a great favour to allow Catholics to live in the bogs and mountains; and even, when the bogs were reclaimed, they were driven from them, and ordered to seek for refuge in more desolate places. Under such circumstances, we cannot be surprised that the Catholics of Ireland should have been reduced to poverty, but it must be a matter of amazement that they were at all, able to preserve their existence in the kingdom.

However, the energy of the Irish race was not to be broken down by confiscation and penal laws; notwithstanding the spoliation and sufferings to which they had been subjected, they displayed a persevering industry, and many of them, overcoming all obstacles, have had their energy rewarded by the acquirement of wealth and station. Yet, as it has been said, the general condition of the country, and the poverty of so many of its Catholic inhabitants, as well as the wealth and prosperity of many Protestants, cannot be explained without continual reference to the history of the past, and showing how the former were robbed and persecuted in order to enrich the latter.

In conclusion, it appears to us evident that it is most useful and edifying, and conformable to the practices of the Catholic Church, to preserve and publish the records of those who suffered for their faith. Their patience and humility edify us, and teach us to be submissive and obedient in the time of trial and affliction; their courage and constancy show us how firmly we ought to be attached to our faith; their prayers for their enemies afford us a lesson of forbearance and charity, and the success with which they fought the good fight, and merited an imperishable crown, must excite our gratitude to heaven, and at the same time convince us that our Faith is " the victory which overcometh the world."

Since this "Historical Sketch" was first published several valuable works have appeared illustrating the period to which it refers, and we have made use of some of them at almost every page. To avoid the necessity of repeated reference, it may suffice to here insert the titles of the works in full :—

"The Cromwellian Settlement of Ireland." By John P. Prendergast, Barrister-at-Law (Second Edition) London: Longmans, 1870.

"Aphorismical Discovery of Treasonable Faction, i. e , A Contemporary History of Affairs in Ireland from 1641 to 1652." Edited by John T. Gilbert. In three Volumes. Dublin : for the Irish Archæological Society, 1879.

"History of the Irish Confederation and the War in Ireland, 1641-1643." By Richard Bellings. Edited by John T. Gilbert. In two Volumes. Dublin : Gill and Son, 1882.

"Cromwell in Ireland." By Rev. Denis Murphy, S.J. Dublin: Gill and Son, 1883.

"Collections Relating to the Dioceses of Kildare and Leighlin." By Rev. M. Comerford, P.P. Dublin: Duffy, 1883.

"Transactions of the Ossory Archæological Society." Kilkenny: Vol. the First, 1879; Vol. the Second, 1883.

"The Rise and Fall of the Irish Franciscan Monasteries, and Memoirs of the Irish Hierarchy in the Seventeenth Century." By Rev. C. P. Meehan. Fifth Edition. Dublin: Duffy, 1877.

"Pii Antistitis Icon; or, The Life and Death of the Most Rev. Francis Kirwan, Bishop of Killala." Edited by Rev. C. P. Meehan. Second Edition. Dublin: Duffy, 1884.

HISTORICAL SKETCH

OF

The Persecutions Suffered by the Catholics of Ireland,

UNDER THE RULE OF

CROMWELL AND THE PURITANS.

General Proscription of the Irish Catholics by the Puritans.

1. Lord Clarendon and others explain the designs of the Puritans to exterminate the Catholics.—2. Acts of Parliament and Orders of the Lords Justices.—3. Fierce spirit of Puritan Writers.—4. Testimony of Various Historians.—5. Conduct of Tichbourne, Sir William Cole, Sir Charles Coote, &c.—6. Fate of Sir Simon Harcourt and Sir Charles Coote.—7. Some instances of barbarous cruelty.—8. Dr. John Lynch describes the sufferings of Catholics.—9. Division of this Sketch.

1. THE persecution carried on by the Puritan Parliament and Cromwell against the Catholics of Ireland has scarcely a parallel in the history of the Church. Without a special providence of God watching over His children, whom He was chastising in His mercy, the Catholic faith could not have been preserved in so

frightful and so trying an ordeal. It is the mercy of the Lord that we have not been consumed. No sooner had the Puritan faction become predominant in England, having dethroned their sovereign, and imbrued their hands in his blood, than they resolved on the utter extermination of the Irish people, who had been true to Cæsar and to God, and they did not hesitate to declare that thus alone could Catholicity be rooted out from our island. In fact, the extermination of the Irish Catholics became a leading feature in their political programme. "The Parliament party," writes Lord Clarendon, "had grounded their own authority and strength upon such foundations as were inconsistent with any toleration of the Roman Catholic religion, and even with any humanity to the Irish nation—and more especially to those of the old native extraction, the whole race whereof they had upon the matter sworn to extirpate" (History, i. 215). Dr. John Lynch in *Cambrensis Eversus* corroborates this statement (vol. iii, pp. 85-90), and adds: "Three thousand Irish Puritans signed a document in which they earnestly insisted either that the Catholic religion should be abolished in Ireland, or that the Irish race should be extirpated." And, page 99, he writes that the Irish Puritans "rioted in the promiscuous slaughter of women, old men, and children; and the English auxiliaries openly avowed that they would strain every nerve to extirpate, without mercy, the Irish race." The contemporary author of the "Aphorismical Discovery" published for the I. A. S. by Gilbert, also states that "it was blazed abroad by the best note of Protestants, that all Ireland by that time twelvemonth must either go to church, be executed, or endure banishment or exile" (i. 12) : and the Irish Bishops, in an official document in 1650, attest the cruelty of the Puritans " whose practice daily is, and hath been, to extirpate the Catholic Religion and the professors thereof, to the loss and profanation of churches, altars, use of sacraments, and everything that is dear to a Catholic, as also the shedding of Prelates' blood even to death, and contrary to the public faith, and the daily persecution of Priests, friars, nuns, and their imprisonment, and banishment by public proclamation."

2. As early as the 8th of December, 1641, an act was passed in Parliament to the effect that the Catholic religion should never be tolerated in Ireland ;* and in order to carry this act into execution, the Lords Justices issued the following order to the commander of the Irish forces : " It is resolved, that it is fit his Lordship do endeavour, with his Majesty's forces, to slay and destroy all the said rebels, and their adherents and relievers, by all the ways and means he may ; and burn, destroy, spoil, waste, consume, and demolish all the places, towns, and houses where the said rebels are or have been relieved and harboured, and all the hay and corn there, and kill and destroy all the men there inhabiting able to bear arms."

All the subsequent acts of Parliament and orders of the Lords Justices are dictated in the same sanguinary strain. As an instance we may cite the enactment by the Lords and Commons of England, on 24th October,

---

* "Rushworth's Collections," p. 455.

1644: "*that no quarter shall be given to any Irishman, or to any papist born in Ireland.*"

3. The writers of the party were animated by the same exterminating spirit; and, though the soul shudders at the recital, we shall present an extract from one of the political pamphlets of the period, that the reader may fully appreciate the virulence of Puritan hatred against the Catholics of Ireland: "I beg upon my hands and knees that the expedition against them may be undertaken whilst the hearts and hands of our soldiery are hot, to whom I will be bold to say, briefly: 'happy is he that shall reward them as they have served us; and cursed is he that shall do the work of the Lord negligently.' Cursed be he that holdeth back his sword from blood; yea, cursed be he that maketh not his sword stark drunk with Irish blood—that maketh them not heaps upon heaps, and their country a dwelling-place for dragons, an astonishment to nations. Let not that eye look for pity, nor that hand be spared that pities or spares them; and let him be accursed that curseth them not bitterly."

4. It would be tedious to enter into full details of the cruel extermination by which the army in Ireland sought to carry into effect the desires of their English masters. The whole history of their sanguinary career may be well summed up in the words of the Protestant historian, Borlase, "the orders of Parliament were excellently well executed" (Hist. of Reb., page 62). Leland and Warner refer to the letters of the Lords Justices themselves for the fact that the soldiers "slew all persons promiscuously, not sparing even the women." And Dr. Nalson, another Protestant historian, appeals

to the testimony of officers who served in the Parliamentary army, "that no manner of compassion or discrimination was shown either to age or sex." Lord Ossory, too, himself a bitter enemy of the Catholics, in a letter to Ormonde, informs him how the Puritan Lord President of Munster " caused innocent and guilty to be alike executed," and commemorates some instances of barbaric cruelty for which we would seek in vain a parallel in the fiercest persecutions of paganism.

At the first outbreak of the revolution the Lords Justices were in great alarm, but when they discovered that the Irish were without arms, " they took courage," says a contemporary writer, "and rushing out with horse and foot completely armed, they slew man, woman, and child, as they came under their lash, as well those that held the plough as the pike, the goad as the gun. Thousands were thus killed; and the Lords Justices were known not to favour any officer that did not, upon his return from these birdings (as they called them) give a good account of their sport, though their game was unarmed men, and too often women and children" (Ap. Prendergast, p. 56).

5. One of their officers, named Tichbourne, who commanded in Dundalk in 1642, was able to boast that in his district " there was neither man nor beast to be found in sixteen miles between the two towns of Drogheda and Dundalk, nor on the other side of Dundalk, in the county of Monaghan, nearer than Carrickmacross."*

* Ap. Curry, p. 169, and *Vindiciæ*, p. 417. *Cambrensis Eversus*, vol. iii., p. 97, states that the Puritans of the North shot down the Catholics as wild beasts, and made it their special delight "*to imbrue their swords in the heart's blood of all the male children.*"

A Protestant dignitary, Dean Bernard, describing this scene of desolation wrote : "By the death of so many men about us, having their houses and all their provisions either burnt or drawn hither, the dogs only surviving are found very usually feeding upon their masters, which taste of man's flesh made it very dangerous for the passengers in the roads, who have been often set upon by these mastiffs, till we were careful to kill them also."

Another officer, Sir William Cole, who commanded in a few counties of the North, slew, in a short period, as Borlase informs us, together with 2,400 swordsmen, "seven thousand of the vulgar sort" (Hist., p. 112). And the same historian adds (p. 113) that "after this manner did the English fight in the other quarters."

When in May, 1642, the Earl of Clanrickard induced the citizens of Galway to submit, and took them under the king's protection, he received a reprimand from the Lords Justices, declaring that he should have persecuted them "with fire and sword." Moreover, to prevent like clemency for the future, "they issued a general order to the commanders of all garrisons, not to presume to hold any correspondence or treaty with any of the Irish papists dwelling or residing in any place near or about their garrisons, or to give protection, immunity, or dispensation from spoil, burning, or other prosecution of war to any of them, but to persecute all such rebels with fire and sword, according to former commands and proclamations in that behalf."

Sir Charles Coote was one of the leading champions of Puritanism in Ireland, and of him in particular, and his associate officers, M'Geoghegan writes : " There were no exceptions in the barbarous orders which they gave to their soldiery, when letting them loose to make their bloody hunts amongst the Irish Catholics." Yet far was the Parliament from reproving the conduct of this sanguinary monster; and when he was slain at Trim, in April, 1642, we are informed by Borlase that "floods of English tears accompanied him to the grave" (Hist. page 104).

One instance of his cruelty will for the present suffice. He received an order from the Council in Dublin, in 1641, to proceed to the county Wicklow, against the O'Byrnes. "His troops killed all that came in their way, both man, woman, and child; nay, they would murder women, in their very travail." One of his troopers carried on the point of his spear the head of a little babe which he cut off, after killing the poor mother, "which Coote observing, said that he was mightly pleased with many such frolicks." (*Aphoris. Discov.*, vol. 1. p. 13.) The younger Sir Charles Coote rivalled his father in those deeds of cruelty. He commanded the army in Ulster at the time of the death of Owen Roe O'Neill. The author of the *Alithinologia* attests that as soon as this Irish leader, the only check to his ravages, was removed, he acted like another Attila, devastating the provinces of Ulster and Connaught, and spreading desolation everywhere, "massacring the inhabitants, destroying the sacred edifices, and putting to death the clergy" (*vastationem agris, hominibus cædem, templis ruinam, Ecclesiasticis exterminium*), p. 71.

6. Sir Simon Harcourt, another of the military leaders, was no less remarkable for barbarity and hatred of the Church. He gave orders for the indiscriminate slaughter

of the Irish, not even the infirm and decrepit or the women and children were to be exempted from this cruelty. His career however was soon brought to an untimely close. A few days after setting out on his campaign he summoned a castle near Dublin belonging to Mr. Walsh to surrender, and this being refused, he declared that the castle should be razed to the ground. When a large piece of ordnance was levelled against the castle, he wished himself to see that it was properly aimed, and in the act of sighting it, was shot dead by one of the nine men who alone formed the garrison. The troops at once abandoned the siege of the castle, and returned to Dublin.

The supplement to the *Alithinologia* states that, at Trim, Sir Charles Coote the elder caused the statues of SS. Peter and Paul, which were held in great veneration, to be hewn in pieces, and thrown into the fire. A very ancient image of our Blessed Lady, engraven in wood, was also venerated there. Sir Charles ordered it to be brought to Mr. Lawrence Hammond's house, at which he stopped. It, too, was accordingly hewn in pieces and put into the fire, at which he sat. Whilst he was yet seated there, it was announced that a body of Irish troops was at hand, and before he could quit the spot he was shot dead (*Aphorism. Discov.* i. 32).

7. When the Government and chief officers were so bent on cruelty, we can no longer be surprised at individual deeds of barbarity perpetrated by the soldiery on the defenceless inhabitants; it is thus we find them deliberately knocking out the children's brains against the walls at Clonakilty, county Cork; we find them turning the Irish into their houses, to

which they then set fire, as in Bantry, to enjoy the screams and agony of their victims; we find them, at Bandon Bridge and Newry, tying the Catholics back to back, and casting them from the battlements of the bridge, to perish in the river beneath. In the Commons' Journals of 1644 (vol. iii, p. 517) it is recorded that Captain Swanley having captured a vessel at sea, and thrown seventy individuals overboard, *because they were Irish*, was summoned to the bar of the House of Commons, " and had thanks there given him for his good service, and a chain of gold of £200 value." And Lord Clarendon (ii. 478) writes, that this was not an exceptional case; but, on the contrary, with officers of the navy, "it was a rule, whenever they made Irish prisoners, to bind them back to back, and cast them overboard."

One of the first acts of the Irish Confederates was to forward an address of loyalty to the king, in which they declared that before appealing to arms " they had, with all submission, addressed themselves, by petition, to the Lords Justices and Council, for a timely remedy against the then growing evils, but that therein they had found, instead of a salve for their wounds, oil poured into the fire of their discontents." They add that they had with a firm hand repressed the attempts of those who appeared bent on plundering the Puritans, " though the measures offered to the Catholic natives here, in the inhuman murdering of old decrepit people in their beds, women in the straw, and children of eight days old; burning of houses, and robbing of all kinds of persons, without distinction of friend from foe, and digging up of graves, and then burning the dead bodies of our ancestors, have not deserved that justice from us." And Carte, in his "Life of Ormonde," writes: "That they did not exaggerate in this particular, is plain from a letter of Lord Clanrickard's, who says, that while he was at Tyrellan, in treaty with Lord Forbes, the commander of a Parliament ship-of-war, though Lord Ranelagh, President of Connaught, was then in the fort of Galway, he saw the country on fire, his tenants' houses and goods burnt, and four or five poor innocent creatures, men, women, and children, inhumanly murdered by Forbes's soldiers, who, having taken possession of Lady's Church in Galway, the ancient burying-place of the town, did, upon their departure, not only deface it, but digged up the graves and burnt the coffins and bones of those that were buried there." (Carte's "Ormonde," vol. iii. p. 109.)

8. Dr. John Lynch, Archdeacon of Tuam, and for some time Vicar-Apostolic of Killala, was eye-witness of many of these outrages, and in his invaluable work entitled "Cambrensis Eversus" thus depicts the excess of Cromwellian barbarity :—"All the cruelty inflicted on the city of Rome by Nero and Attila, by the Greeks on Troy, by the Moors on Spain, or by Vespasian on Jerusalem—all has been inflicted on Ireland by the Puritans. Nothing but that pathetical lamentation of Jeremias can appropriately describe her state—'With desolation is the whole land laid desolate; our adversaries are our lords, our enemies are enriched; the enemy hath put out his hand to all our desirable things; . . . our persecutors are swifter than the eagles of the air; they pursue on the mountains, and lie in wait for us in the wildernesses; we have found no rest; our

cities are captured, our gates broken down, our priests sigh, our virgins are in affliction.' From Ireland all her beauty is departed; they that were fed delicately have died in the streets; they that were brought up in scarlet have embraced the dung; when her people fell there was no helper. All that has ever been devised by the ingenuity of most cruel tyrants, either in unparalleled ignominy and degradation, or in the savage and excruciating corporal torture, or in all that could strike terror into the firmest soul—all has been poured out on Ireland by the Puritans. They plundered our cities, destroyed our churches, laid waste our lands, expelled citizens from their cities, nobles from their palaces, and all the natives from their homes; nay, they forbade countless numbers of men even to enjoy the sight of their native country, or to breathe the air which they had inhaled at the moment of their birth. . . . Some of our priests they put in chains and dungeons—that was the most lenient punishment;—others they tortured with stakes and strapadoes; some were shot to death, others hanged or strangled. From the priests they turned their fury against all sacred things and places consecrated to the worship of God, which were first sacrilegiously pillaged, then all the paintings and images were destroyed, the statues were cloven in pieces with the axe, and either thrown into the flames or consigned to stables and brothels. Those temples where the priest performed his sacred functions, where the sacred canticles of the Church ravished the ears of the faithful, and sacred orators encouraged the people to piety by their ceaseless exhortations, where the people often poured forth their prayers to God, and devoutly attended all the functions and mysteries of religion: these now resound with the yells of drunkards, the neighing of horses, the barking of dogs, the clamours of quarrelsome soldiers, and the howling of women. Within them we now see taverns instead of altars, blasphemy for prayers, the cursing of heretics instead of pious and orthodox sermons, obscenity and impurities instead of chaste conferences" (vol. iii. p. 181).

Division of the present Historical Sketch.

9. To proceed with order in detailing the progress of this dire persecution of the Catholics by the Puritans we shall—

First, see the violence with which it raged in the chief districts in Ireland, down to the year 1652;

In the second part we shall examine the penal laws subsequently enacted by the Cromwellians for the avowed purpose of rooting out Catholicity from this "Island of Saints;"

And in the third part we shall detail some particular instances of the persecution, and trace its course even after the restoration of Charles II.

The matters referred to must be treated very briefly: but the extracts from contemporaneous writers, here produced, will show how intense were the sufferings of our forefathers, and how generously they fought the good fight, and preserved their faith, the most noble of all treasures, though they were stripped of all the earthly property they possessed. To the laws of this period may well be applied the words with which the illustrious Edmond Burke described the penal enactment of a later time:—"The code against the Roman Catholics was a machine of wise and elaborate contrivance; and as well fitted for the oppression, impoverishment, and degradation of a people, and the debasement in them of human nature, as ever proceeded from the perverted ingenuity of man."

PART THE FIRST.

PERSECUTION OF THE CATHOLICS IN THE PRINCIPAL DISTRICTS OF IRELAND.

CHAPTER I.

Sufferings of the Catholics in Dublin.

1. Proclamation of 1641 prohibiting the Catholic Religion in Dublin; Letter of a Capuchin.—2. Sufferings of Fathers Caghwell and Fitzsimon and other Jesuits.—3. Doings of Sir Charles Coote.—4. Extracts from Dr. Talbot's Work, "The Politician's Catechism."—5. From Dr. Lynch.—6. Heroism of the Clergy of Dublin.—7. All Catholics banished from Dublin in 1647—8. The Plague in 1650.—9. Fresh Persecutions and Constancy of the Catholics in Dublin.—10. Orders repeatedly issued banishing Catholics from the City; Number of Catholics according to Dr. Dempsey.

1. Dublin, being the seat of Government, was the first city that experienced the sad effects of the Puritan persecution. Before the close of 1641 a proclamation was published, interdicting there the exercise of the Catholic religion; a rigorous search was made to discover the priests and religious, and no fewer than forty of them being arrested, they were, for some time,

treated with great rigour in prison, and then transported to the Continent. An extract from a letter addressed to his superior in Rome, on the 12th July, 1642, by a Capuchin father, who was sent into exile, will convey some idea of the storm thus let loose against the Catholics: "Whithersoever the enemy penetrates, everything is destroyed by fire and sword; none are spared, not even the infant at its mother's breast, for their desire is to wholly extirpate the Irish race. In Dublin our order, as also the other religious bodies, had a residence, and a beautifully ornamented chapel, in which we publicly, and in our habit, performed the sacred ceremonies; but no sooner had the soldiers arrived from England, than they furiously rushed everywhere, profaned our chapels, overturned our altars, broke to pieces the sacred images, trampling them under foot and consigning them to the flames; our residences were plundered, the priests were everywhere sought for, and many, amongst whom myself and companion, were captured and cast into prison. . . . We were twenty in number in prison, and the Lords Justices at first resolved on our execution, but through the influence of some members of the council, we were transported to France. The masters of the two vessels into which we were cast, received private instructions to throw us into the sea, but they refused to commit this horrid crime. Oh, would to God that we had been worthy to be led to the scaffold, or thus drowned for the faith!"*

2. A narrative of the Jesuit missionaries in Ireland,

---

* Lett. of Fr. Nicholas, superior of the Capuchins of Dublin: from Poitiers, 12 July, 1642.

written about the same time, thus briefly sketches the sufferings endured by the members of that Order: "We were persecuted, and dispersed, and despoiled of all our goods; some, too, were cast into prison, and others were sent into exile."* Amongst the fathers of the society in Dublin, was F. Henry Caghwell, renowned for his learning and zeal: "being confined to his bed by sickness, he was apprehended by the soldiers and hurried to the public square; as he was unable to walk, or even to stand, he was placed in a chair, more for mockery than for ease, and subjected to the derision and cruel insults of the soldiery; he was then beaten with cudgels and thrown into the ship with the others for France." Another holy priest, whose name is well-known in connection with our suffering Church, Father Henry Fitzsimon, though in his eightieth year, "was obliged with the other Catholics to fly from Dublin and seek safety in the mountainous districts. The winter had set in with unusual severity, yet he had to undertake the difficult journey on foot, and to wander stealthily through the woods and mountains. He passed the whole winter in the midst of a bog, being thus secured from the Puritan cavalry. His cabin being only half-covered, he was exposed to the wind and rain; his bed was of straw, always moist from the rain above, or from the stagnant waters of the bog beneath. Yet the good priest was ever joyous, and only intent on consoling those who

* Missio Soc. Jes. usque ad an. 1655. The original text of these Historical Narratives has been printed in *Spicilegium Ossoriense*, vol. i. (1874), and vol. ii. (1878): being written at the very time of the events which they commemorate, they are invaluable in illustrating the history of this period.

were sharers of his sufferings. The children he instructed in the catechism, the sacrament of penance he administered to all that approached. He could not, however, long endure the privations of that painful state and was therefore obliged to embark for the continent, where he soon expired, full of merits, as he was of years."[*] The letters of the Jesuit Fathers give some further details. F. Robert Nugent, a near relative of Inchiquin, writes to Rome on the 24th of March, 1642: "No human pen could describe the miseries of this kingdom; nothing is seen or heard of but depredations, murders of men, women, and children; and burning of property, and utter ruin of families and their homes. . . . Here nothing goes on but burning and slaughter, fire and sword." Again, on the 10th of November, the same year he writes: "Up to last May nothing was more familiar to us than the promiscuous murders of innocent Catholics of every sex, rank, and age; for the Puritans were well armed and furious—they burned villages, hamlets, whole towns, and the mansions and castles of the nobles and gentlemen; they set fire to the barns and cornfields; and they were determined to destroy all Irishmen, and leave no trace of them. But, thanks be to God, Owen O'Neill's arrival in the North has put a stop to their work. . . . Several religious and other clergymen have been put to death already; none of ours has yet received that honour. FF. Quin, Pursell, and Lattin, in spite of all dangers, remain in Dublin to help the persecuted Catholics. F. Quin

---

[*] Relatio rerum quarumdam notabilium quæ contigerunt in Hibernia ab anno 1641, usque ad an. 1650.

especially assumes all kinds of disguises with success—he turns out as a military man, a gentleman at large, a peasant, &c." In February, 1643, he further states that all the Jesuits had left Dublin "except F. Quin, who works day and night among the faithful, and F. Pursell who is ill and lying hid; while F. Lattin is kept in the closest custody in a horrible prison." F. Dillon who in 1641 was the Superior of the Jesuits in Dublin, also writes on the 3rd of August, 1643: "Out of the sixteen or seventeen Fathers of our Dublin Residence, only three remain in that city. F. Caghwell was paralysed and could not be moved without danger to his life. The Puritans cruelly banished him to France, and he has since died, a true confessor of the Faith. Another Father (F. Lattin) while he attended the sick, was captured and imprisoned; a third (F. Pursell) is sick, and keeps within doors, and renders the service of his ministry to all who go to him. As I could not be of any help in Dublin, I have been sent to Galway, the most western corner of Ireland and perhaps of Europe. Galway is a small, but populous, neat, and well-built town, constructed of unpolished marble. Our house is rather near the Puritan fort, and opposite to it; and as our enemies are generously attentive to us, they send us sometimes iron balls that weigh thirty-two pounds, and have knocked down a great part of our roof."

3. Sir Charles Coote, senior, of whom we have spoken in the preceding chapter, was appointed by the Lords Justices to the command of the troops in Dublin and its immediate neighbourhood. He was so violent in his fury that as a rule he was quite beside himself with rage,

and he appeared to those about him to enjoy the use of his reason only at rare lucid intervals. When summoned before the Council in Dublin to receive the command of the troops, he insisted on taking the oath in pagan fashion, putting his right hand on a naked sword and musket, which were placed on the table before him, and he swore that he would not desist from prosecuting the war until all the Irish were cut off "*se nunquam, nisi deletis Hibernis, finem pugnandi facturum*" (*Alithinologia*). In his excursions in the counties of Dublin and Wicklow, the aged, and helpless, and infirm, unable to save themselves by flight, were massacred in cold blood. When the poor people were found to have concealed themselves in the firs and brushwood, the soldiers used to form a cordon all around, and then to set fire to the firs, putting all to death with savage delight. The officers declared that thus to pursue the Irish was the same sport and amusement to them as to hunt the wild beasts *hisce truculentiis patrandis perinde se oblectari ac si venando feras persequerentur* (*Ibid.*). The troops that were most successful in the work of slaughter received the congratulations of the Lords Justices, whilst those who put only a few to death were reprehended for their remissness. Parsons, one of the Lords Justices, gave instructions to the military that no attention was to be paid to the certificates of loyalty or permissions to remain in the city accorded to privileged individuals: all were to be treated alike. Indeed the Lords Deputies from the very outset of the disturbances did not conceal their joy and unspeakable gratification that the Irish Catholics were driven to take up arms, and they openly avowed their wish that for every one who had already joined the movement, 20,000 others would follow suit, nor could any more agreeable message be brought to them than that some wealthy nobleman had quitted the city, for he was at once pronounced guilty of treason and his goods and property forthwith became their booty to be distributed among their friends and dependents.

4. A rare work, entitled "The Politician's Catechism," published in 1658, by Father Peter Talbot, afterwards so illustrious as Archbishop of Dublin, gives precious details regarding the barbarous deeds of cruelty perpetrated by the Puritan soldiery when carrying out the orders of the Lords Justices. In chapter the 10th, we read: " Witness their marches about Dublin, where the inhabitants were all of English extraction, and spoke no other language but the ancient Saxon. There are very few of that once populous country called Fingal left alive—all perished by fire and sword, being a most innocent people, and having nothing Irishlike in them but the Catholic religion. In the march of the Protestant army to the county of Wicklow, man, woman, and child was killed; a gentlewoman, big with child, was hanged at the arch of a bridge, and the poor Catholic that guided the army, for reward of his service at parting, being commanded to blow into a pistol, was shot therewith into the mouth, though there had been no murder committed on the Protestants in that county. In another march into the same shire, one Master *Comain*, an aged gentleman, who never bore arms, was roasted alive by one Captain Gines (Guinness); yea they murdered all that came in their way from within two miles of Dublin.

"In a march into the county of Kildare, in or about February, 1642, some of the officers went into Mrs. Eustace of Cradogston's house, a sister to Sir William Talbot, of eighty years of age, who being unable to shun them, entertained them with meat and drink; after dinner, herself and another old gentlewoman, and a girl of eight years of age, were murdered by the said Protestant officers.

"Walter Evers, Esq., aged and sickly, and for a long time before the war bedridden, being carried by his servants in a litter to shun the fury of the army, was taken and hanged. In Westmeath, Master Ganley, a gentleman of good estate, having a protection, and showing it, hoping thereby to save his goods, lost his life: having his protection laid on his breast he was shot through it, to try whether it was proof. Master Thomas Talbot, a gentleman of ninety years of age, and a great servitor in Queen Elizabeth's wars in Ireland having a protection, also was murdered.

"Seven or eight hundred women and children, ploughmen and labourers, were burned and murdered in a day in the King's land (a tract within seven miles of Dublin), where neither murder nor pillage had been committed on the Protestants. Whensoever the army went abroad, the poor country people did betake themselves to the furze, where the Protestant officers did besiege them, and set the furze on fire: such as shunned and escaped that element were killed by the besieging army, and this they termed a *hunting*, sporting themselves with the blood of innocents. These barbarous and savage cruelties were ordinary, not only near Dublin, but in all other parts of the kingdom, wheresoever the Protestants were, and may be read in divers remonstrances and relations published in the beginning of the late troubles."

5. The statements of this illustrious archbishop are more than confirmed by the Archdeacon of Tuam, Dr. John Lynch, who attests that the soldiers of Dublin garrison "fell on all the inhabitants in the neighbourhood of the city, who either from age or sex, or disease, were detained at home and not able to fly. The poor victims were shot down like birds by those savage sportsmen. The watchword amongst all the reinforcements sent over from England was *Extirpate the Irish root and branch;* as if they would say—Let us cut off the Irish nation from the land of the living, and let its name be remembered no more" (*Camb. Evers.* vol. iii., p. 97).

Not content with this excess of violence, the Puritans were accustomed to display, by mockery and ridicule, their hatred of the sacred ceremonies of our holy Church. More than once, however, Divine Justice delayed not to avenge those insults. One case is mentioned by the author from whom we have just quoted: "A common soldier, an Englishman, contrived to procure somewhere the vestments which the priest wears at the altar, and having put them on, he appeared at noonday within the grating before the house of Adam Becans, in St. Nicholas's-street, Dublin. He had a book lying open before him, and a vessel full of water by his side; and while he pretended to be reading the blessing of the water in the book, he dipped the aspersorium in the water as if he were going to sprinkle the passers-by, mocking all the while the sacred ceremonies used by the priests. In this sacrilegious personation of the priest he continued until the sound of the drum summoned him to drill in Ostmantown orchard. He had not been many minutes there when two bullets from the gun of one of his comrades, which accidentally exploded, pierced his groin. He was carried back in this state to the very house above-mentioned, whilst his comrades gave the priest's vestments to Mrs. Bridget Rochfort, requesting her to restore them to the place from which they had been stolen, protesting that the sacrilegious travesty of the priestly function was, in their opinion, the cause of the catastrophe, and denying any participation in the crime" (*Ibid.*, p. 124).*

6. Though it was death for Catholics to exercise their religion within the walls of Dublin, yet many continued to reside there privately; nor was a devoted clergy wanting to risk every peril in order to administer to them the holy sacraments. The manuscript narrative already referred to details many instances of the arts to which they were obliged to have recourse to thus break to their flock the bread of life. One lived as a hermit, perpetually shut up in a secret place, only a few Catholics being acquainted with his retreat. Another, often changing his disguise, went publicly through the streets;

---

* The history of our Irish Church abounds with instances of the divine chastisements which awaited those who persecuted the ministers of God, and ridiculed the holy practices of Catholic faith. The fate of Brunchard, President of Munster, is especially remarkable. His rage against the Catholics was like that of Antiochus against the Jews, and his death was also similar, for he expired in 1607, devoured piecemeal by vermin. See *Camb. Evers.*, ibid., p. 101; and *Relatio Ec. Hib.*, by David Kearney, Archbishop of Cashel, written in 1608, published in Appendix to "Lives of the Abps. of Dublin," vol. i. (Duffy, 1865.)

at one time he wore a long beard and a soldier's dress; at other times he travelled as a mechanic or merchant; sometimes, too, he carried a bread-basket on his shoulders, thus becoming all to all that he might gain all to Christ. A third disguised himself as a miller, and occasionally as a gardener; and though living in the country, often passed through the midst of the enemy's guards carrying herbs, or fruits, or some such articles, as if he were journeying to market, whilst he was in reality hastening to the bedside of the infirm.

"For the clergy," writes Mr. Prendergast, "there was no mercy; when any forces surrendered upon terms, priests were always excepted; priests were thenceforth out of protection to be treated as enemies that had not surrendered. Twenty pounds was offered for their discovery, and to harbour them was death. . . . To be prosecuted, however, was nothing but what they were used to from the days of Queen Elizabeth. There were statutes in force making the exercise of their religion death. Yet, as Spencer remarked, they faced all penalties in the performance of their duties. They spared not to come out of Spain, from Rome, and from Rheims, by long toil and dangerous travelling to Ireland, where they knew the peril of death awaited them. These laws occasionally slept, but were revived by proclamation when the fears or anger of England were aroused; and then the priests had to fly from the woods or mountains, or to disguise themselves as gentlemen, soldiers,* carters, or

* In a curious pamphlet, entitled "A Catholic Conference, &c." by Barnabie Rych, London, 1612, it is said that a Protestant student of Trinity College recognised in Waterford a priest, his acquaintance, " disguised *in a ruffling suit of apparel, with gilt rapier and a dagger hanging by his side.*"

labourers. They had no fear that any of the Irish would betray them. But pregnant women and others, hastening on foot out of the Protestant parts towards those places where priests were known to be harboured was frequently the cause of their being apprehended. . . . In all parts of the nation there was found a succession of these intrepid soldiers of religion to perform their sworn duties, meeting the relics of their flocks in old raths, under trees, and in ruined chapels, or secretly administering to inviduals in the very houses of their oppressors, and in the ranks of their armies."*

Their stratagems, however, did not always enable them to elude the vigilance of the soldiery. Thus, one aged man—a venerable Jesuit—was seized at the very altar when offering the Holy Sacrifice; the soldiers at once tore off the sacred vestments and cast him into a horrid dungeon. Another priest, though disguised, was assailed by them in the public streets, despoiled of all he had with him, and thrown into the common sewer; and it was only by the interposition of some passers-by, who declared he could not be a priest, that he was rescued from their brutality.

6. When, in 1647, the city was treacherously surrendered by Ormonde to the Puritans, the severest measures were at once re-enacted against the Catholics. By public edict it was commanded that all *papists* should quit the city; it was declared a capital crime for any of them to stop even one night within the walls of Dublin or its suburbs; and it was prohibited, under penalty of death and the confiscation of property, to receive into

---

* *Settlement*, &c., p. 154-162.

their houses any Jesuit or priest, and at the same time large rewards were held out to all who would give information against the violators of this edict.* In the Proceedings of Parliament in 1650, is published a letter from Dublin, of 11th November, that, year declaring that "all the Papists are to be turned out of this city; and for the Jesuits, priests, friars, monks, nuns, £20 will be given to any that can bring certain intelligence where any of them are: and whosoever doth harbour or conceal any one of them is to forfeit life and estate:" and so rigorously was this proclamation enforced that the Governor of the city was able to report on the 19th of June, 1651, that "though Dublin hath formerly swarmed with papists, I know none now there but one who is a chirurgeon, and a peaceable man. It is much hoped the glad tidings of salvation will be acceptable in Ireland and that this savage people may see the salvation of God."

7. Whilst the sword of persecution thus rendered desolate the Church of Dublin,† another scourge was sent by Providence to test the virtue of our suffering people. In the month of June, 1650 the plague commenced its first ravages within the city walls. "In my diocese," writes the archbishop, "almost all the priests have died or have been murdered by the enemy; the

---

* Relatio, &c., *ut supra.*

† The Catholics in the neighbourhood of Dublin were treated with as much severity as in the city itself. Near Clontarf, fifty-six men, women, and children were thrown into the sea by order of a Colonel Crafford. Massacres were also committed at Malahide, Wicklow, Arklow, and other parts of the country. Other instances of barbarity are recorded in O'Connell's Memoir of Ireland, p. 224, &c.

religious are scattered, and my flock, for the greater part, has been destroyed by war and famine, though the pestilence has as yet scarcely made its appearance amongst us." (Letter of 6th June, 1650.) Nevertheless, before the close of that year, the plague had numbered amongst its victims 16,000 of the inhabitants.* Many fled to the country parts to avoid the contagion ; for three years it raged with unabated fury, during which interval the number of its victims was swelled beyond 30,000. It was only in the winter of 1651 that the violence of the disease seemed for a time relaxed, but the rage of the heretics against the Catholics was then increased tenfold.

8. On the Feast of St. Stephen, the Protomartyr, the governor of the city, desirous to slay the souls of those who perchance had escaped from the pestilence, published an edict commanding all Catholics of whatsoever sex or age to present themselves at the heretical churches, or otherwise within fourteen days to remove, under penalty of death, beyond two miles from the city walls ; none were allowed to return to the city without a written permission from the governor, and then only by day, for all Catholics were absolutely prohibited to rest for even one night within the walls. No alternative now remained to the Catholics; " they had to choose between the death of the body or of the soul. Yet of all the dense population of Dublin, only five hundred of the lowest populace, impelled by fear of cold and famine, and other impending calamities, to them far

* Missio Soc. Jesu, &c., written in 1651. Borlase states that "in the summer of 1650, 17,000 persons died of the plague in Dublin."

more dreadful than the sword, presented themselves at the churches of the heretics." A merciful Providence* was not wanting to those who chose to suffer everything rather than imperil their faith. Such Catholics as yet retained some property outside the city walls welcomed the exiles to their houses, and shared with them their remaining goods, till in the following year the rigour of the edict was again relaxed, whilst at the same time all were gladdened by the return in a spirit of penance to the bosom of mother church of the greater part of the five hundred who had fallen away.

9. The order for the expulsion of the Catholics was frequently renewed in the succeeding years, and it was only by privilege that some few were permitted to remain in the city for a short time. Thus, on the 5th June, 1654, "the Governor of Dublin was authorized to grant licences to such inhabitants to continue in the city as he should judge convenient, the licences to contain the name, age, colour of hair, countenance, and stature of every such person; and the licence not to exceed twenty days, and the cause of their stay to be inserted in each licence."† When, in 1656, a general declaration was published, ordering all the Irish and papists to withdraw to a distance of two miles from all walled towns or garrisons before the 26th of May, that year, special orders were issued to the Mayor of Dublin to report what progress had been made in carrying it into effect. On 24th October new instructions were given to the same "to take effectual means to remove

* *Missio* loc. cit.
† Prendergast "Settlement," p. 137.

all the papists that might be then dwelling in the city, and all places within the city, within forty-eight hours after the publication of the order."* Subsequently, on 19th of November, a list of all the papists still remaining in Dublin was returned to the Council, with the view of ordering them to be tried by court-martial. Nor were these mere threats: *the prisons were choked*, to use the words of the Commissioners, and the gallows, too, had its victims. Thus, on the 3rd of April, 1655, we find commemorated that Mr. Edward Hetherington, of Kilnemanagh, being tried by a court-martial, which sat in St. Patrick's Cathedral, Dublin, was led out to execution, and "duly hanged, with placards on his breast and back: *For not transplanting.*"† Sometimes the orders of Council were directed against particular classes of citizens; for instance, on the 10th October, 1656, at the petition of William Hartley and other Protestants, instructions were issued for "all popish shoemakers to be searched for by the mayor and sheriffs of Dublin, and none to be allowed to inhabit in Dublin or its suburbs." Again, on the 3rd of April, 1657, on the petition of the Protestant coopers of Dublin, the mayor and sheriffs were ordered "to report to the Council Board why the Irish coopers had not been removed."‡

It will not, therefore, surprise us to find that, in this very year, 1657, the newly appointed Vicar-Apostolic of Dublin, Dr. James Dempsey, declared to the Holy See that "*there were not, in the diocese of Dublin, Catho-*

* Ibid., 141. † Ibid., pp. 140-1. ‡ Ibid., p. 53.

lics enough to form three parishes." How consoling it is to reflect that, after two hundred years of almost uninterrupted persecution, the mustard seed has grown into a mighty tree, and, instead of 3,000, we find well nigh 390,000 Catholics in the diocese of Dublin.

* "Dublinii non sunt tot Catholici quot constituerent tres Paroecias." Ex actis Sac. Cong., an. 1657.

CHAPTER II.

SUFFERINGS OF THE CATHOLICS IN CASHEL.

1. Barbarity of Inchiquin at the taking of Cashel.—2. Father Stapleton's death.—3. Of F. Barry, O.S.D.—4. Pillage of the Cathedral.—5. Account given by Archdeacon Lynch.—6. Narrative of F. Saul, S.J.—7. Sufferings of the citizens in 1654.—8. Most Rev. Thomas Walsh, Archbishop of Cashel.

1. In 1647, Morrogh O'Brien, Baron of Inchiquin, having administered the *covenant* to his Puritan followers, led them on to the assault of Cashel. Along his march he everywhere burned the crops, and massacred the peasantry; and to the present day his name is familiar in the household traditions of our country as "Murrough of the burnings." All the cruel deeds, however, of that sanguinary monster sink into insignificance when compared with the sack of the ancient city of Cashel. "There is not on record," says the Rev. Mr. Meehan, "a more appalling tragedy;" and the following details, taken from the manuscript narrative of the Irish superior of the Jesuits, written early in 1651, more than justify this assertion.* "Cashel," he says, "became not only a prey to the enemy, but even a slaughterhouse. The city being but badly fortified, it accepted the offer of conditions from Inchiquin, and opened its gates. The garrison, about 300 in number,

* Relatio rerum quarumdam, &c., ut sup.

together with the priests and religious, as also very many of the citizens, retired to the cathedral church, which holds a strong position, and is styled the Rock of St. Patrick. The enemy having taken possession of the city, and in part destroyed it by fire, assailed the cathedral with all their forces, but were heroically repulsed by our troops. After a long combat, the general of the enemy suspended the fight, and, demanding a surrender, offered permission to the garrison to depart with their arms and ammunition, and all the honours of war, requiring, however, that the citizens and clergy should be abandoned to his mercy. It was then that the true heroism of the Catholic soldiers was seen. They refused to listen to any conditions unless the citizens and clergy, whom they had undertaken to defend, should be sharers in them; and they added, that they chose rather to consecrate their lives to God on that Rock of St. Patrick, than to allow that sanctuary to be profaned by heretics. The assault was then renewed with extreme ferocity; the enemy, being seven thousand in number, assailed the church on every side, entering by the windows and the shattered doors. Nevertheless, for some time the struggle was bravely maintained within the church, till our few troops were rather overwhelmed by the multitude of the enemy than vanquished by them.

"When all resistance ceased, then was the cruelty of the heretics displayed against the priests and religious, one of whom was of our society, by name William F. Boyton. Many old men, of eighty years of age, aged females, some of them in their hundredth year, besides innumerable other citizens, who had grown old, not only in years but in piety, and whose only weapons were their prayers, prostrate around the steps of the altar, now empurpled them with their blood, whilst the infirm, who had been borne to the church as to a place of sacred refuge, and the innocent children were slain on the very altar.

"Within the cathedral nine hundred and twelve was the number of the slain, of whom more than five hundred were of the heretical troops, and about four hundred of the Catholics.* Everywhere dead bodies were to be seen, which for some days remained uninterred. The altars and chapels, the sacristy and seats were covered with them, and in no place could the foot rest on anything save on the corpses of the slain."

2. One of the priests who had taken refuge in the cathedral, Father Theobald Stapleton, was remarkable for his piety; clothed with surplice and stole, and holding a crucifix in his left hand, he sprinkled with holy water the enemy's troops as they rushed into the sacred edifice. The heretics, mad with rage, strove with each other who should pierce him with their swords, and thus he was hewn to pieces. At each wound the holy man exclaimed, "Strike this miserable sinner!" till he yielded his soul into the hands of his Creator.

3. In the town itself no fewer than 3,000 were massacred by the heretical enemy,† and twenty priests were

* Ex quibus Catholici fere quadringenti: ex hæreticis supra quingentos.

† Dr. Thomas Walsh, Archbishop of Cashel, in a letter of 20th December, 1650, writes: "Ego plures meas papiros ac libros perdidi per infestissimum Christiano nomini hostem Baronem de Inshequin, cujus milites ter Ecclesiam et ædes meas omni prætioso ornatu et supellectili spoliarunt."

martyred within the sanctuary. In St. Patrick's chapel a number of helpless females had gathered around the statue of the saint, and were there barbarously put to death. This is attested by the Nuncio Rinuccini in the account of his Nunciature presented to Pope Innocent the Tenth immediately after his return to Rome in 1649. The heroic death of Father Richard Barry, of the Order of St. Dominick, is especially recorded:—*

"When the priests had been cut to pieces, Richard Barry alone survived. Him did God reserve for greater trials. The captain, seeing the venerable friar in his habit, and struck by his noble and sanctified appearance, said to him: 'Your life is your own, provided you fling off that habit; but if you cling to such a banner, verily you peril life itself.' When the father replied, that his habit was an emblem of the passion of the Redeemer, and more dear to him than life; 'think more wisely,' rejoined the captain; 'indulge not this blind passion for martyrdom, for if you do not comply with my orders, death awaits you.' 'Be it so,' said the father, 'your cruelties will be to me a blessing, and death itself great gain.' Infuriated at this answer, they bound the venerable man to a stone chair, kindled a slow fire under his feet and legs, till after two hours of torture his eyes flashed their last upon that heaven which he was about to enter. Three days after the sack of the town, Inchiquin's soldiers retired, loaded with booty; and on the fourth day a pious woman found the friar's body amid heaps of the slain. She reported the fact to the Vicar-General who, accompanied by Henry

* See Dominic de Rosario's history of the Geraldines, p. 202.

O'Cuillenan, notary apostolic, who is still living, caused the mutilated remains to be borne in funeral procession to the convent of the Dominicans, where, after chaunting *Te Deum*, his religious brethren interred them with all honours due to a man who died for the Faith. His death took place the 16th September, 1647."

4. The demoniac scenes that followed, most clearly proved how great a share religious hatred had in stimulating the fanatical Covenanters to this fearful massacre:—

"The heretics set to work at once to destroy all the sacred things which had been stored in the cathedral of St. Patrick. The altars were overturned; the images that were painted on wood were consigned to the flames; those on canvas were used as bedding for the horses, or were cut into sacks for burdens. The great crucifix, which stood at the entrance of the choir, as if it had been guilty of treason, was beheaded, and soon after its hands and feet were amputated. With a like fury did they rage against all the other chapels of the city; gathering together the sacred vases and all the most precious vestments, they, through ridicule of our ceremonies, formed a procession. They advanced through the public squares, wearing the sacred vestments, and having the priests' caps on their heads, and inviting to Mass those whom they met with on the way. A beautiful statue of the Immaculate Virgin, taken from one of the Churches, was borne along (the head being broken off), in mock state, with laughter and ridicule. The leader of the Puritan army had, moreover, the temerity to assume the archiepiscopal mitre, and boast that he was now not only governor and lieutenant of Munster, but also Archbishop of Cashel."*

5. Dr. John Lynch, Archdeacon of Tuam, in his MS. History of the Irish Bishops, gives a detailed account of the desecration of this holy place by the soldiers of Inchiquin. It was on the festival of St. Patrick, 1642, that with solemn pomp the cathedral on the Rock of Cashel was dedicated once more to divine worship. The faithful, from a considerable distance, gathered into the city to take part in the imposing ceremony, and many of them wept with joy at seeing this spot so dear to their Fathers, hallowed once more by the sacred rites of religion. The cathedral was soon restored to its former beauty, and nothing was left undone to complete the splendour of its interior ornamentation. But on the 14th of September, 1647, all this was undone. On the approach of Inchiquin's troops, several persons fled to the Rock, which, by nature and by art, seemed to be a place of secure refuge. The city soon became a prey to the Puritan soldiers, and then the Rock was itself assailed. "In the cemetery the fight was for a time maintained on both sides with the greatest determination, but the defenders at length, overwhelmed by the number of the assailants, retreated to the church. The enemy, too, rushed in, scaling ladders being applied to the windows, and the doors broken open, and many were slaughtered on both sides. The Catholic survivors shut themselves up in various recesses, which they refused to leave until the promise of their lives was given them. No sooner, however, had they come forth and surrendered their

---

* Relatio, &c., *ut sup.*

arms than the commander of the enemy broke his promise and ordered all to be put to the sword. A few of the more wealthy were spared, and a few saved themselves by hiding in secret places. Three hundred of the Catholics and more than six hundred of the enemy were slain. Among those put to death were Theobald Stapleton, chancellor of the church, two vicars choral, Thomas Morrissy, bedridden through old age, and another Theobald Stapleton, author of an Irish catechism printed in Roman type: also Richard Barry, of the Order of St. Dominic, prior of the Cashel convent, Richard Butler and James Sall, Franciscans, and William Boyton, a Jesuit. The soldiers slew, moreover, the children and the decrepit and the women, and many of these victims of sacrifice were massacred at the altar. Some women, concealed in the recesses of the church, were stripped of their clothes, and, refusing to come forth, were soon mantled in their blood. Not content with this, the enemy overturned the altars, trampled on the images, plundered all the furniture, sacred and profane, tore off the ornaments, broke the statues to pieces. One who had made a mockery of the statue of the Blessed Virgin came to an untimely end; for whilst he was pulling some iron from a window, a stone from the top of the church fell upon him and crushed him to death. They moreover cast down the richly-carved wood-work of the chapels, and they took down and broke the bell of the high tower of the sacred buildings. In a word, the church, which but a little while before was most beautiful to behold, could now only excite horror in those who gazed upon its desolation."

6. Another narrative, addressed to Rev. John Young, S.J., a distinguished native of Cashel, then residing in Rome, written on the 1st of November, 1647, by Fr. Saul, S. J., who was witness of the tragic scenes which he describes, was published in an Italian periodical a few years ago, and may be seen in full in the Appendix to Father Edward Murphy's "Cromwell in Ireland." Some extracts from it will serve to confirm and complete the account given by the writers already cited:

"The year 1647 was a disastrous one for the whole of Ireland, and the times fell most heavily on Cashel, the metropolitan see of the province of Munster. Lord Inchiquin, who was rightly called the scourge of God, after reducing and burning nearly the whole of this district, moved his Parliamentary army upon Cashel. The garrison of the city numbered only four hundred men, and the citizens were thrown into the utmost confusion by the difficulties of their situation and the sudden approach of the enemy. The garrison deserted the walls, and retired to St. Patrick's Rock, while a great part of the inhabitants, taking with them a supply of provisions and most of their household effects, followed the soldiers thither. The remainder, not trusting to the protection of the rock, concealed themselves in the outlying country, just in time to escape the fast advancing enemy. The Puritan troops entered the city without resistance, and after making merry on the food and drink left behind by the citizens, lay down to sleep. The next day, which was the feast of the Exaltation of the Holy Cross, the enemy reconnoitred the rock and its defences for the space of an hour, although information about its state had already been given by some traitors,

Catholics only in name, who after having lived on our bounty for a long time, were terror-stricken at the enemy's ravages, and had disappeared. We believe that God appointed that day to be the witness, not indeed of our destruction, but of our glory, and it was meet that those who wished to taste the delight of the Cross must first share its ignominy. When the reconnoitring was over, the hostile army divided into three parties, whose points of attack were the three weaker portions of our fortifications. Before attacking, a messenger left their lines and came up to the rock to treat about a surrender on these terms: that the garrison should be allowed to depart with their muskets and with bullets in bouche, but that the clergy and citizens should be left to the mercy of their commander. Here the bravery of the Catholic soldiers shone out, and they replied that they would risk their lives in defence of those whom they had vowed to protect rather than break their word, and that they preferred to dye with their hearts' blood that holy ground to allowing it to be desecrated by heretical miscreants. The Puritan leader was stung to the quick by this generous answer, and ordered the charge to be sounded. On they come with lightning speed, at the same time throwing fire-brands into the air, one of which, happening to fall into the vestibule of the monastery of the Friars Minor, set the hall on fire, and burned it to the ground. They slack not their speed until under cover of the walls, where they are safe out of range, for the turrets and embrasures were too high to admit of aim being taken at the enemy as they lay at close quarters. The besieged, therefore, throw away their guns, and climbing up the steep bastions, hurl down the foe as they appear above the scaling-ladders, until overcome by the numbers that swarmed up the north wall, the least defensible portion of the fort, they fall back slowly, intending to take up a position in the church. Scarcely have they begun to retreat when the enemy press round them on all sides with renewed energy. The very cemetery itself is disputed inch by inch, until of those that remained outside the church not one survived. The issue of the day depended on the capture of the main building, which therefore the enemy make the centre of attack. They charge the north and south doors, but are driven back with no less determination by our soldiers. Unable to effect an entrance in this direction, the Puritans plant their ladders against the walls of the church, and leap through the windows. Hemmed in on all sides, nevertheless our brave defenders fight with the energy of despair, and nothing could be heard in that vast edifice but the clash of arms and the shouts of the combatants. For upwards of half an hour the contest raged in the very nave of the cathedral with equal valour on both sides, but unequal forces, the fanatical enemy polluting the very sanctuary, and dyeing its stones with blood consecrated to God and his Church. At length our brave defenders, now reduced to sixty, turn and ascend the steps of the bell-tower, followed by the enemy, who call on them to surrender. With the alternative before them of death by starvation or by the enemy's sword, they give themselves upon condition of their lives being spared. The deceitful commander gave his word, but as soon as their swords were collected he gave the order to kill all without exception. Many are at once cut down, some of the richer citizens are spared in hope of ransom, others run to hide themselves in the crypts and vaults, of which there was a great number about. All, however, with the exception of one or two, are either despatched by the sword or retained as prisoners. The Bishop, together with the Mayor and his son, and a few others, conceal themselves in a more secure and secret hiding-place, but do not stir therefrom until assured of their safety.

"Thus ended that cruel butchery and the most disgraceful sacrilege that was ever seen in Ireland. We lost about one thousand men, the enemy at least five hundred. Old men on the verge of the grave, whose weapons were their rosaries, defenceless women and children, were struck at the very altars without regard to age or sex. In one word, the enemy, exulting over their prey, hew in pieces and burn all the statues, overthrow the altars, and pollute the sacred vessels. The large crucifix that towered above the entrance to the choir had its head, hands, and feet struck off, the organ was broken, and the bells, whose chimes cheered our soldiers as they fought, were deprived of their clappers and their beautiful tone. Nothing escaped the ruthless hand of the spoiler. The Puritans load themselves with the goods of the citizens, with which the church was filled; they excavate the very crypts, and break open the marble tombs in hope of plunder. All the passages, even the altars, chapels, sacristies, bell-tower steps, and seats were so thickly covered with corpses, that one could not walk a step without treading on a dead body. Those who remember the splendour of the cathedral in the celebration of the sacred ceremonies on holidays and feast-days, and the sumptuous workmanship of the altars and monuments, could not bring themselves to view the scene of horror, or, if they did look upon it, they shed abundant tears the while. Here the course of cruelty and sacrilege did not end, but rather increased in fury. Some dress themselves in the precious vestments, and with birrettas on their heads, invite the rest to Mass. Others dash the holy images against the walls, and others again bear aloft in solemn procession a headless statue of the Immaculate Virgin, exquisitely wrought with golden tracery. The pictures of St. Patrick and St. Ignatius, together with those of other saints, deaf and dumb idols as they called them, were turned into horse-cloths or used as sacks. One man there was, who on catching sight of the smaller statue of the Blessed Virgin at our house, scoffed at it, saying: 'How now, Mary of Ireland, how now? Eat some peas.' But his mockery was the cause of his death, for a little while after, while he was removing the iron bars from the windows of a house, a stone dropped from the topmost storey, and falling on his head broke in his skull. Lord Inchiquin himself put on the Archbishop's mitre, boasting aloud that he was the Governor of Munster and the Mayor and Archbishop of Cashel. Not only the goods of the citizens and the church ornaments suffered from the ravages of the soldiers, but also the dwellings in the city and the houses consecrated to God. Already the burning brands were applied to the wooden partitions, when some of the chief men stepped forward, and by the promise of a large sum of money, to be contributed by all the citizens, saved the city from a deluge of fire. Yet the conflagration could not be got under, and the most ancient city of Cashel, that had seen so long a succession of kings and archbishops, was burnt to the ground. That city, I say, which because it had received the light of the faith from Patrick, suffered it never to be extinguished or obscured, endured such a change that for a long time no priest or sacred rite was seen there. Graced by the trophies of so many victories for the faith, strengthened by the protection of so many patron saints, the city contains a Puritan enemy in its midst. What we hope for is that Cashel will not become a byword among men, and will acquire greater glory by its losses for the faith than by its triumphs. While we mourn that loved ones are no more, we rejoice that they are crowned with the martyr's crown above, and it is not wrong to think that their souls are in bliss. For on the nights preceding the destruction of the city, when we went to the soldiers of the garrison and exhorted them to abstain from swearing and other practices of the camp, we found them compliant beyond measure, and prepared to shed their blood for the faith. Before they engaged the enemy most of them several times, all at least once, cleansed their consciences by confession, and received the Bread of Life. But if they are detained in the cleansing fire of purgatory, I recommend them most earnestly to the sacrifices and prayers of your Reverence and the rest of the Fathers on this day, the Commemoration of the Souls of the Faithful Departed."

7. When, in 1654, the inhabitants of Cashel were ordered to withdraw to a distance of at least two miles (if not transplantable), or to transplant, they forwarded a petition setting forth a special grant made to them

by Cromwell. They state that Cromwell arrived before their walls in a storm of wind and sleet, long after dark on the night of the 3rd of February, 1650. Pressed by the pelting storm, and anxious to house his men, he granted that the inhabitants, on giving him immediate admission, should enjoy their properties and liberties, and that the priests there would be spared. All, however, that they could now obtain from the Puritan Commissioners was a respite for their transplantation till 1st May, 1655. It was remarked that this concession was of little avail. A few days after the respite was granted to them the whole town was burned to the ground, some few slated houses only excepted, which had been occupied by the troops, and thus the inhabitants were driven to seek a shelter in the adjacent country. We will see hereafter how terrible were the hardships endured by our people in the forced migration from their homes. For the present a few words must be added regarding the pastor who at this trying period shared the perils of his flock.

8. Among the many blessings conferred by a merciful Providence on Ireland in latter times, not the least was the illustrious array of bishops who adorned her sanctuary throughout these years of her martyrdom. In the very foremost rank of those distinguished prelates a place must be assigned to Thomas Walsh, Archbishop of Cashel. His parents, Robert Walsh and Anastasia Strong, were remarkable among the citizens of Waterford for their devoted attachment to the Faith, and for the unbounded charity with which they extended a generous welcome to the suffering clergy, for whom their residence was at all times a secure asylum. He

was born in 1588, at a time when his father was shut up in prison on account of his fearless devotedness to his religion. At an early age he was sent to Spain, and entered on his preparatory studies under the care of his uncle, Thomas Strong, Bishop of Ossory, then an exile for the Faith at Compostella. As he grew in years he was remarkable for his virtues and learning, and in 1626 was promoted by Pope Urban VIII. to the Archiepiscopal See of Cashel. Whilst faithfully discharging all the duties of his office, he made it a rule to hold every year a synod of the clergy in some retired place far away from the public haunts, thus the better to avoid giving offence to the Government. On one occasion while the clergy were thus assembled at synod in a wood, some spies who had been put upon their track cried out that they were engaged in treasonable designs, and called on them to surrender. The archbishop might easily have escaped, but he at once presented himself to the leader of the party and voluntarily became their prisoner on the condition that the clergy would be allowed to depart unharmed. He was led to Cashel, and consigned to the custody of the Protestant Archbishop Hamilton, who treated him with some courtesy and next day forwarded him to Dublin in charge of Mr. Hamilton, his son. This gentleman was filled with admiration for the meekness and piety of his prisoner, and throughout the journey sought instruction as to the teaching of the Catholic Church, and pursuing his inquiries, soon afterwards retired to the Continent and embraced the Faith, and throughout all the turmoil of the subsequent years proved himself a devoted son of the Church. Our Archbishop, however, was thrown into prison in Dublin, and detained there in solitary confinement for nine months. At length, being brought before the Lord Deputy Wentworth, he clearly proved himself guiltless of any attempt against the State, and was set at liberty on the security of some friends that he would appear before the court whenever summoned to do so. It is remarkable that when the Confederates appealed to arms in 1641, there was not one of those who were engaged in the arrest of the Archbishop but in some way or other came to an untimely end. During the years that success attended the confederate cause, Dr. Walsh displayed a boundless generosity in relieving the wants of the indigent, frequently despoiling himself of his own mantle to cover the nakedness of the poor. When the Rock of Cashel was assailed in 1647, the Archbishop's house, which adjoined the cathedral, shared in the general wreck. Everything that he possessed, books, episcopal ornaments, and sacred plate, all perished, and he himself had to seek for shelter out in the woods and on the hills. When the storm had passed, he returned to Cashel, and nowise disheartened set himself in earnest to gather together the stones of the sanctuary and to readorn God's temple; and so successful were his labours that on the 18th of July, 1648, the old cathedral was again solemnly restored to the sacred rites of religion. When at length the Puritan arms triumphed, he once more sought a refuge in remote recesses, enduring the greatest hardships, that he might assist his flock. He was in Limerick during its memorable siege, and having quitted the city after the surrender to Ireton, was attacked on the way by Matthew Godfrey, who seized his horse and treated the Archbishop with great brutality. He then sought a refuge in the town of Ballywilliam, but was arrested on the 4th of January, 1652, and thrown into prison in Clonmel. There were several priests shut up in the same prison, and so tranquil and religious was their demeanour that the gaoler, though otherwise a bitter enemy of the Catholics, permitted them all to assemble together with the Archbishop, to converse together, and to recite the Divine Office in common. Whilst they were thus engaged in prayer, he would not permit any of the other officials to disturb them. They were not allowed to say Mass, but the Blessed Sacrament was every day brought to them. Food was abundantly supplied to them through the charity of the faithful: they partook, however, of only one meal, and the rest they distributed to the poor. The Archbishop was offered his liberty and permission to live among his relatives if he would engage not to exercise the sacred ministry; but though the imprisonment and his many hardships had brought on grievous and painful infirmities, he courageously refused to be liberated on such conditions: for this, he said, he was invested with spiritual power, that he would administer the sacraments and exercise the sacred ministry, and he would rather suffer death a thousand times than by any voluntary act of his to forego his right to discharge the duties of his office; wherefore on the 16th of July, 1653, he was transferred to Waterford, and since his infirmities had rendered him quite helpless, he was carried on board a vessel bound for Spain. He landed at Corunna, where every reverential care was extended to him by the Archbishop of Compostella. For a short time he fixed his abode in that Catholic town, whilst strength permitted, administering Confirmation and assisting at the sacred functions; but his infirmities increasing he was carried to the Irish College in Compostella, where he breathed his last in peace the 4th May, 1654, and his remains were interred with solemn pomp in the Cathedral. A more detailed account of his life may be seen in "Spicilegium Ossoriense," vol. ii., p. 136.

CHAPTER III.

SUFFERINGS OF THE CATHOLICS IN CORK.

1. Cork surrendered to the Puritans: description of the city.—
2. Sufferings and constancy of the people.—3. Heroism of the clergy.—4. London pamphlet of 1644.—5. Lynch's narrative.—
6. Colonel Phayre, governor of Cork.—7. Two devoted bishops.

1. IT may be said of the city of Cork, as of Dublin, that throughout the whole period of the triumph of the Catholic cause, it remained in the hands of the Puritans, or at least was subject to Protestant control. Hence it was that not even the voice of calumny attempted to accuse the Catholics of having plundered or put to death on the outbreak of the hostilities a single one of the Protestant citizens. Nevertheless, there as elsewhere the Catholics were persistently treated with the greatest cruelty. The narrative from which many extracts have already been made,* gives the following details as to the city of Cork :—

"The fury of the most cruel persecution, carried on by the Parliamentarians against the Catholics, reached Cork without encountering any obstacle. For, the president of the province, pretending to be a liege minister of the king, was, together with his troops, admitted without difficulty within the walls. Having

---

* Relatio rerum quarumdam, &c. Anno 1650.

thus, under pretence of defending it for the king, got possession of the city, he perfidiously handed it over to the Parliamentarians."

Cork held at this time the fourth rank among the Irish cities. It was remarkable for its harbour and the wealth of its merchants, although its outward features had but little to captivate the stranger. Holingshed calls it a "haven royal, happily planted by the sea." Camden describes the city as being in the form of an egg, with the river flowing around it and through it, not passable but by bridges, and "lying out in length, as it were, in one direct broad street." In a rare tract, published in 1622, we find the following description of Cork: "The city hath its beginning upon the side of a hill, which descendeth easily into one wide and long street; the only principal and chief street of the city. At the first entrance there is a castle, called Shandon Castle, and almost over against it a church built of stone, as the castle is a kind of marble, of which the country yieldeth store. The city hath many houses, built of the same kind of stone, and covered with slate. But the greatest number of houses are built of timber or mud walls and covered with thatch."

2. As early as the year 1644 an order was issued by the governor expelling all the Catholics from the city of Cork. On the 26th of July in that year he sent for the Mayor and Corporation at 6 o'clock in the morning, and when they were assembled he led them into his garden and there gave them in charge to a troop of soldiers who with muskets loaded and matches lighted kept close watch over them. The civic authorities being thus secured, the military governor proceeded

through the streets of the city, accompanied by his officers and a large body of the military, and commanded "all the Irish inhabitants," both old and young, to leave the city, prohibiting them, however, to carry any of their goods or property with them. As each street was cleared, the soldiers took formal possession of the houses and locked the doors. In a few hours the whole city was depopulated, and not an Irish Catholic resident was left therein. Even the wealthiest citizens, with their wives and children, were driven forth from their homes and compelled to seek for shelter in the fields, under hedges and ditches, and to solicit, at the hands of the farmers, a little daily sustenance. (See a Relation drawn up by the Mayor, in 1644, in "Carte Papers" ap Prendergast, p. 167.)

When, in 1648, the peace was proclaimed, the survivors were permitted to return to the city. They did not long, however, enjoy this favour. The English garrison revolted to the Puritan Parliament on the 23rd of October, 1649, and again the Proclamation was published, banishing all the Catholic citizens. An eye witness of the sufferings of those devoted Catholics writing in December, 1649, attests that "they were plundered of all that they had," and so great was the terror and confusion that prevailed that "one citizen did not know the miseries of the other, by which mean the poor inhabitants had a greater sense of the las than of the former plundering." (Letter of Philip Martel, 22nd December, 1649. *Ibid.*)

The contemporary narrative already referred to fully confirms these statements. No sooner was Inchiquin master of the city, it says, than he issued an order com manding the Catholic clergy to depart, but permitting four of the parochial clergy to remain, lest the Catholic citizens, who were as yet too powerful, might be impelled to revolt. As the Puritan forces increased, fresh pretexts were found for new persecutions:—

"The hatred of the heretics for our religion (the narrative thus continues) becoming greater and greater every day, an order was published prohibiting the citizens to carry swords, or to have in their houses any arms whatsoever. This being effected, another proclamation was issued by the president of the council of war, commanding all Catholics either to abjure their religion or to immediately depart from the city. Should they consent to embrace the parliamentary teaching (parliamentariam religionem), they were permitted to remain and enjoy their goods and property. Should they, however, pertinaciously adhere to *popery*, all, without exception, were to immediately depart from the city. Three cannon shots were to be fired as signals at stated intervals before nightfall, and any Catholic that should be found in the city after the third signal, was to be massacred without mercy. It was then that the constancy of the citizens in the faith was seen. There was not even one Catholic to be found in the whole city to accept the proffered impious condition, or to seek to enjoy his property and goods with the detriment of his faith. Before the third signal all went forth from the city walls—the men and the women, yea, even the children and the infirm: and it was a sight truly worthy of heaven to see so many thousands thus abandoning their homes—so many venerable matrons, with their tender children, wandering through the fields, or overcome by fatigue, seated on the ground, in ditches, or on the highway: so many aged men, some of whom had held high offices in the state, and were members of the nobility, with their wives and families, wandering to and fro, knowing not where to seek a place of refuge; so many merchants who, on that morning, abounded in wealth, but now had not a home in which to rest their weary limbs, yet all with joy went forth to their destruction, abandoning their houses and goods, their revenues and property and wealth, choosing rather to be afflicted with the people of God, on the mountain-tops, and in the caverns, in hunger and thirst, in cold and nakedness, than to enjoy momentary pleasures and temporal prosperity with sin."

3. The clergy were not less devoted to the sacred cause of faith than their spiritual children, and some of them, as we will hereafter see, displayed a heroism in death which rivalled the martyrs of the early Church. The Annals of St. Mary's Priory, preserve the names of three zealous Dominican labourers in this city: "Father Thomas Fitzgerald (they record), a Dominican, a good priest, combining great zeal and piety with primitive simplicity of manners, dressed himself as a peasant, and in that assumed garb served the Catholics of Cork, during the entire period of Cromwell's usurpation. Father Eustace Maguire was no less distinguished in the time of terror and persecution for his intrepid courage than for his meek piety and religious zeal. Being chosen by the Catholics as governor of the castle of Druimeagh, near Kanturk, he so guarded and defended it during the period of Cromwell's wars that it was never taken or surrendered. Brother Dominic

de Burgo, a young professed member of the Order of Preachers, and near relative of the Earl of Clanricarde, was made prisoner on board of the ship in which he had taken his passage for Spain to pursue his studies. He was thrown into prison at Kinsale, whence he made his escape by jumping from the top of the jail wall down on the sea shore. For two days he lay concealed in a neighbouring wood, all covered with mud, without clothing, food, or drink. At length he found shelter under the hospitable roof of the Roches in that neighbourhood, probably of Garretstown. He was, at a later period of life, the celebrated Bishop of Elphin, for whose head or capture the Government offered a large reward, and to whom Oliver Plunket, the martyred Archbishop of Armagh, wrote from his dungeon, warning him of the attempts of the Privy Council against his life. He died in exile."*

4. A pamphlet was published in London, in 1644, under the name of Jane Coe, entitled "A plot discovered in Ireland and prevented without the shedding of blood," to palliate in some way the outrages thus committed upon the unoffending citizens of Cork. It pretended that Lord Inchiquin had made the discovery of a plot to murder all the Protestants "invented and practised by the popish priests and bloodthirsty Jesuits," and therefore to be beforehand with them had "put the Irish out of Cork in July last." No one, indeed, except this anonymous scribe ever found the trace of even the

---

* See the interesting "Account of the New Dominican Convent of Cork, &c., with an Abstract of the Annals, &c." Cork, 1850, p. 21, seq.

suspicion of such a projected massacre, but some facts are mentioned in the pamphlet which serve to corroborate the statements of the Catholic writers. Thus it mentions that the priests were put to death, and it adds that it was by a stratagem "the sheriffs and chiefest men of the city were carried off prisoners to the fort," and when these were thus secured "the chiefest aldermen and others in the city were taken and kept prisoners as hostages, to secure the English as well within as without the gates; and in the meantime there was a proclamation made that if the Irish resisted the English the soldiers should shoot them, and if any English were killed in the broil, the chiefest of their city should be hanged over their walls," and thus without any struggle all the Irish were driven forth from the city.

5. Lynch in his MS. History of the Irish Episcopal Sees gives some additional details. The citizens of Cork, he says, gave a cordial welcome to Sir William St. Leger and his troops when, proclaiming themselves royalists, they demanded an entrance into the city. St. Leger, however soon showed himself in his true colours: "He permitted his soldiers to rush into the chapel of the Dominicans, which in a moment they despoiled: they left almost lifeless the Prior who was offering up the Holy Sacrifice, and all the rest of the Catholic clergy they led off to various prisons. The contagion of the hardships which thus oppressed the citizens of Cork soon spread to the inhabitants adjoining the city, and even to those who were at some distance from it, for the Parliament troops, being worsted in several engagements, returning to the garrison in Cork, vented their rage on the inhabitants. The more wealthy were killed

or cuffed: the poor were maltreated and even tortured to death. But fresh troops of Puritans arriving added new severities to those hitherto endured. Imitating the Emperor Adrian, who banished the inhabitants of Jerusalem to such a distance that they could no longer catch a glimpse of their own country, the Puritans drove the citizens, robbed of everything they possessed, to a distance from the city walls. They began their cruelty with Fr. Francis Matthews, a Franciscan, native of Cork: they forced sharp pieces of heated iron under his nails: they then hanged him. After a time he was taken down, and being found to be still alive was a second time strung up and strangled. When they had shown their brutality in the death of this worthy man who had held the office of Provincial of his Order in Ireland, and Guardian of the Convent in Louvain, and was renowned for his preaching, the Puritan troops in their executions throughout every part of the county Cork displayed an insatiable thirst for blood, putting to death men and women, young and old; sometimes they flung whole bands of innocent victims from the rocks into the sea, or from the bridge into the river: others they shut up in houses and then set fire to them; they singed the hair and beard of others so that even their own wives could not recognise them, and then hanged them. Sometimes they put a loaded pistol into the mouth of the unoffending Catholic and fired it off; they took infants by the heels and knocked out their brains against the rocks: other infants they threw to suck the breasts of their dead mothers: in a word as the tract on the murders committed by the Puritans attests, more than 2,800 decrepit men, women, children, and unoffending husbandmen who were serving the Puritans and under their protection, were put to death with barbarous cruelty. Fr. Dominic Roche, Dean of Cork, who had for many years been Vicar-General of the Diocese of Cork, continued faithfully to attend to the spiritual wants of the suffering flock under the Cromwellian rule. He was so beloved by them that even when the storm of persecution was at its height they concealed him in hiding-places, until at length the whole of that country swarming with the enemy, he was by name banished from all that district. Archdeacon Lynch adds: "As regards the rest of the clergy of the city and diocese of Cork, some were put to death, as John Therry of the Order of St. Augustine and Daniel Culan, a Priest; the rest were punished with exile or imprisonment, and most of them died from the hardships endured in prison or in exile."

6. When Cork and the other southern garrisons revolted from the King in 1649, Colonel Phayr was appointed the Governor of Cork. Suffice it to say that he was one of the three selected by the regicides to be witnesses of the execution of Charles the First, and in the language of those times, his appointment as governor of Cork was made "before the king's blood was dry upon his fingers." We can easily realise to ourselves with what cruelty the Catholics were treated in the city and throughout the county under such rulers. Cromwell writing to the Speaker from Cork on the 19th December, 1649, laments the death of Lieutenant General Jones, who died of fever at Dungarvan and was interred at Youghal, but adds: "You see how

God mingles out the cup unto us. Yet there hath been some sweet at the bottom of the cup." The sweet to which he thus refers was that Colonel Touchy had surrounded a number of unarmed Irish, near Passage and had put them all to the sword. Such were the deeds of heroism that brought consolation to the heart of Cromwell.

7. The two devoted Bishops who at this trying period ministered to the faithful flock of Christ in Cork must not be forgotten. William Therry, who was appointed to the united sees of Cork and Cloyne as early as 1623, belonged to one of the wealthiest families of the city, and was reckoned among the most eloquent and learned of the Irish clergy in his day. During the eighteen years that he ministered to his people until the Puritan troops began their ravages, he was indefatigable in his labours, reviving piety, promoting pilgrimages, instructing by word and example, holding synods, and restoring the vigour of religious discipline. The contemporary Archdeacon Lynch in his MS. History of the Irish Bishops, relates that he shared all the sufferings of his flock in the first years of the Confederate war. "The city of Cork, he writes, being occupied by the enemy through stratagem, the governor reckoning it unsafe to place trust in any Catholic, commanded the citizens by edict either to renounce their Roman Creed or to quit the city before evening. Three cannon shots were the signal for departure. Sad was the spectacle of suffering which the city then presented, although a glorious one in the sight of heaven, and meriting the applause of the Christian world. Before the third signal the whole body of the citizens, mothers

with their infants, aged men who had held high posts of dignity, with their whole families, were seen scattered through the fields, going forth to voluntary exile, preferring the Faith of their fathers to their homes and paternal inheritance. At morning they abounded in wealth, before evening they were despoiled of everything save their belief in God and confidence in his mercy. The devoted Bishop, though plundered of everything he had, proceeded to Cloyne, where he assiduously dispensed hospitality to those who were in distress, for the people, seeing his own bitter privations, were stimulated in their efforts to succour his indigence. He was not, however, allowed to remain there long, being summoned to take part in the government as a member of the Supreme Council of the Confederates. Weighed down by this addition to his former cares, he was seized at Fethard with fever which after eight days brought him to the tomb on the 18th of March, 1643 (old style), in the 73rd year of his age. His remains were interred at Cashel."

Robert Barry, of the family of Barrymore, succeeded him. He constantly sided with the Nuncio Rinuccini, throughout the many dissensions that marked the decay of the Confederate cause. He at the same time under various disguises visited his flock and administered Confirmation and the other sacraments to them. Cromwell permitted some of the clergy to go into exile into foreign countries, but being told of his zeal in upholding religion, excepted him from all hopes of mercy. He was thus compelled to seek for shelter for a considerable time in the woods and marshes amid the greatest privations, till at length he was enabled to get on board a friendly ship off the coast and thus to take refuge in France. He spent eight years at Nantes assisting the Bishop of that See in the discharge of the Episcopal duties, and dying on the 6th of July, 1662, was interred in the Cathedral of that city close to the entrance to the choir.

CHAPTER IV.

SUFFERINGS OF THE CATHOLICS IN DROGHEDA.

1. Drogheda remarkable for its piety: besieged in 1642.—2. A price set on the heads of the Irish leaders.—3. The garrison and citizens put to the sword.—4. Massacre in St. Peter's Church.—5. Details of the general massacre.—6. Statement of Froude refuted.—7. Quarter was promised.—8. Hugh O'Reilly and Edmund O'Reilly, Archbishops of Armagh.

1. THE old Catholic city of Drogheda had for a long time been remarkable for the devotedness of its people to the cause of religion. The ruins which still remain attest the many institutions of piety and learning erected there. In the part of the city embraced in the diocese of Armagh, there were not only the parochial church and the convents of Dominicans, Augustinians, and Franciscans, but also the Priories of St. Mary de Ursa, and of St. Lawrence, with a noble church entitled from our Blessed Saviour, and two religious hospitals dedicated to St. John the Baptist, and St. Stephen. On the opposite bank of the river, in the diocese of Meath, there was the church of St. Mary's under the invocation of our Lady of the Assumption, the noblest edifice in the city, besides the Church of St. Nicholas, and a Carmelite convent: there were also two Priories of St. John and St. James, specially devoted to the relief of

pilgrims. The river Boyne, which flows through the city contributed not a little to its wealth. The right of fishery on the Monday after the Feast of St. John the Baptist, which of old belonged to the Dominicans, was appropriated by the Protestant Primate, and so highly prized was the revenue derived from this source that Bramhall, who was appointed by the crown to the Primacy in 1660, refused as insufficient the offer of £40 sterling made by a gentleman, for permission to fish on that day. During the short interval of comparative peace which preceded the war of 1641, Drogheda had begun to resume its position as a Catholic city. The Bernardine Fathers and the Jesuits opened public oratories, and the religious ceremonies were performed with unwonted splendour, whilst the convents of the Nuns of St. Clare and St. Elizabeth, recalled the piety and fervour of the olden times. On the 6th of December, 1641, three or four hundred gentlemen of the pale, having at their head Jenico Preston, Earl of Gormanston, came on horseback to the Hill of Crofty, a mile or two from Drogheda, where the Ulster troops were assembled, and having put the question, for what purpose were they in arms, was it in defence of religion and of the king's rights, and received an authoritative answer in the affirmative, they dismounted, joined the Irish ranks, and promised earnest co-operation. Six days later, 500 soldiers were sent from Dublin to garrison Drogheda. A small detachment of the Irish troops lay in wait for them near Gillanstown-bridge, and favoured by a thick fog assailed them with great ardour. The troops, seized with panic threw away their arms and fled, and most of them were slain in the pursuit. The arms thus obtained were of singular advantage to the Ulster leaders. Lynch adds that the English officer in command of the soldiers cried out on seeing the Irish troops "Countermarch," this the Irish took up to be "Contabhart-bhais" (*i.e.*, our lives are in danger), and they were thus inspired with great courage. In the first months of the war the Puritan troops were fully equipped with supplies, and arms, and ammunition: the Irish were wholly unprovided even with the most essential requirements of war. Most of them were only armed with wooden stakes, some carried scythes or similar weapons; there were but a few muskets, and no cannon. Gunpowder sold for £1 per pound, and it was all but impossible to procure even a small supply of it at that price. Nevertheless the Protestant settlers, particularly in the North, were so struck with terror that great numbers of them began to go to Mass and to learn the sign of the cross. The *Alithinologia* states that so many were thus converted wherever Sir Phelim O'Neill appeared, that he was everywhere applauded as a most efficacious preacher and poems were composed in his honour. The city was besieged by the Northern Confederates for some months in 1641 and 1642, but the fortifications for those times were particularly strong, the gates being strengthened by castles, and the city wall being about 20 feet in height, and from four to six in thickness, diminishing towards the summit so as to allow a space of about two feet behind the embrasures for the soldiers to stand on. The Confederates having no artillery to batter these walls, a small military garrison sufficed to render it impregnable against their assaults. The Catholics, though forming a considerable majority of the citizens, made no attempt to interfere with the garrison. The report was industriously circulated one evening that a night assault was to be made, and that the Catholic citizens were to mark their doors with a cross that thus they might be preserved unharmed in the intended massacre. The Puritan garrison accordingly adopted the singular precaution of marking all the Protestant houses with a cross in whitewash, whilst they depicted a gallows on the door of every Catholic house, hoping thus in the case of the triumph of the Confederates to involve the Catholic citizens in ruin. The report, however, was a mere matter of hoax, and no assault was made that night. So severe was the frost that winter that the Boyne was frozen over, and men and horses could cross from bank to bank upon the ice. The city being badly provided with firing and provisions, the citizens and garrison were soon reduced to the greatest extremities. The Catholics, however, were subjected to special trials, for the Puritan soldiers, under pretence of searching for arms, entered their houses, and appropriated to themselves whatever articles of value they could find. Many of the wealthy citizens had placed their most precious goods in the religious oratories, as in inviolable sanctuaries: but these too were intruded upon and everything found there was carried off and publicly divided among the soldiers like booty taken from the enemy's camp. Nor was this all. On Ash Wednesday, 1642, all the Catholics, excepting a few who had proved themselves benefactors to the Puritan garrison, were relentlessly driven forth from the city. The only alternative allowed was that they would renounce their faith, and some, overcome by the terrors of such a banishment, actually proclaimed themselves Protestants that thus they might be permitted to remain. Even these, however, met with their punishment; for the Protestant ministers serving in the garrison, having detected that there was no reality in their renunciation of Popery, and that they had merely adopted a new name that they might continue to dwell in their parental homes, caused them to be driven forth like the rest. Two armies, one of Scotch forces from the north, the other under the command of Ormonde from Dublin, began their march soon after for the relief of the beleaguered city, whereupon the besiegers, being wholly unprovided with arms or ammunition, broke up their camp and retired to Dundalk, then in possession of the Confederate Catholics.

2. It was about this time that a proclamation was issued by the Council in Dublin, setting a price upon the head of Phelim O'Neill and of several of his associates. This document, which well illustrates the Puritan spirit of those times and the manner of war they waged against the Confederates, is as follows:—

"PROCLAMATION.

"By the Lords Justices and Council.

"We do hereby make known to all men, as well good subjects as all others, that whoever he or they be that shall betwixt this and the five-and-twentieth day of March next kill and bring, or cause to be killed and brought to us, the lords justices, or other chief governor, or governors, for the time being, the head of Sir

Phelim O'Neill, or of Conn Magennis, or of Rory Maguire, or of Philip Mac Hugh Mac Shane O'Reilly, or of Collo MacBrien Mac Mahon, he or they shall have by way of Reward, for every one of the said last persons, so by him to be killed, and his or their head or heads brought to us, as followeth, viz., for the head of Sir Phelim O'Neil, one thousand pounds; for the head of the said Sir Conn Magennis, six hundred pounds; for the head of the said Rory Maguire, six hundred pounds; for the head of the said Philip Mac Hugh MacShane O'Reilly, six hundred pounds; for the head of the said Collo Mac Brien MacMahon, six hundred pounds, and pardon for all his or their offences that shall kill, and so bring in, or cause to be killed, and so brought in, the said head or heads.

"We do furthermore make known and declare unto all men, as well as his Majesty's loving subjects as all others, that whosoever shall, betwixt this and the five-and-twentieth day of March next, kill and bring, or cause to be killed or brought in to us, the lords justices of this kingdom, as aforesaid, the head or heads of the said Patrick M'Gartan, Art Oge MacGlafney Magennis, Rory Mac Brian Oge Magennis, Philip Mac Hugh Mac Shane O'Reilly, Philip Mac Mulmorry O'Reilly, Mul Morry Mac Edward O'Reilly, Hugh Boy MacShane O'Reilly, Owen Mac Shane M'Philip O'Reilly, Rory Magwire, Donogh Bane Magwire, Brian Mac Cowcannaght Magwire, Tirlogh Roe O'Neal, Tirlogh Gorm O'Quinn, Cormack Mac Owen O'Hagan, Patrick Modder O'Donnelly, Art Mac Tirlogh Mac Henry O'Neil, Hugh Oge O'Neal, Donogh Oge O'Murchie, Collo

Mac Brian Mac Mahowne, Neal Mac Kena, Collo Mac Ever Mac Mahowne, Captain Hugh Mac Phelim Birne, Shawn Mac Brian Mac Phelim Birne, Luke, *alias* Feogh, O'Toole; Luke, *alias* Feogh, O'Toole; Luke, *alias* Feogh Mac Redmond Birne; Phelim Mac Redmond Birne, Dermot Mac Dowlin Cavenagh; Lewis, *alias* Lisagh, Mac Owney Dempsie, Art O'Molloy, Herbert Fox, Owen O'Molloy, Florence Mac Shane Fitzpatrick, Barnabie Dempsie, Daniel Doine, Barnabie Fitzpatrick, James Mac Fergus MacDonell, James Faghny O'Farrall, Will O'Farrall, James M'Connell Farrall, Oliver Boy Fitzgerald, Pierse Fitzgerald, Maurice Eustace, Nicholas Sutton Roger, *alias* Rory O'Moore; William Fitzgerald, Robert Preston, James Fleming, Patrick Cusake, Edward Belagh, Gerald Leins, Luke Netterville, George King, Richard Barnewall, Colonel Richard Plunket, Matthew Talbot, John Stanley, John Bellew, Christopher Barnewall, and Oliver Cashel, or any of them, he shall have, by way of Reward, for any of the said last-mentioned persons so by him to be killed, four hundred pounds and pardon for all his other offences; though such person or persons so slaying or killing the said traitors, or any of them, bring not, or cause to be brought to us, the Lords Justices as aforesaid, the head or heads of the said traitor or traitors, yet being justly proved, shall forthwith, upon proof so made, receive the reward of three hundred pounds for every one of the said last-named persons so killed and proved, and shall have pardon for all his or their offences, that shall kill or slay the said traitors or any of them.

"Given at His Majesty's Castle of Dublin, the 8th day of February, 1641.

"John Rotherham,   Ormond Ossory,
Fra. Willoughby,   R. Dillon,
Rob. Meredith,   Cha. Lambert,
F. Temple,   Ad. Loftus,
          Cha. Coote.
       God Save the King."

3. Though in the meantime, many of the Catholic citizens had returned, it was not till the end of June, 1649, that the city was taken from the Puritans, and that the Catholics were allowed to live in peace in Drogheda. Sir Arthur Aston, a brave Catholic English royalist, was appointed governor, and an army of three thousand men most of them Irish, were assigned as its garrison, under the command of Colonels Warren and Wall. The Catholic citizens resumed their practices of piety, the churches which had become ruinous in the hands of the Puritans were purified and restored to divine worship, and religion began once more to flourish as of old.

In the meantime, Cromwell had landed on our shores firmly resolved to acquire popularity amongst his fellow-Puritans by the extermination of the Irish *papists*. On his arrival in Dublin he addressed his soldiers, and declared that no mercy should be shown to the Irish, and that they should "be dealt with as the Canaanites in Joshua's time."*

The city of Drogheda was the first theatre of his exterminating fury. No sooner had the garrison of the

---

* "Dr. Anderson's Royal Gen." p. 76.

town submitted on the promise of quarter, than orders were given for an indiscriminate massacre. The spot chosen for the assault was the part of the city-wall adjoining St. Mary's church. It was a place difficult of access and strongly fortified. The wall was there 20 feet high and strengthened with towers and pierced with portholes: but then that position commanded the whole city and being won rendered further resistance impossible. The old wall, battered by the powerful cannon of the besiegers, soon tumbled down, and at five o'clock on the evening of the 9th day of the siege the assault was made. The Catholic soldiers displayed great valour. Three times did they repel the charge of the 12,000 assailants, till, seeing further resistance fruitless, they accepted quarter that was offered them. Cromwell, nevertheless, writing to Parliament, makes it a boast that he himself gave orders that all should be put to the sword;[*] and subsequently, in the usual Puritanical phrases of that period, he styles that worse than brutal massacre, *a righteous judgment of God upon the barbarous wretches; a great mercy vouchsafed to us; a great thing done, not by power or might, but by the Spirit of God.* Some of the soldiers with Sir Arthur Aston and other officers retreated to the Millmount, also called the Moat, described by Cromwell in his letter to the Parliament as "a place very strong and of difficult access, being exceeding high, having a good croft and strongly palisaded." Unwilling to prolong a struggle which they saw could be of no avail they soon surrendered, but by Cromwell's

[*] Letter, Sept. 17, 1649, to Hon. William Lenthall, Speaker of the Parliament in England.

orders were all put to the sword. All the soldiers being thus removed, the slaughter of the inhabitants continued for five days, and the Puritan troops spared neither age nor sex, so much so, that the Earl of Ormond, writing to the secretary of Charles II., to convey the intelligence of the loss of Drogheda, declares that " Cromwell had exceeded himself, and anything he had ever heard of, in breach of faith and bloody inhumanity." General Ludlow, in his despatches, speaks of it as *an extraordinary severity*, and, indeed, Cromwell's own letters present sufficient data to justify these statements.

4. The church of St. Peter, within the city, had been of old a place of popular devotion; a little while before the siege, as we have seen, the Catholics had re-obtained possession of it, and dedicated it to the service of God, and the Holy Sacrifice was once more celebrated there with special pomp and solemnity on the first Sunday of September, in 1649. Thither many of the citizens now fled, as to a secure asylum, and, with the clergy, prayed around the altar; but the Puritans respected no sanctuary of religion: "*In this very place,*" writes Cromwell, "*near one thousand of them were put to the sword. I believe all their friars were knocked on the head promiscuously but two; the one was Father Peter Taafe, brother to the Lord Taafe, whom the soldiers took the next day, and made an end of; the other was taken in the round tower under the repute of a lieutenant; and when he understood that the officers in that tower had no quarter, he confessed he was a friar, but that did not save him.*" We learn some further particulars about this massacre in St. Peter's church from *Johnston's History of Drogheda:*—"Quarter had been promised to all those who should lay down

their arms; but it was only observed until all resistance was at an end. Many, confiding in this promise, at once yielded themselves prisoners; and the rest, unwilling to trust to the mercy of Cromwell, took shelter in the steeple of St. Peter's; at the same time the most respectable of the inhabitants sheltered themselves within the body of the church. Here Cromwell advanced, and, after some deliberation, concluded on blowing up the building. For this purpose he laid a quantity of powder in an old subterraneous passage which was open, and went under the church; but, changing his resolution, he set fire to the steeple, and, as the garrison rushed out to avoid the flames, they were slaughtered. After this he ordered the inhabitants in the church to be put to the sword, among whom many of the Carmelites fell a sacrifice. He then plundered the building, and defaced its principal ornaments."*

5. The Rinuccini MS. states that besides the garrison, about four thousand of the Catholic citizens were thus deliberately massacred. Lord Clarendon records, that during the five days, whilst the streets of Drogheda ran with blood, "*the whole army executed all manner of cruelty, and put every man that related to the garrison, and all the citizens who were Irish, man, woman, and child to the sword.*"† Dr. Fleming, Archbishop of Dublin, in a letter to the Sacred Congregation (5th June, 1653), says, that four thousand brave men, among whom his own nephew, Colonel Fleming, were slain in this fright-

---

* The old church of St. Peter's, thus desecrated by the massacre of the Catholic citizens, stood on the site of the modern church which was built in 1740.

† "Hist.,' vol. vi. p. 395.

ful massacre; and Cromwell himself* reckoned that less than thirty of the defendants were *not massacred, and these,* he adds, *are in safe custody for the Barbadoes.*

The manuscript narrative often referred to† presents many details regarding this horrid tragedy: "The city being captured by the heretics, the blood of the Catholics was mercilessly shed in the streets,‡ and in the dwellinghouses, and in the open fields; to none was mercy shown, not to the women, nor to the aged, nor to the young. The property of the citizens became the prey of the parliamentary troops; everything in our residence was plundered; the library, the sacred chalices, of which there were many of great value, as well as all the furniture, sacred and profane, were destroyed. On the following day, when the soldiers were searching through the ruins of the city, they discovered one of our fathers, named John Bathe, with his brother, a secular priest: suspecting that they were religious, they examined them, and finding that they were priests, and one of them, moreover, a Jesuit, they led them off in triumph, and, accompanied by a tumultuous crowd, conducted them to the market-place, and there, as if they were at length extinguishing the Catholic religion and our society, they tied them both to stakes fixed in the ground, and pierced their bodies with shot till they expired."

* See let. cit. ut sup.
† Relatio rerum, &c. written in 1651.
‡ The street leading to St. Peter's church retained, even within the memory of the present generation, the name of *Bloody-street;* it is the tradition of the place that the blood of those slain in the church formed a regular torrent in this street.

Father Robert Netterville was another victim of their fury. He was aged and confined to bed by his infirmities, nevertheless, "he was forced away by the soldiers and dragged along the ground, being violently knocked against each obstacle that presented itself on the way; then they beat him with clubs, and when many of his bones were broken, they cast him on the highway; some good Catholics came during the night, bore him away and concealed him; on the fourth day, having fought a good fight, he departed this life to receive, as we hope, the martyr's crown."*

Two fathers of the Dominican Order also at this time attained the martyr's crown. These were F. Dominick Dillon, prior of the convent of Urlar, one of the regular chaplains of the Confederate army, and F. Richard Overton, prior of the convent of Athy: they were seized and taken outside the walls to the Puritan camp. There in the presence of the whole army they were put to death through hatred of their religious profession and of the Catholic faith. (Hib. Dom., p. 566.)

6. Froude in his work "The English in Ireland" (vol. i. p. 124), endeavours to discredit the massacre of the Catholic citizens at Drogheda: "It is possible," he writes, "that in such a scene women and children may have been accidentally killed; but there is no evidence of it from an eyewitness, and only general rumours and reports at second hand." He manifestly relies on the

* *Ibid.* Another MS. history of the Jesuit Order in Ireland briefly states regarding the massacre at Drogheda: "All the Catholic citizens were cut off by Cromwell; one of our Society was tied to a stake and hewn in pieces. Six of our fathers were then there; now there is none."—MS. narrative written in 1665.

fact that all the citizens being massacred it would not be easy to produce eye-witnesses to attest the massacre. Yet what shall we say to the testimony of Cromwell himself who in his letter to the Parliament writes: "It is remarkable that these people, at the first, set up the Mass in some places of the town that had been monasteries, and afterwards grew so insolent that the last Lord's day before the storm, the Protestants were thrust out of the great church called St. Peter's, and they had public Mass there, and in this very place near a thousand of them were put to the sword, fleeing thither for safety." And what will he reply to the statement of Thomas à Wood, who was one of Cromwell's officers, and was engaged in this very work of slaughter? His brother, Anthony à Wood, in the preface to the *Athenæ Oxonienses*, records the vivid description given by that officer of the terrible massacre of the citizens in which he had had a part: "He returned from Ireland to Oxford (he writes) for a time (in 1650) to take up his arrears at Christ Church, and to settle his other affairs; at which time being often with his mother and brethren, he would tell them of the most terrible assaulting and storming of Tredagh (Drogheda), wherein he himself had been engaged. He told them that 3,000 at least, besides some women and children, were, after the assailants had taken part, and afterwards all the town, put to the sword on the 11th and 12th of September, 1649. At which time Sir Arthur Aston, the governor, had his brains beat out and his body hacked (and chopped) to pieces. He told them that when they were to make their way up to the lofts and galleries in the church, and up to the tower where the enemy had fled, each of the assailants would take up a child and use it as a buckler of defence when they ascended the steps, to keep themselves from being shot or brained. After they had killed all in the church, they went into the vaults underneath, where all the flower and choicest of the women and ladies had hid themselves. One of these, a most handsome virgin, arrayed in costly and gorgeous apparel, kneeled down to Thomas à Wood, with tears and prayers, to save her life; and being struck with a profound pity, he took her under his arm, and went with her out of the church, intending to put her over the works to shift for herself. But a soldier, perceiving his intentions, ran his sword through her body. Whereupon à Wood, seeing her gasping, took away her money, jewels, &c., and flung her down over the works." (Edited, in 1848, by Bliss for the Ecc. Hist. Society, p. 51.)

But besides these unquestionable witnesses there were others among the sufferers whose testimony cannot be impeached. Some officers and men, who were wounded and left for dead, escaped under the cover of the night and rejoined the camp of Lord Ormonde. Several others succeeded in concealing themselves during the days of the massacre, and lived to give authentic evidence of the scenes they had witnessed. It was from them that Ormonde and Inchiquin as well as the Catholic authorities above cited learned the various particulars which they attest. Among the non-combatants who thus escaped was Richard Talbot, afterwards so well known as the Duke of Tyrconnel. He was very young at the time, but the sights which he witnessed made a lasting impression on his mind and inspired him with a horror for the Puritans all his life long.

7. Some modern writers have also vainly attempted to prove that no promise of quarter was given to the garrison of Drogheda. However, even Borlase (*Irish Insur.*, p. 282) confesses that this promise was made. Dr. Lynch also expressly writes: "Cromwell, though at the head of a large army besieging Drogheda, could not take the town until its defenders had received a promise of their lives from some persons of high rank in his army; nevertheless, Cromwell instantly issued the savage order for that most atrocious massacre."

This violation of faith was, however, an everyday occurrence with the Puritans. The author just referred to gives another instance of it: "Shortly after the commencement of the late war, the Castle of Sligo was besieged by the enemy. The commander of the besieging force promised in writing to spare the lives of the besieged; but as soon as the castle gates were thrown open, the garrison was shamefully butchered to a man . . . . when the Kilkenny delegates complained to Cromwell of the daily infraction of the conditions granted by himself, he is said to have answered, that as he was now in England, he could not be bound by the stipulations he had made in Ireland."—(*Camb. Evers.* vol. iii. p. 187.)

For the unparalleled brutality displayed at Drogheda a vote of thanks was passed by Parliament to Cromwell, a day of general thanksgiving throughout the kingdom was ordered, and it was decreed "that the house does approve of the execution done at Drogheda, as an act of justice to themselves and of mercy to others who might be warned thereby."

8. Hugh O'Reilly, a descendant of the old Irish

monarchs, was at this time Primate and Archbishop of Armagh. It is recorded of him that he prohibited the use of pewter chalices when offering the Holy Sacrifice, and obliged the clergy to provide sacred vessels of silver or other precious metal for their respective churches. He frequently administered Confirmation in the woods or on the hill-sides, and, surrounded as he was by Scotch settlers, he endeavoured clandestinely as best he could to instruct his flock. He was nevertheless arrested and thrown into prison in Dublin, accused of carrying on treasonable correspondence with the Irish officers on the Continent. The accusation proved groundless and he was restored to liberty. Throughout the Confederation period he displayed a devoted heroism, without fear and without reproach, ever united with his flock. When at length the province of Ulster was overrun by the Puritan armies, he chose for himself a silent retreat in the little island of the B. Trinity in the county of Cavan, where after suffering incredible hardships (*post plurimas ærumnas in eo recessu patientissime toleratas*) he died in 1652, aged 72 years. He was succeeded by Edmund O'Reilly, who had already been well tried in the crucible of suffering. When he sailed for Ireland, after having completed his studies at Douai, the ship was driven in a gale to Dartmouth, and O'Reilly, being recognized as a priest, was arrested, led off to Chester, and kept in prison there for two years. Being appointed Vicar-General of Dublin by Archbishop Fleming in 1636 he remained within the city and continued to discharge the duties of his office throughout all the vicissitudes of that trying period till the Archbishop's death in 1651. Appointed to the Primacy in

1657 he was driven into exile in 1661. An invitation sent to the Irish clergy in 1666 to attend a conference convened in Dublin for the purpose of presenting an Address attesting their loyalty to the Crown, gave him an opportunity to return once more to Ireland. So far, however, was this conference from assuring his safety that he was again put under arrest, and he was liberated only on his friends giving security that he would quit Ireland and never again return. He continued, however, to labour indefatigably to promote the interests of the Irish Church in Rome and in France, till his death on the 8th of March, 1669, at Saumer, where he was interred in the church of the B. Virgin.

CHAPTER V.

Sufferings of the Catholics in Wexford.

1. Massacre in Wexford in 1649.—2. Several priests and religious killed.—3. Letter of the Bishop, Dr. French, on this massacre.—4. Extracts from his apology.—5. Massacre of 300 females at the Cross in Wexford.—6. Savage cruelty of George Cooke and Captain Bolton.—7. Sufferings of the Bishop; fate of Cooke.—8. Martyrdom of Rev. Daniel O'Brien, Dean of Ferns, and others.

1. In Wexford the scenes of Puritan barbarism were again renewed. The town was favourably situated for defence. The walls were high, and protected by towers, and strengthened on the inside by a rampart of earth fifteen feet thick. In the harbour were three vessels, one of them of thirty-four guns. Winter was setting in, and Cromwell was already complaining of the scarcity of fodder for his cavalry. The citizens were brave and well provided with arms. Colonel David Sinnott, the governor of the town, and Sir Edmund Butler, who commanded the troops, were devoted to the royal cause. The castle, however, which stood at the south side of the town, a little outside the walls, was entrusted to the care of Captain James Stafford. The Irish bishops assembled at Jamestown complained of his being wholly unfit for such a post, and they style him "a young man, vain and unadvised;" the author of the *Aphorismical*

Discovery speaks of him as "a vain, idle, young man, nothing practised in the art military;" and indeed his whole merit appears to have been that he was a favourite of Lord Ormonde, who was now the Viceroy and commander-in-chief of the royal army.

On the eleventh day of the siege, which was the 11th of October, Cromwell offered the following conditions: "I shall give soldiers and non-commissioned officers quarter for life, and leave to go to their several habitations, with their wearing clothes, they engaging themselves to live quietly there, and to take up arms no more against the Parliament of England. And the commissioned officers quarter for their lives, but to render themselves prisoners. And as for the inhabitants I shall engage myself that no violence shall be offered to their goods, and that I shall protect the town from plunder. I expect your positive answer instantly, and if you will upon these terms surrender and quit, and in one hour shall send forth to me four officers of the quality of field officers, and two aldermen, for the performance thereof, I shall thereupon forbear all acts of hostility."

Captain James Stafford was one of the four deputed by the governor to proceed to the Puritan camp to discuss these articles of surrender, and Cromwell availed of the opportunity to deal privately with him. The result was not long to wait for. While the proposed terms were still under discussion, the Puritan troops were treacherously admitted into the castle. Carte expressly states that the enemy entered the gates "by the treachery of Captain Stafford;" and adds that "Stafford having privately received Cromwell's forces into the castle, which commanded the part of the town that lay next it, they issued suddenly from thence, attacked the wall and gate adjoining, and soon became masters of the place." (*Life of Ormonde*, vol. ii., p. 63.) The gates being thrown open, the whole army poured in. So sudden was this collapse of the defence that the townsmen were first made aware of Stafford's treachery by seeing the enemy's colours floating from the summit of the castle and the guns turned against the walls.

2. Cromwell, being thus in possession of the town, was heedless of the conditions which he had proposed and "*thought it not good or just to restrain the soldiers from their right of pillage, nor from doing of execution on the enemy.*"* In his opinion the massacre of the inhabitants could only be likened to that of Drogheda, and he adds: "It pleased God to give into your hands *this other mercy*, for which, as for all, we pray God may have all the glory." In the same letter he estimates the number of the garrison thus butchered at 2,000, and recommends the Parliament to send over English Protestants to inhabit the city, as "of the former inhabitants not one in twenty can be found to challenge any property in their own houses. Most of them are run away, and many of them were killed in this service. God, by an unexpected providence in His righteous justice, brought a just judgment on them, causing them to become a prey to the soldiers."

It was thus that on the 11th of October the enemy entered the town of Wexford. The *History of the Jesuits in Ireland*, by Father St. Leger (1655), briefly

* Lett. of Cromwell to the Parliament.

sketches the scene of slaughter that ensued: "On the city being taken, Cromwell exterminated the citizens by the sword." Another contemporary record details the special sufferings of the friars of the Order of St. Francis: "On the 11th of October, 1649, seven friars of our Order, all men of extraordinary merit, and natives of the town, perished by the sword of the heretics. Some of them were killed kneeling before the altar, and others whilst hearing confessions. Father Raymond Stafford, holding a crucifix in his hand, came out of the church to encourage the citizens, and even preached with great zeal to the infuriated enemies themselves, till he was killed by them in the market-place."* The Archbishop of Dublin, in the letter already referred to, repeats the same in a few words: "At Wexford," he says, "many priests, some religious, innumerable citizens, and two thousand soldiers were massacred."†

The following are the names of the Franciscans who, with several others, met their death in the chapel of their Order at the hands of the Puritan soldiers: Fr. Richard Synnott, Fr. John Esmonde, Fr. Peter Stafford, Brother Didacus Cheevers, Fr. Paulinus Synnott, Fr. James Cullime, and Fr. Patrick Synnott.

3. The fullest narrative of the sufferings to which the Catholics were subjected is presented by the venerable bishop of the diocese, Dr. Nicholas French. When Dr. French was appointed Bishop of Ferns, he strenuously resisted his promotion; whereupon some of the leading

* Letter of F. Francis Stafford. See it in full in *Duffy's Magaz.* May, 1847.

† "Multi Sacerdotes, nonnulli religiosi, plurimi cives, et duo millia militum trucidati."—Lett. 5 June, 1650.

priests of the diocese drew up a memorial in reply to the difficulties he had proposed. This memorial is preserved in the library of Trinity College, Dublin, and is dated *Wexford*, 10*th October*, 1645. Amongst other things the memorialists state, that " he was advanced to the episcopate, not by purchase, or solicitation, or interest, but called by God, as the faithful and prudent servant whom God placed over his household. '*It was then*,' says St. Gregory, '*a praiseworthy thing to aspire to the episcopate, when by it one only obtained more sufferings, and when he who ruled the faithful had, for his privilege, to be led out the first to the trials of martyrdom.*' And, perhaps, in the calamitous times in which we now live, these words may be well applied to the bishops of Ireland." These words were in part prophetical, and during the subsequent period of persecution Dr. French was foremost in sharing the perils and privations of his flock. From the place of his exile he thus wrote to the internuncio in the month of January, 1673 :

"On one day I lost, for the cause of God and the faith, all that I possessed: it was the 11th of October, 1649. On that most lamentable day my native city of Wexford, abounding in wealth, ships, and merchandise, was destroyed by the sword, and given a prey to the infuriated soldiers, by Cromwell, that English pest of hell. There, before God's altar, fell many sacred victims, holy priests of the Lord; others, who were seized outside the precincts of the church, were scourged with whips; others were hanged: some were arrested and bound with chains; and others were put to death by various most cruel tortures. The best blood of the citizens was shed; the very squares were inundated with it,* and there was scarcely a house that was not defiled with carnage and full of wailing. In my own palace a youth, hardly sixteen years of age—an amiable boy—as also my gardener and sacristan, were cruelly butchered; and the chaplain, whom I caused to remain behind me at home, was transpierced with six mortal wounds. These things were perpetrated in open day by the impious assassins. From that moment (and this it is that renders me a most unhappy man) I have never seen my city, or my flock, or my home, or my kindred. After the destruction of the city I lived for five months in the woods, with death ever impending over me. There my drink was milk and water, a small quantity of bread was my food, and on one occasion I did not taste bread during five days; there was no need of cookery for my scanty meals, and I slept in the open air without either bed or bed-clothes. . At length the wood in which I lay concealed was surrounded by numerous bodies of the enemy, who anxiously sought to capture me and send me loaded with chains to England. My angel guardian being my guide, I burst through their lines and escaped, owing to the swiftness of my steed."†

4. In the library of Trinity College, Dublin, another letter of this prelate is preserved, written at the same period, and entitled "Apologia," being a defence of the course he had pursued in seeking his safety in exile. In it he thus addresses his accuser:—

"You say nothing about my native city, Wexford,

---

* Fundebatur clarus civium sanguis quo inundabant plateæ, &c.
† Litt. Nicol. Fernens. Ep. ad Internuntium. Anversæ Jan. 1673.

cruelly destroyed by the sword on the 11th of October, 1649; nothing of my palace being plundered, and of my domestics impiously slain; nothing of my fellow-labourers, precious victims, immolated by the impious sword of the heretics before the altar of God; nothing of the inhabitants weltering in their own blood and gore. The rumour of the direful massacre reached me whilst I was in a neighbouring town, suffering from a burning fever. I cried and mourned, and shed bitter tears, and lamented; and turning to heaven, with a deep sigh, cried out, in the words of the prophet Jeremias, and all who were present shared in my tears. In that excessive bitterness of my soul, a thousand times I wished to be dissolved, and to be with Christ, that thus I might not witness the sufferings of my country. From that period I have never seen my city or my people, but, as an outcast, I sought a refuge in the wilderness. I wandered through woods and mountains, generally taking my rest and repose exposed to the hoar frost, sometimes lying hid in the caves and caverns of the earth. In the woods and groves I passed more than five months, that thus I might administer some consolation to the few survivors of my flock who had escaped from the universal massacre, and dwelt there with the herds of cattle. But neither trees nor caverns could afford me lasting refuge; for the heretical Governor of Wexford, George Cooke, well known for his barbarity, with several troops of cavalry and foot-soldiers, searching everywhere, anxious for my death, explored even the highest mountains and most difficult recesses; the huts and habitations adjoining the wood, and in which I sometimes had offered the Holy Sacrifice, he destroyed by fire, and my hiding-places, which were formed of branches and leafy boughs of trees, were all overturned. Amongst those who were subjected to much annoyance, on my account, was a nobleman in whose house he supposed me to lie concealed. He searched the whole house with lighted tapers, accompanied by soldiers, holding their naked swords in their hands to slay me the moment I should appear; but amidst all these perils God protected me, and mercifully delivered me from the hands of this blood-thirsty man."

5. In these extracts the public square or market-place is referred to as the chief scene of this wholesale massacre. M'Geoghegan and Lingard attest that many of the principal inhabitants had assembled there, and no fewer than 300 females are said to have chosen the same place of refuge. They knelt around the great cross which was erected in its centre, and they hoped that their defenceless condition, their prayers and cries, would move the enemy to compassion. The ruthless barbarian, the pagan Goth or Hun, would have been moved to pity, but Puritan fanaticism had steeled the hearts of Cromwell's followers against every sentiment of mercy, and the market-place of Wexford was soon inundated with the blood of these martyrs.

Some have questioned the accuracy of the statement made by M'Geoghegan and Lingard as to the massacre of these females around the cross of Wexford; they say Dr. French and other contemporary writers would not be silent in regard of this particular. But these contemporary writers sufficiently describe the wholesale massacre of the inhabitants, without mercy being shown to age or sex; and any particulars that are added have a special reference to themselves. The same writers, when describing the destruction of Drogheda, are silent as to the massacre of the females in the crypts of St. Peter's Church; and were it not for the narrative of an officer, who himself was engaged in that barbarous deed, some critics, as we have seen, would be found to reject it as fabulous. The constant tradition, not only of Wexford, but of the whole nation, attests the truth of the statement of the above-named historians.

6. In the above extracts Dr. French also describes George Cooke, the commander of the Puritans in Wexford, as especially remarkable for his brutality and cruelty. Some instances recorded by the author of *Cambrensis Eversus* more than justify his description. After stating that a promise had been given by him to the inhabitants of Wexford, that on a certain day they might reside in their own homes, he adds:

"But this same Cooke afterwards authorised Captain Bolton, before the expiration of the stipulated day, to scour that county with his cavalry and plunder it; then commenced an indiscriminate massacre of men, women, and children, by which not less than four thousand souls, young and old, were atrociously butchered. In 1652, the same Governor Cooke shut up 300 men and many infants in a house in the county of Wexford, and then setting fire to the house, all were burned in the flames. But Captain Gore, one of the officers under Cooke, succeeded in concealing on his horse, under his cloak, a little boy that had escaped out of the house. Cooke, discovering the fact before they had retired very far from the house, burst into a violent rage, severely condemned the captain, and returning himself with the poor little innocent boy, hurled him into the raging flames. Little wonder that Captain Bolton, who had formerly executed the savage orders of his commander, should emulate the ferocity and act on the principles of his master, and leave some other monuments of his own treachery and savageness."—(Vol. iii. pp. 191-3.)

7. Dr. French, Bishop of Ferns, who has so vividly described the sufferings of the Catholics of Wexford, shared during the siege the hardships and perils of his flock. He had some time before addressed a letter to Owen Roe O'Neill and the Ulster Catholics, exhorting them to place no confidence in the Puritans, the sworn enemies of the Catholic Church and of Ireland, but to unite cordially with the royal troops. A copy of this letter being found in the plunder of the episcopal palace, excited the rage of George Cooke, the Cromwellian Governor of Wexford, who left no means untried to compass the bishop's death. Dr. Lynch, in his MS. History, repeats that the whole surrounding country was scoured by bands of soldiery in search of him. The secret recesses of the houses were minutely scanned, the woods and morasses were everywhere explored. Dr. French, however, escaped, and made his way to Galway, whence he sailed for the continent in the month of November, 1650. We meet with him in Rome in 1653, and there, presenting a memorial to the Sovereign Pontiff, he writes: "I, a most afflicted bishop, an exile in foreign lands through the barbarous cruelty of the English heretics, having fulfilled a vow

in the holy house of Loreto and made the visit at the shrines of the apostles, now present myself at your Holiness's feet, unable to give any account of my flock and of the church of Ferns entrusted to my care, but that everything sacred has been swept away, the churches are profaned, the ecclesiastical possessions are a prey in the hands of plunderers, the vessels of the altar have become the drinking-cups of drunkards, and the house of God a den of robbers. One thing alone can I say to bring consolation to your Holiness, and that is, that the people under the tyranny of the wicked enemy, though subjected to great sufferings, have not ceased to be Catholics, nay, rather have been madé more fervent by the persecution. Twenty parish priests and three religious, amid hardships and poverty, minister to their spiritual wants; the rest of the clergy have perished by the sword or by sickness. Myself alone wander inconsolable an exile from my flock." Dr. French never revisited his flock, but he laboured indefatigably on the continent to promote its welfare, till his death on the 23rd of August. 1678. As for Cooke, he met with the chastisement which his cruelty deserved. Soon after the restoration of Charles II. he was thrown into prison in London on the accusation of treason, and received himself at the hands of the executioner the punishment of death which he had so mercilessly dealt out to others.

8. Before we pass from this theatre of Puritan cruelty, the martyrdom of the Rev. Daniel O'Brien, Dean of Ferns, deserves to be specially commemorated. Having studied in the Irish College of Compostella, and being

promoted there to the holy order of priesthood, he ever afterwards cherished such an affection for Spain and its people, on whose piety and other merits he loved to dilate, that he was popularly known as Father Daniel the Spaniard. He was indefatigable in the sacred ministry, and was particularly successful in bringing Protestants into the true fold. He led a most holy life, and his flock were so attached to him that they would have willingly shed their blood in his defence. After the capture of Wexford he took refuge in the house of a nobleman who lived in the neighbourhood, and continued there to stealthily exercise the sacred ministry. The heretics, seeing a number of persons proceeding thither, and suspecting that Mass was being said, went unperceived in a boat, and surrounding the house threatened death to anyone who would dare to stir. The officer then commanded them to deliver up the priest, as otherwise he would order the soldiers to shoot them down. The venerable old priest, hearing the tumult, came out from his room and said to the officer: "Why do you trouble these good people, who have done nothing wrong? I am the priest who has offered up the Holy Sacrifice; if that is a fault, it is all mine." He was at once seized, and everything he had was taken from him. The officer insisted particularly on bearing away the chalice, and when about leaving with the prisoner, filled it with ale and triumphantly drank it off in the presence of them all. He had scarcely taken the draught, however, when he fell down in a terrible paroxysm, roaring aloud and tearing himself through an agony of pain. Father O'Brien, seeing his misery, and filled with compassion for the unhappy man, made the sign of the cross over him, whereupon he was freed from his terrible suffering. The officer at once gave back the chalice to him, and marching off the soldiers, allowed him to remain there undisturbed. He was afterwards again and again arrested and thrown into prison, but through the intercession of some of the governor's friends, the Catholics were able to secure his release. At length, in 1655, sentence of death was passed upon him. He received the intelligence with ineffable delight, and though, through his infirmities and long suffering, he had become quite disabled and almost unable to stand, yet, on the evening before his execution, his strength returned, and he walked full of courage and joy to the scaffold. He addressed a few glowing words to the assembled crowd, exhorting them to be devoted children of the faith and of Holy Church, and then sealed his preaching by laying down his life for Christ, on the 14th of April, the vigil of Easter, in 1655. He had for companions in martyrdom the Rev. Luke Bergin, of the Cistercian Order, and Rev. James Murchu (Murphy) a secular priest. They were tried by a jury of twelve Protestants, who returned a verdict that no crime had been proved against them; but the judge, turning to the jury, laid down the law that no crime could be more heinous than to be a priest, and at once the verdict of guilty was pronounced. The citizens of Wexford petitioned that at least they should not be hanged within the city walls, but even this request would not be granted. The bodies of the three holy martyrs were interred within the ruinous enclosure of

St. Francis' monastery, outside the walls of the city, and to the great terror and confusion of the heretics, a brilliant heavenly light was repeatedly seen encircling the spot where they were interred.*

* From the MS. "History of the Irish Bishops," by the contemporary, Dr. John Lynch.

CHAPTER VI.

SUFFERINGS OF THE CATHOLICS IN KILKENNY.

1. The Mass not to be tolerated.—2. Ravages of the plague; heroism of the Rev. P. Lea, and others.—3. Treason at work: bravery of the Irish soldiers at Callan.—4. The defence of Kilkenny.—5. Barbarity of Axtell and the Puritan troops.—6. The market Cross.—7. David Rothe, Bishop of Ossory.—8. Hardships endured by the clergy.—9. Bernard Fitzpatrick, V.G., John Daton, and others, martyrs.—10. A curious fact.—11. F. Fiacre Tobin: all the clergy banished.—12. The decree rigorously enforced.—13. The Catholic citizens driven forth from Kilkenny.

1. AFTER the massacre of Wexford, Cromwell invited the other cities and towns to surrender. Should they consent to receive parliamentary garrisons, their property and goods were to be secured to them, and no inquiries were to be made as to religion. One thing only would be required, that *the Mass* should be abolished; "for," he added, "wheresoever the authority of Parliament extends the Mass shall not be tolerated." However unable the Catholics might be to resist the torrent of destruction that was now bursting upon them, yet they were too devoted to the faith to embrace this impious condition, and, as we learn from Dr. Burgatt (subsequently Archbishop of Cashel), not one was found in the whole island who would consent to barter his religion for the proffered boon. Thus the sword of extermination was again unsheathed.

The city of Kilkenny was at this time the seat of government of the Catholic confederates: its walls were strongly fortified, and its citizens were alike remarkable for their loyalty to the crown and their devotion to the Catholic faith. In the words of a contemporary writer, "Catholicity was flourishing in the city of Kilkenny when the Puritan army, like a devastating torrent, overturning everything in its course, appeared before its walls." Whilst the inhuman foe threatened it from without, another scourge laid it waste within.

2. In the month of August, 1649, the plague made its first appearance on the western coast of Ireland. From the Rinuccini papers we learn that the contagion was brought to Galway by an English vessel carrying supplies for the royal troops. The war during the preceding years, the hardships that had befallen our people, and the widespread desolation of the open country that followed in the train of the Puritan army, prepared too well the soil of Ireland for the seeds of pestilence, and now rich and abundant was the harvest of death. Wherever the Cromwellian troops advanced they plundered the country, and consumed by fire whatever the sword could not destroy. Before the close of the year the terrible disease extended its ravages to Kilkenny. It was not unlike the malady known in England as the Black Death. Few of those who were attacked by it survived more than a few hours, whole families were swept away, and the medical art seemed to have no resource that could stop the contagion or bring relief to the sufferers. Many of the citizens sought for safety in flight, but wherever they went the same terrible malady stared them in the face. The

population of the city was soon lessened by one-third, and the same proportion of deaths was found in the army, the garrison being in a few months reduced by the disease from 1,200 to 400. Several of the clergy caught the contagion in the exercise of their sacred ministry, and died true martyrs of charity. The name of the Rev. Patrick Lea is commemorated with special eulogy. This heroic man was untiring in administering the sacraments to the sick and the dying, but not content with this, he endeavoured moreover to assist them in their temporal wants: he became the servant of the poor, discharging for them the most loathsome duties, and he closed their eyes in death, and when all others had forsaken them he dug their graves and on his shoulders bore their corpses to their resting-place. It was whilst performing this last-mentioned voluntary task of his apostolate of charity that he himself caught the contagion, and he expired a true martyr only a few days before the arrival of Cromwell's army at the city gates. "Rev. Patrick Lea, a man held to be a saint by all who knew him," thus runs the contemporary narrative, "was employed in the service of those who were struck down by the plague. He was well versed in all kinds of learning, even in the knowledge of medicine; for this reason it was the wish of all the citizens that he would undertake that duty. But owing to the excessive ardour of his charity and zeal, which knew no bounds, his career was short. Not only did he untiringly hear the confession of the plague-stricken, give them Holy Communion and Extreme Unction, and bestow on them all the spiritual aid they needed; but, besides, he was unceasing in attending to their bodily wants, supplying them with medicines, preparing their food, and cleansing their sores. It happened that a poor man whom he was attending died, and as the body was spreading contagion all around, Father Lea, without waiting for the help of others, took up the corpse in his arms and carried it to a neighbouring cemetery, and digging a grave, buried it there. Owing to the heated state in which he was, and to the contact with the putrid corpse, he was stricken down by the fatal disease on the 24th of March, 1650, to the edification of those who witnessed his charity and to the great grief of the citizens." Father Fiacre Tobin, of the Order of Capuchins, and Father John Daton, a Franciscan, both natives of the county Kilkenny, were also remarkable for the devotedness of their zeal. A few years later the former had the merit to become a Confessor of the Faith, whilst the latter was further privileged to seal his teaching with his blood.

3. Early in February, 1650, Cromwell left his winter quarters, and after occupying Fethard, Cashel, and Thurles, marched towards Kilkenny. He looked on the Capital of the Irish Confederates as already his own; for one of Ormonde's officers, named Tickle, had covenanted to surrender the city to him on condition of receiving £4,000, with a high command in Cromwell's army, and the post of Governor of Kilkenny. "If your excellency will draw before this town" (thus wrote the traitor), "I shall send a messenger unto you upon your first approach, and shall give you an account of the weakest part of the town and the force within exactly, and what else I shall find or you may direct me to be most necessary for you." (*Carte MSS.*, vol.

xxvi.) The correspondence, however, was discovered, and the traitor suffered the penalty of death, which he so justly deserved. Cromwell, on hearing of his fate, retired from the city and laid siege to Callan.

Callan was at this time a walled town of considerable strength and defended by three castles. Sir Robert Talbot, one of Ormonde's officers, was appointed governor and chief in command, and it was said that he had already arranged with Cromwell for its surrender. A small castle or outwork, however, was held by an Irish officer named Mac Geoghegan, who, with his small company of 100 men, offered a determined resistance. Three times they repulsed the assault of the enemy, but no succour being sent to them by the Governor, and being overwhelmed by numbers, they were at length every man put to the sword. Three hundred Puritans had been killed in the repeated assaults, and at the last attack Captain Mac Geoghegan, before he succumbed, was said to have slain twenty of the assailants with his own sword. His wife displayed no less valour. She hurled stones and other missiles upon the assailants, and was herself left for dead, being covered with wounds. Next day, however, this brave woman was picked up alive, and she was still living thirty-five years later, in the reign of James II., when the Aphorismical Discovery which relates the fact was written. (See this valuable work, edited by Gilbert, vol. ii., p. 64.) Talbot, with his troops, at once surrendered, and were allowed to march away with their baggage, but without their arms, and so enraged was Cromwell at the opposition which he had met with at the hands of these few devoted Irish soldiers, that he gave up the town to be pillaged, and ordered all its inhabitants to be put to the sword.

4. It was not till the 22nd of March, 1650, that Cromwell began operations against Kilkenny. James Archdekin was at this time Mayor; James Walsh had the charge of the Castle; but Sir Walter Butler, of Paulstown, was military governor of both the Castle and the city. The garrison was so reduced by the plague that it did not number more than about 400 fighting men, besides one troop of Lord Ormonde's cavalry; nevertheless, aided by the citizens, their defence of the city was most heroic. The Rinuccini MS. in a few words commemorates the bravery of the defendants as beyond all praise. Taylor, in his "History of the Civil Wars in Ireland," also speaks of the defence of the city in terms of the highest eulogy, and adds that were it not for the treachery of some of those within the walls Cromwell would have abandoned the siege.

Sir Walter Butler had left nothing undone to strengthen his position and to gather additional troops for the garrison. Lord Dillon, and his detachment of 2,000 men, were ordered by the general-in-chief for Leinster to repair to Kilkenny, but he replied that his men were so terrified by the reports regarding the plague that they refused to march towards the doomed city. The small garrison at Sandford's Court, then known as Cantwell's Castle, a few miles from Kilkenny, were asked to come in haste to join in the defence of the city; "but the officers, being English, Welsh, and Scotch, sent some of their number to Cromwell, offering him possession of the castle, and asking money and passes to go beyond the sea to serve in the armies of foreign states. He accepted their terms, on condition that they should do nothing to the prejudice of the Parliament of England."

Cromwell's head-quarters were placed at the Moat, beyond the Black Quarry, now known as Cromwell's Hill. His cannon soon shattered the old city wall, and a large breach was effected in front of the present parochial church of St. Patrick's, but Sir Walter Butler erected earthen breastworks within the wall, strengthened with palisades. A storming party, led on by Lieutenant Colonel Axtell, twice attempted to enter the breach, but were each time repulsed with great slaughter, no fewer than six hundred of the Puritan assailants being slain. The assault was ordered a third time, but they refused to advance, for they had learned to their cost that the counterworks completely commanded the breach on the inside. Cromwell himself, when he had got possession of the city and examined all the works, wrote: "It was a mercy to us that we did not further contend for an entrance there, it being probable that if we had it would have cost us very dear." Irishtown, which embraced St. Canice's Cathedral, and that portion of the city which lay beyond the Bregagh, had its own line of defence. The first assault made there was also repulsed, but all the garrison being required for the main point of attack, that part of the city was, after the first few days, left undefended, and was occupied by the enemy. On the 27th of March, a breach was made with pickaxes in the wall adjoining St. Francis's Abbey, close by the place where the Bregagh joins the Nore. A considerable body of the Cromwellian troops obtained an entry here, but they were quickly driven back, and most of those who had entered were slain. Eight companies of foot, under Colonel Gifford, next attempted to storm St. John's Gate and thus effect an entrance into the city. They advanced very resolutely, but were received with a galling fire, which compelled them to retire, leaving more than a hundred of their men wounded or slain. So many repulses were enough to make Cromwell hesitate as to the expediency of continuing the siege, but the Governor, seeing that his brave soldiers were exhausted by continual watching at their posts, and despairing of any succour from without, resolved to make as good conditions as he could by a timely surrender. The garrison was allowed to march out with military honours; the citizens were to be protected in their persons, goods, and estates; but with the exception of a hundred muskets and a hundred pikes, the soldiers were to surrender their arms to the troops appointed to receive them at the distance of two miles from the city. The city surrendered on the 28th of March, and as the soldiers marched out, with Sir Walter Butler at their head, they were complimented by Cromwell for their bravery: he said that they were gallant fellows, and that he had lost more men in the endeavour to storm the place than at Drogheda.

Colonel Axtell was appointed Governor of the city for the Puritan Parliament, and throughout the whole period of his government displayed a barbarous cruelty in his dealings with the Catholic citizens, and in particular in his enmity against the clergy. He had held the command of the foot guard on the memorable 30th of January, when King Charles was executed on the scaffold erected at the gate of the Royal Palace. After the Restoration he was one of the leading regicides who were excepted from pardon, and suffered the penalty, they so justly deserved, of death at Tyburn. Before execution he declared that nothing so afflicted his soul at that moment as some of the deeds of blood in which he had had a part in Ireland, and the writer who records this fact adds that the following was one of those deeds of cruelty thus particularly referred to: Sixteen or seventeen of the Catholic citizens of Kilkenny had been taken under special protection, but Axtell ordered them all to be put to death, and seized on everything that belonged to them.

The Puritan troops, enraged at the losses they had sustained from a handful of brave soldiers, though they were pledged to respect the lives and property of the citizens, did everything in their power to show their hatred of our Catholic people and of the religion which they professed. The churches were profaned, the altars overthrown, the paintings and statues destroyed, and, in a word, a relentless war was waged against everything held sacred by the citizens. Search was made for the vestments and religious ornaments that had been concealed, and when discovered they were desecrated and plundered. The religious books, crucifixes, and other articles of devotion found in the private houses were thrown into the streets, and either burnt or carried off as booty. In one of his letters Cromwell had used the emphatic words: "As regards the clergy, they know what to expect at our hands." The manner in which they were treated by the victors in Kilkenny was no exception to the general rule. Dr.

Patrick Lynch, of Galway, writing to the Secretary of Propaganda on the 1st of May, 1650, states that a report had reached him of the cruelties exercised in the city of Kilkenny, and "of a number of priests, religious, and citizens" having been put to death there. A regiment of cavalry was quartered in St. Canice's Cathedral, and the aisles were converted into stabling for the troopers' horses. The beautiful stained-glass windows were broken to fragments, the altars demolished, the stone-work ornaments defaced, and in a few weeks the work of centuries was, at the hands of these iconoclast barbarians, well nigh reduced to ruin. The Protestant Bishop Williams, in plaintful language, laments the sad disaster that had befallen this noble edifice: "The great and famous and most beautiful cathedral church of St. Kenny they have utterly defaced and ruined. They have thrown down the roof of it, taken away five great and goodly bells, broken down all the windows, and carried away every bit of glass, which they say was worth a very great deal, and all the doors of it, that hogs might come and root, and the dogs gnaw the bones of the dead; and they broke down a most exquisite marble font, wherein the Christians' children were regenerated, all to pieces, and threw down many goodly marble monuments that were therein, and especially that stately and costly monument of the most honourable and noble family of the house of Ormonde, and divers others of most rare and excellent work, not much inferior, if I be not much mistaken, to most of the best, excepting the Kings' that are in St. Paul's Church or the Abbey of Westminster." He further states that most of the religious edifices throughout the diocese were desecrated in like manner. The "fanatick limbs of the beast," he says, beheaded most of the churches, the roofs of them, both slates and timber, being quite taken off, and the walls thrown down even to the ground. Even when the monarchy was restored, under Charles II., these fanatics continued to display their hostility against these religious structures. "I found," he says, "the Cathedral Church and the bishop's house all ruined, and nothing standing but the bare walls, without roofs, without windows, but the holes, and without doors. And when I desired Mr. Connel, my registrar, to begin to repair some places of that church, and to set up benches and forms, some of the Anabaptists (as we have good reason to think) came in the night time, the church having no doors, and with axes and hammers or hatchets brake them down and carried them quite away, and did other unseemly abuses besides."

6. The large cross situated in the public square was a special mark for their irreligious fanaticism. Father Archdekin, himself a native of Kilkenny, in his *Theologia Tripartita*, published a few years later, thus writes: "There stands in the market-place of Kilkenny a magnificent structure of stone, of elegant workmanship, rising aloft after the manner of an obelisk. It is supported by four lofty columns, which bear the weight of the whole superstructure. You ascend it on the four sides by flights of stone steps; and above all on the highest point was placed a sculptured figure of the Crucifixion. After the occupation of the city by Cromwell's soldiers, some of them who were particularly remarkable for their impiety, assembled in the market-

place, armed with their muskets, and directed many shots against the symbol of the Crucifixion, in order that they might fully complete their irreligious triumph; and this their persecuting fury at length accomplished. But behold! the wrath of an avenging God quickly pursued the authors of this sacrilege. A mysterious malady seized on them so that none survived more than a few days." Another contemporary narrative gives some further details of this deed of sacrilege: "Seven soldiers of the Cromwellian army, like seven unclean spirits, set themselves to destroy the crucifix. After firing at it for some time, they broke off the lighter portion of it, and returned in triumph to their dwellings. But of the number, six died almost immediately after, three on that same day and three on the day following. The seventh I know not what happened him. The facts became known to the whole city, and served to confirm the Catholics in their veneration for the cross and to terrify in no small degree the heretics, its enemies."

7. The illustrious David Rothe was at this time Bishop of Ossory. He was the son of Geoffrey Rothe, a wealthy merchant of Kilkenny, and was born in the year 1568. Being consecrated Bishop of his native diocese in 1618, he displayed the zeal of an Apostle ministering to the wants not alone of his immediate flock but of the faithful throughout all Ireland, for plenary jurisdiction was given to him on account of the persecution which prevailed, and of the few Bishops who now remained in the kingdom. Dr. Rothe was chosen a member of the Supreme Council of the Confederates and laboured assiduously to preserve union in the

Confederate ranks. At the same time he left nothing undone to promote a spirit of piety among his devoted people. Early in 1642, the whole city was with solemn religious ceremonies dedicated to the Blessed Virgin. The statue of our Immaculate Lady was borne in procession from St. Mary's Church, and erected in the market-place, in a shrine of exquisite and costly workmanship. The bells of all the churches and the peals of the artillery, proclaimed the general jubilee, and at night festive bonfires illumined every street. The citizens assembled before the sacred image on Saturdays to chant Our Lady's Litany, and from that time Kilkenny has never ceased to be OUR LADY'S CITY. The Cathedral of St. Canice, having been allowed to fall to ruin by its Protestant occupants, was restored by Dr. Rothe at considerable expense, and was rededicated to the worship of God on the 1st of October, 1644. Weighed down by infirmities and years, Dr. Rothe was unable to take that active part which he would have desired in the important deliberations of the Supreme Council during the last years of the Confederation. Whilst the plague raged in the city, the aged Bishop, helpless as he was, caused himself to be carried from house to house to bring consolation to the sufferers and to minister to their wants. The city having at length surrendered he resolved to accompany the soldiers as they marched from the city. They had proceeded only about two miles, when a marauding party of the enemy fell upon the rear-guard and seizing on the aged Bishop dragged him from the carriage in which he was concealed, and treated him with the greatest indignity. They deprived him of everything he had, and then threw him more dead than alive into a wretched hovel on the roadside, with a tattered cloak full of vermin as his only covering. He was soon after thence conveyed to his friends in the city, but the days which he survived were to him a prolonged martyrdom. He expired on the 20th of April, 1650, in his 82nd year, and such was the esteem in which he was held by all, that his obsequies were allowed to be performed with due solemnity in St. Mary's Church, and his remains were deposited there in the family vault, the cathedral in which his own tomb had been prepared being occupied by the Cromwellian soldiery.

8. The years of Puritan sway which followed the demise of Dr. Rothe were a period of sorrow and persecution for the widowed Church of Ossory. The Catholic clergy were classed by the Puritans with the wild beasts, and were hunted down with a persistent intensity of hatred for which we can only find a parallel among the Pagan persecutors in the early annals of the Christian Church. No detailed narrative of their sufferings has been handed down to us, but the occasional glimpses which contemporary records afford suffice to make known how much the heroic Priests of those days had to endure that they might be faithful in their duty towards their flocks and break to them the strengthening Bread of Life.

In a narrative compiled by the Jesuit Fathers, of which the original Latin text may be seen in the *Spicilegium Ossoriense* vol. ii., p. 43, the sufferings of the members of the Society are thus briefly sketched: "A few days after the death of Father Lea the city of Kilkenny was taken. . Our Fathers sought to avoid the danger in various ways. One of them armed himself with a weapon and passed out with the soldiers, who were leaving the town. Another acted as servant in the house of a certain nobleman, and when waiting at table often poured out wine and ale to the enemy. A third, in the disguise of a merchant, remained at large in the city and employed himself in administering consolation to the Catholics. Meanwhile the army of the heretics entering the town, overturned the altars, and profaned the images, crosses, and all other sacred things. They destroyed our house and oratory, sparing nothing that they thought belonged to a Jesuit. The sacred furniture of the altar had been hidden away; yet it was found and plundered. The books were thrown out in the streets and burned. The soldiers who were struck down by the plague were put into our house, which was turned into an hospital, and everything was profaned."

From the Rinuccini MS. we learn that Father Barnaby Barnewall, Commissary-General of the Capuchins, was in the city of Kilkenny during the siege. He made his escape in the disguise of a soldier, but was exposed to incredible hardships on the road from hunger and cold, intensified by old age and infirmity. He made his way, however, to his relative, the Countess of Fingall, in Meath, and during the following years, despite the bitter persecution, continued to reside at her mansion, attending during all that time to the spiritual wants of the vast adjoining district. As regards the secular clergy the same MS. adds that they all either attained the martyr's crown or were cut off by the plague or driven by the terrors of the most cruel persecution to seek a refuge in some remote recesses of the kingdom.

The Memorial of the Langton family as we read in the Transactions of the Kilkenny Archæological Society for 1864, sets forth in one short sentence the whole history of the clergy of Kilkenny, so far as the arm of the Puritan Government could reach them, "all our clergy were expelled by the Parliament and the usurper Cromwell." Dr. Patrick Lynch, Provost of Galway, writing to Propaganda on the 1st of May, 1650, also attests that, according to the reports which had reached him, the heretics had raged with great cruelty in the city of Kilkenny, and had put to death a number of priests, religious, nobles, and merchants.

9. After the death of the Bishop, the Diocese of Ossory was administered by the Vicar-General, Bernard Fitzpatrick, or as his name is given in the Irish records, Bryan Mac Turlogh Fitzpatrick, who, towards the close of 1651, was confirmed as Vicar Administrator of the See by Edmund O'Dempsey, Bishop of Leighlin, the only Bishop of the province, then residing in Leinster. In the *Aphorismical Discovery* it is said of this heroic ecclesiastic that he was "a zealous, religious, and pious priest, but within a short time after God did call him unto a better choice into glory, in remuneration of his virtues." In the *Threnodia Hiberno-Catholica* (cap. vi), and also in the *Elenchus Encomiorum de Joanne Scoto*, by Father Bonaventure O'Connor, O.S.F. (printed at Bolzano, in the Tyrol, in 1660, p. 307), it is further stated that this Father Bernard Fitzpatrick, Vicar-General of Ossory, was of the noble family of the Lord Barons of Ossory, and having taken refuge in a cave, that he might shelter himself from the fury of the persecutors, he was tracked thither by the heretics,

"who, there, beheaded the most holy man, who was famed throughout the whole kingdom, and was remarkable alike for his life and learning, and lineage: his head was set upon a stake at the gate of one of the towns as food for the birds of the air, and the rest of his body was left to be devoured by the beasts of the earth."

Father Denis Murphy, S. J., in his *Cromwell in Ireland*, thus writes: "There is a tradition still current in Kilkenny, that after the surrender of the town, some distinguished ecclesiastics took refuge from the violence of the soldiery in a secret chamber of the Dominican friary attached to the Black Abbey. None knew of their place of concealment except a few trusted friends, among whom was a woman named Thornton, who engaged to supply them every night with milk. This woman, for a bribe, betrayed the secret, and indicated to the Cromwellian soldiers where their victims could be found by spilling the milk along the road from the outer gate to the spot where the entrance to the secret chamber should be sought. The consequence was that the ecclesiastics were dragged from their concealment and put to death. Their betrayer received a grant of land as her reward" (p. 314). This tradition is undoubtedly accurate in its general details of the massacre of "distinguished ecclesiastics" who had sought a refuge in some retired spot from the terrors of the persecution that encompassed them. In one circumstance, however, the modern narrative appears to have deviated from the old tradition. It was not in the convent at the Black Abbey, but rather in one of the caves at Thornback, the site of the old Dominican novitiate, that the clergy were concealed, and it seems to me most probable that one of those distinguished Ecclesiastics who, in that silent retreat, received the martyr's crown, was precisely the Vicar-General, Bernard Fitzpatrick, of whom we have just spoken.

Among the clergy who, under the Puritan tyranny, laid down their lives ministring to the faithful of Kilkenny, Father John Daton, of the Order of St. Francis, deserves particular mention. A native of the county of Kilkenny, he at an early age embraced the Franciscan rule of strict observance, and was remarkable for his piety, gravity, prudence, and spirit of penance. Throughout the fierce controversy regarding the censures and Interdict in 1648, he was always found at the side of the Nuncio, and his name appears in the address presented by the clergy to Monsignor Rinuccini, on the 5th of November, 1648. When the Guardian of the Franciscan Convent, Kilkenny, was thrown into prison for refusing to abide by the instructions of the Supreme Council in the matter of the ecclesiastical censures, Father Daton, being the next in authority, became temporarily Superior, and fearlessly followed the very course for which the Guardian had been imprisoned. After the surrender of the city to Cromwell he remained in Kilkenny in secular dress, and proved himself indefatigable by night and day attending the sick and comforting the dying by bringing to them the consolations of religion. On the 2nd of August, 1653, he was at length discovered and arrested together with a Capuchin lay-brother and two Franciscan Nuns. It was the Feast of the Portiuncula, and the crowds of the faithful who, on that day, flocked to the house in which Father Daton was concealed, that they might approach the

Sacraments and gain the indulgences, led to his discovery. At ten o'clock at night he was seized by the Puritan soldiers, and by order of the Governor of the city was thrown into prison. Next day he was brought before Axtell. He was interrogated as to his priestly character, his religious profession, the saying of Mass, the administering of the Sacraments, all of which he publicly avowed, and from which no earthly command would induce him to desist. He was sentenced to be hanged on the second next day with all the additional torture and indignities usually attendant on death for treason. He spent the interval in the most fervent exercises of penance and prayer, and was led to the scaffold on the 5th of August, 1653. With every manifestation of joy and thanksgiving to God, he went to the place of execution "and being hanged and embowelled while yet alive, and quartered," he received the martyr's crown.

The two Franciscan Nuns, arrested on the same day with Father Daton, were sisters by birth as well as by religious profession. They lived retired in their house and privately wore the habit as Tertiaries of the Order of St. Francis. They, too, were sentenced to death, but an interval of twelve days was granted them that they might have an opportunity if they so willed of saving themselves by renouncing their religious life. They had the consolation of being imprisoned in the same dungeon with Father Daton on the vigil of his martyrdom, and with dauntless heroism they resolved to emulate his fortitude and prepared themselves for death. Through the interposition of some friends, however, their sentence of death was commuted into banishment. They were put on board a vessel sailing for Spain, and they were received with joy into one of the religious houses of that Catholic nation.

The Capuchin lay-brother arrested on the same memorable 2nd of August, 1653, was called in his religious Order Brother John of Dundalk, but his secular name was John Verdun. He was advanced in years and paralyzed, and was at death's door through dysentery. He lived in a house adjoining the temporary Capuchin Convent, and all the books and furniture and religious ornaments of the scattered community had been consigned to his care. All this was now seized by the Puritans, and he himself was sentenced to death. Owing to his infirm condition, however, the sentence was not executed, and for ten months he lingered on in the common prison, enduring with the greatest constancy all the sufferings of a prolonged martyrdom. For some time he was not allowed even a bed to lie upon, and had scarcely any food. He had no means of his own to pay for food, and the Catholic people were so overwhelmed with calamities, and so ground down by spoliation and oppression of every sort that they could afford him but little aid. At length, in the beginning of June, 1654, he was taken from gaol, and in company with twelve priests, who had been seized and sentenced to exile, was hurried off, surrounded by a body of soldiers, to Waterford. There they were again thrown into the common prison, where they were associated with the worst characters, and detained for six months awaiting a vessel to sail for the Continent. The Governor of Waterford, William Leigh, was a savage Puritan, and made use of every endeavour to induce his prisoners to renounce Popery and embrace what he was pleased to call his Gospel tenets. At length, on the 25th of July, 1654, the good lay-brother was put on board a vessel bound for France.

On the 14th of August he landed in that Catholic country, and was there welcomed by his religious brethren as a Confessor for the faith, and every comfort was ministered to him, but weighed down by infirmities and the hardships of his imprisonment, he expired at the Capuchin Convent, Charleville, on the 15th of March, 1655.

10. All the exiles at this time sent into exile or transported to serve as slaves in the Tobacco Islands, were not as submissive as Brother Verdun and his companions. The Rinuccini MS. mentions one instance of a large number of sufferers, whose only crime was their love of country and their faith, who, a few years later, were shipped in an English vessel from Waterford for Barbadoes. Every evening the captives were put in irons, and the hatches were closed down on them for the night, but by day they were allowed to roam freely on board the vessel. Their treatment on board was of the worst. The contemporary record states that they were fed like slaves, or rather like brutes. And yet several of them were of noble birth. They were nearly all from the counties of Kilkenny and Waterford, and there were not a few skilled seamen among them. As they conversed together in the Irish tongue, which was not understood by the sailors, they arranged, when a few days at sea, to distribute themselves among the crew and the officials, and at the signal " Dia agus Padruic linn "—*God and St. Patrick be with us*—to seize them and make them their prisoners, and then to steer the

vessel for France. The next morning, the sea being calm, and the officers and men all basking in the enjoyment of undisturbed tranquillity, two or three of the exiles ranged themselves near each of the crew and others on board, and no sooner was the signal given, than each of the exiles re-echoed again and again the same invocation, " God and St. Patrick be with us," and almost without a struggle they seized on all the officers and men, and put them in the irons from which they themselves had been just freed. They steered the vessel to Brest, and sold it there after setting free the crew. Brest was at this time the great rendezvous for the Irish merchants, some of whom at their private expense fitted out cruisers, received letters of marque from the king, and became rich beyond measure by their depredations on the merchant vessels of the Puritans. Such numbers of our countrymen had settled at Brest, which, under the patronage of Cardinal Mazarine, was just then growing into importance among the French ports, that it seemed as if transformed into an Irish colony. The descendants of these exiles spread themselves over the neighbouring territory, and the names of many of them became illustrious in the annals of their adopted country.

11. We have already referred to the charity displayed by the Capuchin, Father Fiacre Tobin, a native of Kilkenny, who, from the first commencement of the plague, had devoted himself with most perfect self-sacrifice to the service of his suffering fellow-citizens. After the surrender to Cromwell, he continued with unwearied zeal to pursue his apostolate of charity, assuming at times various disguises the better to elude

the vigilance of those who were in eager pursuit of the clergy. For a few months he was thus enabled to exercise the sacred ministry with impunity, but he was at length detected by a Puritan whose suspicions were aroused by the very appearance and demeanour of Father Fiacre, and judging him to be a priest engaged in the administration of the sacraments, pretended to be a Catholic and saluted him with the title of Father. This salutation threw the good Capuchin off his guard. He was at once arrested, loaded with irons in prison, and threatened with death, and for a time subjected to many hardships. Soon, however, the gaoler was appeased by gifts, and the prisoner was enabled to say Mass in prison, and even to converse with the faithful who came privately to visit him and to receive at his hands the Sacraments of Penance and the Blessed Eucharist. After a time sureties were accepted for his peaceable demeanour; the city itself was assigned him for his prison, and he was allowed full liberty within the city walls. When the decree of banishment was published against the clergy in 1653, he was sent into France, and on the 3rd of May of that year he addressed from Nantes a letter to his Superior at Charleville on the Meuse, from which a few extracts will suffice to set before us in faithful and vivid colours the deplorable state of ruin and desolation to which the nation was at this time reduced: "Under penalty of death the clergy are now banished from every part of Ireland; not only the priest, but the person who shelters him, shall be judged according to the statutes enacted against such persons in England in Elizabeth's reign. As regards the Catholic laity, they are permitted to live in Ireland, but they are so ground down by the crushing weight of taxes and other burdens that they cannot endure it very long. When Kilkenny came into the enemy's hands, Father Barnabas, who was then Commissary, directed me to remain in the city, and I did so, although with reluctance, for it was painful to me and quite contrary to my wishes to lay aside the religious habit and to assume the secular dress. I went around from house to house, administering to the families and their household the Sacraments of Penance and the Blessed Eucharist, and when summoned to assist those attacked by the plague I hastened at once to them. At length I was arrested by the heretics in the streets of Kilkenny, and hurried off to the Governor, who interrogated me as to the houses in which I had said Mass, and as to the presence of other clergy in the city. I replied that I could not, with a safe conscience, bring others into trouble by answering such questions. He then cried out: 'You will be hanged on to-morrow.' I said: 'I am prepared to die.' He used these words merely to terrify me. I was led back to prison, and all that night prepared myself for death; but my imprisonment was prolonged for nine months. . . . At the end of nine months the local magistrate allowed me to have the city as my prison, the Catholic citizens giving security that whenever called upon I would be ready to appear before the court. I was thus enabled to administer the sacraments more freely than when I was in gaol, and sometimes I gave Holy Communion to forty, and even fifty or sixty persons, besides the instructions on the Catechism, which were given on the Sundays and holidays. The English always showed me the greatest civility, but they made me pay for their hospitality. I had every night to pay fourpence for lodging, but food and other things I stood in need of were abundantly supplied by the charitable Catholic citizens. Should it be in your power to forward missionaries to the island of San Christofe, I would ask you to send me thither, unless I may be permitted to return to Ireland, for that island, even more than Ireland, is in need of missionary aid, and moreover the Religious have full liberty at San Christofe to instruct the ignorant, as a Jesuit, who is stationed there, lately wrote to a priest in Kilkenny. Should you not have the faculty to send missionaries thither, it will be a matter truly pleasing to God to obtain it from the Sacred Congregation, for in that island there are several thousand Catholics, with none but one Jesuit to break the bread of life to them."

12. The writer of the Rinuccini MS., himself an Irish Capuchin, referring to the decree of banishment against the clergy, published on the 6th of January, 1653, in consequence of which Father Fiacre was exiled to France, attests that it was "most rigorously carried out, so much so that among the thousands of soldiers at that time scattered throughout Ireland, there was scarcely a single one who was not either a spy, or a judge, or some such official of this barbarous persecution, so unrestricted was their power against the clergy and their harbourers and friends, and to such a degree was the fury of their cruelty intensified by the premium of £5 set upon each ecclesiastic's head. Wherefore it happened that the Irish clergy who had survived the famine and pestilence, the sword, fire, and halter, were,

after this truculent decree, which showed forth the English barbarity in its true colours, divided into two ranks: some sought a refuge in France, Spain, Belgium, Germany, or Italy; but others, yearning to die for Christ, remained in Ireland. It being impossible for those who remained at home to live in the houses of the Catholics, they sought a secure retreat in the woods or desert places, or in subterraneous caves, or the haunts of wild beasts (for they entrusted themselves rather to these than to the English), and in other like out-of-the-way hiding-places, where they constructed houses of reeds or huts or cabins; but even thus they dared not to continue for any time in the same place through fear of the spies, whole herds of whom were scattered throughout every corner of the kingdom, with an inconceivably perverse and malignant eagerness to ferret out the priests."

The law against harbouring a priest, to which reference is made in the above narrative, was not a mere matter of threat, but was rigorously enforced, and hence it was that the clergy, rather than run the risk of adding to the hardships of their suffering flocks, refused in many cases to avail themselves of the generous hospitality offered to them, and chose to live out in the bogs, or to seek a safe retreat in some hill-side cave or other out-of-the-way places. Fr. Morison, in his *Threnodia*, published in 1659, relates what he himself had witnessed: "I myself have seen this iniquitous law put in execution in the city of Limerick by Henry Ingoldsby, the governor of that city. A gentleman of Thomond, named Daniel Connery, was accused of harbouring in his house a priest, and being convicted on his own confession, although the said priest had a safe-conduct from the Governor himself, he was sentenced to death, and the sentence being as a matter of mercy mitigated into confiscation of all his goods, and imprisonment was afterwards commuted for perpetual exile. He had a wife of a noble family of Thomond, and twelve children; his wife fell ill and died through want of the mere necessaries of life; and of his children, three handsome and virtuous girls were shipped as slaves to Barbadoes, where, if yet alive, they live in miserable slavery. The rest of his children, who were too young to work, are either dead of hunger or drag out a miserable life in the hands of their enemies. I also saw the law for denouncing a priest put in force in the same Limerick, under the same Governor, in the year 1652, against a noble and honest Catholic of the name of Daniel Molloy of Thomond, who, coming to Limerick on account of some business, chanced to meet, at a Protestant inn, a priest, a relative of his, named David Mollony. This priest was afterwards betrayed and taken prisoner, and Daniel was summoned to answer why he had not informed the magistrates that there was a priest there. He answered that he was a Catholic, and that there was no law obliging a person to denounce a priest, although there was one not to harbour or feed him; and this was correct, for this clause was not added to the law till three years later. But notwithstanding this prudent answer, the Governor ordered his ears to be cut off by the executioner, which was done. I could give a thousand such examples." The same writer gives his own experience of the treatment to which the priests were subjected in prison, for he had the privilege of being himself a sufferer for the faith : " I myself passed thirty months in a dark dungeon thirty feet underground, with irons of forty-seven pounds weight on my feet and hands, sometimes alone, sometimes in company of robbers, often beaten and wounded, and at last sent into exile. Now there are so few priests left, that there are many Catholics, especially in Munster, who have not been able to receive the sacraments for one, two, three, and even six years, and some have journeyed 120 miles to confess and receive the Blessed Eucharist once."

Father Fiacre Tobin, having received the permission of his superiors, which he had solicited, returned to Ireland, and with the merciless sword of the persecutors at every instant impending over his head, continued in season and out of season to instruct and console the faithful, and to encourage them in the practice of virtue. About the year 1656, however, he was again arrested, thrown into prison, and treated with great cruelty, and at length sentenced to perpetual slavery in the Barbadoes, a slow martyrdom which for many of the victims of the Puritan tyranny had greater terrors than death itself. Father Fiacre, however, accepted his sentence with joy. He had yearned to proceed to those islands as a missionary for Christ, and now, in the mysterious ways of Providence, it would seem as if his prayer had been heard, and that the very enemies of the Church, in the frenzy of their persecuting spirit, would lead him thither. But heaven was content with his desire for martyrdom. He was put on board a vessel in Dublin, despoiled of everything that he possessed. The vessel, however, was compelled by stress of weather to put into a southern port, and as he was seized with fever he was transferred to the prison in Waterford. Here he spent five months in the greatest misery. Overcome by the fever and the hardships of his imprisonment, he expired at Kinsale, in the hands of the Puritan persecutors, whilst being again shipped on board the vessel for Barbadoes. I have been particular in putting together these details connected with the life of this zealous confessor for Christ, as in those days of peril and of martyrdom the history of one priest may be regarded as the history of all the clergy. Even in the darkest hour devoted men were not wanting to minister to the spiritual needs of the faithful of Ossory. A Carmelite missionary, who presented in Rome a report on the Irish Church, and in particular on the Leinster province, in the beginning of 1662, writes: "I know that in the county of Kilkenny there are several priests, as well of the regular as of the secular clergy, who have their own Vicar-General, as I have been informed by a priest of that county." (*Spicilegium Ossoriense*, ii. 210.)

13. Two petitions presented to the king and to Lord Ormonde by the citizens of Kilkenny soon after the restoration of the monarchy, portray in the liveliest colours the many hardships which they had been compelled to undergo during the Cromwellian *regime*, and which they were still destined for some years longer to endure. Their address to the King is styled, "The humble petition of the distressed, banished, and dispersed late native inhabitants and citizens of the city of Kilkenny." They proclaim that they had always been noted for their loyalty, "in so much as that town in all times of peace and hostility hath been a refuge

to all true subjects of the crown of England, and a terror to their enemies," and they had surrendered the city to Cromwell only when there was no hope of relief, "after suffering in a high degree all the extremities of the plague, fire, and sword, and four several storms in several parts of the city." They had, however, obtained quarter and fair conditions from the enemy, but Colonel Daniel Axtell being approved Governor of the city, "hath in the year 1653, without any order or direction, even according to those times, being out of his wilful and imperious disposition and innated quarter, breaking mind and quality, seized upon your petitioner's charters, muniments, and ensigns of authority, and dispersed and banished as well their mayor and aldermen and other officers as the petitioners themselves, into several quarters; forcing them in an unseasonable time of the year to remove their habitations and sell their goods at an under-value, and for the most part to lose their household stuffe (property) for want of buyers. Since which time they lived and do live in a distressed and sad condition after they had been formerly impoverished in their personal estates and fortunes by heavy and unsupportable contributions, and other taxes and charges far beyond their abilities. All which the said Governor Axtell did merely by the violence of the soldiery, and so contrary to the said Quarter, he having then the command of a regiment of foot and a troop of dragoons, sufficient forces to oppress your poor, naked, armless, and distressed petitioners." The mayor of the city referred to in this petition as deposed by Axtell was Elias Shee, and at the time this petition was drawn up was "living in Connaught in a distressed condition."

In the letter to Lord Ormonde they set forth the calamities that befell them at the hands of the Puritan enemy, "subjecting us to the anarchical government of usurping, assassinate, and regicide men (if they may be so termed), who, casting off all humanity, turned into and became savages in cruelty, so as, to express ourselves in the civillest language that we can, we have endured the worst of miseries, and far worse than Egyptian slavery." The object of their writing to him, they say, is that he may present their petition to his Majesty: "We presume, out of our coverts and lurking-places, to present an address to his Majesty of some of our manifold grievances: we know well that we being not able to prosecute the same, it will die unless your Excellency will be pleased to give life to it by your countenance and favour."

On the 6th of March, 1653-4, the order was issued commanding all the Irish to quit the city of Kilkenny. In the country parts none were allowed to remain but ploughmen, labourers, and those whose land or goods was of less than ten pounds value. Even such, however, were now banished from the city, and forbidden to reside within two miles of its walls, for the Puritans of England had resolved to fill the cities and towns with a goodly race, and they deemed it inconsistent with their security that any Irish Papist should reside among them. It was difficult, however, to execute all at once this general decree of banishment, and on the 15th of May, 1655, the English and Protestant inhabitants of the city obtained a further order from the Commissioners of Parliament, that "for the better encouragement of an English plantation in the city and liberties" all the houses and lands lately belonging to the Irish, and now in possession of the State, should henceforward be demised to English and Protestants, and to none others." But even this was not judged sufficient, and it was also ordered that no English merchant should employ Irish agents or servants, and that all Irish should quit Kilkenny before the 4th of June, 1655, "except such artificers as any four justices of the peace, for the convenience of that corporation shall licence to stay for any period not exceeding one year." Neither did the Commissioners allow those orders to slumber, and, as an instance of their ferocity, it is mentioned in a letter of March the 25th, 1655-6, that Daniel Fitzpatrick was sentenced to death by the Commissioners in Kilkenny for refusing to transport himself into Connaught.

If the Kilkenny Catholics hoped by the interference of Lord Ormonde to have their rights secured and their property restored to them, they relied upon a broken reed. Ormonde's chief anxiety just then was to enlarge his own estates, and to uphold the English interest. Strange to say, it would seem as if the banishment of the Irish Catholics were even more strictly carried out now than hitherto. "Worthy cousin," writes Richard Shee from Kilkenny, at the close of the year 1660, "there are thirty-two artificers and shopmen whom the late Usurper thought fit to dispense from transportation, and are now commanded by strict order in twenty-four hours' warning, given them last Friday, to depart with their families." The Act of Settlement brought no relief to the banished Irish citizens, for it was so contrived that the new occupiers were not to be disturbed in the towns, and the native Irish were thus to remain deprived of their dwellings and properties, even though they should establish their unvarying attachment to the royal cause. The king, indeed, had the right of issuing Letters for restoring individual Papists, but the Commissioners were ordered, in 1663, to suspend the giving of any decrees of innocence to Papists "who would claim house property in towns," and in 1665 the king declared that he surrendered altogether this special power. Thus the Irish Catholics, so far as the law could effect, were for ever debarred from their city possessions. No wonder that a contemporary writer should declare that such legislation was dictated by no privilege save that of "the Cannibal English interest."

CHAPTER VII.

SUFFERINGS OF THE CATHOLICS IN CLONMEL.

1. First Assault on Clonmel, in November, 1649.—2. Cromwell baffled in his attempt to get possession of the town by treachery. —3. Heroism of Hugh O'Neill and the Irish troops during the siege in 1650.—4. The town surrenders on honourable conditions. —5. Cromwell's rage.—6. The citizens plundered; Martyrdom of Fr. Mulcahy—7. Heroism of Geoffry Baron—8. Martyrdom of three Dominican Fathers and others.—9. Hugh O'Neill.

1. WHEN the Puritan soldiers made their first appearance before Clonmel, in November, 1649, the burgesses wisely chose for their governor Hugh Duff O'Neill, nephew of the deceased leader of the Ulster troops, the illustrious Owen Roe O'Neill. Cromwell, now advancing upon Waterford, sent forward a detachment to occupy Clonmel. Lord Ormonde, indeed, looked on its defence as hopeless, and withdrew the ammunition and other stores; but Hugh O'Neill thought otherwise. With a small body of Ulster Catholic soldiers he threw himself into the town, restored the confidence of the people, and when a fierce assault was at length made, repulsed the enemy with great slaughter.*

* The Rinuccini MS. expressly attests that at this first assault upon Clonmel, Cromwell withdrew his troops—"magnam suorum rebellium cladem et confusionem passus."

2. In the month of March, 1650, the Puritan army again showed itself before the walls of Clonmel, although it was not till after the surrender of Kilkenny that Cromwell took the command in person, and the regular siege began. The garrison numbered only about 1,500 men; but with the exception of a small body of Ormandist Cavalry, under the command of Major Fennell, they were heart and soul devoted to Ireland, and full of confidence in their brave governor. The town was well protected on the south side by the Suir, and on the other three sides was defended by a strong wall. Ormonde had repeatedly promised supplies of provisions and ammunition, but those supplies were never sent. Early in April, the mayor and O'Neill wrote to him, declaring their resolve to defend the town to the utmost of their power: they told him that "the garrison was of good courage and resolution," and now that the safety of the kingdom was in the balance, they besought him "to prevent any bloody tragedy to be acted there, as in other places, for want of timely relief; that the army should march night and day to their succour, and, in the meantime, that the promised relief might be sent them, accommodated with provisions for themselves and the garrison."

To Cromwell's summons to surrender, Hugh O'Neill replied that he was resolved to defend the town as best he could, and "so wished him to do his best." The besiegers planted their heavy artillery, and left nothing undone to give a speedy account of this small garrison. O'Neill, however, was not disheartened, and made repeated sallies, to the great annoyance and loss of the besiegers. In the words of the *Aphorismical Dis-*

SUFFERINGS OF THE CATHOLICS IN CLONMEL. 147

covery, he behaved himself both wise, courageous, and fortunate against Cromwell and his party, not only in a defensive, but offensive way, with many valiant sallies, and martial stratagems, to the enemy's mighty prejudice, who did lose some days 200, other days 300, or 400, or 500 men. This loss was so often, and so common, that my Lord Cromwell was weary of the place, that if his honour did not impede, his lordship would quit the place, and raise the siege. Resolving this and many other things in his breast, and among the rest that he was confident that no relief would come to the town, and that it would be a stain on his honour to quit such a place, the conquest of a whole kingdom being at stake, he sought by repeated attacks to tire out the garrison, whilst at the same time he endeavoured by the usual golden key to open the gates to his army. He entered into a secret correspondence with Major Fennell, who was in command of a detachment of Ormonde's cavalry, and who, on the promise of full pardon, and of a gift of £500, undertook to open one of the city gates on the north side of the town, at twelve o'clock the next night, and to admit 500 of the besieging force. A party of the Ulster troops were on guard there: these he withdrew, substituting some of his own men in their place. Everything was ready for the deed of treason, but O'Neill took care to visit the posts himself to see that his orders were observed. Finding that the Ulster soldiers had been removed from the gate, contrary to his command, he ordered the arrest of Fennell, who, to secure his pardon, revealed the conspiracy in all its details. O'Neill accordingly placed a picked body of men in ambush close to the gate by which the enemy would be admitted, and directed Fennell to deal with Cromwell according to his covenant. The result is told in a few words in the *Aphorismical Discovery:*—" The enemy was watching his opportunity, and observing the signal, marched towards the gate ; five hundred did enter, the rest, *nolens volens,* were kept out; all that entered were put to the sword."

3. The same writer adds: " My Lord Cromwell, certified of the preposterous issue of his late bargain with Fennell, was mighty troubled in mind, and therefore did send for other armies and great ordnance." Lord Broghill came with fresh forces from the southern garrisons, and the siege was pushed on with increased vigour. At length, " with continual thundering, a long breach was made near one of the gates " in the western wall, a few yards south of the tower called the Magazine, where a portion of the old town walls may still be seen. Whilst the besiegers were rejoicing at this success, and awaiting the orders for the assault, O'Neill sent, unobserved, 200 chosen men along the banks of the river, and falling on a detached body of the enemy who were in guard of an unfinished fort, cut them off before any relief could come. Nor were the citizens idle within the town. Men and women, townsmen and soldiers, drew clay and stones and timber, and fenced "a long lane, a man's height, about eighty yards in length on both sides, up from the breach, with a foot-bank at the back of it." Two pieces of cannon were masked at the end of this lane, and the defence of the breach was entrusted to a picked body of soldiers and volunteers. The storm began at eight o'clock in the morning. An officer who was present thus de-

scribes the result: "The Puritans entered without any opposition; but few were to be seen in the town till they so entered that the lane was crammed full of horsemen, armed with helmets, backs, breasts, swords, musquetoons, and pistols, on which those in the front, seeing themselves in a pound, and that they could not make their way further, cried out, 'Halt! Halt!' Those entering behind at the breach thought by those words that all those of the garrison were running away, and cried out, 'Advance! Advance!' and so advanced that they thrust forward those in before them, till that pound or lane was full, and could hold no more. Then suddenly rushed a resolute party of pikes and musketeers to the breach, and scoured off and knocked back those entering. At which instance, Hugh Duff's men within fell on those in the pound with shots, pikes, scythes, stones, and casting of great long pieces of timber, with the engines amongst them; and then two guns firing at them from the end of the pound, slaughtering them by the middle or knees with chained bullets, that in less than an hour's time about a thousand men were killed in that pound. About this time Cromwell was on horseback at the gate, with his guard, expecting the gates to be opened by those entered, until he saw those in the breach beaten back, and heard the cannons going off within. Then he fell off, as much vexed as ever he was since he first put on a helmet against the king, for such a repulse he did not usually meet with."

A second storming party was formed, led on by some of Cromwell's bravest officers. The onset was so fierce that the defenders were driven from the breach; but as the assailants entered they found themselves exposed to a galling cross-fire from the neighbouring houses. For four hours troop after troop was hurled into the breach, but most of the assailants were slain, and the survivors were forced to retreat, leaving the dead bodies of about two thousand of their companions as a barrier against any further advance. Whitelock attests that "Cromwell found at Clonmel the stoutest enemy his army had ever met with in Ireland, and never was seen so hot a storm, of so long continuance, and so gallantly defended, neither in England nor in Ireland." MacGeoghegan and Borlase estimate the loss of the Puritans at 2,500. Carte states that 2,000 of Cromwell's best men were slain at the storming. A contemporary narrative, published in the *Spicilegium Ossoriense* (vol. ii. p. 59), says "he lost more than 2,000 men before Clonmel, a greater number than he had lost by all the towns which he had stormed and taken since he came to Ireland." Cromwell could not conceal his admiration of the gallant conduct of O'Neill, and declared the garrison to be invincible, and he now resolved to change the siege into a blockade.

4. O'Neill, however, had exhausted all his means of defence. Without ammunition and without provisions a speedy surrender should very soon be inevitable. He accordingly quitted the town silently at night with his brave troops, permitting any of the clergy and townspeople who so pleased to accompany him. As had been arranged with O'Neill, the mayor, Mr. White, sent the next morning messengers to Cromwell's camp with offers to capitulate. The terms were easily agreed upon, the more particularly, says the Rinuccini MS., in that no mention was made of O'Neill or his soldiers, whom

Cromwell was thus in hopes of getting into his hands. It was expressly covenanted that "the inhabitants of Clonmel shall be protected in their lives and estates, from all plunder and violence of the soldiery, and shall have the same rights, liberty, and protection, as other subjects under the authority of the Parliament of England have or ought to have and enjoy within the dominion of Ireland." It was only when the articles were duly signed that Cromwell asked the mayor if Hugh O'Neill was aware of the surrender. He replied that O'Neill had gone with all his men on the preceding night. Cromwell stared and frowned at him, and said: "You knave, have you served me so." The mayor answered that his excellency, at their conference, had not asked any question on that head. Cromwell foamed and raged; but the keys of the gates were delivered, and during the few days that he remained the conditions were kept. Troops, however, were sent in pursuit of O'Neill, and the women and children, as well as the stragglers and wounded, who were obliged to fall back from the main body, were put to the sword.

The neglect shown by Ormonde in the matter of supplying the town with ammunition and provisions was severely censured by the whole nation, and the citizens of Limerick, in an address presented to the bishops before the close of the year, reproached him in that "he had pledged his honour that within twenty-one days he would furnish the garrison with abundant supplies, whereas twenty-one weeks passed by without the promised aid being given. Truly, the inhabitants of Clonmel have reason to pronounce a malediction on such *honour*."

5. Two or three days after the surrender of Clonmel, Cromwell took occasion to return to England, leaving in his stead Ireton to prosecute the war. A letter from the camp, in May, 1650, published in Cary's *Memorials* (vol. ii., p. 218), shows how humiliating to Cromwell's pride was the check which he had received: "In the taking of Clonmel you may think we paid dear. Having lain long before it, and in the meantime taken Kilkenny, much loss by sallies being sustained, an onslaught was resolved. It was done with great loss, and the town carried. But the inner entrenchments, devised by the governor, a kinsman of O'Neill's, cost far dearer gaining. After all which, they were by main force cast out of all, and with much entreaty of Cromwell persuaded to lodge that night under the walls, that their siege might be believed not absolutely to be quitted. In the night, little powder being left to defend, all was drawn away, persons and things worth anything. Cromwell himself says he doubted of getting on the soldiers next day to a fresh assault. Towards morning a parley beat, and was gladly received, so that conditions were granted to their desires, not being above eighty defendants in all, out of 2,500. They were mad when they came in, and sending to pursue, cut off 200 women and children. Since a review of their force, which consisted of all the strength they could make, their troopers dismounted to boot, nearly all the officers of Ireton's regiment are wanting; and you may guess shrewdly at Hercules by his foot; and the business is at this pass, that he that undertook to have Ireland at his command so by last Michaelmas as a child should keep it under with a rod, can't now assure

his soldiers two miles from home, and promise them a safe return."

6. The scenes which in other towns had followed upon the success of the Puritan arms were now repeated in Clonmel, and the author of the *Aphorismical Discovery* expressly attests that "the inhabitants were rifled, pillaged, and plundered, without respect of persons, or mercy of degree" (ii. 79). It is related by Bruodin, that during the siege, Fr. Nicholas Mulcahy, parish-priest of Ardfinnan, in the county of Tipperary, was seized by a troop of the Puritan cavalry, that had been sent out to reconnoitre. Immediately on his arrest he was put in irons, conveyed to the camp of the besiegers, and offered his pardon, if he would only consent to use his influence with the inhabitants of Clonmel, and induce them to give up the town. This he steadily refused, and was in consequence led out in view of the besieged city, and there his head was struck off, whilst he prayed for his faithful people, and asked forgiveness for his enemies.

7. Geoffry Baron, of Clonmel, was subsequently put to death at Limerick. Being asked at the court-martial what had he to say why sentence should not be passed against him, he replied : "that it was not just to exclude him from mercy, because he had been engaged in the same cause as the Parliament pretended to fight for, which was for the religion and liberty of his country." (Ludlow's *Memoirs*, p. 144.) He was at once sentenced to be hanged. He asked to be allowed to return to his house to dress himself before his execution. This he was permitted to do, accompanied by a guard. He accordingly proceeded to his house, "and

finding there a new suit of white taffitie, with all the addresses suitable, as if to be presently married, adorning himself therewith, rode gallantly, as he was accustomed, with the guard towards the place of execution." In his countenance and words he showed great joy, and being asked why he put on such a dress for the scaffold, replied: "that, if to marry a creature he did no less, and now that he was of belief that his soul departed at this instant from this body, did straight enjoy the pleasures of heaven, in the consummation of the eternal nuptial felicity, and to bestow this last livery upon the relict companion of his soul, was the least of his duty." (*Aphor. Discov.* vol. iii., p. 20.)

8. De Burgo preserves in his *Hibernia Dominicana* the following account of the death of two holy priests of the Dominican Order :—

Father James O'Reilly, O.S.D., was a learned theologian, an eloquent preacher, and a famous poet. He had been sent a short time before from Waterford to Clonmel, to train the youth of the town in polite literature, and in the Christian doctrine. When the garrison abandoned the town, he too sought safety in flight. Not knowing whither the road led, he wandered about, and fell in with a troop of Puritan cavalry. They asked him who he was. He replied fearlessly: "I am a priest and a religious, although an unworthy one, of the Order of St. Dominick. I have lost my way, and while trying to escape you, have fallen into your hands. I am a member of the Roman Catholic Apostolic Church. So have I lived, and so will I die. May God's will be done.." The soldiers fell on him, and covered him with wounds. For a whole hour he lay weltering in his blood. He did not cease to invoke the holy names of Jesus and Mary, and to beseech his patron saints to intercede for him. At length, exhausted by his numerous wounds, the holy martyr gave up his soul.

Father Myler Magrath, O.S.D., was put to death after the town had come into the hands of the Puritans, and by his heroism in martyrdom made amends for the disgrace which the apostate promoted by Queen Elizabeth to the See of Cashel, had brought upon the name. Fr. Magrath had come to Clonmel to give the consolations of religion to the afflicted inhabitants. He was seized whilst engaged in his holy work at the bedside of a sick man. The Puritan satellites hurried him off to the governor. His trial was a brief one. He was condemned to death, and hanged immediately after.

F. Dominick de Rosario further records that Fr. James O'Reilly was arrested whilst reciting his office on the mountain-side near Clonmel, and that Fr. Magrath, being led to the scaffold, "addressed the spectators in a stirring appeal, exhorting them to continue true to the faith, and thus merited the martyr's crown." He adds that some time after the surrender of the town, the Puritan garrison siezed on another Dominican, Fr. Thomas O'Higgins, and having kept him for awhile in prison, led him to the scaffold. This was, indeed, the fate of all the priests who fell into the hands of the Puritan soldiers. Thus, for instance, as we learn from the *Aphorismical Discovery*, a priest was seized at Gowran, in the county of Kilkenny, and was at once hanged : and when Castledermot was plundered, three friars were arrested and cruelly put to death.

9. The reader will be anxious to learn the fate of the brave Hugh O'Neill, who so heroically defended the town against the enemy's assaults. We will again meet with him at the siege of Limerick. After the fall of that city he was sent a prisoner to London, and detained there for more than a year. At length, in 1653, he, at the urgent request of the Spanish Court, was set at liberty, and proceeded to Flanders, and thence to Spain. On the death of his relative, the Earl of Tyrone, about this time, he, with the sanction of the Spanish Government, assumed that title, and with it received a high military post in the Spanish army. He won new laurels for his name and country in the subsequent war with Portugal, but fell mortally wounded on the battle field. He bequeathed the title of Earl of Tyrone to the grandson of Owen Roe O'Neill, who was now completing his education in Rome, under the patronage of the Sovereign Pontiff, and who, a few years later, entered the Spanish service, and soon gave proof that with the name he inherited the chivalrous spirit of his ancestors.

CHAPTER VIII.

SUFFERINGS OF THE CATHOLICS IN WATERFORD.

1. Letter of the Bishop of Waterford, Dr. Comerford.—2. Defence of the city against Cromwell.—3. Plague; Ireton occupies the city. —4. Sufferings of the clergy and citizens.—5. Official statements.— 6. Fr. Nugent.—7. Patrick Comerford, Bishop of Waterford.

1. In the Barberini archives in Rome, is preserved a letter written on the 9th of March, 1642, by the venerable Bishop of Waterford, Dr. Comerford, to an Irish gentleman resident in Paris, which presents many valuable facts connected with the glorious struggle in which Ireland was then engaged. A few extracts from it will suffice to illustrate our present subject :—" I attribute your silence to the calamities of these turbulent times. I write this letter to acquaint you with the state of this kingdom, which, for the greater part, is now engaged in a great and unexpected struggle. It commenced in Ulster, thence it passed to Leinster and Connaught, and in fine to Munster. Its scope and object was to prevent the massacre and utter extermination of the Catholics of this kingdom, which our enemies sought for, and to repel the tyrannical persecution which they had already planned against us, as also to recover the liberties and privileges of our oppressed nation, and to defend and maintain against the Puritans

the ancient and loyal prerogatives of our most gracious monarch."

He then details the wants of the Irish army, the ports to which succour could be safely sent, the plunder of the country by the Puritans, and adds:—"Last week the President of Munster having received reinforcements, once more took the field, together with the Earl of Cork, the Earl of Barrymore, Lord Broghill, and Sir John Browne. Marching to Dungarvan, and seizing on the castle, they set fire to the town, and put to death Father Edmund Hore and Father John Clancy, both priests, together with other of the principal citizens; they then sacked the place and retired, leaving a strong garrison in the castle."

2. Throughout the whole eventful period of the confederation, Waterford had proved itself most loyal to the national cause, and most devoted to the Nuncio Rinuccini. When, through the intrigues of the Ormondist faction, the Nuncio was forced to quit Kilkenny in 1647, he found a secure refuge in Waterford, and thence soon after returned in triumph to the seat of government. The bishop being threatened with the seizure of the temporalities of the See, unless he forsook the Nuncio's cause, replied: "Though I were to be stripped of all that the world could give me, for my submission to the decrees of Holy Church, I will, nevertheless, persevere in my obedience; nor will I cease to pray God that He may guide faithfully the counsels of the Confederates of this Kingdom." On the approach of Cromwell, the citizens refused to admit Lord Castlehaven with his English regiments, and Ormonde declared that he would send them no other

SUFFERINGS OF THE CATHOLICS IN WATERFORD. 159

help. When, however, the deputies from the city obtained 500 men from the Ulster camp, he revoked his order, and permitted 1,500 Irish Catholic soldiers from his own camp to join the garrison. Lieutenant-General O'Farrell was appointed governor, and as he allowed no communication to be held with the besiegers except through himself, the enemy was unable to apply the usual golden key to the city gates. Ormonde's army of 10,000 men was not far distant, and Cromwell, disheartened at the prospect of a tedious siege in mid-winter, broke up his camp on the 2nd of December, 1649, to take up his winter quarters in those towns of the south, whose English garrisons had declared in his favour. During the short time of the siege he had lost more than 1,000 men by sickness, and among them some distinguished officers. " Finding the indisposition in point of health increasing, and his foot falling sick near ten of a company every night they were on duty, and his numbers not above 3,000 healthful foot in the field, being necessitated to put so many into garrison, the enemy mustering about 12,000 horse and foot, having well near as many in the town as he without, bread and other necessaries not coming to them, and the dripping weather having made the ground so moist that it would not bear the guns, the council of war in consequence advised him to rise from before Waterford, and to retire into winter quarters to refresh the sick and weak soldiers."

3. In the beginning of June, 1650, Ireton again led the Puritan army towards Waterford. Lieutenant-General Preston was now the governor. The citizens, decimated by the plague, and weary of supporting the garrison,

more than once expressed their readiness to surrender on favourable conditions. At length, on the 6th of August, the articles of surrender were duly signed. After three days the garrison was to march, with military honours, to Athlone, life and property were guaranteed to the citizens, and any strangers or others dwelling in the city had permission to accompany the garrison. Thus, on Friday, the 10th of August, 1650, the city of Waterford came into the enemy's hands. Ireton, in his letters to London, expressed his wonder that a city so populous, and strongly fortified, and well provisioned should have so soon surrendered; but the Bishop of Waterford, writing to Father Luke Wadding, in Rome, on the 3rd of July, 1651, assigns the true cause. Five thousand of the citizens had been carried off by the plague, and only a few now remained able to bear arms; their resources were well nigh exhausted, for the whole support of the garrison during the eight months that intervened since the first siege had been thrown upon the citizens; and what was of greater importance, from the military point of view, only a few barrels of gunpowder now remained, without any hope of a further supply being available.

Four days later the fort of Duncannon surrendered on the same conditions. Thomas Roche, who for a long time had been its governor, having died a few months before, the chaplain of the garrison, Rev. Gelasius Smith, was appointed to succeed him. The handful of troops who formed the garrison displayed the greatest bravery, but after the surrender of the city, further defence being fruitless, Fr. Smith, by order of the general in command, signed the articles, not as priest, but as governor, and with his men marched out with all the honours of war.

The Narrative of events in Ireland, written in 1655, to which reference has been already made in the preceding chapters, gives a few interesting details relating to the Catholic city of Waterford at this period.

As the year 1650, it says, spread mourning and sorrow through all parts of the kingdom, so, in a special manner, did it put an end to the happiness of Waterford. Pestilence, famine, and the sword at the same time assailed the city. The enemy, when laying siege to the city the first time, offered liberal conditions, together with the privileges of the citizenship of London, and the free exercise of their religion. But the inhabitants held in mind the interpretation that had been put upon this latter article on the surrender of Ross, when Cromwell declared that it extended only to the interior belief, and not to the open practice of that religion, and hence they resolved on resisting to the last the heretical foe. Dreading the treachery of the royal officers, they refused to admit within the walls the reinforcements which Ormonde offered them; and though the siege was carried on with unremitting vigour from September to December, so heroic was the defence, that on the feast of St. Francis Xavier the enemy abandoned the siege in despair.

However, those whom the parliamentary forces could not subdue were gradually wasted away by pestilence, till at length the city became a prey to the enemy. Of the many thousands who then defended it, four hundred alone survived, when Ireton, after the siege of Clonmel, advanced a second time against its walls. Nevertheless, it again resisted for nine weeks, " and it came into the enemy's hands, not so much overcome by force, as because it had become a solitude through the violence of the pestilence." For a little while no persecution was proclaimed, but ere long the virulence of Puritanism was seen; an edict commanded all Catholics to depart from the city within three months, and thus citizens and clergy were involved in a common ruin; "*and now, glorious confessors of Christ, they seek a secure asylum, scattered over the various regions of the earth.*"*

4. From a letter of a Capuchin father (30th June, 1651), written from Waterford to his superior in Rome, we learn that no ecclesiastic dared to appear publicly in the city, and that neither friendship nor reward could induce the heretics to allow the slightest toleration.† "As for me," he adds, "I pass freely through the city, for I serve as gardener the chief heretic of this city; sometimes, too, I work in carrying loads, passing as one of the coalporters." We learn further details from the bishop of the diocese, who, writing from his place of exile to Rome (3rd March, 1651), thus depicts the ruin that had fallen on his once chosen flock: "War and the pestilence have laid waste the whole country; our churches and altars are profaned and transformed into stables or barracks, or hospitals; no longer is the sacrifice offered up, nor the divine word preached, nor the holy sacrament administered; the ecclesiastics who were spared by the plague, have been sent into banish-

* Ibid. "In varias mundi partes gloriosi Christi confessores emigrarunt.

† "Nullus ecclesiasticus audet apparere: nullum enim horum tolerant aut favore victi aut muneribus."

ment; the pestilence swept away five thousand of the citizens and soldiery, and still continues its havoc there. Truly this dire scourge is a chastisement for our sins."

Another manuscript, entitled, "Narratio Brevis Status Regni Hiberniæ," &c., written on 13th August, 1651, thus briefly sketches the state of Waterford at the same period:—" From Waterford all the citizens and old inhabitants were driven forth in the month of May last, being deprived of all their possessions and houses and lands; neither is there any hope of their being able to return. The same has happened to the Catholics in Dublin and elsewhere. The enemy searches out with the greatest rigour for all priests and religious. Any priests that are arrested are cast into dungeons and chains; they are barbarously and cruelly treated, and are thence, for the most part, banished to foreign lands. In the month of April, this year, a priest of the Order of St. Dominick, for celebrating Mass and administering the Sacraments, especially that of Penance, endured a glorious martyrdom, being hanged in the public square of Clonmel. All such as receive a priest or religious into their houses, or give them any assistance are grievously fined and oppressed."

5. The official government records published by Prendergast fully corroborate the statements of the Catholic writers. When the city surrendered to Ireton, on 6th August, 1650, its garrison was permitted to march to Athlone, with standards flying, trumpets sounding, and all the other honours of war. Its wealthy merchants, however, were all dispersed and banished, its thronged

streets became desolate, its houses dilapidated, and the breast of the broad river shipless. Colonel Richard Lawrence proposed a scheme to raise in England a regiment of 1,200 men, who would inhabit the city and serve at the same time to guard it. The proposal received the approval of Ireton, and Colonel Lawrence was appointed governor of the city. On the 10th December, 1650, the Commissioners for Ireland report that Waterford, as well as Limerick, Galway, and Cork, had become ruinous, the houses falling down, and by indigent people pulled down. Year after year such reports were repeated. Men with means could not be got to settle there, and only such persons flocked thither as hoped to have dwelling-houses without rent for their habitations. At length the Restoration came. Many of the former citizens hastened back from Connaught and other places of refuge, hoping now, at least, to enjoy their old inheritance in peace. They were quickly undeceived. On the 10th December, 1661, the Lords Justices issued a proclamation commanding all such Papists, and all merchants and tradesmen who had been tolerated under the late usurpers, to depart from the city within twenty-four hours, with their goods and families, and this was so rigorously enforced that many poor women who had hoped to escape unobserved, were, in the depth of winter, dragged through the streets, and thrust out of the town. Several of the old merchants, on hearing the glad tidings of the restoration of Charles II., petitioned from Ostend, St. Malo, Nantes, and Rochelle, in France, and from St. Sebastian and Cadiz in Spain, on behalf of themselves and others in far-off Mexico, to be allowed to return and to exercise in their native city the skill and the fortune they had gained by trafficking during their eleven years' banishment. Such petitions were at intervals repeated, yet to none of them was a favourable answer given; and the reason was, lest the English interest of the new planters should be encroached upon by these old Catholic families.

6. Yet, during all this time, some Catholics had remained in the city, and priests had not been wanting who braved every peril in order to minister to them the sacraments of life. In the very household of the Puritan governor, Colonel Lawrence, Fr. Nugent dwelt. He was a skilful gardener, and he made himself useful in a thousand other ways. Sometimes Chief Justice Cook, Chief Justice of Munster, who was "a most sweet man, and a great comfort to the godly," would borrow this able servant for a few days. Yet, all this time F. Nugent was with imminent risk of his life visiting and instructing the remnant of the Catholic citizens.

7. Patrick Comerford, who at this time ruled the united Sees of Waterford and Lismore, was the child of Robert Comerford and Anastasia (White), and a native of the city of Waterford. Throughout the sixteenth century the citizens had proved themselves so devoted to the Catholic faith, that the city was popularly known as "Parva Roma," a miniature Rome. Born about the year 1586, Patrick, at an early age, resolved on embracing the ecclesiastical state. The house of his widowed mother was ever open to shelter the devoted priests who suffered persecution for the faith, who in return instructed her son in the rudiments of learning, and trained his heart to piety. Father Dermod

O'Callaghan, one of the zealous ministers of religion who had found a secure refuge there, had taken an active part in restoring the churches of the city to divine worship on the death of Queen Elizabeth. For this reason he was pursued with special enmity by the heretics, and being obliged to fly to the Continent, was mainly instrumental in establishing the Irish College at Bordeaux, for which the necessary funds were provided through the munificence of Cardinal de Sourdis, Archbishop of that city. The young Comerford accompanied F. O'Callaghan to France, and became one of the first, as he was destined to be in after life one of the most illustrious students of the new college. He applied himself to the higher studies of philosophy and theology in Lisbon and Coimbra, and being enrolled in the Order of St. Augustine, was distinguished as a professor at Terceiro and in Brussels. He was remarkable for his stature, and obtained considerable repute as poet, theologian, and orator. Being summoned to Rome to assist at a general chapter of the Order, he was appointed by Pope Paul V. commendatory Prior of Kells in Ossory, and received the decree of Doctor in Theology at Florence. Returning to Ireland, he, with the sanction of the illustrious bishop, David Rothe, applied himself, though residing in Waterford, to administer the sacraments from time to time, and to instruct in the doctrines of life the faithful of the district intrusted to his care. His brother being captured by pirates, and led off to Morocco, Father Comerford collected among his friends the sum of money demanded for his ransom and proceeded to Spain to procure his release. His brother, however, thus restored to liberty, was almost immediately on landing in Spain carried off by the plague. This, however, did not dishearten the good religious, for it is recorded that he procured from the Moors the release of one hundred slaves. From Spain he proceeded to Rome, and the clergy of Waterford and Lismore, having presented a petition to the Holy Father in his favour through Lawrence Lea, Vicar-General of the united dioceses, and Dean of Waterford, he was appointed bishop of the vacant sees in the Consistory of the 12th of February, 1629, and was consecrated by Cardinal Bentivoglio, assisted by two other bishops, in the oratory of St. Sylvester, at the Quirinal, on the 18th of March following. Returning to Waterford, he laboured strenuously in the conversion of Protestants to the true faith, and such was his success in refuting their errors that he was called "*malleus hæreticorum*," "the hammer of heretics." At a later period, during the Confederation, he printed at Waterford a controversial work which he composed at this time. His life was often exposed to great risk from the pursuit of the enemies of the faith, and he had repeatedly to seek for safety in concealment or flight. Soon after his return to Ireland, he wrote a letter to Fr. Wadding from Waterford, on the 22nd of November, 1629, in which he describes Ireland in the gloomiest colours: "It is the moistiest, the stormiest, the poorest, and most oppressed country that I saw since I left it until I returned . . . As for trading or stirring in mercantile affairs, which is the support of this kingdom, it is so much forgotten, that scarce a man doth know (of) what colour is the coin in this miserable island ; the dearth of the two last years, the universal sickness, the oppression (by the) soldiers, beside other incumbrances, have made Ireland to seem to be in very deed the land of ire. At sea, a merchant cannot navigate two days when he is taken by a Hollander, or a Dutch, or a French pirate, or a hungry Biscayner. The weather is so rainy and drowsy continually, that it doth imprint and indent in a man's heart a certain saturn quality of heaviness, sluggishness, laziness, and perpetual sloth. Our (Lord) Deputy is gone for England, and in his stead do govern the kingdom the Lord of Cork and the Lord Chancellor. What is their mind we do not know yet, but if they will not expel us out of the kingdom, I know not what other punishment can they inflict upon us, for money or means they cannot find in any place of Ireland." A year and a half later (12th of March, 1631) he writes more cheerily to the same : " The country here doth begin a little to respire after the tedious wars, dearth, and sickness, with which it was afflicted all these six years past. As yet we see no great persecution since the peace was proclaimed, although we may not presume much on this little toleration, fearing such another devastation and desolation as came upon us this last year. This, your native place, lifts up its head from the waves, as if it were after a long storm, and if any place of the kingdom have any stirring or trade, this will not overslip it." During the triumph of the Confederate cause, the ceremonies of the Church were performed in Waterford with such decorum, exactness, and splendour, that the Nuncio attested he had nowhere seen the usages of Rome more faithfully reproduced. The bishop, by Pontifical authority, attached to the Cathedral, the Church of St. Catherine, of old belonging to the

Canons Regular of St. Augustine, and in exchange gave to the religious of his Order the chapel of the Blessed Virgin, hitherto dependent on the cathedral. During the terrible visitation of the plague he was untiring in visiting the sick and administering every spiritual aid and consolation to his flock. When at length the city fell into the enemy's hands, he was ordered to quit the kingdom within three months. He accordingly sailed for Brittany; but on the journey was twice seized by pirates, and plundered of everything he had. Writing to the Archbishop of Fermo, on the 23rd of March, 1651, he states that after his exile from Ireland "the few priests who had survived the pestilence, and concealed themselves among the remnant of the Catholics, were banished." He adds: "I hear that the plague has begun its ravages again, and is carrying off the few Catholics that remained. Since my departure, my nephews, Paul Carew and John Fitzgerald, and several others, have died. The same tale of misery comes to us from Dublin, Wexford, Kilkenny, Ross, Clonmel, and the adjoining districts." The States of Brittany made ample provision for the exiled bishop's support; but worn out by his infirmities and sufferings, he died at Nantes, on Sunday, the 10th of March, 1652, and was interred in the episcopal vault in the cathedral. When, seven years later, the same vault was opened to receive the remains of Robert Barry, Bishop of Cork, the body of Dr. Comerford was found quite incorrupt. The epitaph inscribed upon his tomb by his nephews, Patrick Hackett and Nicholas Fitzgerald, may be seen in the third volume of the Spicilegium Ossoriense. During the exile of the bishop, and throughout the whole dismal period of Ireland's suffering, till John Brennan was appointed bishop, the vacant sees were administered by the Rev. Robert Power, Dean and Vicar-General. He was descended from the Barons of Curraghmore, and displayed great energy and prudence, and throughout the perilous times of his administration never abandoned the flock. Repeated attempts were made by the Puritans to ensnare him, but the affection of his people guarded him from every danger, and when each storm subsided he was again found at his post labouring indefatigably to impart instruction and dispense the bread of life to the children of Christ.

CHAPTER IX.

SUFFERINGS OF THE CATHOLICS IN LIMERICK.

1. Ardour of the people of Limerick in the Catholic cause; Letter of the Bishop.—2. Citizens determine not to receive Ormonde; their Letter.—3. Ireton besieges Limerick; is repulsed by Hugh O'Neill.—4. St. Vincent sends Missionaries to Ireland.—5. Their labours in Limerick.—6. Praised by Archbishop of Cashel and Bishop of Limerick.—7. Piety of Limerick.—8. Letter of Dr. O'Dwyer.—9. Limerick taken by Ireton; several put to death.—10. Two facts attested by Fr. Dominick O'Daly.—11. The articles of surrender violated; Death of the Bishop of Killaloe.—12. Fanning and others put to death.—13. Extracts from the official diary.—14. Execution of Thomas Stritch and Sir Patrick Purcell.—15. Prophetic words of St. Vincent de Paul.—16. The Bishop of Limerick.

1. From the very commencement of the confederate war the citizens of Limerick were remarkable for the ardour with which they entered on the struggle: they were subsequently still more distinguished by the heroism with which they drove Ireton from their walls; but their renown received its brightest lustre from the true Christian spirit which they displayed, and in which, when overcome by the pestilence and the number of their foes, they chose rather to endure every suffering than abandon the Catholic faith.

As early as the 8th October, 1646, the bishop of that

see, writing to the secretary of the Sacred Congregation, declared that no longer did any alternative remain: "We shall either restore the Catholic Religion in its full splendour, or be all cut off to a man (*aut fidem Catholicam stabilire aut omnes ad unum perire*): one spirit pervades us all . . . but unless timely succour comes from foreign parts, we shall surely be overcome, and the Catholic religion will be rooted out, in defence of which alone this war was begun."

2. True to their principles, the citizens, even when the Puritan army was marching to the attack, refused to admit Ormonde or his troops within the walls. Perhaps one of the most remarkable documents of this period is the protest which they presented to their bishop in the beginning of 1650, and which they again solemnly laid before the Archbishop of Cashel and the other bishops of Ireland, when assembled in Limerick on the 24th of October, the same year. In it they sketch the career of Ormonde and Inchiquin, whom they justly stigmatized as traitors:—"What succour, they ask, can we expect from Ormonde and Inchiquin, the sworn enemies of the Catholic cause? What good can this nation look forward to from the government of those who persecuted her with fire and sword, and displayed such tyranny, and sacrilege, and profanation, as surpass all former persecutions of the Church? . . . Should we be necessitated to surrender, will it not be better to enter into negotiations with the Parliament, and secure some conditions, than to open our gates to a domestic enemy, by whom we shall be first despoiled of all our goods and properties, and then, as has happened in so many other cities, be sold to the enemy?

Can any city or town be named which admitted Ormonde within its walls, and was not betrayed by him? Who will dare to deny that it happened so in Dublin, Drogheda, Dundalk, Carlingford, Trim, Athlone, Navan, Naas, Wicklow, Carlow, Ross, Waterford, Wexford, Kilkenny, Carrick, Fethard, Cashel, and so many other towns, all of which endured such miseries and dire calamities through the treacherous designs of Ormonde, as no volume could contain, no pen describe, no tongue express?"

They, moreover, add an important fact that although, according to the official returns, £533,564. 10s. 11d., that is to say, more than half a million of ready money had been raised from the 1st of January, 1649, to the 1st of January, 1650, for the expenses of the war, in addition to the corn which was gathered, and the civil taxes, which were collected as usual; yet of all this sum only £28,000 had been devoted to the payment of the troops—£16,000 having been given to the Protestant soldiers, and only £12,000 to the Catholic army.

3. It was in the month of September, 1650, that Ireton, with his army, greatly reduced in numbers, appeared for the first time before the walls of Limerick. Coote, with the northern troops, being repulsed at Athlone, was unable to take part in the siege, and Ireton's army was of itself insufficient to assail the city, except on the south side; but he hoped that the treason of some of the Ormondist officers would open the gates after a show of resistance. The citizens had chosen Hugh Duff O'Neill for their military governor, with full confidence in his loyalty, as well as in his military skill. Even he, however, had lost all hope of being able to

defend the city. Writing to Ormonde, he declared that there was not in the garrison an officer or soldier in whom he could implicitly confide. However, when Ormonde proposed to enter the city with his army, the citizens refused them admittance, and offered themselves as volunteers for its defence. Ireton, seeing their determination, broke up his camp, and for the present abandoned the siege.

In the summer of 1651, Ireton sat down a second time before the walls of Limerick. Its heroic garrison, though small, repulsed the enemy at every assault. For a long time the issue appeared doubtful. The author of "Brevis Narratio Status Regni Hiberniæ" thus writes from Connaught, on the 13th of August, 1651: "Ireton, at present, by a close siege, hems in Limerick on every side; mounds and batteries and fortresses are everywhere erected around the city; by a repeated bombardment the wall at the western bridge of the city was thrown down, whereupon the enemy attempted an assault, their regular army attacking it by land, whilst by a number of boats and small vessels, they sought to penetrate into the city on the river side; yet, the citizens of Limerick not only bravely resisted and repelled the assault, but pursued the enemy without the walls, utterly discomfiting them, the number of Ireton's slain being 1,500. The boats and vessels too became a prey to the victors. More than once the assault was repeated, but always with a similar result; so that up to the present time the loss of Ireton's army is reckoned at more than 3,500."

However, famine and the plague soon effected what the power of the enemy could not achieve. Whilst the city was thus laid desolate by the pestilence, it witnessed many scenes of Christian heroism, of which our country may be justly proud. It is chiefly from the memoirs of St. Vincent de Paul that we glean the particulars of the heroic charity, and of the fervour of piety which the citizens then displayed.

4. St. Vincent de Paul, that angel of charity, cherished a special affection for the persecuted Church of Ireland. " The sole detail," says M. Collet, " of all he did and procured to be done in favour of the ecclesiastics banished from Ireland by Cromwell would exceed my limits, and wear out the patience of my readers ;" and the Archives of Paris yet preserve many records of the untiring efforts of the saint to provide a home and a refuge for the multitude of our countrymen who, despoiled of all they possessed, and exiles from the land of their birth, were cast upon the shores of France. The Bishop of Waterford, who had been an eye-witness, gave an account to Clement IX. of the assistance in money, and ornaments, and clothing, sent by the saint to the suffering Catholics in Ireland, declaring at the same time, that as St. Patrick and St. Malachy in earlier ages, so Father Vincent was raised up by God in this period of persecution, to be the salvation of our country.

5. It was in 1646 that the first missionary fathers landed in Ireland, having accompanied the bishop from Paris ; and during the five years that they remained, Limerick was the chief scene of their labours. The happy fruits of their zeal were soon visible to all ; and it is recorded, as a striking fact, that none of the clergy who assisted at their missions were found to abandon their spiritual

charges: "All remained with their flocks entrusted to them, assisting and defending them until they were banished, or suffered death for the Catholic faith; and, in effect, it was granted to all to endure one or the other."*

A fact, incidentally mentioned in the Life of St. Vincent, speaks volumes for the persecution to which our clergy were then exposed: "It happened," says the author of his life, "that one of those heroic parish-priests came to a missionary father (who lived in a cabin at the foot of a mountain) to make his annual retreat; on the following night, he was discovered in the act of administering the sacraments to some sick persons, and was cut to pieces on the spot by the heretical soldiery. His glorious death," adds the same writer "crowned his innocent life, and fulfilled the great desire he had to suffer for our Lord, as he himself had declared in the preceding year at a mission given by the Vincentian Fathers in Limerick."

6. On the 16th of August, 1648, the Archbishop of Cashel wrote to St. Vincent that, through the zeal of his good fathers, "the people had been excited to piety, which was increasing every day; and although these admirable priests have suffered inconveniences of every sort since their arrival in this country, they, neverthe-

---

* See Abelly's "Vie de St. Vincent," lib. iv., chap. 8, "tous demeurerent constamment pour les assister et defendre jusqu' à ce qu' ils furent mis à mort, ou bannis pour la confession de la foi Catholique," &c. Fathers James Waters, Gerald O'Brien, and Philip Dalton were the three first missionaries sent by St. Vincent to Ireland. Father Waters died after a short time, and Father Barry was sent in his stead. Lynch states that eight priests were sent to Ireland by St. Vincent.

less, have not ceased for an instant to apply themselves to their spiritual mission, and, blessed by heavenly grace, they have gloriously propagated and increased the worship and glory of God." At the same time the Bishop of Limerick wrote that, " by the example and edifying deportment of these fathers, the greater part of the nobility of both sexes had become models of piety and virtue. It is true that the troubles and the wars of this kingdom have been a great obstacle to their functions; nevertheless, the truths of faith have been so engraven by them upon the minds of the inhabitants of both the cities and the country parts, that our people bless God in their adversities equally as in prosperity."

7. When the plague raged with all its violence in 1650, only three priests of the order remained in Ireland, but their labours were incessant, and an abundant spiritual harvest was their reward. At that time there were 20,000 communicants within the walls of Limerick; "the whole city assumed the garb of penance to draw down the blessings and the graces of heaven. To this the magistrates contributed not a little; for besides the good example which they gave by their assiduous attendance at the exercises of the mission, they employed their authority to root out vice and to banish scandal and public disorders. Amongst other things they established laws, and ordained certain punishments against cursing and swearing, so that these detestable vices were almost entirely banished from the city and the neighbourhood, and Almighty God Himself seemed to authorise these wise proceedings by the most manifest chastisements which came on the transgresssors of such holy

ordinances." In April, 1650, St. Vincent wrote to the superior of the community, encouraging them to meet courageously the dangers which then threatened them. In his letter he says: "You have given yourselves to God, to remain immovably in the country where you now are in the midst of perils, choosing rather to expose yourselves to death than to be found wanting in charity to your neighbour. . . . You have acted as true children of our most adorable Father, to whom I return infinite thanks for having produced in you that sovereign charity which is the perfection of all virtues. I pray Him to fill you with it to the end, that exercising it in all cases and everywhere, you may pour it forth into the breasts of those who want it. Seeing that your companions are in the same disposition of remaining, whatever may be the danger from war and pestilence, we are of opinion that they should be allowed to stay. How do we know what God intends in their reward? Certainly He does not bestow on them such a holy resolution in vain. My God, how inscrutable are thy judgments! Behold, at the close of one of the most fruitful missions we have ever as yet witnessed, and perhaps, too, one of the most necessary, Thou didst stop, as it were, the course of thy mercies upon this penitent city, and dost lay thy hand still more heavily upon her, adding to the misfortune of war the scourge of pestilence; but all this is done in order to gather in the harvest of the elect, and to collect the good grain into thy eternal granary. We adore thy ways, O Lord!"*

8. Dr. Edmund O'Dwyer, the Bishop of this city, to

---

* Abelly. Ibid., pages 215-216.

whom we have already referred, writing about the same time to the holy founder of the congregation, details some particulars of the missionary labours of these good fathers : " I have often, in my letters to your reverence, given you an account of your missionaries in this kingdom; to speak the truth, never in the memory of man was so great progress in the Catholic religion heard of as we have witnessed within the few last years, owing to their piety and assiduity. . . . The whole city seems to have changed its face, being compelled to have recourse to penance by the war, the famine, the pestilence, and the great danger impending on every side, all which we receive as manifest signs of the anger of God. The Divine Goodness has been pleased to do us this favour, although we are but useless servants, and God has been pleased to make use of the weak things of this world to confound the mighty. Even the persons of highest quality in the city attend so assiduously to the sermons, the catechetical instructions, and all the other exercises of the mission, that the cathedral is scarcely large enough to contain all. We know of no better way to appease the anger of God than by destroying the sins which are the root and cause of all these evils. Verily it is all over with us if God does not stretch out to us a helping hand. To Him it belongs to have mercy and to pardon. . . . I know not, under heaven, a mission more fruitful than that of Ireland, for although we should have a hundred missionaries, the harvest of souls would be still exceedingly great, and the labourers too few."

Well did this worthy bishop declare that no human aid could now avert the impending ruin. In a few months the plague alone numbered eight thousand victims within the walls of Limerick, and amongst them was "the brother of the bishop, who chose to expose his life going with the missionary fathers to visit the sick and console them, and relieve their wants. It was wonderful to behold the poor people supporting this plague, not only with patience, but even with peace and tranquillity, declaring that they died happy because they had been relieved of the burden of their sins in the tribunal of penance; others said that they lamented not their death, since it had pleased God to send them the holy fathers (thus they styled the missionaries), to purify their souls." . . . Twenty thousand general confessions repaid the zeal of the devoted missionaries. The bishop beholding all this could not refrain from crying out: "Although Mr. Vincent never did anything else for the glory of God than the good he has done for these poor people, he ought to esteem himself a happy man."

9. At length this last bulwark of Ireland was compelled to submit* to the army of the Parliament. Conditions, indeed, were granted; but, with the Puritans, condi-

---

* Amongst the Wadding Papers, Rome, is the following list of the war material found by Ireton in Limerick, on the 31st October, 1651: "Barrels of powder, 83; barrels of mixed shot, 23; match, three ton and a-half; powder and fixable muskets, 1165; broken muskets and musket barrels, 1610; fowling-pieces, firelocks, and carbines, 215; lpikes 512; half-pikes, 30; halberts, 93; brownbills, 27; pistols, most unfixed, 109; colours of bandelieurs, 246; old swords, 140; old saddles, 72; (*brass*) demy-cannon, 2; demy-culverin, 1; saker, 2; faulknet, 2; small-drake, 1; (*iron*), culverin, 1; saker, 2; menion, 7; falken, 2; faulknet, 3." This was the whole military store of the Irish garrison.

tions were only made in order to be violated, and no sooner were they admitted within the walls, " than they cruelly massacred many of the inhabitants on account of the Catholic faith which they professed."*

The Bishop of Limerick, with Thomas Stritch, Mayor of the city, and Oliver French, Mayor of Galway, on the 11th of January, 1651, addressed a letter to the Duke of Lorraine and the other Catholic princes on the Continent soliciting aid for their suffering country. "Alas! (they say) Catholic Ireland has now become a prey to the caprice and malice of the heretics, for the fort of Duncannon, the strongest bulwark of the kingdom, Waterford, Kilkenny, Wexford, the mistress of the sea, Ross, Clonmel, and all the Catholic cities and towns have fallen into the enemy's hands. The cities of Limerick and Galway alone now remain to the Confederates, and they survive only as a spark of the all but expiring Catholic cause." No aid, however, could be procured from the Continent, and Athlone being shamefully abandoned by Clanricarde the Puritan troops of Ulster under Coote united with Ireton's army, and encamped before the devoted city early in the summer of 1651. It was not so much, however, by the valour of the assailants, as through the dissensions that prevailed within the walls, that the city was to be taken; and Ireton, writing to the Speaker of the Parliament in London on the 3rd of November, 1651, a few days after its surrender, attests that there were many among the citizens, some of them, too, of high position, who having heretofore, and in particular during this siege, " given

* Abelly, loc. sit., p. 218.

proofs of constant affection for Englishmen and the English interest, deserved to be permitted to remain in the city, and to have consideration shown them in the matter of their estates."

The Rinuccini MS. gives us a few particulars relating to the siege. As early as the third day of the siege the Ormondist party within the city endeavoured to have the city surrendered. Through the exertions of the bishop and some of the citizens this attempt failed. They secured for themselves, however, the possession of the City Gate, called the Water Gate, and sent out at night one of their party named Andrew White to arrange for the introduction of Ireton's troops. For three days and nights the whole city was in alarm, expecting every moment to find themselves betrayed into the power of the enemy. The vigilance of O'Neill, however, baffled their treachery, and inspired the citizens with fresh courage. Ireton soon after attempted to occupy by night an island close to the city, that by fortifying it he might annoy the garrison, and render the defence of the city impracticable. A considerable detachment of picked troops was chosen for this task. O'Neill had closely watched their movements, and having set an ambush for them, not only prevented their design, but completely annihilated the whole detachment. After this check Ireton abandoned all thought of assault upon the city, content to cut off the supplies, and thus to force the garrison to surrender. For about five months this went on, till winter was again at hand threatening to compel the enemy once more to abandon the siege.

On the 6th of October Peter Creagh entered on the

duties of Mayor of the city. When taking the oath of office at the Dominican convent in the presence of the bishop he pledged himself that he would take no step towards the surrender of the city without the approval of the clergy and the military authorities. The defence of the city was practically in his hands, for the corps of citizen volunteers was under his command, and they divided with the garrison the custody of the city gates. The new mayor was himself an Ormondist, and he was now so worked upon by that faction, who had become the more powerful owing to the plague and the long-continued distress that preyed upon the citizens, that he was scarce a fortnight in office when he sent his namesake, Peter Creagh, an ex-Mayor of Limerick, and two other citizens, with full powers to negotiate the surrender of the city. It was in vain that the clergy and bishop condemned these proceedings. The Ormondists and their adherents carried the day by their violence and clamour, the conditions offered by Ireton were accepted on the 27th of October, and St. John's Gate was thrown open to his army. Colonel Fennell, the same who had well nigh betrayed Clonmel into Cromwell's hands, had received from the mayor the charge of this gate of the city. He turned its batteries against the garrison, and rendered any further resistance impossible. It was by a just retribution that this officer, though soon after promoted to a commission in the Puritan army, was before the close of the year accused of some crime in Cork, and hanged "with more than ordinary justice."

By the articles agreed upon between the mayor and the enemy the city was to be surrendered to Ireton for the Puritan Parliament on the 29th of October, 1651; the citizens were to "have quarter for their lives and liberty for their persons," and they were guaranteed "their clothes, money, and other goods, so as to be free from pillage, plunder, or other hostile violence in their persons or goods during their continuance under the said deputy's safe-conduct or protection." The following, however, were excepted from quarter:—Major-General Hugh O'Neill, governor; Major-General Purcell, Sir Jeoffry Galway, Lieutenant-Colonel Lacy, Captain George Wolf, Lieutenant Sexton, the Bishop of Limerick, the Bishop of Emly, the Bishop of Killaloe, Rev. John Cuillin, a Dominican friar; Rev. David Roche, a Dominican friar; Captain Lawrence Walsh, a priest; Rev. Francis Wolf, a Franciscan friar; Rev. Philip O'Dwyer, priest; Alderman Dominick Fanning, Alderman Thomas Stritch, Alderman Jordan Roche, Edmund Roche, burgess; David Rochefort, burgess; Sir Richard Everard, Doctor Higgins, Maurice Baggot, of Baggotstown; Geoffry Baron, Evans, a Welsh soldier who had deserted from the Puritan camp; and all persons who had acted as spies in the camp since the 4th of the preceding month of June; as also "such persons as shall be found to hide or conceal any of the said excepted persons, or be privy to their concealment or attempt to escape." (*Aphor. Disc.*, vol. 3, appendix, p. 255.)

On the surrender of the city, as the Rinuccini MS. attests, "1,200 officers and men of the garrison alone survived, 2,000 soldiers having died during the siege, besides more than 5,000 of the citizens cut off by the sword, famine, or pestilence: 4,000 citizens alone were found able to bear arms, but they were for the most part not trained to war, being merchants or artizans of different trades. The enemy also seized in the city 8 pieces of brass cannon, 16 of iron, besides 24 demy-cannon, part of brass, part of iron, and 83 barrels of powder, and arms for 3,500 men, with muskets and other military stores of little importance, and some old cavalry equipments, but no horses."

Ten of those excepted from quarter voluntarily surrendered, including Hugh O'Neill and Sir Richard Everard, whose lives, however, were spared—the latter, on account of his advanced years, being imprisoned in Ireland, whilst the former was sent to the Tower of London to await the decision of the Parliament. Ireton, in his official despatch to the Government in London, on the 3rd of November, 1651, announces that Major-General Purcell, Thomas Stritch, the ex-Mayor, and the Bishop of Emly had been already hanged, and their heads set upon poles on the tower on Limerick Bridge. A few days later four others were executed after the same manner—that is, Sir Jeoffrey Galway, Dr. Higgins, Captain George Wolf, and Jeoffrey Baron, nephew of Fr. Luke Wadding. The Rinuccini MS. adds that Fr. James Wolf, O.S.D., brother of the above captain, and Fr. David Roche, O.S.D.; Fr. John O'Cuillin, O.S.D.; with Fr. Lawrence Walsh and Alderman Dominick Fanning, "the pillar of the Catholic cause in Limerick," were also soon discovered. Of the first it is merely recorded that "his head was struck off;" the second was sentenced to slavery in the Barbadoes—a sentence more cruel than death itself; the rest were hanged. A writer who was present throughout the whole time of the siege adds that the three Dominican Fathers could easily have escaped from the city had they so wished, but that yearning for martyrdom they braved every peril in the discharge of their sacred duties, and died with true heroism.

10. Two facts, mentioned by Fr. Dominick O'Daly, in his *History of the Geraldines* deserve to be recorded. His work was published at Lisbon in 1655, only four years after the surrender of Limerick to Ireton, but what adds greater weight to its authority, its statements relating to the Limerick siege were derived not only from James Dowley, whose name is mentioned by O'Daly, but also, as the Rinuccini MS. attests, from Fr. Fabian O'Mulreany, a Dominican Father, who was in Limerick during the whole time of the siege. This Fr. O'Mulreany was a man of learning and prudence, and had written a narrative of the events of which he was witness. He was, moreover, held in high esteem by his contemporaries, and when the Archbishop of Cashel, just before those disastrous days of the Puritan triumph, petitioned His Holiness for a Coadjutor, the name of this learned Dominican was one of those presented by the bishops of the province to the Holy See. The portentous signs are thus recorded in the History of the Geraldines:—" A most extraordinary phenomenon was observed on the 17th of July, 1651, a little before midnight, of the day sacred to St. Alexis. The Irish garrison had been six weeks working at the walls and strengthening the fortifications, when, just as all was completed, there appeared, on the eastern side of the mountain that is north of Limerick, a luminous globe, brighter than the moon, a little

inferior to the sun, which, for two leagues and a half, shed a vertical light on the city, and then faded into darkness over the enemy's camp. The second wonder was the apparition of the blessed Mother of God, at about 3 o'clock in the afternoon, on the summit of the great church dedicated to her honour. She was seen by some simple people who were at work in the fields, and she was accompanied by St. Francis and St. Dominic, and five other heavenly beings, who seemed to follow her to the Convent of the Dominicans, and thence to the Franciscan Church, without the walls. From those who beheld this apparition, Father James Dowley, a man famed for his merits and learning, received information of the details as I have narrated them, and he himself is still living." The statement of the Dominican historian is corroborated by an unlooked-for witness. In the appendix to the *Aphorismical Discovery*, Mr. Gilbert has published the diary of some Puritan officers during this siege, and precisely, on Thursday, July the 17th, we find the entry :—" This night, about 11 of the clock, a flame of fire passed over Limerick, giving that light by which one might read. It moved from the north-east, continuing about half a quarter of an hour" (vol. iii, page 244).

11. As was usual with the Puritan troops, wherever they became masters, the plighted conditions were not kept. "Bad as the articles were," says the Rinuccini MS., citing the words of an officer who was present, "they were not observed. The citizens were compelled to deliver to Ireton all their gold and silver, their precious plate and jewellery, and many were driven forth, with their wives and children, from their residences

and from the homes of their fathers." What was regarded as a just judgment of God, some of the very citizens, who lost all that they possessed, were among the leaders of the Ormondist faction who had clamoured for the surrender of the city.

One of those marked out for execution was snatched by death itself from the cruel hands of Ireton. The name of the Bishop of Killaloe was on the list of those excepted from quarter, as the Rinuccini MS. bears witness, nevertheless that name does not appear upon the printed list forwarded to London by Ireton. The venerable bishop, more than seventy years of age, had prayed, like St. Augustine of old, that he might not live to see the desecration of the churches that he so loved. His prayer was heard. He was struck down by sickness the very day that the articles of surrender were signed, and he expired before the Puritans, who thirsted for his blood, could glut their vengeance by his martyrdom. He had pursued his philosophical studies at Galway, in the school of Alexander Lynch, which, in the beginning of the seventeenth century, was reckoned among the most flourishing academies in the kingdom. It was famed for its observance of discipline as well as for the ardour of its scholars in the pursuit of sacred science, and youths flocked to it for instruction from all parts of the kingdom. Very soon, however, that able master was obliged to dismiss his scholars and to desist from his fruitful task of teaching. The heretics, like Julian the apostate, who ordered all the Christian schools to be closed, would not permit the Catholic youth to be instructed by Catholic masters, and the students, being forced by order of the Lord

Chancellor Jones to forego the advantages of the Galway Academy, O'Molony proceeded to Paris, where he devoted himself, for several years, to sacred studies. He was subsequently appointed Bishop of Killaloe, and consecrated in the Church of St. Victor, in Paris, by the Bishop of Auxerre, assisted by two other bishops, in the month of November, 1630. Returning home he, for twenty years, laboured in season and out of season, proving himself a pattern of virtue to his clergy, and instructing his flock by word and example. Throughout the whole course of the Confederate war he was heart and soul with his people, rejoicing in their triumphs and comforting them in their sorrows. A short time before the siege of Limerick he was arrested and plundered of everything he had, by order of some of the Ormondist officers; but, in compensation for this outrage, a sum of about £600 was given him by the Lord Deputy. He availed himself of this wealth and of everything else that he possessed during the siege, first, to redeem the sacred vessels and Ecclesiastical treasures, which had been pledged for the public wants, and, secondly, to pay the soldiers of the garrison, and it was said that the siege was prolonged for a fortnight, mainly through his resources. This was well known to the Puritan enemy, who had resolved to lead him out forthwith to the gallows, but death saved him from their cruelty. Not for this however (says the contemporary Archdeacon Lynch) is the title of martyr to be denied him, for he was marked out for martyrdom, and the Puritans, unable to torture him after death, seized upon his books and papers and consigned all to the flames.

12. Of Dominick Fanning, a former mayor of the city, the *Aphorismical Discovery* records, that when the Puritan army entered the city, he concealed himself in his family tomb, at St. Francis's monastery; but being overcome by the cold and hunger, came forth " to the body of the church, where there was a guard with a great fire," and all besmeared as he was sat down to warm himself. The captain soon recognised in him a person of quality, but moved with compassion, the better to conceal him, " gave him a kind kick, asking what did the rogue there, and commanded him away, threatening if ever again he found him there to hang him." The servant of Fanning, who was present, happened to be a traitor, and whispered to the captain who he was. The captain paying no attention, the servant gave information elsewhere, and Fanning being at once arrested was forthwith hanged. The captain, however, to punish the servant's perfidy, who was exulting in his master's execution, gave orders to one of the soldiers to run his sword through him, so that he met with the deserved punishment for his perfidy.

The *Aphorismical Discovery*, just cited, adds that " several others of both clergy and laity were pitifully mangled, massacred, hanged, and dragged, man, woman, and child, excepting the betraying traitors." And, again, the same unexceptional authority attests that the Puritans, instead of observing the conditions, were " running here and there, massacreing and killing every mother's child they met, other than the exempted traitors: three days and so many nights were they in this bloody execution, no grotto, cellar, prison, church, or tomb was unsearched, and all therein found made piecemeal, and hanged and quartered" (vol. iii., page 20).

13. A few extracts from the "Diary of the Parliamentary forces," already referred to, will serve to place the true circumstances of this famous Siege of Limerick in their true light. Setting out from Waterford, Ireton issued a strict order prohibiting, under severe penalties, any of his officers or men from intermarrying " with any of the women of this nation that are Papists, or have lately been such, and whose change of religion is not and cannot be judged by fit persons such as shall be appointed for that end, to flow from a real work of God upon their hearts convincing them of the falsehood and evil of their own ways." (*Aph. Disc.*, vol. iii., page 226.) As early as the 20th of May, 1651, Colonel Ingoldsby "with 1,000 horse, foot, and dragoons," appeared before Limerick, hoping "by correspondency with some within" to capture the city. The plot however failed. Though these troops immediately retired towards Killaloe, the siege may be said to have begun on that day. The regular operations of the siege, however, by the Puritan army did not commence till the 3rd of June. On Monday, the 16th of June, a small party of 14 Irish soldiers, at one of the outstations of the city, surrendered after quarter given, but they were by order of Col. Totthill all put to the sword. Two days later, provisions being scarce, some decrepit men and their families, about forty in all, were sent out from the city. Ireton ordered four of them to be put to death to deter others from quitting the city. It was then that a decrepit father, seeing his daughter amongst those marked out for death, offered himself to be hanged

in her stead. However, instead of four, the whole party, about forty in number, were put to death by the Puritan soldiers (page 240)! This fact, so plainly attested by the Diary of the Siege, will serve as a proof of the little reliance that is to be placed on the statements of the Puritan officers, when referring to the deeds of cruelty perpetrated by those under their authority. Lieutenant-General Ludlow, who was present on the occasion, states in his Memoirs, that Ireton ordered "one or two to be executed," and adds, that "a gibbet was erected in the sight of the town walls and one or two persons hanged up, who had been condemned for other crimes, that those within might suppose that execution to be for coming out." (*Memoirs*, published in London in 1751, page 142). Thus does he attempt to travesty the horrid deed of cold blood massacre which would seem incredible were it not recorded in all its deformity in the authentic Puritan Diary. Webb, in his *Compendium of Irish Biography*, would make us believe that those famished citizens were only driven back into the city. Under the head of Ireton, he writes: "One of the most thrilling incidents in *Ludlow's Memoirs*, is his account of how they (the besiegers) beat back into the town a crowd of famished and plague-stricken non-combatants, who sought to leave it." It is thus that Irish History has been hitherto written. The poor people, instead of being driven back, were all put to death, and their murder was officially described as a mistake. The *Diary* adds, that in one of the sallies from the city, Ireton and his staff ran imminent risk: "His lordship with other principal officers were then laying a new fort, when the enemy so sallied, there not being works or guards between them and the party sallying near them; but God otherwise disposed it diverting the danger and carrying the enemy another way, they not seeing their advantages" (page 245).

The losses of the Puritan army were very great. In one of the sallies, as Cox records, no fewer than 300 of their soldiers were slain. The plague also made great havoc amongst them, but new troops were poured in from England, and thus, as one of their officers triumphantly records, their army was kept immortal. From Waterford alone no fewer than 10,000 men marched to the camp during the siege. The garrison within the city were quite exhausted by the incessant anxieties and labour of the six months' siege without relief or succour. They were, moreover, quite disheartened by the pestilence which swept off so many brave men. As they marched out after the surrender of the city, two or three of them fell down dead of the plague, and several were found lying unburied in the churchyard. Ireton made show of admiration for Hugh O'Neill, and anxiety to save his life. A Puritan officer, however, who assisted at the court-martials, records that the Lord Deputy had not forgotten "the blood shed formerly at Clonmel, where this O'Neill was Governor," and that, at two successive court-martials, he, by his authority, led a majority of officers to pronounce sentence of death against him; but, as circumstances prevented these sentences from being carried out, at the third court-martial, the officers being left to their own judgment, his life was spared.

14. In 1650, Mr. Thomas Stritch, on terminating his spiritual retreat, had been elected mayor, and he ever

proved himself an unflinching defender of his country's cause.

"On receiving the keys of the city, he laid them before the statue of the most holy Virgin, praying her to receive the city under her protection, whilst, at the same time, as an act of homage, all the public guilds marched in procession to the church; he then made a most Christian address to the whole assembly, encouraging them to an inviolable attachment to God, to the Church, and to the king, offering to lay down his own life in so just a cause. God was pleased to accept his offering, and, on the city being taken, he* received the martyr's crown, together with three other

---

* We wish to present to the reader the following extract of a letter written in 1653 by two Vincentian Fathers, Fathers Barry and Gerald O'Brien, to Rome, which gives some interesting particulars connected with this illustrious family:—

"The news I hear from Ireland are, that there is no hope of accommodation or liberty of conscience for the poor Catholics of Ireland there. Those of the Irish army who forced us to render the city of Limerick unto the enemies, upon so base conditions, were hanged at Cork, viz., Col. Ed. Fenell and Lieut.-Coll. William Burke of Brittas. All the clergy were banished except very few; as I am informed, there is the matter of three score of these exiled priests for the present at Nantes: little James Stritch wrote unto me from St. Malo's; he tells me his mother, great mother, brethren, sisters. and uncles remain in a little island upon the river of Limerick, called Augnish. His uncle Patrick Stritch died four days after his arrival at St. Malo's. You have been informed, I believe, of your cousin James Creagh FitzAndrew's death, and his daughter's marriage. I would wish you had there one of Thomas Stritch's children, to be presented unto some cardinal."

The "little James Stritch" of whom mention is here made was a few years later (in 1660) received as student into the Irish College, Rome, and towards the close of the century we again meet with him as Bishop of Emly.

persons, who, having been his companions in his spiritual retreat, were likewise partakers of his reward. They all four marched along, not only with firmness, but even with joy; and before execution they severally addressed the bystanders, moving the very heretics to tears, and declaring before heaven and earth that they laid down their lives for the confession and defence of the Catholic faith. Their heroic example greatly encouraged the other Catholics to preserve their faith, and to suffer all extremities of persecution rather than be wanting in the fidelity which they owe to God."*

Father Anthony Broudin, in his *Descriptio Regni Hiberniæ*, tells of the death of a few others:—

"The most illustrious Sir Patrick Purcell, Vice-General of all Munster, a noble-hearted and most accomplished warrior (for in Germany, under Ferdinand III., he acquired an immortal renown, combating against Sweden and France), after the taking of Limerick, was hanged; then his head was cut off, and exposed on a stake over the southern gate, called St. John's Gate, A.D. 1651. The illustrious and most noble Sir Geoffrey Barron, a sincere Catholic, of the highest fidelity, and of singular eloquence, who had been deputed by the confederate Catholics of Ireland as their envoy to his Most Christian Majesty, was hanged at the same time, and beheaded and quartered. The noble Dominick Fanning, too, ex-Mayor of Limerick, and alderman, a man well known, and of the highest integrity, who had rendered many services to the confederated Catholics, and had, in his public

* Abelly, loc. cit., pp. 218-9.

offices, conferred much benefit on the whole kingdom, as well as on the city, was in like manner executed at the same place, and happily exchanged life for death: on the same day, and at the same place, and by the same martyrdom, Father Laurence Wallis, a priest, also passed to a more blissful life; and with him Daniel O'Higgin, a medical doctor, a wise and pious man, was led to the scaffold."*

15. It would be easy to multiply these extracts, but suffice it to say that the city was laid desolate, and that those who escaped the sword were despoiled of all they possessed, and then driven from its walls. St. Vincent, having been informed by the Superior of the Order in Ireland of the number of those who had suffered death for the faith in Limerick, cried out: "The blood of these martyrs will not be forgotten before God, and sooner or later will produce an abundant harvest of Catholicity." (Abelly, loc. cit., p. 220.) And this prophecy is wonderfully fulfilled in our days, when religion is producing such admirable fruits in Limerick and in every part of the kingdom, and restoring, even in the midst of poverty, its former splendour and glory. In the last two centuries, as well as in the early ages of the Church, the truth of the maxim of Tertullian has been fully confirmed, "The blood of martyrs is the seed of Christians."

16. Edmund O'Dwyer, Bishop of Limerick, has been frequently named in the preceding pages. Born in the

* Broudin, cap. 8. All the facts here mentioned are also commemorated by Morison, in his *Threnodia Hiberno-Catholica*, Œnoponti, 1659, who styles himself "an eye-witness to the unheard-of cruelty to which the Irish were subjected."

county of Limerick, he pursued the higher studies at Rome, Paris, and Rheims, and having laboured for some time on the Irish mission, proceeded to Rome in 1634, as Procurator of Archbishop O'Queely of Tuam and other Irish Prelates, and continued for eight years to discharge the duties of that responsible office in the Eternal City. Returning to Ireland in 1642, he was seized by Moorish pirates off the British coast; for twenty-one days he was kept in iron chains and wooden fetters, and was sold as a slave at Sale on the northwest coast of Africa. A Calvinist of Rochelle trading along that coast purchased him soon after for £40, and set him at liberty in France on the promise of receiving for his ransom a sum of £60. Two years later he was again sent to Rome to solicit prompt aid in the name of the Irish Confederates and bearer of a petition addressed to Urban the Eighth, that Fr. Luke Wadding, O.S.F., would be promoted to the Cardinalitial dignity. Pope Urban, however, died before O'Dwyer reached Rome, and thus that petition becoming informal could not be presented. Innocent the Tenth, who next ascended the Papal throne did not cherish the same esteem for Wadding as his predecessor, and the petition of the Confederates was not renewed. O'Dwyer, however, was appointed Coadjutor Bishop of Limerick, and was consecrated by the Bishop of Senlis, in the Church of St. Lazare, in Paris, on Sunday the 7th of May, 1645. Sailing for Ireland from one of the ports of Brittany, the ship was captured by a Turkish corsair, and being led to Smyrna, he was again sold as a slave and obliged to grind corn with a handmill, and to wear a gag upon his mouth (*ne farinam voraret*), lest he should feed upon the meal. Providence, however, had again prepared a refuge for him. An Irish lady, married to a French merchant in Smyrna, discovered that there was a countryman among the slaves and at once procured his release and sent him back to France. We have already spoken of his labours for the welfare of his spiritual flock. He suffered a great deal during the siege of his Episcopal city. The citizens being rent by factions, and the Ormondists manifesting their joy that the city was to be surrendered, their opponents formed a plan to avenge their rejoicing by blowing up the house in which they were assembled. The Bishop, however, vigorously remonstrated with the leaders of the party and induced them to desist from this wicked design. On the surrender of the city to Ireton, he was excepted from quarter, but made his escape disguised as an officer's servant, carrying a load upon his back, and having his face singed with gunpowder. He made his way to the Irish camp under the command of Lord Muskerry, and Ireton having heard of the course which the Bishop had pursued to prevent the blowing up of the Ormondists who had procured the surrender of the city, sent him a safe-conduct, empowering him to return and to remove from the city any property that still remained to him. He remained in the city for only a few days, mourning over the desolation of his flock, and then proceeded to Brussels where he died on Easter Sunday, in 1654.

CHAPTER X.

SUFFERINGS OF THE CATHOLICS IN GALWAY.

1. Clanrickard appointed Lord Deputy; the remedy comes too late.
—2. Galway taken after a long siege.—3. Dr. Kirwan, Bishop of Killala's, sufferings in his place of refuge.—4. The enemy enters Galway; military exactions.—5. Plunder of the house of Martin Kirwan.—6. Dr. Kirwan arrested and sent into exile with other ecclesiastics.—7. Calamities that befell the citizens.—8. Extracts from the Annals of Galway.—9. Dr. Fallon, V.G., of Achonry; decree of banishment against the clergy.—10. Violence and brutality of the troops.—11. Some account of the Bishop of Meath and other illustrious sufferers for the Faith.

1. To review in detail the sufferings of the other cities of Ireland, would be to repeat the scenes which we have already described. There is, however, something peculiar in the rigour displayed by the Puritans in the capital of the western province that claims a special attention. A gleam of sunshine broke in upon the gloom of despondency that hung over the nation, when, in the year 1650, a Catholic nobleman, the Earl of Clanrickard, was proclaimed Lord Deputy with authority from the crown to govern the kingdom of Ireland. A little while before, the Bishops and other representatives of the Irish Church, assembled in solemn deliberation at Jamestown. Charles O'Conor towards

the middle of the last century, thus describes this classic spot: "It contains an area of four or five plantation acres in an oblong square, surrounded by a strong wall six feet in thickness, about twenty feet high: the two gates are broken down. It stretches along the Shannon (about nine miles from Belanagare), under a rising ground to the west; no fortification was ever worse situated for defence." But if its position as a fortress did not make it memorable in history it won immortal fame by the Bishops' decrees. They impeached the whole administration of Lord Ormonde, they set forth the resources of the nation which he squandered, and the ruin which he brought upon the royal cause, and as sole remedy they called upon him to resign to abler hands the trust which the Sovereign had reposed in him. To the Episcopal indictment no satisfactory answer could be given. Ormonde fled the kingdom, and the reins of government passed into the hands of Clanrickard. There was great rejoicing in Loughrea on the feast of the Purification in 1651, when the Lord Deputy in Viceregal State, assisted at High Mass in the Church of the Blessed Virgin. The sword of State was borne before him, the chief military officers accompanied him, the Archbishop of Tuam with the Bishops of Killala, Kilmacduagh, Limerick, Cork, Emly, Kilfenora, Down, and Clonfert, were there to do him honour; banners were displayed, congratulatory addresses were presented, and the humiliations of a hundred years appeared to be forgotten in the tardy tribute to Catholic devotedness and loyalty. These expressions of congratulation and joy were repeated in Galway on the 17th of March, where he assisted with the same viceregal pomp at solemn Mass, in the presence of the above-mentioned prelates, and at the Panegyric of our National Apostle delivered by the Bishop of Dromore.

All this gave promise of united exertions, and revived the drooping courage of the friends of Ireland in the west. But the remedy had come too late. The past misgovernment had exhausted the resources of the country, and the seeds of dissension so industriously sown were destined still to bear their bitter fruits. Clanrickard was found to pursue the same course as Ormonde; he viewed with distrust the old Irish soldiers who alone could check the Puritan enemy, and disaster and ruin soon began to follow in his train.

Many particulars of the sufferings which soon fell to the lot of the Catholic citizens of Galway are set forth in "the Life of Dr. Francis Kirwan, Bishop of Killala," written by his friend, Dr. John Lynch, and published at St. Malo's, in 1669.*

2. The city of Galway was remarkable amongst the other cities of Ireland for the wealth of its inhabitants, and the beauty of its edifices. The walls were of green marble, flanked by numerous towers; the waters of Lough Corrib flowed through its centre, whilst the regularity of its streets, the fair proportions of its buildings, its noble squares, and its palaces built of native marble, gladdened the eye. All this was soon to become a prey to the ruthless enemy. A band of adventurers under the command of Lord Forbes, were the first to plunder this Catholic city. These adventurers were

---

* See reprint and translation of this work, by Rev. C. P. Meehan, 1884.

enrolled under an Ordinance of the House of Commons of 14th of April, 1642. They stipulated for the hanging and shooting of rebels, and the keeping of what castles they took and for the dividing amongst them of all the spoil. They had no special service, but were to make waste and havoc. Having landed at Galway in the summer of 1642, they broke the truce made by Lord Clanrickard, got possession of St. Mary's Church, dug up the graves, and burnt the coffins and bones of the dead, and required the citizens to sign a submission, expressing their belief that there was no other means of saving them from extirpation and banishment.*

The ruin thus begun was completed by the Cromwellian soldiery. It was in the month of June, 1651, that the Puritan army marched into Connaught, laying waste the whole province with fire and sword, and on the 8th of July they encamped before the walls of Galway. The city had already been decimated by the pestilence, yet it was only after nine months' combat that the enemy entered within the walls.

3. Dr. Francis Kirwan was at this time lying hid in a country house, at a short distance from the city. For eight months he continued there in a small, narrow room, which, besides two beds for himself and his chaplain, was barely able to contain a chest. This served for an altar; and whilst the Holy Sacrifice was offered up each day, one bed had to be removed to afford standing room for the celebrant. The intense cold of winter was endured without a fire, and during the whole eight months only thrice did the bishop go for an

---

* *Prendergast,* p. 75.

instant from this hiding-place; on one occasion he was carried out wrapped in a sheet, whilst the enemy were engaged in searching every corner of the house for arms, and when met by the soldiers he was recognised only as a feeble and worn-down old man; and well does his biographer compare his many sufferings at this period to those of the early pastors of the Catholic Church.

4. Within the city the soldiery displayed a *rabid detestation* of the Catholic priests, and with an insatiate avarice plundered the Catholic citizens of all they possessed. When the bishop deemed it more secure to enter the town, "he was obliged to take refuge in the topmost stories of the house aneath the tiles, and this, too, at mid-winter, without one spark of fire. Sometimes, too, he was forced to go out on the roof, and when the pursuers approached, to descend into a neighbouring house by the dormant-window" (p. 123). We must allow this contemporary writer to depict some of the frightful scenes of persecution to which the citizens were at the same time subjected:—

"Along with the three scourges of God, famine, plague, and war, there was another which some called the fourth scourge, to wit, the weekly exaction of the soldiers' pay, which was extorted with incredible atrocity each Saturday, bugles sounding and drums beating. On these occasions the soldiers entered the various houses, and, pointing their muskets to the breasts of men and women, threatened them with instant death if the sum demanded was not instantly given. Should it have so happened that the continual payment of these pensions had exhausted the means of the people, bed, bedding, sheets, tablecloths, dishes, and every descrip-

tion of furniture, nay, the very garments of the women, torn off their persons, were carried to the marketplace and sold for a small sum, so much so, that each recurring Saturday bore a resemblance to the day of judgment, and the clangour of the trumpet smote the people with terror, almost equal to that of doom's day."
—(Page 123.)

5. The scene of plunder in the house of Mr. Martin Kirwan, which he next describes, is only an instance of the fearful course which was pursued by *these harpies*,* when the country was parcelled out to their devastating fury :—

"In the house they found only young children and servants, together with the mother, who superintended their education, for the father and his son were in prison. Having ransacked the whole house, the soldiers entered an inner room, where they saw some glittering rays of light, and, in this recess, they discovered a wooden tabernacle, ornamented with gilded mouldings, and wooden candlesticks, likewise gilt, which the bishop was about to place in some church. All these sacred objects did the soldiers drag out of the house, nor could they be induced, by supplication or money, to restore them. They subsequently tore them all to pieces, and scattered many relics that had been deposited in the tabernacle."

6. When at length the good bishop, finding it impossible to remain any longer concealed, surrendered to the Government, he and several other ecclesiastics were treated as galley slaves. They were marched along

* This is the designation given them by the contemporary author.

in bodies, surrounded by soldiers, drums beating and bugles sounding, and when, by the diligence of priest-catchers, many other ecclesiastics were cast into prison, the former were locked up in houses hired for the occasion, and for which the prisoners themselves had to pay. During his imprisonment the holy man found occasion frequently to celebrate the sacred mysteries, and, at a window in the rere of the prison, administered to the children the sacrament of confirmation.* No sooner was it discovered by the Government that the bishop and his companions were thus engaged in conferring spiritual blessings on the Catholics than their banishment was resolved on. The confessors of Christ "were suddenly carried off to a ship, and, on their way, were surrounded by a terrible escort, nor had they any previous notice of the decree of banishment, lest their friends might succour them with some viaticum."— (Page 129.)

7. During the siege the enemy had sustained serious losses from the garrisons and citizens. As early as the 27th of May, 1651, the Puritans, having occupied an island opposite to Galway, began to fortify it. The strait, however, that separated it from the city being fordable at low water, a number of the citizens crossed over unawares, retook the island, and put to the sword a considerable number of the enemy who were rioting there. Even towards the end of March, 1652, the great majority of the clergy, when interrogated by the Lord Deputy Clanrickard, were of opinion that the city should not be surrendered. Out of one hundred and

* Ibid., page 127.

twenty-six, whose opinion was thus asked, only six counselled the surrender, whilst one hundred and twenty urged that the defence should be prolonged. Clanrickard, however, saw no prospect of relief from any quarter, and the citizens, being weary of the burden of the garrison's support, and terrified by the ravages of the pestilence, the city was handed over to the Puritans on the 12th of May, 1652. Fr. Gregory French, prior of the Dominicans of Galway, writing to Rome from France, in July of the same year, sketches the consequences in a few words :—" Those citizens of Galway who were most eager to throw open its gates to the English are now reduced to a miserable plight, without sacrifice, without priest, without sacraments, and every day they are more and more plundered and worried by the Puritan soldiers."

In *Cambrensis Eversus* we find some further details of the calamities that fell on the citizens of Galway, and it must be borne in mind that its author (Rev. John Lynch) was present in Galway throughout the whole time of the siege :—" Galway," he says, " was the last of all the towns in England, Scotland, and Ireland that remained faithful to the king, but it, too, fell at last into the hands of the enemy. . . . . The commander of the besieging army was not a man of ordinary rank, but Charles Coote himself, commander of Connaught and Ulster, which provinces he had subjugated for the Parliamentarians. From him the besieged extorted honourable conditions, . . . but the men appointed to the chief government of Ireland by the parliament refused to ratify these conditions. In a short time they commenced to rob the citizens of their property. These were allowed to remain within their native walls only so long as they had money to support the common soldiers and to glut the avarice of their officers, but when the daily contributions levied on the city had, by degrees, exhausted its wealth, they were deprived of the magisterial offices three years after the capitulation. Then, as each roll of citizens was drained of all its property by these taxes, they were cast out of the city, but the more wealthy were allowed to remain, so long as they had any money, until at last nearly all were cast out and compelled to wander through the country, endeavouring to support themselves by agriculture, of which they knew nothing."—(Vol. iii, p. 189.)

8. The MS. Annals of Galway, preserved in the library of T.C.D., written in the reign of Charles the II., give us some important details, in the following words :—" Upon the surrender of Galway, there was such a dearth in the county, that many thousands died by the second plague, and three scourges of God were then reigning, viz., dearth, plague, and sword, and many, to whom life was spared, had no great means left to maintain themselves. Upon an information of Colonel Stubbers, Governor of Galway, of the multitude of vagabonds and idlers in the country, he obtained an order to ship them for Barbadoes, and this order was so carried out, that many housekeepers, going to see their cattle and their children were pressed on board, and all others that were registered in the contribution book, so that there were two thousand persons sent off, and were sold there as slaves. The unruly crew of soldiers broke down the monuments and

coffins of the dead, taking from them the winding-sheets, as though some treasure had been within the said coffins, nay, breaking down crucifixes and such spiritual costly works engraven on fine marble. Sir Peter Tench's tomb, gilt with gold and all made of fine marble, being in St. Francis's Abbey, the building of which cost more than £500, was, along with the rest, demolished and converted by the governor of the said town into a chimney, and the rest of the said grand stones or marbles of the said abbey were sold and sent beyond sea, and the monuments left wide open for the dogs to drag out and eat the corpses interred there, and likewise they erased the king's arms, and converted the church and abbey to stables, and they were, for the most part, illiterate and covetous to hoard up money by the ruin of the poor inhabitants, without any regard to conscience or public faith, the sword then being in lieu of the law, our unhappy iron age. The mayor, sheriffs, and the English made freemen of their own, viz., cobblers, butchers, tinkers, and all sorts of artificers.
. . . About this time you might see whole families destroyed, and streets not having six families, and soldiers, or poor bakers, that ought to content themselves with one cellar, had great houses to live in, till they burned all the lofts, and wainscots, and partitions thereof, and then removed to another house till they made an end of all the town, and left them full of excrement and filth, so that it was poison to enter into any of the said houses, formerly fit to lodge kings or princes, being the completest and best fitted in all Ireland. The inhabitants thereof, being the best and greatest merchants in the kingdom for hospitality, liberality,

and charity, both at home and abroad, accompanied with good education, were now in the midst of frost and snow, lying in hedges, in smoky and miserable huts, and barracks in the country, being all removed, excepting families who were forced to quarter the most part of the soldiers of the town, and to pay excessive tributes and bribes, but were, at last, turned out with the rest. The clergy, being about fifty in number, were sent to Arran and Boffin, where they were almost starved, being allowed but two pence *per diem*, and, even that not paid, and strict proclamation was made against the lives and goods of such as would entertain any clergyman. The images of our Blessed Lady and of other saints were burned, chalices were made common cups to drink out of, and priests' vestments were made secular clothes of."

9. Throughout the whole province of Connaught the persecution raged with the same fury. Thus, when Dr. James Fallon, who governed the diocese of Achonry as vicar-apostolic " was arrested in Iar-Connaught, the heretics so plundered him of his copious collections of books, that not even a breviary was left with him. Before he was made prisoner he for a long time was exposed, day and night, to the inclemency of the winter, till he at length erected a small hut at the base of a rock, which he covered with leafy branches. Here he remained till the goats, brousing on the foliage, stripped the branches, and then he was obliged to seek elsewhere a place of refuge." (*Ibid.*, page 15.)

In the articles of surrender of the various garrisons, a clause was generally inserted to the effect that such articles did not extend to the Catholic clergy. To say

Mass was an act of treason, and to be a priest was to be an enemy of the commonwealth. Thus in the articles granted to Colonel Edmund O'Dwyer, for the Irish Brigade in Tipperary and Waterford, the 23rd of March, 1652, the clause is added: " Provided that the benefit of all or any of the articles aforesaid, extend not to any priest or other of the Romish clergy in orders; nor to any that sat in the first General Assembly, nor to any that sat in the first Supreme Council." (*Aphoris. Discov.*, vol. iii., p. 295). Again, when Colonel Murtogh O'Brien surrendered on the part of the Irish troops in the county of Clare, it was covenanted "that the benefit of these articles extend not to any priest or other of the Romish clergy in orders, further than the Major-General (Waller), doth undertake industriously to solicit the Commissioners of Parliament that such of the clergy in orders, having no other act or crime laid to their charge than officiating their functions as priests, not being suffered to live in quarters or protection, shall have passes and liberty to go beyond the seas." (*Ibid.*, p. 313.) In the articles granted to the Leinster troops the clause was added on the 31st of July, 1652 : " All of the popish clergy submitting to a trial, and not being found guilty of offences, &c., shall have passes to go beyond the seas." (*Ibid.*, p. 318). In the articles with Lord Muskerry and the army of Munster: "That the benefit of all or any of the articles aforesaid extend not to the exemption of any person from being questioned, &c., nor to give protection to Priests and Jesuits or others in Popish orders to live in the Parliament's quarters " (*Ibid.*, p. 326) ; and the same clause is repeated in the articles for the

Ulster army. (*Ibid.*, p. 348.) No mention, however, of any such clause was made in the surrender of Galway, and some of the clergy deluding themselves with the vain hope that toleration was accorded them, began privately to say Mass and to bring the consolations of religion to the suffering citizens. They were speedily undeceived. On the 7th of May, 1652, the following decree was published by the Commissioners in Galway :*

" Whereas we have strong reason to suspect that to the offence of God and the displeasure of those who fear Him and walk in his paths, many clandestine Masses and other idolatrous ministrations of the Roman Church are frequently practised by several of the Popish clergy, who not being able to depart were permitted by the articles of surrender to remain in this garrison, we hereby ordain and declare that all Jesuits, Seminary Priests and others of the Romish clergy, who are known to have exercised any part of their ministerial functions or any of the rites or ministrations of the said church, are by the very fact deprived of all right to the said articles, and also all those who assisted at the said ministrations or were cognisant of them, and within forty hours will not make them known to the Governor and one or more of the Commissioners for the administration of Justice. We further require and command under the above penalties that the mayor, aldermen, citizens, inhabitants, and men of whatever condition they may be, residing in this municipality, shall not use movable crosses, crucifixes, relics, or pictures,

---

* I translate it literally from the Latin text in the Rinuccini MS., as I have not met with a copy of the original English text.

according to the service of the Romish Church aforesaid, nor shall they keep any such in their houses, and further, that they shall demolish, or cause to be demolished, all fixed crosses and crucifixes, whether within or without the gates. And this edict, when it has been published, at sound of trumpet, shall be affixed in the public places of this city, that no one can plead ignorance thereof."

9. All that we have said in this article is authenticated, from official documents by Mr. Prendergast, who thus writes :—" The town of Galway, the last fortress of the Irish, surrendered to Ludlow on the 20th of March, 1652, on articles securing to the inhabitants their residence within the town, and the enjoyment of their houses and estates. The taxation was soon so great that many of the townspeople quitted their habitations and removed their cattle, unable to endure it, consequently the contribution fell the heavier on the remaining inhabitants. This tax was collected from them every Saturday by sound of trumpet, and, if not instantly paid, the soldiery rushed into the house and seized what they could lay hands on. The sound of this trumpet, every returning Saturday, shook their souls with terror, like the trumpet of the day of judgment. On the 15th of March, 1653, the Commissioners for Ireland, remarking upon the disaffection thus exhibited, confiscated the houses of those that had deserted the town. Those that fled were wise in time. On 23rd July, 1655, all the Irish were directed to quit the town by the 1st of November following, the owners of houses, however, to receive compensation at eight years' purchase; in default, the soldiers were to drive

them out. On 30th October this order was executed. All the inhabitants, except the sick and the bedrid, were at once banished to provide acccmmodation for such English Protestants, whose integrity to the State should entitle them to be trusted in a place of such importance ; and Sir Charles Coote, on the 7th November, received the thanks of the Government for clearing the town, with a request that he would remove the sick and bedrid as soon as the season might permit, and take care that the houses, while empty, were not spoiled by the soldiery."*

10. Hardiman, in his " History of Galway," adds some further particulars. "The surrender," he says, "was followed by a famine throughout the country by which multitudes perished. This was again succeeded by a plague which carried off thousands, both in the town and the surrounding districts, so that the severest vengeance of heaven seemed now to have been poured down on the heads of this devoted community. Many, driven to despair by the severities inflicted upon them, instead of avoiding the pestilence, sought refuge in death from their merciless persecutors. This dreadful visitation continued for two years, during which upwards of one-third of the population of the province was swept away, and those who survived were doomed to undergo sufferings to which even death itself was preferable. . . . The most violent acts of oppression and injustice openly took place without any control. The king's arms and every other emblem of royalty were torn down, the churches and abbeys

* *Settlement*, &c., p. 146.

were converted into stables for the dragoons, the chalices and sacred vessels used as drinking-cups, and the old and valuable libraries of the clergy burnt or sold to the shops. The mayor and aldermen, though expressly protected by the articles, were repeatedly abused and dragged to prison for daring to remonstrate with the licentious soldiery, who set no bounds to their brutality and violence. The annals (of the town) relate that their avarice went so far as to break open the tombs and root the dead bodies out of the graves in hopes of finding riches interred with them; and that when disappointed they left the carcasses uncovered, so that they were often found mangled and eaten by the dogs. The inhabitants having repeatedly, but in vain, appealed to the governor against these atrocities, at length ventured to represent their grievances to the commissioners in Dublin; they received, however, such replies as showed they were to expect no relief from that quarter. After several specious and evasive answers, to preserve the appearance of justice, orders of reference were made to the very persons complained of; they were finally informed that the articles of surrender, being still under consideration in England, could not be interfered with; and they were thus dismissed to undergo even worse treatment than before for at all presuming to complain." (Pages 134-5.)

11. It was when the siege of the city was about to commence that the venerable Bishop of Meath, Dr. Thomas Dease, passed to his reward. He had pursued his higher studies in Paris, where he subsequently taught the course of philosophy with great applause. Among his disciples was Francis de Harlay, afterwards Archbishop of

Rouen and Abbot of St. Victor, in Paris, at whose public thesis, held under Dr. Dease's presidency, Louis XIII., as yet a minor, and all the ` nobility of the French Court, assisted. Many high posts of distinction were offered him, but he declined them all, devoting his leisure time to assist the culprits under sentence of death, and earnestly co-operating with Thomas Messingham, as well by his ample means as by the exercise of the sacred ministry, to put on a permanent footing in the French capital the Irish College, which has since borne such abundant fruit, and of which, a few years before, the foundations had been successfully laid by the Rev. John Ley. As early as the year 1611, as Fr. Fitzsymon attests, many friends of Ireland petitioned the Holy See for the appointment of Dr. Dease to the diocese of Meath. It was not, however, till ten years later that he accepted the proffered dignity, being privately consecrated in a little town near Paris on the 14th of May, 1622. I will not speak of his labours in gathering together the scattered stones of the sanctuary and building up anew the Church of his fathers among his faithful people. Suffice it to say that he collected ample funds, which he consigned to the Jesuit Fathers, to establish in Athlone a college for the education of youth, and further endowed that college with lands to the value in those days of £100 a year for the maintenance of students belonging to his family. One other fact, perhaps, should not be omitted. In his boyhood he had, with some companions, injured the garden and crops of a neighbouring farmer, who, however, had readily forgiven them this wild freak. The first care of the bishop on his return to the diocese was to compensate the good farmer for every injury which he had sustained. Dr. Dease was highly esteemed as a poet in his native Celtic tongue—so much so that, as Lynch attests, his poems were sung and recited through the length and breadth of the kingdom. He died in the Jesuit College at Galway in the month of May, 1651, at the age of seventy-two years, and was interred in the Church of St. Nicholas, close to the sacristy door, at the right-hand side as you enter the sacristy.

Three months later he was followed to the tomb by Thomas Fleming, Archbishop of Dublin. The life of this illustrious prelate has been sketched in considerable detail in the " Lives of the Archbishops of Dublin." Only for two short intervals was he able during the whole time of the Confederation to penetrate within the limits of his metropolitical see. Worn out by fatigues and infirmities, he died at Galway, during the siege in August, 1651.

Among the distinguished laity who came into the enemy's hands on the surrender of the city was Jeoffrey Browne, for many years a leading member of the Supreme Council of the Confederates. He was a citizen of Galway, and throughout the whole period of the Confederate war was so intent on this service of the State that he scarcely spent a month each year at home: he was remarkable for his ability and skill in conducting public negotiations, and for his eloquence. He was for this reason repeatedly selected by the General Assembly and the Supreme Council to treat of the most weighty matters with foreign princes and with the Viceroy. In all this he sought no aggrandisement or self-interest, but only to discharge faithfully the duty which he owed his country and his sovereign. He was summoned to England by the Cromwellian Government, and after an imprisonment of two years was arraigned for high-treason, but, being acquitted, was permitted to return to Ireland.

John de Burgo, Archbishop of Tuam, and the Bishops of Kilmacduagh, Kilfenora, and Clonfert, were also in the city during the siege, and bore its hardships with heroism, but they consulted for their safety by flight whilst arrangements were being made for surrendering to the enemy. John de Burgo, of the race of the old Earls of Connaught, and connected by birth with most of the magnates of the West, was appointed Vicar Apostolic of Clonfert in the year 1627. He availed of his influence with the nobility of the province to check the Plantation schemes of the Viceroy Wentworth, whose agents scoured the country to arrest him. On the return of peace he was, on the 16th of October, 1641, promoted to the episcopal ranks, but his consecration did not take place till the 19th of May of the following year. He held a high place among the members of the Supreme Council of the Confederation, and was translated to the Archiepiscopal See of Tuam on the 11th of March, 1645. With princely munificence he applied all the revenues of the see and the rich gifts of his friends to the decoration of the cathedral and the erection of a college and other institutions connected with religion. He continued for about two years after the loss of Galway to labour among his flock, travelling from district to district, concealing himself as best he could, and often exposed to imminent danger. At length, on the 1st of March, 1654, he was arrested at Ballymote, together with some priests who accompanied him, and despoiled of all the episcopal ornaments that remained to him. Even his episcopal cross and ring, which were of great value, were appropriated by his captors, and he was set at liberty for a time, only on security being given that he would surrender when called upon. In the following June he was thrown into prison in Galway, and though through the many hardships to which he was exposed he was struck with paralysis and weighed down by other infirmities, he was kept in close confinement for fourteen months. He was then hurried on board a ship bound for France, which in four days was wafted by favourable winds to the coast of Armorica. He lived at Nantes for five years, and then passed to the seaport town of Dinan, that, being near St. Malo, he might have greater facilities for holding communication with his flock. Seeing that the storm of persecution had in part subsided, he returned to his diocese in 1662, and though unable through his many infirmities to endure much fatigue he administered the Sacrament of Confirmation to vast numbers who flocked to him from other dioceses widowed of their pastors. He every year on Holy Thursday consecrated the holy oils for his own province and for the province of Cashel, and foreseeing that his death was at hand, he, in 1667, anticipated by a week this sacred ceremony, availing himself of the privilege granted him by the Sovereign Pontiff, and on Holy Thursday of that year calmly expired, being seventy-seven years old. He had caused to be repaired the oratory in which the relics of St. Jarlath were enshrined, and there, with all the religious pomp that the circumstances of those times would permit, his remains were deposited on Easter Eve of 1667.

His brother, Hugh de Burgo, of the Order of St. Francis, was appointed to the See of Kilmacduagh, in the consistory of the 11th of March, 1647. He was remarkable for his ability in administration and skill in languages, and had held with distinction high posts among his Franciscan brethren in Spain, Portugal, Belgium, Bohemia, and other countries of Europe. He, in 1649, roofed in a portion of the old Cathedral of Kilmacduagh, which he dedicated once more to divine worship, and he continued to minister faithfully to his flock, almost driven to despair by the Puritan oppression. He was at length compelled to quit Ireland about the year 1656. He took refuge in England, and being protected by some powerful friends administered confirmation, and promoted piety among the scattered children of the Church, till his death, which, as Lynch asserts, took place probably in 1660. A letter which he addressed from London to Cardinal Barberini in Rome, without date, faithfully depicts the sad condition of the Irish Church subsequent to the Puritan triumph. "Of twenty-six bishops (he says) who previous to this recent persecution of the Church resided with their flocks, four only, or at the most six, now survive, namely, John, Archbishop of Tuam ; Francis, Bishop of Killala; Edmund, Bishop of Limerick ; Eugene, Bishop of Kilmore ; and Hugh, Bishop of Kilmacduagh. Since the rigour of the persecution allows no intercourse of letters between Ireland and the Continent, I was sent hither by my colleagues of the province of Connaught, that I might from hence make known to his Holiness and to your Eminence the state of that province and neighbouring parts; also, before I departed from Ireland, Thomas, Archbishop of Cashel, was still there, bedridden from old age, and the heretics, as I understand, dragged him from his bed, hurried him from Clonmel to Waterford, and put him on board a ship bound for Spain, without the food or assistance requisite for one so feeble. By this cruelty the heretics sought to accomplish the bishop's death, a penalty they were unwilling to inflict on him publicly within the kingdom, lest his martyrdom should prove a solace to the Catholics. In consequence of a most rigid inquisition concerning all priests and other ecclesiastics throughout the entire kingdom a very great number of them fell into the hands of the heretical enemy. They were all sentenced to banishment, and shipped on board of vessels bound for various parts—Spain, France, Belgium, or the Indies—just as the first opportunity of vessels offered, and that without food or any other provision, after the heretics had taken all their goods and possessions for themselves. Not one-tenth of the clergy escaped this inquisition, and they who did escape it, lead now a life full of extreme misery in hiding-places in mountains and forests, for the Catholics cannot aid them, unless with loss of all their chattels and farms; and, lest this should happen, the good ecclesiastics prefer to continue in the woods and to suffer every hardship rather than put Catholics to such risk. By day they lie concealed in caves and on the mountains, and at night they sally forth to watch for a few hours over the spiritual needs of Catholics. They are in great want of faculties, ordinary and extraordinary, which they humbly and earnestly request may be speedily sent to me for secure transmission to them. . . . In times of such most cruel persecutions of the Church the spiritual consolations ought to be abundant. It would be hard to suffer extremes for the Church if the Church refused to compassionate the sufferers. This hardship will be removed by your Eminence in your zeal for the salvation of so many souls." (*Spicilegium Ossoriense*, vol. i., p. 405.)

Andrew Lynch, Bishop of Kilfenora, was one of the few Irish Bishops destined to outlive the Puritan storm and to see comparative peace restored to the Irish Church. The house of his parents in the city of Galway was a secure refuge for the persecuted clergy during the reigns of Elizabeth and James the First, and his father, Mark Lynch, had the further merit of being for a considerable time imprisoned for the faith. Andrew studied in Paris, and soon after his ordination was successively promoted to the posts of Vicar-General of Killaloe, Vicar-Apostolic of Killala, and Warden of Galway. He was remarkable for his knowledge of the Canon and Civil Law, and he spent a considerable sum in the purchase of books, for anything like a Catholic Library was a rare thing in Ireland in those days of persecution. Though appointed to the See of Kilfenora in the month of March, 1646, the Bulls did not reach him for two years, when he was consecrated by the Nuncio, Archbishop Rinuccini, on Sunday, the 21st of April, 1648. During the short interval that he was allowed to watch over his flock in peace, he restored the old Cathedral Church dedicated to St. Fachtnan, and was indefatigable in administering the holy Sacraments. When at length the Puritan sword laid waste the fold of Christ in the West, he took refuge for a time in Inisbofin, and thence sailed to France. He lived for several years at St. Malo, exercising the episcopal functions amid a people in great part composed of his exiled countrymen. The only treasure he brought with him was a remnant of his rich library, and even in France these loved books were his chief delight.* The survivors of the Irish Bishops and clergy deputed him to appeal to the French Government in their behalf, which he did in a printed address remarkable alike for lucid reasoning and fervid eloquence. Moved by this appeal, an agent was despatched from Paris to Cromwell, to plead the cause of the Irish exiled for the faith. He replied with that cant and hypocrisy which were characteristic of all his utterances, that the Parliament persecuted no one for religion and interfered with no one's belief. The French Government allowing itself to be deceived by this response, voted the paltry sum of £300, to enable the Irish exiled Bishops to return to their flocks. In 1655, the Bishop of Kilfenora returned to Ireland, and with the Primate and the Bishop of Ardagh and other representatives of the clergy, met in Dublin in the following year, to present to the king a declaration of loyalty, and thus to disabuse the government so far as in them lay of its prejudices against the Irish Catholics. Dr. Lynch was chosen to preside at their deliberations, but so far were the Lord Lieutenant Ormonde and the court from appreciating the peaceable

* " Instructissimæ Bibliothecæ magnis impensis a se quondam comparatæ reliquias tanquam tabulam naufragio subductam ad se dudum patria delatas assidue evolvebat." (MS. Hist.)

efforts of the good Bishop, that no sooner had the assembly concluded its labours than an officer was sent by Ormonde to the Bishop's house to arrest him and lead him off to prison. The door was opened in person by the aged Bishop, and the officer mistaking him for the servant, asked was the Bishop at home. He replied in the affirmative, and the officer rushed in to secure his intended captive. Without a moment's delay the aged Bishop quitted the house through the opened door and made his escape to France. He spent the closing years of his life at Rouen, assisting the Archbishop of that See in the discharge of the episcopal duties, and he appears to have died there about the year 1674.

Walter Lynch, Bishop of Clonfert, was also a native of Galway. Having studied rhetoric and philosophy in the Irish College at Lisbon, he returned home and for some years, despite the laws that proscribed Catholic education, opened a school and taught with applause, first at Gort, and subsequently in Limerick. He then proceeded to Paris and completed his theological studies and received the Laurea in that Faculty. Appointed Rector of St. Nicholas's, and Warden of Galway, he was remarkable for his zeal and eloquence, and it is in particular recorded of him that in the humble chapel in which the faithful, ere the Confederates restored peace to the Church in 1641, were accustomed to assemble, he added to the decorum of divine worship by constructing an organ, probably the first that since the accession of Queen Elizabeth, was introduced into any Catholic chapel of Ireland. He also collected a large and well-assorted library, but the heretics set fire to it, and the whole collection of books was destroyed. In the year

1647, he was promoted to the See of Clonfert, and shared with his people in all the vicissitudes of the closing years of the Confederation. When all was lost in the West, he for a time took refuge in the island of Inisbofin, and then sailed for the Continent. After a short stay in Brussels he proceeded to Taurin, in Hungary, where he was enrolled in the Cathedral Chapter, and assisted the Bishop in the discharge of the episcopal duties. He was engaged making preparations to return to his flock when he received the summons to a happier world in the year 1664.

CHAPTER XI.

SUFFERINGS OF THE CATHOLICS DURING THE PLAGUE.

1. The Plague rages in Ireland.—2. Puritans anxious to bring on Famine and Pestilence.—3. Pestilence commences in the West.—4. Heroism of Father Wolf of Limerick.—5. Of Fathers O'Cleary and White in Waterford.—6. Desolation of the Country described an English Priest-hunter and others.—7. Ireton's Death foretold by Dr. O'Brien, Bishop of Emly.

1. From the preceding narrative it is manifest that the whole kingdom was subjected to a dire persecution, which surpassed in ferocity the sufferings of any nation recorded in history: "Everywhere agriculture and commerce ceased. Each one's thoughts were solely devoted to preserve life, and to avoid the impending destruction. Hence resulted a dearth of all articles of food, and with famine, a pestilence, too, assailed us. Thus the three scourges of God, of which David had to choose but one, were all at the same time inflicted on us—famine, pestilence, and war. Urged by the famine, numbers fled from all parts of the kingdom to seek shelter in the cities, whilst others, too, fled thither, driven from their estates, or escaping from the sword of the heretical enemy, so that no longer could a place be found for them within the walls, and the outcasts filled the highways and the country around." *

* Missio Soc. Jesu, &c.

So dreadful, indeed, was this scourge, that the learned Dominican father, Dominick de Rosario, cried out: "Oh, look upon us to-day, ye nations. Are we not a spectacle to men and angels? Learn of us what a terrible calamity it is to fall into the hands of the living God, and let him who stands take heed lest he fall." *

No wonder that an Irish poet would give expression to our nation's sorrow in those pathetic words, published by Mr. Gilbert, in the Appendix to the *Aphorismical Discovery*, vol. iii., p. 90. Erin, clad in mourning, appears to the poet as he knelt beside the graves of the Irish Princes, on the hill of St. Peter, in Montorio, in Rome:—

" Wailing she uplifted her arms
And, with eyes raised to heaven,
Addressed the King of the sky
In these doleful words:
O Great God! I pray thee to hear me.
Is it sinful to ask a brief question? . . . .
Why should punishment be inflicted
Most heavily on one race?
Why should lowly slaves be freed,
Why should those once free be now enslaved?
Why are the poor and innocent hanged,
And the guilty left joyful?
Why are not heretics extirpated.
Why are the faithful persecuted by evil-doers?
Why are not Lutherans punished,
While true believers are done to death?

---

* *Hist. of the Geraldines*, page 103.

Why are the lambs left bleeding,
Why are the wolves allowed to prey on the flocks?
By what justice is Erin cast down,
Why are her groans unheeded?
Why are not the Gaels exalted,
A people who at all times obeyed God?
Since the coming of holy Patrick
With the faith to Erin,
Neither reverse, nor pain, nor affliction,
Nor foreign might, nor sore oppression
Could take Christ's faith from the hearts of the Gaels.
Their light was brilliant as the sun,
It glittered as an Angel,
On it there fell neither blemish, stain, nor spot,
Throughout Ireland, on the sons of Miled.
Alas! O Christ! this is true indeed.
What dost Thou require of us? Wilt Thou not listen?
Or is it Thy will never again to look upon us?
Upon us, who have always adored Thee,
Now punished unjustly under the Saxons.
Surely, it was the Saxon blood, low
And treacherous, which deserved to have been forsaken."

2. It was from the commencement a main object of the Puritans to bring on this famine. Ormonde's letters inform us* that "Sir William Parsons advised the governor *to the burning of corn,* and to put man, woman, and child to the sword; and Sir Adam Loftus wrote to

* Vol. ii., p. 350.

the same effect." It was, indeed, the renewal of the policy pursued at the time of Elizabeth, and which was so strongly recommended by Spenser, "in order that thus," he said, "the Irish might be driven to devour each other." That the parliament hoped for this result is clear from the *History of Lord Clarendon*, who records (ii. 323) that, when an armistice was ageed to between Ormonde and the Catholic forces, the parliament passed a vote of censure on the commander for betraying, as they said, the interests of the Protestant religion, " since the rebels were now brought to their last gasp, and reduced to so terrible a famine that, like cannibals. they eat one another, and must have been destroyed immediately, and utterly rooted out."

Hence it was that amongst the military weapons distributed to the soldiers from the store of Waterford, we find not only swords, and pikes, and shot, but also " eighteen dozen of scythes with handles and rings; forty reape-hooks, and whetstones and rubstones proportional,"* which were destined to cut down the growing crop. The Commissioners of Ireland writing to the parliament of England, 1st July, 1651, state that Colonel Hewson had started with his troop for Wicklow, where he "doth now intend to make use of scythes and sickles that were sent over in 1649, with which they intend to cut down the corn growing in those parts."† The result of such a warfare is thus given in

* *Order of Council,*, ap. Prend., p. 14.
† *Ibid.* Another Order of Council, ordered 3rd August, 1652, "that the Governor of Dublin do give warrant to the commissary of the stores in Dublin, to issue the Bibles now in the stores, to the several companies of foot and troop of horse within the said precincts of Dublin;" again on 17th August, 1652: "You are desired forth-

the words of various government records by Mr. Prendergast : " To place garrisons near their fastnesses, to lay waste the adjacent country, allowing none to inhabit there on pain of death, was the course taken to subdue the Irish. The consequence was that the country was reduced to a howling wilderness. Three-fourths of the stock of cattle were destroyed. In 1653, cattle had to be imported from Wales into Dublin: it required a licence to kill lamb ;* tillage had ceased ; the English themselves were near starving. . . . The revenue from all sources, even in 1654, did not amount to £200,000, whilst the cost of the army exceeded £500,000." Hence the commissioners, in the letter above referred to, describing the general state of the country, say : " The stock of cattle is almost spent ; above four parts in five of the best and most fertile lands in Ireland lie waste and uninhabited."

3. The pestilence which resulted from the famine first appeared in the west, and thence soon spread itself through the whole country. The Provost of Galway, writing on the 1st of May, 1650, says : " The pestilence has changed this city into a desert, by the flight of nearly all the inhabitants, and the death of three thou-

---

with to deliver out of the stores under your charge one hundred Bibles unto Mr. Robert Clarke to be by him disposed of, for the use of the forces and others, as may be, for the propagation of the Gospel within the precinct of Galway."

* The following order is dated at Dublin, 17th March, 1652: "Upon the petitions of Mrs. Alice Bulkely, widow, and consideration had of her old age and weakness of body; it is thought fit and ordered that she be permitted to kill and dress so much lamb as shall be necessary for her own use and eating, not exceeding three lambs for this whole year," &c.—Ibid., pp. 16, 17.

sand persons." Another letter, in the following month of June, estimates the total amount of deaths in that city, from famine and pestilence, at 3,900.

We have already seen how in Dublin no fewer than 30,000 citizens were mowed down by the same disease. In Limerick, too, it made many victims. "Truly these were disastrous times," cries out Father Dominick de Rosario, "for the sword was ever unsheathed without the walls, whilst Death was mowing down his victims within."*

4. The heroism of Father James Wolf, in assisting the sick in Limerick, is especially recorded. He was absent when the city was taken by the enemy; but, "on learning that all the ecclesiastics there had been either expelled or butchered, he contrived to get into the city for the purpose of administering the sacraments to the sick and dying." He was only allowed to continue eight days in this ministry of charity. Being arrested by the heretics, he was led forthwith to execution, and from the scaffold exhorted the assembled multitudes to remain steadfast in the faith, addressing to them these memorable words: "We are made a spectacle to God, men, and angels; but the angels rejoice, whilst men scorn us."†

5. In Waterford the plague also raged with great violence, and the number of its victims soon swelled to 5,000. We are informed by Father Dominick de Rosario, that as soon as it made its appearance there, "the bishop called his priests together, and exhorted them to

---

* Hist., &c., page 224.

† See *Dom. de Rosario*, loc. cit., page 210, and *Hib. Dom.*, page 568.

strain every nerve in order to console the afflicted. This they did with great assiduity, administering unceasingly the holy sacraments of penance and the Eucharist."* He mentions two as particularly distinguished in this city: Father Michael O'Cleary, prior of the Dominican convent, and Father White, a secular priest. "Three days did they pass in solitude and prayer before entering on that harvest of death; and when they had received the sacramental confessions of thousands, they themselves died of the infection."

The disease, however, was not confined to any particular district; it spread throughout the whole island, and prepared the way for the triumph of the Puritans. "The success of Cromwell and Ireton, and his followers," writes a contemporary author, "must be ascribed, not so much to their own strength as to the dreadful pestilence that desolated the country. For the anger of God being kindled against us on account of our sins, his chastening angel so afflicted us with a direful pestilence in almost all the towns and cities of the entire kingdom, that the soldiers and citizens being swept away by it, the enemy often got possession of little more than empty cities and fortifications, so few were those that remained to oppose them."

6. But we shall allow an English Protestant historian, who was himself employed at this very time in hunting to death the Irish, to describe the frightful miseries which then fell upon our devoted country:—

"About the year 1652 and 1653, the plague and famine had so swept away whole counties, that a man might travel twenty or thirty miles and not see a

* *Relatio rerum*, &c., an.

living creature, either man, beast, or bird; they being either all dead, or had to quit those desolate places; our soldiers would tell stories of the place where they saw a smoke: it was so rare to see either smoke by day, or fire or candle by night. And when we did meet with two or three poor cabins, none but very aged men, with women and children, and those, like the prophet, might have complained: 'We are become as a bottle in the smoke; our skin is black like an oven, because of the terrible famine.' I have seen those miserable creatures plucking stinking carrion out of a ditch, black and rotten, and been credibly informed that they digged corpses out of the grave to eat."* And some instances are added, too horrible to be here related.

Mr. Prendergast also writes:—"Ireland now lay void as a wilderness. Five-sixths of her people had perished. Women and children were found daily perishing in ditches starved. The bodies of many wandering orphans, whose fathers had embarked for Spain, and whose mothers had died of famine, were preyed upon by wolves. In the years 1652 and 1653 the plague and famine had swept away whole counties, that a man might travel twenty or thirty miles and not see a living creature. Man, beast, and bird were all dead, or had quit those desolate places."†

7. Amongst the victims of the plague was the com-

---

* Colonel Laurence's *Interest of Ireland*, Part ii., pp. 86-7.

‡ *Settlement*, p. 149. He gives in note a declaration of the Council of Ireland, on 12th of May, 1653, in which, amongst other things, it is stated that, "*Many times poor children who lost parents, or have been deserted by them, are found exposed to, and some of them fed upon, by ravening wolves and other beasts and birds of prey.*"

mander-in-chief of the Puritan forces. On the surrender of Limerick, the heroic Bishop of Emly, Albert O'Brien, was, with several others, excepted from hope of pardon. When brought before Ireton, he fearlessly announced to the tyrant that before many days he himself should answer for his crimes at the tribunal of God. The holy martyr was at once led to the scaffold, but before a month elapsed his prophecy was verified, Ireton being stricken with the plague, and with his last breath exclaiming that the bishop's blood was the cause of his death.* Lynch, in his MS. History of the Irish Bishops, attests that Ireton, when seized with the plague, in the paroxysms of his agony, broke out into the following words, interrupted by his groans:—" It was not I, but the Council, that condemned him to death. I could have saved his life, but it would give displeasure to my friends. Oh! that I had never met that Popish bishop." Some writers have assigned the 26th of November as the day of Ireton's death; others assign it to the 13th of that month. Lest this event should be regarded by the Catholics as a triumph, the English of Limerick for some years observed Thursday, the day on which Ireton expired, as a solemn festival.† His body was embalmed and brought to England, where it was buried with great pomp in Westminster Abbey; but after the Restoration his remains were, with Cromwell's, disinterred, exposed on a scaffold, and burned at Tyburn.

* Dom. de Rosario in *Hist.*, &c., pp. 204-7.
† Letter of Dr. John O'Molony from Paris, 10th May, 1652.

PART THE SECOND.

CHAPTER I.

PENAL LAWS ENACTED AGAINST THE IRISH CATHOLICS—GENERAL STATE OF THE KINGDOM IN 1652.

1. Sad State of Ireland in 1652.—2. Its Sufferings depicted by a Jesuit Writer.—3. Destruction of Religious Houses; the Franciscans; Testimony of Dominican Chapter.—4. Sufferings of Jesuits and others—5. Of Nuns.—6. Sufferings of the Irish likened to those of the Jews, or those described by St. Jerome.

1. OUR country, once the Island of Saints, was now wholly become a prey to the persecutors. As Judea of old, its cities were desolate, its altars were overthrown, everything sacred was trampled on, its priests were led to the scaffold, and the inhabitants that yet survived were subjected to a worse than Assyrian captivity :—

"Neither the Israelites were more cruelly persecuted by Pharoah, nor the innocents by Herod, nor the Christians by Nero, or any other of the pagan tyrants, than were the Roman Catholics of Ireland at this fatal juncture."*

A great part of the kingdom was now quite desolate. The Commissioners of Parliament, in their report of

* Morison's *Threnodia*, p. 14.

1st January, 1651-2, describe the country as almost everywhere interlaced with great bogs, with firm, woody grounds like islands in the centre, approached by a narrow pass, where only one horse could go abreast, easily broken up, so as no horse could attack them; but in and out the Irish could pass over the wet and quaking bog by ways known only to themselves. To reduce these fastnesses to submission, the Commissioners ordered a network of garrisons to be placed near them, the adjacent country to be devastated, and no Irish to be allowed to dwell there, under pain of death. These parts were thus reduced to a howling wilderness. Already, in November, 1650, Ireton, when marching by a circuitous route from Waterford to Limerick, a distance, he says, of about 150 miles, found whole districts of thirty miles together " with hardly a house or any living creature to be seen, only ruins and desolation in a plain and pleasant land." (*Prendergast*, p. 79).

The Protestant pamphleteers of those times made no effort to conceal their glee that the Irish Catholics were thus got rid of with a vengeance. A pamphlet entitled *The Present State of Ireland*, published in London, in 1673, made the calculation that, in the three years, 1650, 1651, and 1652, almost seven eighths of the population of Ireland had been carried off by the sword and pestilence and famine : " In less space than three years there was scarce an Irishman through all Ireland that durst hold up his hand against the English, and, by a necessary severity put in practice for the soon finishing of the war, the whole kingdom became upon a sudden so depopulated, that, considering what vast numbers of the people were destroyed by the sword, famine, and plague, it is thought that, in the conclusion of the said war, there was not left living the eighth part of all the Irish nation—a just judgment of God inflicted on them for their notorious barbarism."

2. In the history of the Jesuit missions in Ireland this sad picture of our country's history is thus depicted*:—

"The heretical enemy, having overcome every obstacle, and obtained possession of the whole kingdom, raged with such fury against all ecclesiastics and everything dedicated to religion, that the Turks or the very demons from hell could not display greater impiety or ferocity. Everywhere the public crosses and other emblems of the Catholic religion were overturned: the altars were destroyed; the chapels profaned, and used as storehouses or stables; the stained glass windows, on which the sacred history of our Saviour's life and the images of saints were represented, were everywhere demolished; the sepulchres and monuments of the dead were broken open and destroyed, that no memory should remain of the Catholic religion; the bells were thrown down and broken; the sacred images and vestments were torn to atoms; the statues of the Blessed Virgin and the saints were dragged through the public streets, with ropes around the neck, besmeared with filth, and hanged from gibbets; the priests and religious were treated with a thousand indignities, cast into prison, and butchered; the Catholics were despoiled of their goods, laden with oppressive burdens, and treated as slaves.

* *Missio Soc. Jesu in Hib. usque in an.* 1655.

"I could mention a thousand horrible instances of such cruelty; and many, too, were the miraculous interpositions of Providence to avenge this impiety. Frequently were seen in the public squares heaps of Catholic books and sacred ornaments and images to be destroyed by fire; the Catholic citizens were expelled from their houses and possessions; and the most noble families were subjected to the lowest and most degrading offices; children and youths were torn from their parents; aged matrons and noble ladies were seized on as servants, and employed in the most menial occupations. Truly this persecution of the Catholics was direful, envenomed, cunning, astute; the heretics feigned that they did not persecute individuals, but only the superstitions and abominations of popery (this was their language). However, these things they persecuted in individuals, and individuals suffered death for them.

"There was no restraint on the soldiery when pursuing the Catholics; the persecutors were at the same time accusers, witnesses, and judges; by day and by night they burst into the houses of the Catholics; they broke open rooms and desks and private drawers, under the pretence of searching for ecclesiastics, and even when no resistance was offered them, they invented whatever suited their designs, and took away with them whatsoever they pleased. It was a capital crime for any ecclesiastic to enter a city, or town, or garrison, to offer the Holy Sacrifice, or to administer the sacraments; and for doing so many suffered death; the same penalty was incurred by whosoever received a priest into his dwelling. No individual could sleep in any of these places without signing his name and receiving an express permission from the governor; those who came were minutely examined as to who they were, whence they came, what their business, &c."

3. Some of the religious orders have, happily, preserved accurate statistics of the sufferings which they endured at this period: the Franciscan Order had sixty-four flourishing houses in Ireland in 1641, each with a numerous community, and there were, besides, ten convents of nuns of the Order of St. Clare. In 1656 not one of all these remained; and an official record, drawn up in 1662, gives the names of thirty Franciscans who, during the Puritan persecution, suffered death for the faith.* The acts of the General Chapter of the Dominican Order, held in Rome in 1656, also commemo-

---

* The important record referred to in the text is preserved among the Wadding Papers, and is dated 16th July, 1662: "Nomina religiorosum O.S.F. qui ab ultima regni Hiberniæ commotione passi sunt ob odium fidei et religionis:—R. A. Pr. Franciscus Matthæus, Provinciæ Pr.; fr. Eugenius Colin, laicus; Pr. Richardus Butler; fr. Jacobus Saul, laicus; R. A. D. Thomas O'Morisa, tertiarius; Pr. Joannes O'Kearney; Pr. Richardus Sinott; Pr. Joannes Esmonde; Pr. Paulus Sinott; Pr. Raymondus Stafford; Pr. Petrus Stafford; fr. Didacus Chivers; fr. Jacobus Rochford; Pr. Eugenius O'Cahan; fr. Antonius Ferrallus; Pr. Gabriel Hicquaeus; fr. Thadeus Becan, laicus; fr. Guillelmus (name illegible); Pr. Joannes Daton; Rev. adm. P. fr. Franciscus Sullevanus cum esset in actuali ministerio Provincialatus; Revmus D. Boetius Eganus, Epus. Rossensis, olim Definitor Gen.; fr. Nicolaus Wogan; Pr. Olanus Conrius; Pr. Benedictus Luchranus; Pr. Marianus Vardaeus initio hujus belli a piratis suspensus ex malo navis; Pr. Christoph. Ultanus die qua morti adjudicatus erat in carcere mortuus; Pr. Joannes Dormer; Pr. Joan. Donagh; Pr. Franciscus Geraldinus, postremi tres in vinculis obierunt; Pr. Hugo Mageoin squalore carceris quamvis libertati restitutus obiit."

rate the glory which redounded to the Irish province from the heroism of the Fathers: "An abundant harvest of those who, in our Irish province, have suffered cruel torments for the Catholic faith has been gathered, in these our days, into the celestial granary; since, of forty-three convents which the Order possessed in that island, not a single one survives to-day which the fury of the heretical persecutor hath not either burned or levelled to the ground, or diverted to profane uses. In these religious establishments there were counted about six hundred, of which but the fourth part is now in the land of the living, and even that number is dispersed in exile; the remainder died martyrs at home, or were cruelly transported to the island of Barbadoes."*

* See De Burgo, *Hib. Dom.*, page 525. A letter presented to the Sac. Cong. on the 4th June, 1657, says: "Più di 30 Domenicani sono stati fatti morire in Irlanda dal 1641, in quà, molti altri relegati nelle isole Barbadoes, e piu di 500 con publico editto esiliati, vanno dispersi per il mondo, ma con il medesimo desiderio di esporre la vita per quella misera patria."

Fr. Dominick de Rosario gives the following list of Dominican Friars who were slain by the heretics: "Peter O'Higgins, Richard Barry, Terence O'Brien, James Woolf, Myles Magrath, Laurence O'Farrell, Thadeus Moriarty, James O'Reilly, Thomas O'Higgins, Ambrose O'Cahill, Dominick Dillon, Gerald Dillon, William Lynch, Stephen Petit, John Collins, Peter Costello, William O'Connor, Gerald Geraldine, William O'Luin, Dominick O'Luin, Arthur MacGeoghegan, David Fox, Donatus Black." He also gives the following as "some of those who died of the plague, contracted in the discharge of their duties: Michael Cleary, John Gerald, Donald O'Brien, Gerald Baggott, Gerald Fitzgerald, and Thadeus O'Cahasy." Fr. Dominick de Rosario was a contemporary, and had the best opportunities for receiving accurate information regarding the facts which he narrates. He held high offices in the Spanish Court, not the least remarkable being that of Extraordinary Ambassador of the Spanish monarch to the French Court. He died Archbishop-elect of Coimbra, on the

4. The sufferings of the Jesuits were not less severe. Before the Puritan invasion they were eighty in number, fifty-six of whom were priests; they possessed six colleges, eight residences, besides many oratories and schools; but in the universal desolation only seventeen fathers remained, and they, too, lost everything, not even retaining an image or book, or the breviary itself; and when the Holy Sacrifice was to be offered up, it was only in some cave or granary, or other obscure corner, and anticipating the morning aurora, the doors and windows being closed, and few being admitted. The fathers being dispersed and scattered, sought a refuge in various places: some in the towns and huts of the poor, others in the mountains and woods, with difficulty dragging along a miserable existence, that they might assist and console the Catholic outcasts: some there were who, in the disguise of rustics or mendicants, visited the cities and towns, and now in one house, now in another, offered the Holy Sacrifice, and administered the Sacraments.*

* "Missio, &c., citat." Another paper, entitled "*Status Societatis in Hibernia nuperi belli tempore*," adds the following particulars: "Patres summo cum fructu et satisfactione tenebant scholas Dublinii, Pontani, Kilkenniæ, Rosponti, Wexfordiæ, Waterfordiæ, Clonmeliæ, Casseliæ, Corcagiæ, Limerici, Galviæ. Ab initio belli cessarunt scholæ ad tempus Dublinii: semper Pontanæ et Corcagiæ quod civitates illas occuparent hæretici et Catholicos ibi crudelius opprimerent: in aliis civitatibus floruerunt liberius; præterea Athloniæ novæ sunt apertæ, sed et Kilkenniæ et Galviæ tradebatur Philosophia. In omnibus hisce civitatibus erant numerosæ sodalitates B. Virginis." Even those that were sent into exile continued to labour for our suffering country, and we learn from a letter of Thomas Quin, 24th Feb., 1660, that three Irish Jesuits were then busily engaged at *Solidor*, near St. Malo, teaching the children of the Irish exiles."

From a petition presented to the Sacred Congregation in 1654, we learn that all the Capuchins were likewise banished, some few alone remaining in the island, who lived "as shepherds or herdsmen, or tillers of the soil."

It would be easy to add to the list of the heroic missionaries who thus suffered for the Faith. Fr. Cornelius O'Driscoll, O.S.B., Abbot of Bangor, was thrown into prison in London on account of exercising his sacred office; and, though subsequently released, died at Douai, in the year 1662, of sickness contracted in prison. Fr. Luke Bergin was put to death at Wexford in 1656, accused of no crime but that he was a priest (*in patibulum ea tantum de causa, quod sacerdos fuerit, actus est*). Laurence Harries, Abbot of Tintern, was subjected to the hardships of imprisonment for a long time, and died in exile. Fr. John Cantwell, Abbot of Jerpoint; Louis Cantwell, Abbot of Holy Cross; James Tobin, Abbot of St. Mary's, Kilcooley; Thomas Lombard, Prior of St. John the Evangelist's in Waterford, were all banished from the Kingdom by the Puritans, and, after suffering a great deal, attained their crown in exile.

5. At the same time the convents of the nuns were destroyed, and their inmates, wheresoever they had not consulted for their safety by flight, were treated with inhuman barbarity. De Burgo has preserved the memory of two (page 572) who were crowned with a glorious martyrdom:—

"In 1653, Honoria Burke, daughter of Richard Burke of Mayo, took the habit of the Third Order; that is, of St. Catherine of Sienna, at the hands of our

Irish Provincial, when she was but fourteen years of age. She erected a residence or small monastery near our convent of Burishool, and led there a sanctified life during the reigns of Elizabeth, James I., and Charles I., devoting herself to holy works, till the decrepitude of old age. In the famine time, He to whom she was espoused did not forsake her; for it is related that in answer to her prayers for daily bread there came daily an unknown youth to the convent-door (an angel from heaven in mortal guise) who provided her and the other sisters with all necessaries of life abundantly, and then disappeared. In the Cromwellian persecution she, with Sister Honoria Magan and a lay-sister, fled to Saints' Island (Mayo), whither they were pursued by the fanatics, seized, and despoiled of their garments, and left in this state in the depth of winter, for what I now narrate occurred in the month of February. After breaking three of her ribs the Cromwellian ruffians flung her, as they would a bundle of rags, into a boat and left her to her fate. In her last agony she besought the sister who accompanied her to take her to the convent of Burishool, and this request was cheerfully complied with, for the sister carried her in her arms and laid her down before the altar dedicated to the Blessed Virgin. This done the sister went to the wood in search of another member of the community who was hiding there, and on her return found the aged sister keeling before the altar, with head erect, and placidly sleeping in the Lord.

" As for Sister Honoria Magan, who was also of the Third Order, she would not be separated in death from her whose pains and labours she had shared in life.

She also was seized by those satellites of Satan in the same island, despoiled of her habit, and wounded. Apprehending something still more terrible, she tore herself from their sacrilegious hands, fled to a neighbouring wood and hid herself in the hollow trunk of a tree, and next day was found there frozen to death."

The Rinuccini MS. briefly refers to the hardships endured by the religious communities of nuns dispersed by the triumph of the Puritan arms, and states that those who escaped death at home fled to the Continent and found an asylum in Flanders, or France, or Spain. Of one of them in particular, a Miss Browne, of Galway, it is recorded that she ended her days in great repute for sanctity (*in Hispania cum magna sanctitatis opinione diem obiit*, vol. v, fol. 2, 267).

Sir Richard Bellings, in his *History of the Irish Confederation*, gives some particulars relating to the convent of St. Clare, called Bethlehem, situated on a promontory jutting out from the southern banks of Lough Ree, about six miles from Athlone. This was one of the first convents established in Ireland since the beginning of Elizabeth's reign, and several religious ladies were gathered there in silence and solitude, leading a life of unostentatious piety in the exact observance of the rule of St. Clare. When, at the commencement of hostilities, Sir James Dillon surrendered the town of Athlone to the Lord President of Connaught, he retired with his troops to the county of Longford, and conducted to a place of greater security the inmates of the convent of Bethlehem. Three hundred of the enemy, under the command of Captain Francis Bertie, " were sent to the convent deserted by the nuns, where they had left all their provisions, some of their habits, some pictures and other ornaments for their chapel and altar." The soldiers, who had as little reverence for things consecrated to God as they had temperance to abstain from drink, "fearless of any enemy, and secure, as they took it, from all danger, filled themselves liberally. So as when a party, sent by Sir Thomas Dillon, who was advertised how they were employed, came upon them the next morning, most of the soldiers and officers were as unfit to fight as they were incapable to obey the commands of their leader, who, striving in vain to draw his men into a posture of making resistance, and giving proof in his own person of much resolution and valour, was slain, and with him most of his men, the Irish being incensed at the copes and (religious) habits which some of the soldiers had put on to make themselves sport" (p. 86).

A somewhat more detailed account of the just judgment that thus befell the despoilers of this hallowed retreat is given in the *Aphorismical Discovery* : " In Dillon's country there is a nook of Lough Ree, where some nuns of St. Clare thitherunto did inhabit. Upon intimation that those enemie forces approached the country (the nuns) deserted their habitation and retired themselves unto an island of the said lough, their flight being so sudden and unexpected that the most part of their household stuff, nay, their very habits, for fear to be surprised, were left behind. The Roundheads issuing to the country, ranging the matter of four score, went to Bethlehem (the place where those nuns did dwell was so called), demolished the house, carried away what they found in it, and hitting on some of the habits, some of the rogues did wear those weeds in a gibing manner, telling their comrades that he was a poor nun. Away they went to their garrisons, as they thought. But against God's divine providence there is no wisdom. One Captain Charles Mellaghlin, of Sir James Dillon's regiment, and Oliver Boy Fitzgerald, with the matter of four-score men in their company, lay in ambush before those Roundheads, and seeing their fit opportunity started to them and slaughtered them all there, neither had they the courage to strike one blow in proper defence. None did the Irish lose but one, and he was killed by his own comrades, reputing him one of the enemy, as having a brave coat of bluff on; for, coming to the field, none of their party had any such wear. In the commencement of the skirmish this soldier killed the owner of that bluff, exonerating the dead thereof, did marshal it on himself, and cost him no less than his life, though by a friendly hand, thinking him to be a foe. See how those were paid for plundering the nunnery and gibing the holy habit" (vol. i., p. 58). Forty years later, Sir Henry Piers (A.D. 1682) wrote, in his *Corographical Description of Westmeath*: "That the abbess of this convent, a daughter of Sir Edward Tuite, was still living in a great old age, and that Ballinacloffy was pointed out as the place where the Puritan soldiers met with their chastisement."

6. Dr. John Lynch, in his *Cambrensis Eversus*, published in 1662, likens the sufferings inflicted on the Irish Catholics by the Puritans to those prepared by Antiochus against the Jews: he also applies to them the words of Tobias (iii. 4): "We are delivered to spoil, and to cap-

tivity, and death, and are made a fable and a reproach to all nations." And, again, those of St. Jerome: " The bishops are taken prisoners, the priests slain, the churches thrown down, horses stabled at the altar of Christ, everywhere grief, everywhere lamentation, and death in a thousand shapes. But," he adds, " we have long been familiar with such scenes; and, as nail drives nail, our fresh wounds efface the memory of our former ones" (vol. i., p. 9).

It would be difficult to find any parallel for all the sufferings which our country thus endured. The writers of this period continually re-echo the passage of the Lamentations :—" The child and the old man lie without on the ground : my virgins and my young men are fallen by the sword: thou hast slain them in the day of thy wrath : thou hast killed and shown them no pity." The author of *Cambrensis Eversus* just referred to (pp. 21-5) well remarks that the cruelty of the Puritans combined the malice of all preceding persecutions, and no better parallel can be found for the dread desolation of the whole kingdom than what we read in Sacred Writ, when the chosen people saw their temple razed, their sanctuary polluted, their cities laid waste, and the people become a byword among the nations. In the words of Bruodin :—" Ireland being entirely subjugated, and scourged by God with pestilence, famine, and the sword, the churches were everywhere profaned, the altars overthrown, the sacred images broken to atoms, the crosses trampled under foot, the priests banished or led to the scaffold, . . . and no words can express how many and how great were the evils which the Catholics that survived were compelled to endure."

7. The state of the diocese of Leighlin will serve as an individual instance to illustrate the desolation of the whole Irish Church; but first, a few words on the illustrious Edmund O'Dempsey, who was at this time bishop of this see. He was the son of Terence O'Dempsey, Viscount Clanmalyre. At a very early age he entered the Irish College at Compostella, and after completing there his philosophical course embraced the Order of St. Dominick. He was remarkable among the religious brethren for his fervour; and prolonged prayer, the hair shirt, and the discipline were his favourite weapons of defence when assailed by temptation.* Returning to Ireland, he was, in 1634, chosen Provincial of the Order, in which office he displayed great earnestness and zeal in promoting piety and the exact observance of the rule. His nephew, Sir Christopher Dempsey, who was an excellent Catholic, was married to the daughter of Viscount Falkland, the Lord Viceroy of Ireland, and had very often to defend his faith against the attacks of Protestant dignitaries and other officials. He noted down from time to time the objections thus proposed to him that appeared to be of any weight, and forwarded them to his uncle, Fr. Edmund, who gave him in writing the necessary response. One of the difficulties proposed by a Protestant bishop is recorded by Lynch in his MS. History. The MS. Gospels of St. Columbkille, he said, afforded abundant proof of the tenets of the Protestant Church. Lynch remarks that the MS. to which reference was thus made was probably the gospels written by St.

---

* "Animum precibus, pectus cilicio, manum flagello armavit.' (*Lynch's MS.*)

Columbkille, at this time preserved at Durrow, and held in the greatest veneration by the people. It soon after passed into the hands of Henry Jones,* Protestant Bishop of Meath, and is now preserved in the Library of Trinity College, Dublin. At the request of Fr. O'Dempsey, the MS. was carefully examined by Dr. Mac Geoghegan, Bishop of Kildare, who was well versed in the antiquities of our country, and who proved beyond all question that the gospels referred to were perfectly in accordance with the teaching of the Catholic Church. All the queries thus proposed to Fr. O'Dempsey, with his answers in English, were arranged in one volume, under the title "Feede your Flocke," and sent to Louvain to be printed, but the priest with whom they were forwarded was shipwrecked, and the work perished with him. Dr. O'Dempsey being promoted to the See of Leighlin in the year 1642, gave frequent proofs of consummate prudence and of unbounded charity towards his suffering flock. Lynch styles him the constant protector and father of the poor, whom every day he welcomed to his house, washing their feet, and feeding them at his own table, and clothing them.† Faithful

* "Rochus Kildariensis Quatuor Evangelia, quæ a S. Columba exarata esse creduntur et apud Durrow in Comitatu Regis, jam servata in maxima veneratione habebantur, ita ut liber ille pro religiosissimo juramento adhiberetur (forsan hic liber est qui nunc in archivio Henrici Jones, Protestantis Ep. Mid. qui membraneus est S. Columbae manibus exscriptus, auratis literis capitalibus et in diversimodos nodos variegatis ornatus) interpretatus," &c. (*Lynch's MS.*)

† "Pauperum etiam perpetuus patronus et pater fuit ut qui quotidie hospitio eos excipere, pedibus aquam effundere, mensæ convivos adhibere, vestitu etiam eos instruere consuevit, ita ut penus pauperum appellari potuerit." (*Lynch's MS.*)

to the traditions of his family, he took a leading part in uniting the Irish Confederates in defence of religion and country, and was one of the last to uphold the Confederate cause. Being at length arrested, he was sent to exile with such precipitancy that he was not allowed an interview with his most immediate relations. He stopped for a short time in Madrid, where the Dominican Nuns lavishly extended to him every care and attention due to a confessor of the faith. Thence he proceeded to the convent of the order at Pontevieda, where he resided till his death on the 6th of September, 1658. His remains were interred with solemn pomp in the Cathedral of Compostella, and on his marble monument was inscribed:—

"Edmundus mundum tempsit Christumque secutus,
Dominicus terris alter et ille fuit."

From Pontevieda, on the 12th of November, 1656, he addressed the following letter to Rome, depicting in vivid colours the deplorable condition of the Irish Church:—"After the Nuncio's departure from the kingdom the whole country was laid waste by fire and famine and the sword. . . . Notwithstanding all this, during three years I spared no fatigue or labour to watch over the flock entrusted to my care, and God alone knows what dangers, hardships, hunger, and misery I endured for the cause of God and His Church during this time in the woods and mountains and deserts and hiding-places. At length I saw my Erin, once the Island of Saints, but now almost entirely deprived of the public profession and practice of the Catholic faith—its churches profaned, its convents reduced to ruin, the altars overthrown, the sacred crucifixes, the images of the Blessed Virgin and the saints, the sacred vessels and ornaments and books trampled on or torn to pieces, and sacrilegiously cast into the flames."

During the exile of the bishop and the subsequent vacancy of the see, the Vicar-General, Charles Nolan, laboured with great zeal to provide for the spiritual wants of its faithful people. A *Report on the State of Ireland*, presented in Rome in March, 1662, gives the following details :—" In the diocese of Leighlin I was acquainted with Dr. Charles Nolan, the Vicar-General, a most learned and holy man, who has undergone much suffering, and exposed himself to many dangers on account of his flock, remaining constantly amongst them, surrounded by enemies, and in circumstances of the utmost danger. He used to conceal himself in the woods and in mountain caves by day, and to nourish the faithful with the sacraments of Holy Church under cover of the night. I received a day's hospitality from this venerable ecclesiastic, and to my great edification we conferred together on religious matters ; but thrice in the course of that day was it necessary to fly from the house and take refuge in the woods, in consequence of soldiery passing the way. In a certain town in that district I have administered the sacraments to one hundred persons who, for three years previously, had not received the Sacraments of Penance and the Blessed Eucharist; many of them even stated that they had hardly ever had an opportunity of assisting at Mass, in consequence of the local priests being known to the heretics who resided in the town. Among these heretics I passed myself off by day as a soldier like one of themselves, and at night I heard confessions, and in due time administered Holy Communion. There are in that district two other priests, one of them a Franciscan, and the other an Abbot of the Order of St. Bernard." (*Spicilegium Ossoriense*, vol. ii., p. 209.)

CHAPTER II.

Edict against the Clergy.

1. Forty Thousand Irish Soldiers leave Ireland.—2. Persecution more violent after their departure: Secular and Regular Clergy Exiled or Condemned to Death.—3. Severity with which this Edict is carried out.—4. Zeal of Clergy: many devote themselves to the mission.—5. Letter of Dr. Burgatt, Archbishop of Cashel.—6. Spies and Informers: the same price on the head of priest and wolf.—7. Several instances of priests in prison and exile.—8. Dr. Lynch's account of the persecutions.

1. Whilst some Catholic soldiers remained in the island, the Puritan persecutors dared not display the full excess of their fury. Their first care, therefore, was to rid themselves of that check to their ferocity. Every facility was given to the foreign courts to transport the Irish soldiers to their service. "The agent of the Spanish Government (writes a contemporary author in 1654) transferred thousands and thousands of them every month, partly to Spain and partly to Belgium."* Borlase estimates the number of those transported in the year 1654 alone at 27,000; and another historian adds, that altogether no fewer than 40,000 Catholics were thus banished from Ireland to the Continent, to

* MS. "Status Rei Cath. in Hibernia hoc anno 1654."

be a standing monument of the persecuting spirit of Puritanism, whilst they, at the same time, filled all Europe with admiration of their valour.*

Spain was, at this time, at war with France, and as the latter had afforded a secure asylum to Charles the II., the Government in England lent its aid and used its influence to ship the Irish soldiers for Spain. It happened that some of those, under the command of Colonel Grace, finding themselves opposed to the king and to their old comrades-in-arms, betrayed to the French army the post entrusted to their care. This so enraged the Spanish officers, that for some time the fresh arrivals from Ireland were left starving and penniless and wholly unprovided for on the coasts of Gallicia. On the other hand, the officers and men who engaged in the service of France were reproached with ingratitude to the Spanish people, who had given such important aid throughout the Confederate war. These found it necessary to publish a manifesto to justify the course they had pursued. " Ireland and Spain (they said) were, indeed, linked together by many special ties. The Irish race had come from Spain, and for centuries so close was the union between both countries that when the Royal Family became extinct in the parent kingdom, they sent to Ireland to choose a prince to wear the Spanish Crown. Under Henry VIII. the Irish chieftains had invited the emperor, Charles V. to take the oppressed kingdom under his pro-

---

* Another contemporary document in my possession states that no less than 20,000 Irish took refuge in the Hebrides and other Scotch islands.

tection. So, too, they sided with Philip II. and Philip III. against Elizabeth, and the noblest families proved their devotedness by the sacrifice of their vast possessions and their lives. But in later times all this was forgotten by Spain. That Government had entered into league with Cromwell and the Puritan Commonwealth of England, and partly through the insidious arts of English officers and partly through the promises of Spanish agents, several troops of brave men had been led to forsake their country and to engage in the service of Spain against their own lawful king. Many of them had been allowed to perish through neglect and want, but those who had chosen the service of France only made use of their undoubted right to enrol themselves under the standard of their sovereign to engage in honourable service and to be ready, when occasion would present itself, to draw the sword once more in defence of Ireland, and to avenge the wrongs they had endured from the enemies of their country." (Rinuccini MS.)

When, a few years later, Cromwell made peace with France, and the king was obliged to shift his quarters into Spanish territory, it was feared that the Irish soldiers in the service of France would change sides and follow the fortunes of their sovereign. Hence it was deemed expedient to march them towards Italy, to remove them, as far as possible, from Spanish intrigue. Being quartered in the neighbourhood of Geneva, a body of Calvinists, from that hot-bed of heresy, recklessly insulted their religion, and, in their presence, treated some priests and Catholics with great cruelty. The Irish legion could not be restrained. They assailed the Calvinists, put a number of them to the sword, and then devastated the whole country for miles around Geneva. This lesson was not soon forgotten, and thenceforth the Calvinists, in the service of France, took care not to offer insult to the Catholic Faith in the presence of Irish soldiers.

2. The troops, being removed, the first edict of persecution was published against the Catholic clergy on the 6th of January, 1653. By it* all ecclesiastics, secular and regular, were commanded, under penalty of treason, to depart from the kingdom within twenty days, and should they not comply with this edict, or should they return to the kingdom, they incurred the penalties specified in the 27th of Queen Elizabeth, that is, they were " to be hanged, cut down while yet alive, beheaded, quartered, embowelled, and burned ; the head to be set on a spike, and exposed in the most public place." The preamble of this edict sets forth that several priests, who had obtained permission to be transported to foreign parts, had, nevertheless, under various pretexts, deferred their departure from the kingdom, and continued to preach their pernicious doctrines. In usual form it then decrees that henceforth the Act of Parliament (27th of Elizabeth) shall be in full force in Ireland in all its parts. It invests not only the judges and magistrates, but the officers and soldiers, and all persons having any civil or military authority, with power to search for and to imprison any of the clergy, who, twenty days after the

* See this edict in full in Dominick de Rosario, pages 227-8, also in De Burgo and others.

proclamation of this edict, in their respective districts, would remain in the kingdom, and the clergy, so imprisoned, were to receive the full penalty of the law. Some of the clauses of the Elizabethan Act of Parliament thus enforced had a far-reaching severity. For instance, all students in foreign parts who would not within six months abjure their faith, were to be regarded as guilty of treason. All persons sending aid to the Catholic exiles were to be deprived of their goods and liberty. Any person sending his son or servant to foreign parts, without the written licence of the chief magistrate, was to be subjected to heavy fines, and any person concealing or harbouring a priest, or knowing of the presence of any such in the kingdom and not notifying it to the civil or military authorities, was to be punished "at the discretion of the chief magistrate."

Thus did the persecutors seek to deprive the fold of its pastors, and we cannot but here adopt the words of Dominick de Rosario:—" Right well did England know that her triumph would never be secure as long as the ministers of the Catholic religion, who kept watch over the flock, were suffered to live in the land" (*Loc. cit.* 229).

A petition, presented at this time to the Commissioners, set forth that there were several of the clergy infirm, aged, and bedridden, some, too, who had become weak in mind through the anxieties and hardships they had endured, and asked that at least these would be permitted to remain in the kingdom. The reply sent by Miles Corbet, one of the Commissioners, declared that no such permission would be granted.

The agents of the Government lost no time in publishing this edict throughout the kingdom. For instance, we read that it was published in Clonmel on the 21st of January, 1653, and Justice Cook seasoned the publication, by declaring from the bench that all Irishmen living on the 23rd October, 1641, or born since in Ireland, were rebels.

3. An example of the severity with which this edict was carried into execution, is recorded in the narrative of the condition of Ireland in 1654.*

"When this edict was published the Superior of the Jesuits was lying sick of fever in the house of a respectable citizen, unable to move in bed, not to say to journey on foot or on horseback; a petition was therefore presented to the governor of the city that he might be allowed to remain some few days till his strength should return. But the governor replied that, though the whole body of the Jesuit was dead, and life remained only in one hand or one foot, he must at once quit every inch of Ireland. The sick man was forthwith seized in bed, hurried along for about seventy Irish miles, in the midst of a severe winter, to a seaport, and there with two other Jesuits and forty secular priests was cast into a vessel bound for Spain."

4. The annual letters of the Society of Jesus (anno 1662), having referred to the just mentioned decree, add:—

"It is easy to imagine what whirlwinds of dangers then assailed the Catholic community in this island and yet the assault evinced how little the persecutors gained

---

* MS. Status rer. Cath., &c., 1654.

by that edict, for the more their fury raged against the priests, the more courageous did these become to encounter every danger; and although very many of them in each city of the kingdom were cast into prison, of whom some were hanged on gibbets, some expired overcome by the sufferings of their filthy dungeons, some were sent into exile to Spain, and others transported as slaves to the Barbadoes, yet those who escaped from the enemy's pursuit were not deterred by such impending dangers from the discharge of their ministry; and others who, scattered through the various academies of Europe, were engaged preparing themselves for the Irish mission, on seeing the harvest now ripe for the sickle, and hoping for more abundant spiritual fruit amidst these temporal disasters, in greater numbers than was known for many years, abandoned their studies and entered on their field of labour.

"In the meantime the magistrates, lest the edict might fall into oblivion, and in order to strike greater terror into those who would give shelter to the clergy, caused it to be proclaimed anew each year throughout the entire kingdom; whence it happened that a great number of the priests, unwilling to create danger for their flocks, lived in caverns, or on the mountains, or in the woods, or in remote hiding-places, and often, too, were obliged to pass the winter without any shelter, concealed amidst the branches of the trees. This deplorable condition of the kingdom fills all the Catholics with terror."

5. This decree was carried into execution with the greatest rigour, and no mercy was shown to whosoever was found to violate it. Dr. Burgatt presents us with

the following details as to the number of the clergy who were sent into exile, or suffered extreme penalty at this direful period:—

"In the year 1649," he writes, "there were in Ireland twenty-seven bishops, four of whom were metropolitans. In each cathedral there were dignitaries and canons; each parish had its pastors; there was, moreover, a large number of other priests, and innumerable convents of the regular clergy. But when Cromwell, with exceeding great cruelty, persecuted the clergy, all were scattered. *More than three hundred were put to death by the sword or on the scaffold,** amongst whom were three bishops; more than a thousand were sent into exile, and amongst these all the surviving bishops, with one only exception, the Bishop of Kilmore, who, weighed down by age and infirmities, as he was unfit to discharge the episcopal functions, so too was he unable to seek safety by flight. And thus for some years our island remained deprived of its bishops—a thing never before known during the many centuries since we first received the light of Catholic faith."†

6. To discover the clergy that remained in the kingdom, spies and informers scoured the country on every side, impelled partly by hatred to religion, partly by the proffered reward. Five pounds was the sum held out by Government for the apprehension of a priest‡ (the

---

* Supra trecentos gladio et crucibus extincti, &c.

† Brevis Relatio, &c., by Dr. William Burgatt, agent of the Irish clergy in Rome, afterwards Archbishop of Cashel, presented to the Sacred Congregation, in 1667.

‡ A MS. entitled "Missio Hibernica, anno, 1652," says: "Jam diminuto multis in regni partibus habitantis populi numero, excrescentibusque pro vastitate sylvis excrescere simul cœperunt rabidæ

same price that was offered for the head of a wolf) together with a third part of the property of the person on whose lands he should be discovered; moreover, the profession of informer was declared an honourable one, and such persons were, by virtue of the edict, to receive the special favour of the Crown, and to be promoted to offices and dignities, as men *well deserving of the State.**

The country was at this time greatly infested with wolves. A Major Morgan, member for Wicklow, declared in parliament, in 1657:—" We have three beasts to destroy that lay burdens on us. The first is a wolf, on whom we lay five pounds a head if a dog, and ten pounds if a bitch. The second beast is a priest, on whose head we lay ten pounds ; if he be eminent, more. The third beast is a tory."† So great was the number of wolves killed in 1655, that in March that year there was due from the district of Galway alone £243 for rewards paid on this account. Two years earlier we find lands in the neighbourhood of Dublin, and a great part of the barony of Dunboyne leased by the State, " the rent to be discounted in wolves' heads."‡

Sometimes the clergy seeking shelter in solitary places were devoured by the wolves. Thus the *Alithinologia* relates that in Gostelach, a district of Connaught, a

luporum catervæ quæ cum novos colonos infestarent, excitata venatorum industria, propositis præmiis, et promissis argenti libris quinque in singula luporum capita, et simul in opprobrium religionis Catholicæ eadem summa promissa est cuicumque sacerdotis delatori. Adeoque lupi caput et sacerdotis eodem venale pretio fuit."

* Morison, *Threnodia*, p. 227
† Ap. *Prendergast*, p. 150.
Ibid. p. 153.

priest in 1654, lying concealed in a wood sent his servant to the neighbouring town for food: the servant was away only a short time, but on his return found the priest torn to pieces and almost wholly devoured by wolves. The words of St. Cyprian may well be applied to such a case: "If the confessor of Christ be struck down by robbers in the deserts or mountains, if the wild beast devour him, or hunger and thirst and cold afflict him, Christ looks down upon His soldier wheresoever he may combat, and bestows on him, suffering for His name, the martyr's reward."

7. On the part of the agents of the Government, the pursuit of the clergy was not less active than the pursuit of the wolves. "Such orders as the following (writes Mr. Prendergast) are abundant:—10th of August, 1657, five pounds on the certificate of Major Thomas Stanley to Thomas Gregson, Evan Powel, and Samuel Ally, being three soldiers of Colonel Abbott's regiment of dragoons, for the arrest of Donogh Hagerty, a popish priest, by them taken, and now secured in the county gaol of Clonmel. To Arthur Spunner, Robert Pierce, and John Bruen, five pounds, for the good service by them performed in apprehending and bringing before the Chief Justice Papys, on the 21st of January last (1657), one Edmund Duin, a Popish priest.* To Lieutenant Edward Wood, on the certificate of Wm. St. George, Esq., J.P. of the county Cavan, dated November, 1658, twenty-five pounds for five priests and friars by

---

* A small silver chalice that belonged to this heroic priest is preserved in the Diocesan Museum, St. Kieran's College, Kilkenny. It has the inscription: "Edmundus Duin me fieri fecit, A.D., 1652, Kilkenniæ."

him apprehended, viz. : Thomas Mac Kernan, Turlogh O'Gowan, Hugh M'Geown, Turlogh Fitzsymons, who upon examination confessed themselves to be both priests and friars. On 13th of April, 1657, to Serjeant Humphry Gibbs and Corporal Thomas Hill, ten pounds for apprehending two Popish priests, viz. : Maurice Prendergast and Edmund Fahy, who were secured in the gaol of Waterford, and, being afterwards arraigned, were both of them adjudged to be and accordingly were transported into foreign parts. On the 4th of January, 1655, the sum of five pounds for having arrested, on the 27th November preceding, a priest with his appurtenances in the house of one Owen Byrne, of Cool-ne-Kishin, near Old Leighlin, in the county Carlow, which said priest, together with Byrne, the man of the house, were brought prisoners to Dublin."

The condition of the priests whilst detained in prison was miserable in the extreme. Of Father Tobin of Kilkenny it is recorded that, though in a violent fever, he was obliged to sleep on the floor, and his only food was a small quantity of half-boiled beans.* It was made a privilege to allow them to transport themselves to foreign parts, as appears from an order of 29th May, 1654 : and then the clause was added that each one should provide the five pounds which had been paid for his arrest. Sometimes, too, on account of infirmity or disease they were released from prison : thus, we find Roger Begs, on 4th August, 1654, dismissed from prison "on account of his miserable condition," after nine months' imprisonment; but two clauses were added,

* Lett. in S. C. de Prof. Fid. 14 March, 1656.

viz., that within four months he should transport himself out of the country, and, during that interval, "should not exercise any part of his priestly functions." Another priest, named William Shiel, was also dismissed from prison, on account of his "being old, lame, and weak, and not able to travel without crutches;" but two conditions were also added in his release, viz., that he should never exercise his priestly function, and should not move *beyond one mile* from the spot in Connaught which would be assigned to him for residence by the Governor of Athlone.* There is one other petition which merits our attention. On the 8th of January, 1655, Richard and Thomas Tuite, Edmund and George Barnewall, and William Fitzsimons, held the Castle of Baltrasna in the county Meath, in defence and rescue of a priest who had repaired thither to say Mass. For this they were arrested and their goods seized; and the soldiers claimed the booty, on the ground that the castle was defended against them "with arms and ammunition by those who maintained a priest in his idolatrous worship, in opposition to the declaration of the State in that behalf."†

Owing to the diligence of the persecutors, the number of the Catholic priests that escaped their search was comparatively few: "The prisons were everywhere filled with prelates, priests, and religious, some of whom were executed on the scaffold, others were privately butchered, whilst the greater number were sent into exile." Thus writes the Superior of the Jesuits in 1652.

* *Settlement*, p. 159.
† *Ibid.*, p. 160.

Another writer, to whom we have more than once referred, describes the state of Ireland in 1654, and contrasts the comparative ease with which the Catholic clergy had in former years evaded the penal statutes, with the difficuty of remaining concealed amidst the present perils, and adds:

"Now the whole aspect of the kingdom is changed; difficulties and dangers are met with at every step; no human industry can enable us to avoid them, but all must be left to a watchful Providence. The cities and towns are now wholly occupied by the heretics, and the Catholics are banished from them; the castles and country residences of the gentry are converted into barracks, or, if not, are held by heretical new-comers.

"No one is allowed to travel through the country without being examined at every mile by the soldiery; you have to show the letters patent of the magistrate of the district from which you come, and in them your age, stature, beard, colour of hair, condition of life, and many other special characteristics are mentioned, and if you are found wanting in any one of them, you are immediately arrested as a spy or a priest, nor is there any hope of the soldiers' sentence being reversed, for each soldier has the judicial right by martial law to arrest any person he may suspect, and inflict capital punishment.

"The same martial law authorises them to enter the house of any Catholic, at any hour of the day or night, and explore every corner of it, under the pretence, forsooth, of detecting and arresting priests. And lest any of the soldiery should be enticed by bribes to allow any priest to escape, the English Government offers a larger reward for each discovery than could be hoped for from the oppressed and impoverished Catholics. The soldiers, therefore, partly impelled by hatred for the Catholic religion, and partly urged on by avarice and the hope of lucre, never cease by day or by night to beset the houses of the Catholics, and explore their most secret recesses: moreover, they hire spies, and keep them in various quarters, that they may thus receive information of any rumour that may be heard of the arrival of a priest in the neighbourhood."*

8. Dr. John Lynch, Archdeacon of Tuam, one of those who were thus compelled to seek a home in a foreign land, in his *Cambrensis Eversus*, written during his exile, gives a vivid description of the rigour with which this edict was carried into execution:—

"Edicts," he says, "were issued, commanding all priests to depart from Ireland before a certain day, and prohibiting them, under penalty of death, to remain beyond that time. All who harboured them were to forfeit all their property, to expiate that act of hospitality. As the wolf in the fable was ready to make a friendly alliance with the sheep, if they would drive away the dogs, as they could then slaughter the poor flock without resistance; so these men banished the priests from the Catholics, that the latter, when deprived of their pastors, might fall more easy victims to the proselytising attempts of heretical teachers. Of the priests who did remain in the country after the appointed day, some were executed, others wasted away their life in the tedious and loathsome horrors of a dungeon, others

* *Status Rei Cath*, &c., an. 1654.

are still barred up in prisons; some were banished to the remote isle of Inisbofin, and delivered in charge to the garrison, who tortured them with great cruelty; many were banished to the West Indies, where they were sold as slaves, and condemned to work in twisting tobacco, and other slave labours. The magistrates prided themselves on what they considered extraordinary lenity, in allowing a great number of priests to escape from their talons to various Catholic countries of Europe" (vol. iii., p. 199).

CHAPTER III.

Other Penal Laws.

1.—Confiscation of Catholic Property.—2. Dr. Lynch describes the Cruelty and Perjury of Puritans.—3. Mock Justice of Tribunals.—4. Parliamentary Commissioners in Dublin; Fines on all who do not attend Protestant worship; all children over fourteen years declared the property of the State; any Irishman travelling a mile from his residence liable to be killed.—5. Effects of those persecutions.—6. Degraded strangers occupying Irish Soil.—7. Detailed account of Penal Laws by Dr. Lynch; Education Proscribed: Children of Catholics obliged to become Protestants, and to marry Protestants, &c.; thus the Irish nobility destroyed.

1. FURTHER penal enactments against the Catholics were passed in quick succession. One of the first measures was to confiscate the estates of the Catholic gentry. No fewer than five millions of acres were parcelled out amonst the Puritan soldiers and favourites of the Protector; and so complete was the extermination of the natives, that when the Government commissioners were distributing some estates in Tipperary, none of the inhabitants could be found to point out the bounds of these estates.*

"Thus," writes Curry, "the sword of extermination passed over the land, and the soldiers sat down to ban-

* *Privy Council Book*, A, 5, in *Haverty's History of Ireland*, p. 595.

quet on the hereditary possession of the natives."*
Captain William Heald in a Report on the State of
Ireland drawn up at the close of the year 1652, attests
that "they who thought all quiet in reference to their
persons and estates, find the sword wrested from them,
their persons on strange and unexpected pretences
arrested, their estates contrary to faith and engage-
ment confiscated, and no less than life and all exposed
by faithless and arbitrary tyranny of those to whom
they had so tamely made surrender of their freedom,
lives, and properties." (*Aphor. Discov.*, iii., 352.)

And Dominick de Rosario cries out:—

"It was not enough for them to torment and slay all
the Irish who fell into their hands; on the contrary,
they resolved to proscribe all those who had not been
taken in their impious toils; they contemplated the
extirpation of the Irish people, in order to secure their
triumph and their new-fangled religion."†

2. *Cambrensis Eversus* also vividly portrays the
severity of this penal enactment: "Not content," he
says, "with driving the priests to exile or death, they
turned their fury against all Catholics, and condemned
all who would not renounce the Catholic faith to forfeit
two-thirds of all their property. All that the Catholics
had suffered before this time was mercy compared with
the injuries now poured out on them. In former times
the magistrates had, it is true, severely oppressed the
Catholics, but they never violated their word, and they
often relaxed the rigour of persecution. But the present rulers of Ireland, or rather her persecutors, have

* *Review of the Civil Wars of Ireland.*
† *Hist.*, &c., p. 227.

blackened the most atrocious cruelty by perjury the most foul—perjury which, worse than any injury, provokes the indignation of man." He then remarks that many had sought by a speedy submission to obtain favourable conditions from the Parliamentarians.

"But experience soon proved that they had been under a most fatal delusion. The character given of the Puritans by King James is perfectly true: *I call the great God to witness, that greater ingratitude or perfidy was never found among mountaineers or border robbers than among those fanatical rogues.* For, when the Irish were stipulating for themselves, they reserved as much wealth as would barely support their family; and when, in violation of treaty, even this was taken away, they were reduced to the last extremities.

"In this manner noble princes, whose mansions were ever open to supply the guest and the stranger with all the profuse delicacies of the festive board, were now reduced to the necessity of wandering about to the houses of their former tenants and servants for as much food as would support life, or to enlist as sailors or marines, or serve under foreign banners, far from their native homes, for the scanty pay which was their only support. Our tyrants did not shear, but grub; they left no roots to produce another crop of wool; they did not imitate the prudent hive-keeper, who leaves as much honey in the hive as will support the bee, but takes away all the rest."—(Vol. iii. p. 201.)

In the Supplement to the *Alithinologia*, the same writer thus describes the condition of the Irish Church after the Puritan triumph:—

"The profession of the Catholic religion was abolished by law (*omnem religionis Catholicæ professionem lege sublatam*); in the churches you no longer find altars, but pig-sties; the priests driven to exile, or deceased in prison, or liberated to die of the diseases contracted in prison; some of them, in their hiding-places in the woods, were devoured by the wild beasts; some dragged to the scaffold from their concealment in the bogs and marshes; others made targets by the soldiery, and riddled with bullets; and others put to death by various other kinds of torture. And as *pro patribus nati sunt filii* (Ps. xliv.), a new generation of vigorous defenders, taking the place of the athletes fallen in the arena, comes to the battle-field of the Church, their toil preserves the ripeness of the old and enriches the Church with a new harvest; heedless of the impending dangers, they minister to their flocks in the recesses of the forests and woods, imitating the example of St. Gratian, Bishop of Tours, who administered the Sacraments in the caverns when the malice of men interdicted their public administration. And things are now come to this pass, that our Nicodemuses, thus secretly solaced by their priests, are deprived of every other comfort. The very fibres of the laws are now broken; it is no longer the natives, but strangers, who are the law-makers; the citizens are driven from the senate, whilst foreigners are invited to it; and the condition of the Jews, deprived of their Synedrium, was not more deplorable than that of the Irish deprived of the right of suffrage, which is given over to aliens, whilst our enemies are our judges. The old citizens are expelled from the cities built by the munificence of their ancestors, and are less encouraged to traffic than the merest foreigners. Wherefore each city has become the home of strangers, but closed against its own sons. Our youths are no longer trained to learning, so that they must grow up adding ignorance to their other miseries. The nobility are dispossessed of their ancestral estates, so that they are worse off than the lowest plebeians: the other proprietors are driven from their holdings, and forfeit the wealth handed down by their fathers or earned by their own industry. Most of the people who retained some small fragment of property are ground down by continual exactions, and it may justly be said of them that they are compelled to pay even more than they possess. For our enemies have adopted the words of Nero: *Hoc agamus ne quis quidquam habeat* (Let us contrive that nobody will have anything). Wherefore I look upon it as a sort of miracle that a single farthing remains to our people after the repeated plundering of all that they possessed, the persecutors, in imitation of Julian the Apostate, overwhelming us by poverty rather than by death, so that, life being prolonged, the torment would be prolonged also, thus adopting the course pursued by Caligula, who, according to the well-known decree, wished his victim to be punished with light but repeated blows, that thus he would the more feel his death. Even so, our people are overwhelmed with great torture, but slowly inflicted, lest we be cut off all at once."

3. That the persecution might be carried on with some semblance of justice, a new tribunal was instituted, called a high court of justice: in it all the ordinary forms of law were set aside; and so iniquitous

and bloody were the sentences pronounced in these courts, that they were commonly called "Cromwell's slaughter-houses"*

It will be well, perhaps, to learn from a Protestant writer, the author of the "History of Independency," the reason why this designation was given to the new tribunals. They were thus called, he says, because " no articles were pleadable in them ; and against a charge of things said to be done twelve years before, little or no defence could be made ; and that the cry was made of blood, aggravated with expressions of so much horror, and the no less daunting aspect of the court, which quite confounded the amazed prisoners, so that they came like sheep to the slaughter."

4. The parliament commissioners in Dublin, for their part, were not idle. It was enacted that anyone absent from the Protestant parish church on Sunday should incur a fine of thirty pence ; and it was made obligatory on the magistrates of Ulster, Meath, Leinster, and Munster, to take away the children of the Catholics and send them to England to be educated Protestants.† All Irish noblemen, whose fathers were not English, were obliged, under pain of death, to wear a distinctive mark on their dress; the Irish of inferior rank were likewise compelled to wear a black round spot on the right cheek, under pain of being branded with a similar

* "The Israelites in Egypt (writes De Burgo) could cry to Pharaoh from their oppression, yet this was not granted to the Irish : if the former were oppressed, they had, however, the fleshpots and abundance of food ; the Irish, whilst enduring a worse than Egyptian slavery, were exterminated by famine and the sword."— *Hib. Dom.*, p. 707.

† Act of Parl., 1657. De Burgo, loc. cit., page 707.

mark for the first offence, and of being hanged for the second.* No office was to be conferred on an Irishman if a fit Englishman could be found; if an Englishman were killed, the Irish of his district forfeited their lives; if an Englishman lost any of his property, the Irish had to compensate his loss threefold. Moreover, all Irish beyond fourteen years of age were declared the property of the Republic, to be employed on sea or land; and any Irishman going one mile beyond the district in which his name was registered without a passport, or anyone taking part in an assembly of *four persons*, forfeited his life.†

Nor were matters much improved when the Commissioners' powers were withdrawn, and Fleetwood apappointed Lord Deputy. He received instructions "to improve the interest of the Commonwealth of England in the dominion of Ireland, for the advancement of religion in that country, and suppressing idolatry, popery, superstition, and profaneness: to give encouragement, and provide competent maintenance to all such persons as are of pious life, and as shall be found qualified for preaching the Gospel: to execute all laws in force against Papists and Popish recusants: to consider of all due ways for the advancement of learning, and training up youth in piety and literature; to see that no Popish

* Porter, *Compend. Annal.*, p. 202.
† See these and other enactments in Porter, loc. cit.; also, De Burgo, and Cambren. Evers, vol. i., p. 51. Another Act, which, perhaps, even still more reveals the rapacity of the persecutors, commanded all Catholics throughout the kingdom to surrender, on the 24th of February, 1653, all the horses that in any way might be deemed fit for the saddle. See *Vita Francisci Kirovani, Ep. Alladen.*, p. 119.

or other malignant persons be employed in administration of the laws or execution of justice, nor practise as counsellors, attorneys, or schoolmasters: to put in execution all the Acts of Parliament now in force in this Commonwealth for sequestering all forfeited estates of popish malignants, archbishops, bishops, deans, and chapters, &c." Thus the rulers might be changed, but the law and rule of oppression remained the same.

5. The history of the Jesuit mission in Ireland, written in 1662, thus describes the condition to which the country was now reduced:—

"The Catholic nobility and gentry, and the inhabitants of the cities and towns are deprived of their lands and goods, and partly banished to foreign countries— partly driven to the remote and uncultivated parts of the kingdom; some, too, were sold as slaves for the American islands, and some were privately butchered. . . . . Thus, all the Catholics are in exile, and in their stead, in the cities and castles, and towns, and garrisons, none are to be found but Parliamentarian heretics, for the most part of the lowest class of artisans, and the scum and outcasts of society.* Hence, the ecclesiastics have nowhere a resting-place, and they are forced to fly to the herds of cattle, or to seek a refuge in the barns, or stables, or desert places; sometimes they seek to conceal themselves by paying for their lodging in the houses of the heretics. As regards the fathers of the Society, some dwell in ruined edifices, others sleep by night in the porticoes of the temples, lest they should occasion any danger to the Catholics."

---

* Viles opifices, populi fæx et quisquiliæ.

6. Again we read:

"The heretics being now masters of the kingdom, the clergy are scattered and destroyed, and the Catholic religion is almost extinct.* The nobility, and gentry, and native citizens are despoiled of their goods and properties, and in their place foreign heretics have been imported, the vilest of men, persecutors and capital enemies of the Catholic religion; so that Ireland no longer seems to be Ireland, and there are no longer any persons there to harbour the clergy and religious, but only to pursue them, and lead them to imprisonment torture, and the scaffold. Such is the sad condition of Ireland under the most cruel tyrant, Oliver Cromwell the Nero, Domitian, and Julian of our age. . . . Hence, Ireland is in a far worse condition now than it was one hundred years ago, for it is inundated with foreign enemies and heretical persecutors; it is an uncultivated field, overrun with briers—an immense and frightful wilderness—a new and unexplored land, to be once more cultivated and reclaimed."†

7. The following still more minute and invaluable narrative of the many penal enactments of this time enforced against the Catholics, is extracted from another contemporary writer:

"The Irish nation, besides many other gifts of nature, has two traits especially remarkable and most innate in her, which seem as two talents most liberally bestowed on her by God, namely, constancy in the Catholic religion, and an insatiable thirst for knowledge,

---

* Delctus et expulsus est clerus; Catholica religio pene extincta.
* Relatio rerum quarumdum, &c., anno, 1650.

in both which qualities I know not if she yields to any other nation. All who are acquainted with the nation know well these her characteristics. The heretics, too, know them by experience; ever since the commencement of the Anglican schism they oppress the Irish with an iron yoke, and renewing the cruelty of the enemies of the Jews towards the shorn Samson, they unceasingly strive, by every art, to destroy them in the eyes of religion and learning; having proscribed the true pastors of souls, they imported mercenary pastors, whose only aim is to plunder, and slaughter, and destroy.

"The Catholic schoolmasters being expelled, now no one can open a school but a heretic, that, forsooth, the poison of Satan may be instilled into the children's minds.

"All Catholic books are prohibited, and wheresoever they are found, they are destroyed by fire, and in their stead we are inundated with pestiferous books that scatter everywhere the cockle of heresy.

"The use of printing is interdicted to the Irish, lest, forsooth, any book might be circulated that did not come forth from a heretical source.

"Nay, more, whilst the Catholic religion yet flourished in the kingdom, the English Parliament decreed that no university should be erected in Ireland, lest, perhaps, the eyes of the people might be opened to see the tyranny of the yoke imposed on them. It is strictly forbidden for an Irishman to send his children for education to foreign parts, excepting to England, where he will be sure to imbibe the asp's milk.

"The jurisconsults are expelled from the tribunals, nay, the Irish are expelled from every office, unless they attest, by oath, the supremacy of the crown in matters of the Church and religion.

"*The eldest sons of the nobility, when young, are handed over to the guardianship of heretics, and those guardians, or rather wolves, devour the innocent lambs, and seize on all their goods and revenues; they consign, moreover, the youths to heretical schools as to so many prisons, where, by daily threats and punishments, they compel them to attend at the Protestant conventicles.* They cannot contract marriage except with one selected by these guardians, wherefore it often happens that the most noble youths, are bound to receive wives from the very lowest class, and from families that have only just emerged from the scum of society by rapine and fraud, the daughters, to wit, or relatives of the tutors, who, moreover, are always heretics, and deeply imbued with the poison of Calvinism.

"All the Irish are excluded from the viceroyalty of the kingdom; they are even declared incapable of this office by the very fact of being born in Ireland.

"Merchandise and commerce are subjected to so many taxes and restraints, that they are almost wholly taken from the hands of the Irish, and given to strangers.*

"The lands and territories of the gentry, by new interpretations of the law, are extorted from those who possessed them for centuries, and are given to upstart heretics. We ourselves have seen many most respectable men who, were it not for the oppression that prevails, would abound in wealth, but who now are seated

---

* Dr. French, in *Unkind Deserter*, p. 186, writes: "The Catholics of Ireland are excluded from all commerce, which the very Turks do grant to their Christians."

in ruined edifices, by an uncheering fireside ; and when interrogated as to the reason of their carelessness, they replied that they did not dare to live otherwise, and were they to repair or ornament their houses, the harpies would at once seize on them, and they themselves be deprived of the little that remained. Hence is the whole nation now reduced to such poverty, that it is no longer reckoned by the foreign countries, and none but poor and outcasts now go forth from that island, whence formerly, as St. Bernard writes, went forth so many swarms of holy men, and countless bands of philosophers, who illumined France, Germany, and Italy, by their learning and the splendour of their virtues."

CHAPTER IV.

PERILS OF THE CLERGY.

1. Heroism of the Clergy of Dublin; *Note.* Many Priests executed.—2. Father Carolan dies of starvation; Father Netterville; Priests carry Holy Sacrament with them.—3. Ludlow's account of Massacre near Castleblaney.—4. Further details of the sufferings of the clergy.—5. Fears that the Irish clergy would become extinct.—6. Edict compelling all Catholics to inform on priests; Number of priests in the country in 1658.—7. Imprisonment in the Islands of Arran and Inisbofin.—8. Father Finaghty.

1. THE reader can now easily picture to himself the perils that on every side beset the Irish priesthood. Yet, heedless of danger, many clung to their flocks to break to them the bread of life. History does not afford examples of more heroic fortitude, more fearless courage, more enduring constancy, than that displayed at this period by the Catholic clergy of Ireland. Mr. D'Alton, in his History of the Archbishops of Dublin, quotes from a Latin manuscript, written in 1653, the following extract :—*

---

* Archbishops of Dublin, p. 424. Hewson was at this time Governor of Dublin. He was an Englishman, and a tailor by trade, and having put himself at the head of a band of robbers, rendered some services to the Cromwellian army. In a letter from Dublin on the 15th of September, 1651, published with the approval of the Parliament in London, he breathes a prayer that the fate of Charles the First might soon fall to the lot of "the younger Tarquin," that is, Charles the Second.

"The keen-eyed vigilance of persecution has driven the Catholic laity into the country, and the priests and monks scarcely presume to sleep even in the houses of their own people; their life is warfare and earthly martyrdom; they breathe as if by stealth among the hills or in the woods, and not unfrequently in the abyss of bogs or marshes, which their oppressors cannot penetrate; yet, hither flock congregations of poor Catholics, whom they refresh with the consolation of the sacraments, direct with the best advice, instruct in constancy of faith, and confirm in the endurance of the cross of the Lord. These things, however, could not be effected without the knowledge of the heretics, who, in a simultaneous impulse, are hurried through the mountains and the woods exploring the retreat of the clergy; and never was the chase of the wild beast more hot and more bitter than the rush of the priest-destroyers through the woods of Ireland, many of whom deem it the most agreeable recreation to run down to death those beasts of the woods, as they term the Catholic clergy."*

---

* It is surprising how some writers have been so barefaced as to assert that no priests were executed during this period. Every contemporary document refers to the great number of ecclesiastics who were led to the scaffold. In addition to the many proofs we have already given in the preceding pages, we may cite a "Narratio brevis status Regni Hibernici," written on the 13th August, 1651, which the writer thus concludes:—" Absoluta hac narratione certo nuncio accepimus sacerdotes quatuor, ex illis sæculares duos, alios duos ex sacra S. Dominici familia religiosos in castro quodam nuper ab hoste in hac Connaciæ provincia capto, in patibulum actos esse et suspensos." Dominick de Rosario also writes: "On a stormy night there came a strong body of the enemy to our monastery of Kilmal-

2. The narrative of the state of Ireland in 1654* presents many additional particulars:—

"We live, for the most part, in the mountains and forests, and often, too, in the midst of bogs, to escape the cavalry of the heretics. One priest, advanced in years, Father John Carolan, was so diligently sought for, and so closely watched, being surrounded on all sides, and yet not discovered, that at length he died of starvation. Another, Father Christopher Netterville, like St. Athanasius, for an entire year and more, lay hid in his father's sepulchre; and even there with difficulty escaping the pursuit of the enemy, he had to fly to a still more incommodious retreat. One was concealed in a deep pit, from which he at intervals went forth on some mission of charity. The heretics having received information as to his hiding-place, rushed to it, and throwing down immense blocks of rock, exulted in his destruction; but Providence watched over the good father, and he was absent, engaged in some pious work of his sacred ministry, when his retreat was thus assailed. As the Holy Sacrifice cannot be offered up in these receptacles of beasts rather than of men, all the clergy carry with them a sufficient number of consecrated hosts, that thus they themselves may be comforted by this holy Sacrament, and may be able to administer it to the sick and to others."

3. Every art of the most refined cruelty was deemed lawful when pursuing to death these doomed victims,

lock, for the purpose of destroying the community. Some of them contrived to escape, but Fitzgerald and Fox (a lay-brother) were slain between the porch and the altar" p. 217.

* Status rei Catholicæ, &c., 1654.

the Catholic clergy; and many are the instances which have been handed down to us of priests who were dragged from their hidden recesses and subjected to the most brutal excesses. One scene, recorded by Ludlow in his memoirs (vol. i., p. 422 edition Vevay, 1698), sufficiently illustrates the rage of the persecutors. When marching from Dundalk to Castleblaney, and passing by a deep cave, he discovered that some Irish were concealed therein. Two days were spent by his party in endeavouring to smother the fugitives by smoke. At the close of the first day, thinking that all should be dead, some of them entered the mouth of the cave, but as they advanced the foremost was wounded by a pistol-shot fired from within. It appears that the inmates preserved themselves from suffocation by holding their faces close to the surface of some running water in the cavern; and one, who was placed at the entrance as guard, took his post near a crevice through which the air was admitted. On the next day all the crevices were stopped, the fires were kindled anew, and, as Ludlow expresses it, "another smother was made." The soldiers then entered with helmets and breastplates: they found the only armed man dead inside the entrance, but they did not enjoy the brutal gratification of finding the others suffocated, for they still preserved life at the little brook. A crucifix, chalice and sacred vestments were found in the cave, and fifteen of the surviving fugitives were at once massacred by the soldiery. One of the victims is supposed to have been a Catholic priest. It is evident they had assembled to assist at the Holy Sacrifice, and it became their happy privilege, by martyrdom, to pass from the temporary altar to the presence of the Lamb in His unveiled splendours in heaven.

4. The treatment of the priests in prison was of the harshest kind. They were for the most part wholly unprovided with means of support, and as the number of prisoners was so great, whilst the remnant of the Catholic nation was weighed down by taxes and oppression of every sort, the charity of the faithful was quite inadequate to relieve their misery. Hence many of them perished through want in prison.

A letter written from Galway, by Fr. Christopher O'Kearney, a Capuchin, on the 18th of July, 1655, sketches for us the daily perils that beset the missionary priest whilst he endeavoured to bring to the faithful the consolations of religion. "In order to evade the persecution (he writes), I have had to wear a number of disguises and to assume various characters, particularly since I was betrayed in Waterford where I served as the governor's gardener and as one of the city porters, that I might thus the better administer the sacraments and instruct the heretics desirous to be received into the Church. Being thrown into prison, I providentially made my escape, and after many adventures I at length settled in Galway, where I pass off as a Scotch peddler, hawking about cheap goods for sale. What shall I say of the hardships and risks to which I have been exposed? During the past two years I was three times detected by the spies, but I always succeeded either in purchasing their connivance or in making my escape. At present, however, I am quite at a loss as to the course I should pursue, for I lack even the necessaries of life. Fr. Bernard, discharges the missionary duties in the neighbourhood, but I have no doubt he will soon end his life on the gallows, for he exercises his ministry in the most dangerous places and is eagerly pursued by the heretics. God has hitherto kept him safe from their hands. But how now are we to support ourselves? our Catholic benefactors and friends have either perished or been transported beyond the seas, and the few that remain are in the same misery as ourselves and in equal need of the charitable aid of others. Fr. Gregory is in the county Cork, but we dare not visit him, the road is so beset with dangers and so many guards of soldiers are stationed everywhere . . . We have here an abundant spiritual harvest, for the leading Catholics of the other three provinces are all transported hither to Connaught. A few missionaries still remain despite the havoc made by the persecution . . .The gallows is always impending over us; yet we never were in better spirits than in those evil days, although like Nabuchodonosor we have to feed with the beasts of the field. In the ship that brings this letter, thirty priests are being sent into exile to France from Galway, eight from Limerick, and others from Cork. I pray you to send others to take their place, for of necessity this kingdom must soon be in want of apostolic labourers for there are many traitors amongst us who every day betray and arrest some of the clergy." (*Spicilegium Ossoriense*, vol. ii., p. 148.)

5. As early as the year 1653, a paper was presented to the Congregation of Propaganda, by Dr. French the exiled Bishop of Ferns, to enlist the aid and authority of the Holy See, in securing a succession of zealous and devoted priests to minister to the spiritual wants of

the suffering children of Christ in the Irish Church: "The present labourers in that vineyard," he says, cannot much longer endure the hunger, thirst, and afflictions, the bitter persecution, the watchings and sicknesses, living for the most part in the woods, and sleeping in the most wretched huts or sand-pits, or caverns, where in twenty-four hours they will hardly get a morsel of bread and a little milk or butter, often having no other drink but water, and sometimes eating the grass for want of bread (*aliquando defectu panis mordent herbam*). Of the truth of this I can bear witness, for I myself have lived out in the woods for five months that I might bring some solace to my scattered flock. Some of the priests have been put to death by the Puritan enemy, others have been cut off by famine and the hardships of imprisonment, and others put on shipboard and banished into exile. There are some who being remarkable for their zeal, integrity of life, and learning, and on that account more hated by the heretics, are sought for, to be thrown into prison or to suffer death, and the houses of the people are explored in search of them, so that to remove the imminent danger that awaits all who would shelter them they are compelled to fly to foreign parts lest their presence at home would lead to the ruin of others. The Religious who were accustomed to assist the pastors of souls in the spiritual vineyard, now that their monasteries are scattered by the Puritans, in great numbers proceed to foreign parts that they may there observe their rule. Take one instance. In the diocese of Ferns where there were three monasteries of Franciscans, one of Augustinians, and one small College of Jesuits, now only three Religious remain. There is no nook in which the Bishops can be safe, and since their presence stirred up a more violent storm against their flocks, for inevitable death awaits those who would shelter them, they have sought a home beyond the seas, and disconsolate, separated from their beloved flocks they weep for religion overthrown, their country ruined, freedom lost, and so many thousands of their countrymen driven into exile. From this flight and exile of the bishops it will result that priests cannot in future be ordained at home to take the place of the veteran workmen worn out by labours, hunger, thirst, and old age. From all this it must be manifest that very soon the vineyard of the Lord in Ireland shall be deserted and desolate, for the spreading briers and thorns of abominable heresy prevent the growth of the good seed of religion, and the shepherds are put to death who should protect the lambs and strengthen them for suffering whilst the wolves rage for their destruction : and it is to be feared lest the sad fate that has fallen on England and Scotland may also be the lot of Ireland, that is, that the priesthood being banished, the Puritan heresy may destroy every vestige of discipline in God's church and root out virtue and religion from the minds of men" (*Spicilegium Ossoriense*, vol. ii., p. 112).

6. Wholly peculiar to this Puritan persecution was the edict published at the same time, commanding the Catholics, under the severest penalties, to give information against their loved pastors, should they merely chance to meet them even in the public streets :—

"If anyone shall know where a priest remains concealed in caves, woods, or caverns, or if, by any chance he should meet a priest on the highway, and not immediately take him into custody, and present him before the next magistrate, such person is to be considered a traitor and an enemy to the republic. He is accordingly to be cast into prison, flogged through the public streets, and afterwards have his ears cut off. But should it appear that he kept up any correspondence or friendship with a priest, he is to suffer death."*

No edicts, however, could sever the bonds that united together the pastors and their flocks. A letter of the Archbishop of Tuam, written from Nantes, in September, 1658, informs us that, even then, whilst the persecution raged with its greatest violence, there were 150 priests in his province, and a like number in the other provinces, "attending to the care of souls, seeking refuge in the forests and in the caverns of the earth." The same illustrious confessor of the faith informs us that "the priests lately arrested were not put to death, as formerly, in consequence of the remonstrance of the Catholic princes on the Continent, but they were transported to the island of Inisbofin, in the diocese of Tuam, where they were compelled to subsist on herbs and water."

7. Mr. Prendergast has published some further details connected with this new place of imprisonment. On 27th of February, 1657 (he writes), the Commissioners referred to his Excellency to consider where the priests, then in prison in Dublin, should be most safely disposed of, and, in reply, an order was received to transport them " to the isles of Arran, lying out

---

* Morison, loc. cit. p. 27.

thirty miles in the Atlantic, opposite the entrance of the bay of Galway and the isle of Inisbofin, off the coast of Connemara." In these storm-beaten islands they lived during the remaining years of the Commonwealth; and from a Treasury warrant, dated 3rd July, 1657, we learn that *cabbins* were ordered to be built for them on these islands, and that the Governor of Galway, Col. Thomas Sadleir, was commissioned to allow them sixpence *per diem* for their support.

A letter from a priest in Nantes, on 19th October, 1659, also states that for some time past the Puritans had "resolved to put none of the clergy to death, and, instead of sending them into exile, to sentence them to perpetual imprisonment. This was partly because they envied us that incredible joy with which the priests went out to death, and partly because they thus hoped to cut off all chance of return to their flocks, and all possibility of administering spiritual assistance to the Catholics. Hence, out of fifty-two priests who were in custody, thirty-six were lately sent to the islands of *Inisbofin* and *Arran*, where there are heretical garrisons, and where they can neither offer up the Holy Sacrifice nor see the face of a single Catholic, and not even are they allowed to administer to each other the last rites of religion."

8. One of the priests arrested at this period was Father James Finaghty, Vicar-General of the Diocese of Elphin, a man much maligned, even in some of our Catholic histories. The short record of his sufferings handed down to us, in a narrative of the visitation of that diocese made in 1668, sufficiently proves that, if

the penalty of death was suspended for awhile, yet no toleration was allowed to the Catholic clergy :—

"Father James Finaghty frequently suffered many tortures and cruel afflictions from the common enemy for the faith of Christ; five times was he arrested, and once he was tied to a horse's tail, and dragged naked through the streets, then cast into a horrid dungeon; nevertheless, being again ransomed by a sum of money, he continues to labour untiringly and fearlessly in the vineyard of the Lord."*

* Relatio visitationis diœc. Elphin. factæ an. 1668, ab Edmundo Teige.

CHAPTER V.

Transplanting to Connaught.

1. The cry to Connaught or hell.—2. Lord Clarendon describes this transplanting.—3. Why Connaught was selected.—4. The Commissioners carry out the Transplantation Scheme; exceptions in favour of those who would renounce the Catholic faith.—5. The persecution sanctioned by the Protestant clergy: letter of Peter Talbot.—6. Other regulations.—7. Particular instances.—8. New trials in Connaught.—9. Catholics obliged to renounce all claim to their former lands; and other severities.—10. Famine and pestilence in Connaught.—11. Seventy stations of Puritan soldiers preying on the natives: constancy of the Catholics.

1. As the sword and subsequent persecuting edicts did not succeed in exterminating the Catholic Irish, the ingenuity of the Puritan masters was set to work to discover some new means of attaining that end. The province of Connaught was chosen, the most desolate and devastated in the whole kingdom, and thither, by public proclamation, all Catholics were commanded to repair. This was, in fact, nothing less than a frightful imprisonment of all the survivors of the nation. To Connaught or the scaffold was the fiendish cry of the persecutors throughout the country; and yet it was not even the province of Connaught, but only the barren portions of it, that the bounty of the Puritans set aside for the Irish Catholics. The heretics retained for themselves a breadth of four miles along the shores

of the Atlantic, and of two miles along the rich banks of the Shannon. The Irish, moreover, were not allowed to reside in the capital of the province or in any of the market towns. Pent up within these precincts, it was expected that the Catholic race would soon become extinct by famine and disease; for, throughout this barren district, the newcomers were friendless and unpitied, without food to eat, or house to afford them a protection; there was no seed to sow, nor cattle to stock the land. It was death for an Irishman to step beyond the limits thus cruelly traced, and any *mere Irishman* found in any other part of the kingdom could be butchered without further inquiry.

2. We shall allow Lord Clarendon to sketch this refinement of Puritan policy:—

"They found the utter extermination of the nation, which they had intended, to be in itself very difficult, and to carry with it somewhat of horror, that made some impression on the stone-hardness of their own hearts. After so many thousands destroyed by the plague which raged over the kingdom, by fire, sword, and famine, and after so many thousands transported to foreign parts, there remained still such a numerous people, that they knew not how to dispose of; and though they were declared to be all forfeited, and so to have no title to anything, yet they must remain somewhere; they, therefore, found this expedient, which they called an *act of grace*. There was a large tract of land, equal to the half of the province of Connaught, that was separated from the rest by a long and large river, and which, by the plague and many massacres, remained almost desolate. Into this space they required all the Irish to retire by such a day, under the penalty of death ; and who should, after that time, be found in any other part of the kingdom, man, woman, or child, should be killed by anybody who saw or met them. The land within the circuit, the most barren in the kingdom, was, out of this grace and mercy of the conquerors, assigned to those of the nation as were enclosed, in such proportions as might, with great industry, preserve their lives."—(Clarendon's *Life*, vol. ii., p. 116.)*

3. Connaught was indeed particularly well adapted for the imprisonment of the surviving Catholics. It is, in fact, a peninsula, surrounded all but ten miles by the Shannon and the sea ; and the erection of a few forts sufficed to completely cut it off from all communication with the remainder of the island. Connaught was, moreover, the most wasted province of the kingdom. Sir Charles Coote, the younger, disregarding the truce or cessation made, by order of the king, with the Irish in 1644, had continued to ravage it with fire and sword. The order was for the transplanting of the Irish nation thither in winter time, their nobles, their gentry, and their commons, with their wives and little children, their young maidens and old men, their cattle and their household goods. . . . They found the country a waste. The county of Clare was totally ruined and deserted of inhabitants. Out of nine baronies, comprising thirteen hundred ploughlands, not above forty ploughlands at the most, lying in the

---

* See also Scobell's *Statut.*, p. 258. The 1st of May, 1654, was the day fixed, after which any Irishman found in any part of the three provinces of Ireland might be arbitrarily put to death.

barony of Bunratty, were inhabited in the month of June, 1653. There was scarce a place to shelter in. The castles were either sleighted by gunpowder, as dangerous to be left in the hands of the Irish, or occupied by the English soldiery, or by the ancient Irish proprietors, who looked upon the transplanters as enemies liable to supplant them, and therefore encouraged their followers to give them a rough reception. Besides this, the Loughrea Commissioners gave some of the earliest transplanters assignments in the barony of Burren, in the county Clare, one of the barrenest, where it was commonly said there was not wood enough to hang a man, water enough to drown him, or earth enough to bury him.*

4. No sooner had the Leinster army surrendered, on terms signed at Kilkenny, 12th of May, 1652, than the Commissioners proceeded to carry out the plantation scheme. The *Adventurers*, as they were called, having advanced the sum of £360,000 for the extirpation of the Irish race, were ordered to receive in payment the moiety of ten counties in Ireland. The Government reserved for its own special favourites, the Regicides, and the most active of the English rebels, all the ecclesiastical lands† and revenues. The remainder of the island was to be set out amongst the officers and soldiers as payment for their arrears, which amounted to

* *Prendergast*, pp. 30 and 47.

† All archbishops, &c., being abolished, an individual named Thomas Hicks was installed in Chichester House on College-green, and authorised by the Government "to preach the Gospel at Stillorgan and other places in the barony of Rathdown, as often as the Lord shall enable him," &c.—*Prenderg.*, p. 24.

£1,550,000, as also in discharge of debts incurred in maintaining the Puritan army, which amounted to £1,750,000. On the 26th of September, 1653, the Act for planting Ireland with English was definitively passed in Parliament, and all the Irish that still remained in the provinces of Leinster, Ulster, and Munster were commanded to remove to Connaught at latest by the 1st of May, 1654, " except Irish women married to English Protestants before the 2nd of December, 1650, provided they became Protestants; except also boys under fourteen and girls under twelve in Protestant service, and to be brought up Protestants: and, lastly, those who had shown, during the ten years' war in Ireland, their constant, good affection to the Parliament of England in preference to the king. There they were to dwell, without entering a walled town, or coming within five miles of same on pain of death."* Another exception was also tacitly, at least, made, viz., that such of the common people, who might be required as earth-tillers and herdsmen for the new settlers, might be permitted to remain, for "being deprived of their priests and gentry, and living among the English, it was hoped they would gradually become Protestants."† The officers and soldiers were forbidden to intermarry with any of the Irish, "for the first purpose of the transplantation is to prevent those of natural principles becoming one with these Irish, as well in affinity as in idolatry, as many thousands did who came over in Queen Elizabeth's time."‡ In a subsequent

* Ibid., p. 30.   † Morison s *Threnodia*, p. 25.
‡ *Mercurius Politicus*, 1653, and *Prendergast*, p. 105. It is singular that many, even of the Cromwellian settlers, soon identified themselves with the Irish. A pamphlet written in 1697 thus laments

scheme, approved of by the Commissioners, all landlords were obliged to make such Irish servants or tenants as remained with them "to speak English within a limited time, and their children were to be taught no Irish. They were to observe the manners of the English in their habit and deportment. Their children were to be brought up under English Protestant schoolmasters; they were to attend the public preaching of Protestant ministers; they were to abandon their Irish names of *Teige* and *Dermot*, and for the future were to name their children with English names, especially omitting the *O'* and *Mac;* and lastly, should build their houses with chimneys as English in like capacity do."* An order published on the 21st of May, 1655, again renewed the injunction that all Irish servants and tenants that were permitted to remain should become Protestants in six months, and their children were to learn the Protestant Catechism in the English tongue.

5. Colonel Lawrence, who was himself one of the Committee of Transplantation, in a tract published in London in 1655, gives us one particular not noticed by most of the other writers. Not only was this new scheme for the extirpation of the Irish Catholics ap-

---

this degeneracy: "We cannot so much wonder at the degeneracy of the present English when we consider how many there are of the children of Oliver's soldiers in Ireland who cannot speak one word of English: and, what is strange, the same may be said of some of the children of King William's soldiers, who came but t'other day into the country. This misfortune is owing to the marrying Irish women. 'Tis sure that no Englishman in Ireland knows what his children may be as things are now; they cannot well live in the country without growing Irish."—(Ap. *Prenderg.*, p. 130.)

* Ap. *Prendergast*, p. 119.

proved by the Protestant statesmen of Ireland, but it had the full sanction of the Protestant clergy. Several solemn meetings, he says, were held, and several goodly ministers and other pious Christians had been desired to attend to seek the Lord for direction in this work. Instead of remonstrance, the only communications addressed to the Commissioners from these meetings were complaints "of the limitations and slow pace" of the transplantation. Colonel Lawrence fully sympathised with such complaints, and as some persons were opposing the Government scheme, he prayed them not to allow the sword to slumber, but " to let out that dram of rebellious blood, and cure that fit of sullenness."*

Rev. Peter Talbot, who a few years later was promoted to the Archbishopric of Dublin, having visited Ireland in the year 1654, addressed a letter from Antwerp on the 3rd of July to the Bishop of Clonmacnoise, then sojourning in Rome, in which he vividly depicts the deplorable state of ruin to which the whole kingdom was now reduced. " You will desire, no doubt, to learn something about our most afflicted country (he thus writes). No history, sacred or profane, presents anything to be compared to its miseries. Such tyranny has never been heard of. . . . It is now fourteen days since I quitted London, where everything was in indescribable confusion, stirred up in great part, as many suppose, by Cromwell himself, that thus he might have an opportunity of throwing into gaol those that could thwart his government. He is now busy im-

* Lawrence: *The Interest of England in the Irish Transplantation*, p. 9.

prisoning the Papists and priests. Of the latter four have been arrested, and a vast number of the former, twenty of whom were Irish, all of them being quite guiltless of any conspiracy. . . . As regards Ireland, the Transplantation scheme is being carried out; for although a promise was made to Sir Robert Talbot and the other Irish agents that it would not be proceeded with—and in fact it was suspended for six weeks—nevertheless, just when I was summoned hither, a new edict ordered it to be carried out with the greatest rigour, which is the same as to cut off by famine in one year all the nobility and people of Ireland. Through Colonel Axtell the Puritans made the offer that any Papists renouncing the Mass and Popery would be exempt from the Transplantation, but not even one individual accepted this condition. It was ordered by the clergy that the whole people would fast on bread and water for three Saturdays, and purify their conscience in the Sacrament of Penance, and receive the Blessed Eucharist. Everyone in the kingdom complied with the order: even the infants only three or four years old kept the fast, to the great confusion of the heretics. The condition of things in Connaught is this: Lands are assigned to the natives in proportion to the number of their cattle, and this is but little indeed. For instance, they have adjudged thirty acres to Lord Dunboyne, and so, in proportion, to the rest. Even thus provided for, however, they must maintain in Connaught seventy English garrisons; and, when all their means are exhausted, the men and women are sold to agents at twenty shillings each, to be transported to the American islands, as has already happened to some respectable persons of noble birth and hereditary possessions. Thousands of the poorer class are forced away in like manner, and are sold at twenty shillings per head. Throughout the whole kingdom there is nothing but lamentations and tears and striking of hands in grief. . . . There are not in Ireland ten families who have wherewith to support themselves for six months on bread and milk: this I learned by my own experience in the districts which I visited, and I have heard the same from the first noblemen of every quarter of the kingdom."

6. The *transplantation* was carried out with the utmost rigour. One of its regulations commanded each proprietor to bear with him from the local officer to the Commissioners in Connaught a certificate in which his name, age, stature, &c., should be set forth. Many of these certificates are still preserved, and they prove that none were spared in this cruel scheme. Thus the certificate of Sir Nicholas Comyn of Limerick describes him as " numb at one side of his body of a dead palsy, accompanied only by his lady, Catherine Comyn, aged thirty-five, flaxen-haired, middle stature, and one maid servant, Honor ny M'Namara ;" and it adds that they were "without substance," *i.e.*, were deprived of all means of support. Another describes: "Ignatius Stackpoole of Limerick, orphan, aged eleven years, flaxen hair, full face, low stature ; and Catherine Stackpoole, orphan, sister to the said Ignatius, aged eight years, flaxen hair, full face ; having no substance."*
Thus none were spared, and all, no matter how circum-

Prendergast, pp. 32-33.

stanced, were commanded to hasten to the wilderness marked out for their imprisonment.

Many, however, resolved to risk death rather than accept the Puritan boon of *transplantation*. Hence, the Commissioners of Parliament often complain that " the gaols were choked" with the number of those who refuse to transplant, and still the untractable Irish refused to obey their orders. The Irish Catholics, too, in 1660, declare that, " pursuant to the said pretended Act (27th Sept., 1663), some were put to death with inscriptions on their breasts and backs, for not transplanting. And, for the more strict and effectual executing of the said pretended Act, it was a frequent practice to make general restraint of all the Irish generally that were found out of the said province of Connaught, which were put in execution at one and the same time through all the other provinces, by troopers and soldiers dragging the poor people out of their beds in the dead time of the night, and bringing them in such troops as there was not gaol room enough to contain them. Therefore, some were put to death, others sold as slaves into America, others detained in prison till they were not able to put bread into their mouths, other sent to Connaught."*

The Rinuccini MS. presents precious details relating to the cruelty of the Puritans in carrying out this edict : " They had recourse to various devices," it says, " to extract whatever substance, marrow, or blood, remained to the Catholics; and not the least cruel of these was to hold out the hope that the transplantation to Con-

* *Carte MSS.*, vol. iii., p. 6.

naught would not be carried out. Enticed by this hope the Catholics disposed of everything they had, and almost starved their wives and children, selling the very necessaries of life that they might realise the large sums that were demanded that they might be permitted to remain in their homes, no matter how oppressive the taxes might be. But when every resource was exhausted, the English in this, too, breaking their plighted faith, with an unheard-of cruelty caused all the Catholic proprietors, some sooner, some later, to transplant to Connaught or Thomond; and this was so carried out that even those of Connaught and Thomond were themselves compelled to quit their ancestral lands and migrate to other districts. Only the labourers and those who had no holdings escaped this transplantation, not through any mercy on the part of the English, but partly preserved by their very indigence, and partly through a new device of Puritan cruelty, that thus they might be separated from those who of old protected them, and might be compelled to till the soil for their new masters. And yet their lot was better than that of the nobility and gentry and others expelled from their ancestral lands, for they were inured to toil, whilst these had no strength for manual labour, without which nothing now remained to them but to perish. Moreover, immense taxes were imposed by Cromwell, now invested with more than regal power; and they were exacted and extorted with such violence that no one could conceive how a man could exercise such tyranny against his fellow-man, or how the Irish Catholics, even with all their toil and sweat and starvation, and all the arts that dire necessity could alone suggest, were able to meet such demands, which were not only prolonged but increased from day to day."

7. Some particular instances that are happily recorded, illustrate the manner in which the Irish proprietors were expelled from their hereditary possessions. The Viscount Roche of Fermoy and his daughters were forced to walk on foot to Connaught, to die in a poor cabin there, whilst his lands were divided amongst the troopers of Cromwell. The estate now called Woodland, the seat of Lord Annaly, adjoining the Phœnix Park, Dublin, was formerly known as Luttrellstown, and under the Puritan *regime* passed first into the hands of Lord Broghill, and then to Colonel Hewson, Governor of Dublin, whilst the proprietor, Thomas Luttrell, "got permission, in 1652, to occupy the stables, and to till the land;"* even from this, however, he was now compelled to transplant. Elsewhere we read of the soldiers entering at once into possession, and "proceeding without mercy to turn out the wives and children of the transplanted proprietors, without giving them even a cabin to shelter in."†

The Viscountess Thurles was the Earl of Ormonde's mother. It was thought that she at least would be allowed to remain undisturbed. The town of Thurles, with 4,000 acres adjacent, was her dower. She had dwelt there in peace throughout the whole period of the Confederation, and she had given her powerful protection to many English who fled to her friendly shelter. When Major Peisley was forced to yield his neighbouring garrison of Archerstown to the Irish forces, and he

* Ap. Prendergast, p. 36.   † *Ibid.* p. 37.

and others of his company were wounded, she invited him, and his whole company to her house, and entertained them for some weeks and sent them forward with abundant supplies to the English garrison of Doneraile. But she was a fervent Catholic. Her son, as yet a child, had been taken from her care on the death of his father, and as a king's ward was brought up a Protestant, the only Protestant of his family. The Adventurers who claimed her land describe her as "a Popish recusant and transplantable," and her dower was forfeited to them.

So too, Lady Dunsany clung to her castle and lands in the rich territory of Meath. To the Adventurers she replied that she would deny them possession unless she was forcibly removed thence. On the 4th of July, 1656, the high constable with his force received peremptory orders to put the Adventurers in possession, and the poor lady with her children was driven by main force from her home.

8. Even when the sufferers arrived in Connaught, new trials awaited them. The officers there had to be bribed by money if the poor transplanter had any money left, or by a secret promise of a portion of the lands to be allotted to him.* None of the inhabitants of Kerry, Cork, or Limerick were allowed to dwell in Clare, lest they might thence behold their native hills and plains. Inhabitants of the same county or sept were to be dispersed as far as possible in different places. The best portions of the remnant set aside for the Irish nation were again appropriated by some new English claim-

* *Ibid.* p. 67.

ants. For Henry Cromwell was reserved Portumna with the 6,000 adjoining acres, and, other grants were made to Sir Charles Coote, Colonel Sadlier, and Major Ormsby.* The barony of Tirrera is bounded on the west by the fine estuary which leads up to Ballina in Mayo. Opposite is the barony of Tyrawley, with a belt of fine, rich feeding and grazing land along the estuary, commencing at Killala, near the mouth, and extending to Ballina. The rest, westwards to Erris, partakes of the nature of that barony, and is a waste of heath and bog. The Cromwellian officers took to themselves the good part of Tyrawley, on the ground that, by means of such an English plantation, the sea coast would be greatly secured, but they left the bad half for the transplanted families. What wonder, then, concludes Mr. Prendergast, "that the transplanted, who could find means to fly, or were not tied by large families of children, sold their assignments for a mere trifle to the officers of Government, and fled in horror and aversion from the scene, and embarked for Spain. Some went mad; others killed themselves; some laid their bones in Connaught, as Lord Trimbleston, on whose gravestone, within the ruins of the Abbey of Kilconnel, that overlook the fatal fields of Aughrim, may be still read the epitaph : 'Here lies Mathew, twelfth Lord Baron of Trimleston, one of the Transplanted.'"

As was to be expected, those who prolonged their existence for a time were forced to live in the greatest misery. "Many opulent persons of good quality,"

* *Ibid.*, p. 194.

writes the contemporary, Bishop of Ferns, "yea, and many of them peers and lords of the realm, were lodged in smoky cabins, and, as might well be said, buried there and starved to death, together with their wives and children."

9. The persecutors, however, were not satiated by thus *transplanting* the Irish inhabitants. They, moreover, obliged all, to whom some portions of land were marked out in this barren district, to sign conveyances or releases of their titles to their former properties, that thus they and their heirs might be for ever debarred from their old inheritance.* We also find recorded that when some of the transplanted Irish erected cabins or creaghs, as the hurdle houses were then called, in the vicinity of Athlone, orders were sent from Dublin Castle to banish all *the Irish and other Popish persons* from that neighbourhood, so that no such gathering should be allowed within five miles of the English garrison.†

10. No pen can describe the frightful scenes of misery that ensued. With famine and pestilence, despair seized upon the afflicted natives. Thousands died of starvation and disease; others cast themselves from precipices, whilst the walking spectres that remained seemed to indicate that the whole *plantation* was nothing more than a mighty sepulchre.‡

* *Clarendon loc. cit.*, vol. ii., p. 116.
+ *MS. Orders of Council*, cit. by Haverty, p. 595.
  See *History of the Irish Catholics*, by M. O'Connor, p. 87. "Thousands perished of cold and hunger, many flung themselves headlong from precipices and into lakes and rivers, death being the last refuge from such direful calamities." Also *De Burgo in Hib. Dom.*, p. 706.

A *Relatio*, drawn up in 1656 by one who had just before escaped to the Continent from this terrible scene, declares that :—" The persecution under Elizabeth was never so violent as that which now rages in Ireland, for then only ecclesiastics were persecuted, now even the nobility and females are subject to it. Women may be seen running after their husbands who are sentenced to exile, nay, they plunge into the depths of the sea that they may be allowed to share in their banishment. Children are seen hurrying after their mothers, and dying in the public streets. Whole towns are transported to the Barbadoes. Many persons, through sadness and terror, run through the country insane. Houses are seen empty, a prey to anyone who may wish to enter them. Virgins are insulted, children are murdered, crowds of the natives are carried off into exile. Oh ! how sad a spectacle !"*

11. The Puritans, however, were still attentive to extort from the suffering transplanted Catholics whatsoever might, perchance, have yet remained to them. A contemporary writer thus describes these new arts of the Puritan persecutors :—†

"There is one thing that now perplexes us very much, the transplanting of our nation to the province of Connaught. This is a tract of Ireland, for the most part, rocky and mountainous, and wholly reduced to a wilderness by the constant whirlwind of wars, uninterrupted for so many years. Nowhere, throughout all that region, can a house be met with. Scarcely is there

* Wadding MSS., Rome.
† Status rei Catholicæ, anno 1564.

a particle of a wall left standing, the edifices being destroyed by fire, and levelled to the ground lest any habitation or defence should remain for the Catholics. Two cities alone remain, and from these the inhabitants are expelled, and they are now filled with English Anabaptists. Some of the ports, too, are inhabited by the same pest. The remainder of the province is wholly devastated and everything levelled to the ground.

"To this desert all the nobility and gentry of the kingdom and all that had any land or possessions are now transported. Amidst these mountains they receive some small particles of land, for the most part sterile and rocky. There they must fix their dwellings and build for themselves, as best they may, or otherwise be exposed to the hoar frost. Nor is the evil confined to this.

"The Catholics, thus transplanted, although deprived of nearly all their fortunes and goods, are, nevertheless, obliged to support, in this Connaught wilderness, seventy stations of Puritan soldiers, which are arranged at stated distances throughout the country, under the pretence, indeed, of their own security, and lest Catholics might plot against the State and excite fresh disturbances, but in reality that they may keep away all priests, and prevent the exercise of the Catholic religion; and, moreover, that thus any property that still remained amongst the persecuted natives might be wasted away and consumed in supporting such a number of guards, and so the whole nation might become gradually extinct. for they see that no violence or artifice can force them to abandon the Catholic faith.

"Indeed, the magistrates more than once notified to some of the Catholic gentry, whom they were anxious to protect, that all this vexation would cease, should they only consent to renounce the Roman Pontiff and especially the Mass. They sought also to persuade not a few of the Catholics, that it was folly for them to precipitate themselves into voluntary banishment, which could be prevented by so easy a remedy; but the Catholics closed their ears with the holy fear of God against these siren enchantments, and they chose to suffer even death rather than to tarnish their glory, holding in mind that they are children of saints, and that an eternal inheritance awaits them."

CHAPTER VI.

Puritan Colonists.

1. Ireland confiscated.—2. Protestant settlers from New England; Vaudois from Piedmont.—3. Their character.—4. Manuscript account of the same.—5. Lord Clare's description.—6. Mr. Thomas Wadding.—7. Cambrensis Eversis.

1. IRELAND was now, indeed, become the spoil of her merciless heretical enemy. The whole kingdom was ordered to be surveyed, and "the best land was rated at only four shillings per acre, and some only at one penny."* The towns were rated at even a lower price. The whole city of Limerick, with 12,000 acres contiguous, had been offered in the beginning of the war for £30,000, with a small rent to the State. Galway, with 10,000 acres, was offered for £7,500 ; and Wexford, with 6,000 acres, was only valued at £5,000. The repeated orders which were issued in 1652, 1654, and 1656, to clear all the towns of their Catholic population, rendered many of them well nigh desolate. In the impeachment of Lord Inchiquin before Parliament, it is set forth that his soldiers destroyed three thousand houses "void of inhabitants" in the city of Cork, and an equal number in Youghal. "For such a scene of desolation," writes Mr. Prendergast, "as the cities

* Morrice, *Life of Orrery*, vol. ii., p. 117.

and towns of Ireland presented at this period, recourse must be had to the records of antiquity, and there, in the ruined state of the towns of Sicily, when rescued by Timoleon from the tyranny of the Carthaginians, there is to be found a parallel. Syracuse, when taken, was found comparatively destitute of inhabitants. So little frequented was the market-place that it produced grass enough for the horses to pasture on, and for the grooms to lie in by them as they grazed. The other cities were deserts, full of deer and wild boars; and such as had this use for it hunted them in the suburbs round the walls. And such was the case in Ireland. On the 20th December, 1652, a public hunt, by the assembled inhabitants of the barony of Castleknock was ordered by the State, of the numerous wolves lying in the wood of the ward, only six miles north of Dublin."

Colonel Jones, one of the Commissioners for Parliament in Ireland, in a letter to Major Scott, on the 1st March, 1652-3, does not hesitate to set forth that this desolate condition of the kingdom afforded a cheering prospect for its future tranquillity : " There is no way (he says) to reduce this land to a perfect and lasting peace, but by removing all heads of septs and priests and men of knowledge in arms, or otherwise in repute, out of the land, and breaking all kinds of interest among them, and by laying waste all fast countries in Ireland, and suffering no mankind to live there but within garrisons; for which end declarations are going out to lay waste the whole county of Kerry, and a great part of the counties of Cork, Limerick, Tipperary, Clare, Galway, Roscommon, Sligo, &c.; the whole counties of

Leitrim, Fermanagh, Cavan, Tyrone, Monaghan, and Armagh, except parts of baronies in some of them not considerable: likewise part of Longford, Meath, and Louth, bordering upon those counties; the whole county of Wicklow, and part of King and Queen's Counties." (*Aphoris. Discov.*, vol. iii., p. 271).

To encourage the Adventurers in the work of planting, as it was called, the Committee of Parliament in England made the following orders on the 12th of May, 1652 :—

"Resolved: That in consideration the Adventurers shall forthwith set upon planting their proportions following, and within three years from the 29th of September next, shall fully plant the same with Protestants of any nation, saving Irish, in such manner as shall be directed by Parliament: that the House be moved that there be set out unto them as many forfeited lands within the counties of Limerick, Kerry, and Tipperary, or within the counties of Limerick, Kerry, and Cork, or within the counties of Waterford, Wexford, Wicklow, and Kilkenny, at their election, as their present Adventurers amount to :

"That upon the considerations aforesaid, the Parliament be moved that 500,000 acres more be given them towards their further charge in erecting buildings, planting the said lands, and forbearance of their monies, &c. :

"That also such houses and buildings belonging to the Commonwealth, and not already disposed of, in the respective towns and cities within the counties which they shall make election of, be demised to the Adventurers for twenty-one years, or three lives, &c. :

"That the Adventurers have liberty to export into Ireland all commodities mentioned in their proposals, which shall tend to the advancement of their plantation, for seven years, from the 29th of September next:

"And that, for the term of ten years, not above a fifth part of the true yearly value of the lands aforesaid be paid in lieu of all taxes, &c."

And lest the Adventurers would be dilatory in securing Protestant settlers for the now uninhabited country, a proviso was added, that any of the said lands not properly inhabited within three years "shall be forfeited to the Commonwealth."

2. At the same time nothing was left undone to provide for the security of the English Protestant settlers, and to attract them to our shores. The following letter from the Commissioners in Dublin to the Secretary of the Government in London, will serve to show how earnest they were in their resolve to remove all Irish Catholics from the path of these new colonists:

"Dublin Castle, 4th March, 1656-7.
"RIGHT HONOURABLE,—

The Council having lately taken into their most serious consideration what may be most for the security of this country, and the encouragement of the English to come over and plant here, did think fit that all Popish recusants, as well proprietors as others, whose habitation is in any port-towns, walled-towns, or garrisons, and who did not before the 15th September, 1643, and ever since, profess the Protestant religion, should remove themselves and their families out of all such places, and two miles at the least distant therefrom, before 20th May next; and being desirous that the English people may take notice, that by this means there will be both security and conveniency of habitation for such as shall be willing to come over as planters, they have commanded me to send you the enclosed declaration, and to desire you that you will take some course, whereby it may be made known unto the people for their encouragement to come over and plant in this country?"*

Notwithstanding all these attractions, however, a sufficient number of English Puritans could not be got to come to Ireland. Hence, to supply inhabitants to the desolate country, Protestant settlers were, from time to time, invited from New England, and liberal offers were likewise made to the Vaudois of Piedmont, should they choose Ireland for an " evangelical colony."† In 1651, Mr. Harrison, minister of the Gospel in New England, " was affectionately urged to come over to Ireland, which he would find experimentally was a comfortable seed-plot for his labours."‡ It was hoped that on his return " the hearts of many others would be stirred up" to plant in our island, and the letter of the Commissioners adds : " they should have freedom of (Protestant) worship, and the advantages of convenient lands, fit for husbandry, in healthful air, near to maritime towns or secure places, with such encouragement from the State as should demonstrate that it was their chief care to plant Ireland with a godly

* Hutchinson, *History of Massachusetts*, p. 190 : *Thurloe*, vol. ii., p. 459.
† *Settlement*, p. 120. ‡ *Prendergast*, p. 284.

generation." In 1655, proposals were made for the planting of the town of Sligo and the lands thereabouts with families from New England, and on the 10th of April, that year, "lands on the Mile line, together with the two little islands called Oyster Island and Coney Island (containing 200 acres), were leased for the use of such English families as should come from New England in America." In 1656 we find some families arriving from America at Limerick, and permission was granted to them to introduce, free of tax, "the tobacco they had brought with them for the use of themselves and families." The lands of Garristown, about fifteen miles to the north of Dublin, were also allotted to such Anglo-Americans as would undertake to colonize our island, and one individual, named John Barker, received thirty acres there on the sole condition that he should dwell on his lot, and not consign it to another.* Even the Dutch and other Protestants had offers made to them; and Samuel Hartlib, dedicating a work on the Natural History of Ireland to Oliver Cromwell, declared that he "looked upon the hopeful appearance of replanting Ireland shortly, not only by the Adventurers, but partly by the calling in of exiled Bohemians and other Protestants also, and partly by the invitation of some well affected out of the Low Countries."† These offers, however, were for the most part made in vain; and so universal was the horror of the brutality displayed by the Puritan officers in Ireland, that none but the very dregs of society

* Order of Council Chamber, Dublin, 30th July, 1656. *Ib.*, p. 121.
† *Ireland's Nat. History*, by Boate. 4to. London, 1652.

could be found, even in England,* to seek a share in the spoil.

3. There is a passage in Dominick de Rosario's *History of the Geraldines* that sketches for us the character of the new settlers, and the rapacious spirit with which they rushed to plunder our Island of Saints:—

" That raging mass, besprinkled with the monarch's blood, burst upon the land of my birth. The butcher, the buffoon, and the hired cut-throat, each led his band; and the very dregs of English cities and towns were invested with centurion authority. Then came hideous woes, as though God would lash us with a triple scourge, discord, famine, and pestilence. Well was it for those who died by the plague, for they passed away without dishonour; and happier were they who perished by the edge of the sword, for they thus escaped the lingering pangs of hunger. Cities and towns were seized by those ruthless slayers; the nobility were ruined, the temples of God razed, altars polluted, everything sacred profaned, whole families destroyed, smiling plains reduced to barrenness, and the lowing herds slaughtered to feed an unbridled soldiery. Blessed, then, were they who possessed nothing. But how shall I describe the horrors which those fiends heaped on the heads of the Catholic clergy? In their private houses, in the caverns of the earth, in the recesses of the mountains and woods, naked and unarmed, were they not maimed, stabbed, struck with stones in their very transit to the gibbet?

---

* Many citizens of London, at the time of the great fire, in 1666, looked on it as a chastisement from God for the cruelties exercised against the Irish.

Oh! how many of them breathed out their souls exhorting their countrymen to deeds of heroism, and undying attachment to the Catholic religion!"*

The Rinuccini MS. after describing the mournful scenes of the year 1655 adds:—" To the whole nation may be applied the words of Joel (i. 4): *That which the palmer-worm hath left, the locust hath eaten: and that which the locust hath left, the bruchus hath eaten; and that which the bruchus hath left, the mildew hath destroyed.* For through the war, and famine, and pestilence, only a fourth part of the clergy and people survived, and these were crushed and ground down by the unchecked and unparalleled cruelty of English heretics, under whose slavery they were so oppressed that all the sufferings endured by the Church under the Diocletians, Neros, and other heretical or pagan princes and emperors, whether in the Old or New Testament, can scarcely deserve the name of persecution, compared to the Cromwellian torture of the Catholics of Ireland. If even to this remnant of the people some peace were accorded, the past might be forgotten; but so far was this from being the case, that new opportunities for oppression were every day sought out, according to the words of Solomon (Prov. i. 11): *Let us hide snares for the innocent without cause;* so that the whole island was red with blood, and bedewed with tears, and ever resounding with the cries and lamentations of the sufferers."

4. Amongst the manuscripts belonging to the King's Library in the British Museum there is a work entitled

* Loc. cit., p. 298.

An Account of Ireland, written in 1773, which, speaking of the Cromwellian era, thus describes well the hordes of sectaries that overspread the three confiscated provinces of Ireland : " An army of new settlers, and mostly of a newer religion, whether Anabaptists, Socinians, Muggletonians, Brownists, or Millenarians, now obtained large grants of forfeited lands in Ireland ; and from these adventurers are descended some of the principal persons in the kingdom in opulence and power. Most of these settlers were men of the sourest leaven, who eagerly adopted the most harsh and oppressive measures against those upon whose ruin they rose."*

5. This description of the sectaries of every hue that divided amongst themselves the possessions of the exterminated or transplanted Irish is confirmed by Lord Clare, in his celebrated speech on the Union :—

" A new colony of new settlers, composed of all the various sects which then infested England—Independents, Anabaptists, Seceders, Brownists, Socinians, Millenarians, and dissenters of every description, many of them infected with the leaven of democracy—poured into Ireland, and were put into possession of the ancient inheritance of its inhabitants."

Indeed nothing else was to be expected considering the condition of England in those evil days. I will allow a Presbyterian writer who from the outset of the revolution had fought in the ranks of the Parliament-

---

* See *The Irish Church, its History and Statistics*, by W. Shee, Sergeant-at-law, &c., 1852, p. 9.

ary party to describe the irreligious confusion into which the whole country was plunged:

"Things every day grow worse and worse; you can hardly imagine them so bad as they are. No kind of blasphemy, heresy, disorder, and confusion, but it is found among us, or coming in upon us. For we, instead of reformation, are growing from one extreme to another; fallen from Scylla to Charybdis; from Popish innovations, superstitions, and prelatical tyranny, to damnable heresies, horrid blasphemies, libertinism, and fearful anarchy. Our evils are not removed and cured but only changed: one disease and devil hath left us, and another as bad is come into the room. You have broken down the images of the Trinity, Virgin Mary, Apostles; and we have those who overthrow the doctrine of the Trinity, oppose the divinity of Christ, speak evil of the Virgin Mary, and slight the Apostles. You have cast out the bishops and their officers, and we have many that cast down to the ground all ministers in all their reformed churches: you have cast out ceremonies in the sacraments as the cross, kneeling at the Lord's Supper; and we have many who cast out the sacraments of baptism, and the Lord's Supper: you have put down Saints'-days; and we have many who make nothing at all of the Lord's-day and fast-days: you have taken the superfluous, excessive maintenance of bishops and deans; and we have many that take away and cry down the necessary maintenance of ministers. In the bishops' days we had singing of psalms taken away in some places, conceived prayer and preaching, and, in their room, anthems, stinted forms, and reading, brought in; and now we have singing of psalms spoken against and cast out of some churches; yea, all public prayer questioned, and all ministerial preaching denied. In the bishops'-days we had many unlearned ministers; and have we not now a company of Jeroboam's priests? In the bishops'-days we had the fourth commandment taken away, but now we have all the ten commandments at once, by the Antinomians; yea, all the faith and the Gospel denied. The worst of the prelates, in the midst of many Popish Arminian tenets and Popish innovations, held many sound doctrines, and had many commendable practices; yea, the very Papists hold and keep to many articles of faith and truths of God, have some order amongst them, encourage learning, have certain fixed principles of truth, with practices of devotion and good works; but many of the sects and sectaries in our days deny all principle of religion, are enemies to all holy duties, order, learning, overthrowing all, being whirligig spirits. What swarms are there of all sorts of illiterate mechanic preachers: yea, of women and boy preachers: what liberty of preaching, printing of all errors, or for a toleration of all, and against the Directory, Covenant, monthly fast, Presbyterial government, and all ordinances of Parliament in reference to religion?" And then he enumerates in another part of his work, no less than a hundred and seventy-six heretical and blasphemous tenets, which were the growth of that period. (Edward's *Gangraena*, p. 16.)

6. It cannot be expected that many virtues would be found in the train of these ruthless colonists; on the contrary, they seemed to wage war against every virtue, and to have become the champions of every vice.

An eye-witness, Mr. Thomas Wadding, thus writes, on the 21st October, 1656 :—" There is no corner of Ireland but is now filled with heresies, and atheism, and iniquity of every sort; never was the Catholic name so persecuted; malice is triumphant, all vices flourish, justice has decayed; true faith, and mercy, and modesty, and sincerity are banished; violence and audacity everywhere prevail; no one has any property but what he acquired by fraud and violence; the good are exposed to persecution and misery; the bad alone are prosperous, and abound in wealth. . . . So that we are tempted to cry out—' O, God! what an age have you made us spectators of!' "*

7. In *Cambrensis Eversus*, vol. iii., p. 75, we find an additional testimony as to the vile character of the new colonists:—" Nobles of high descent," says that contemporary author, " were robbed of two-thirds of their hereditary estates, and ordered to confine themselves within the contracted limits of the remaining third; while the properties wrested from them were assigned to swarms of Englishmen, collected from the barbers' shops, and highways, and taverns, and stables, and hog-sties of England."

* Deus ad quæ nos tempora reservasti! Letter of Thomas Wadding from Nantes, 21st October, 1656, to Mgr. Rinuccini; preserved in Barberini Archives, Rome.

CHAPTER VII.

Irish exported as Slaves.

1. Irish exported as slaves; Testimony of Alithinologia; Sir William Petty and others; *Note.* Rev. J. Grace, in 1666, found 12,000 Irish slaves in Barbadoes, &c.—2. Method of making Irishmen Christians, *i.e.*, selling them as slaves; Cruelty of the Puritans.— 3. Slave trade to Barbadoes legalised.—4. Sale of Irish natives.— 5. Particular instances.—6. Seizure of Paul Cashin, P.P. of Maryborough, and other priests.—7. Irish children exported; St. Christopher's; Irish there.—8. Dr. James Lynch.—9. Irish treated barbarously, according to Father Grace; *Note.* Letter of Bishops of the province of Tuam to propaganda.—10. Faith and piety of the Irish during their captivity.

1. It was not enough to import foreigners of every hue and every denomination into Ireland; the Puritan rulers deemed it further necessary to export, as slaves, to the American islands, as many of the natives as yet survived the miseries and vexations of Connaught. The Rev. Dr. Lynch, who was himself witness of the sufferings of our people at this dismal period, in the very commencement of his valuable work, entitled *Alithinologia*, thus writes:—" In the present calamitous condition of Ireland the clergy are subjected to imprisonment, or exile, or the scaffold; nor is it even permitted to the priests to be shut up in the city prisons, lest perchance the sight of them or their lamentations would excite the pity of the passing crowd of Catholics;

but they are transported to Arran and Inisbofin, the most remote islands of the West, there to be tortured by hunger, and cold, and solitude, and the cruelty of the guards; and whereas in olden times numerous choirs of monks devoted themselves there to continual prayer and other exercises of virtue, now savage bands of soldiers apply their wits to starve the priests of God in prison. . . . The clergy who are not as yet arrested either lie hid in the woods, bogs, caverns, and recesses of houses, or under the garb of husbandmen, or artizans, or labourers, or other disguise, live secretly in Catholic families, whose piety they foster by the sacraments and pious exhortations, although repeated edicts threaten them with death, and enact severest penalties, with the forfeiture of property, against all those who harbour or assist them. So that our clergy at home have to face the hardships of prison, or extreme misery, or death, whilst most of those who are abroad have only the stinted bread of exile for their maintenance. As for the laity, some of them, expelled from their homes and hereditary possessions, are driven far away from the sight of their native land, so that the decree of the Emperor Adrian forbidding the Jews to see Jerusalem even at a distance from an elevated spot would appear to hold good in their regard. A great many being transferred to one province, they are, I will not say located there, but rather packed together like herrings in a barrel, *more halecum in dolio,* so that amid hardships and in poverty they eke a miserable life, whilst even the remnant of their fortunes is wasted by almost daily exactions. Thus their weary bodies are wasted away through misery, and at the same time their minds are tortured, being deprived of religion, and their hearts are rent by the thought of the banishment of those who are dear to them. In one year, since the late war, forty thousand men were transported from Ireland into foreign countries; and since then we have repeatedly seen husbands torn from their wives, children from their parents, servants from their masters, and all forcibly carried off to the West Indies, there to be sold as slaves."

Jamaica and the adjoining islands had lately passed into the hands of England, and slaves were wanting to cultivate the sugar and tobacco plant on that deadly soil. Sir William Petty,* writing in 1672, states that six thousand boys and women were thus sold as slaves from Ireland to the undertakers of the American islands. Bruodin estimates the total number of the exiles from Ireland at 100,000, and adds that of these some thousands were transported to the tobacco islands.† A letter, written in 1656, cited by Dr. Lingard, reckons the number of Catholics thus sent to slavery at 60,000. "The Catholics are sent off in shipsfull to the Barbadoes and other American islands. I believe 60,000 have already gone; for the husbands being first sent to Spain and Belgium already, their wives and children are now destined for the Americas."‡ The Irish his-

---

* Political Anatomy of Ireland, p. 187.

† Propugnac., p. 672, " Aliquot millia in diversas Americæ tabaccarias insulas relegata sunt."

‡ When the Rev. John Grace visited these islands in 1666 he found that there were as yet no fewer than 12,000 Irish scattered amongst them, and that they were treated as slaves.—(From his letter of 5th of July, 1669.)

torian, M'Geoghegan, also writes that, exclusive of the women and children, "from fourteen to twenty thousand, both soldiers and country-people, were sold as slaves, and transported to America" (p. 577).

The contemporary author of the supplement to *Alithinologia* published in 1666, thus writes:—"The Puritan Government, in July, 1654, decreed that the Irish nobility should lose their rank, the people their liberty, wives their husbands, youth the opportunity of learning their religion; and further, that every Irishman would wear some servile badge or token by which to distinguish him from the English, and would be so weighed down by poverty that he could have but little means by his labour and industry for the bare support of his family (*ad familiam parcius alendam*). The people should either give their labour at home for a small hire (*tenui mercede*), or, as the early Christians were sent to the stone-quarries, so were the Irish Catholics now banished to the most remote Indian islands, there to discharge the most abject duties for the colonists, and the women were sold in the public markets in those Anglo-Indian colonies at a trifling price (*vili pretio*), to gratify their masters' passions, or to be their slaves."

2. This transportation to slavery was even viewed by the Puritan persecutors as a boon they were conferring on the Irish Catholics. When Secretary Thurloe wrote to the Lord Deputy of Ireland to inform him that a stock of Irish was required for the peopling of Jamaica, the Lord Deputy replied:—

"Concerning the supply of young men, although we must use force in taking them up, yet it being so much for their own good, and likely to be of so great advantage to the public, it is not the least doubted but that you may have such a number of them as you may think fit to make use of on this account. I shall not need repeat anything regarding the girls, not doubting to answer your expectations to the full in that; and I think it might be of like advantage to your affairs there and ours here if you should think fit to send fifteen hundred or two thousand boys to the place abovementioned. We can well spare them, and who knows but that it may be the means of making them Englishmen—I mean, rather, Christians. As for the girls, I suppose you will make provision of clothes and other accommodation for them."*

The Rinuccini MS. in two or three places refers to the slavery to which the Irish Catholics were subjected in the West Indian islands: "To the island of St. Christopher (better known as St. Kitt's) several thousand Irish Catholics (it says), and whole colonies were transported as slaves, and this for two ends, first, to extirpate from the kingdom the Irish race and the Catholic Faith, and second, to extend by this means the British dominion in those distant regions. And the Irish transported thither, are held like slaves under a cruel lash, and it may be truly said that with them the Catholic Faith has been banished from a great part of Ireland to America." Again it describes from the narrative of

* Thurloe "Memoirs," vol. iv., p. 75. In Porter, "Comp. Annal.," p. 292, we find the following decree of the Irish Commissioners:—
"That Irish women, as being too numerous now, be sold to merchants, and transported to Virginia, New England, Jamaica, or other countries, where they may support themselves by their labour."

one who was present, the scene witnessed in the gaol of the city of Kilkenny in 1653. A husband and wife were kept in the gaol for three months in extreme misery. After that time the husband was seized and "most cruelly torn from his loved wife to be transported with so many of his countrymen who through hatred of the Catholic faith were banished to the American settlements, his wife crying aloud to heaven in vain, and asking as the greatest of favours that she would not be separated from the husband whom she loved and whose slavery she was ready to share. But the English heretics deadened by crime to every sentiment except greed of gain, tore away the wife because she had not strength enough to serve in the Indian islands and threw her into prison, and sent off the husband into slavery." At greater length the same MS. elsewhere thus sketches the condition of the kingdom in the year 1654: "How mournful was the ruin that fell upon this thrice Catholic nation! How sad was the change! Where once the nobility and magistrates and Catholic people crowded around the Apostolic Nuncio, and the Archbishops and Bishops and Priests and Religious, to return thanks to God amid public rejoicing for the victories achieved over heresy and the heretical enemy, those venerable men being driven into the woods and deserts and other hiding-places, or slain by the sword, or strangled at the gallows, or exiled from the kingdom, now none are seen but swarms of Ministers of Calvinism or Lutheranism or the thousand other Anglican heresies, and spies and executioners, and judges, thirsting for Catholic blood, and Puritan soldiers who have turned the religious houses into stables and the churches into cloacas. The sacred images of our Lord, or the Blessed Virgin, or the saints were first treated with every mockery, and then turned to profane purposes, or used as firing by the military. In every corner of the cities and towns some vulture or other was found lying in wait to seize upon persons or things dedicated to God. Then came the terrible scourge of pestilence which for several months laid waste the greater part of the island, Ulster alone being exempt from its ravages. The sword and plague were followed by famine such as hardly any nation from the beginning of the world had ever before endured. And how shall I recall the sending into exile, and banishments, and transportations, recurring every day since Cromwell landed upon our shores in 1649, and more cruel than death itself. At one time we see English ships laden with Catholic priests and people who are led off to the American islands and other parts to endure in the service of those heretics all the horrors of slavery, whilst at another time they bear away our countrymen to serve in the armies in Belgium or Spain. Those sold to the heretics in America, are treated by them more cruelly than the slaves under the Turks; nor is any attention paid to the youth or the decrepitude of age, to sex or rank, or sacerdotal orders or religious life, and with inhuman barbarity the wife is torn away from the husband, and the husband from the wife. Nothing is more painful than to witness the shipment of those exiles, the father separated from his child, brother from brother, sister from sister, relative from relative, friend from friend, spouse from spouse: and the closest ties of nature being sundered by the most heartless heretics the whole island resounds with cries of grief, property confiscated, those most dear led off to death or chains or prison, and the rest driven to exile or transportation. At one place we see the sons of noble families, the hope and consolation of their aged parents, youths delicately reared and carefully educated, who are not only robbed of every chance of their hereditary property, but even despoiled of their more valuable clothes, receiving tattered rags instead, and flogged with rods, and branded like sheep on their skin and flesh, and then driven among a crowd on board these infamous transportation ships : elsewhere we see respectable maidens trained in their father's house to piety and chastity and the love of religion, some of them of noble birth, and engaged to contract honourable marriage corresponding to their social rank, yet in one week are they deprived of their parents hanged on the nearest tree, and of their nearest relatives also put to death, despoiled moreover of their rich patrimony by the greed of heretical monsters, and now almost naked and piercing heaven with their shrieks they are dragged off to the ships : and again husbands and wives, one of their sons being killed in war and another executed on the scaffold, and the rest reduced to beggary or to a soldier's life in foreign lands, their whole family being thus destroyed or scattered, whilst themselves were hoping to be allowed by living according to the articles of surrender and paying the tributes exacted from them, to end their days in sadness in their own homes and holdings, are nevertheless with unparalleled violence driven forth without mercy, the wife thrown into prison in Ireland, and the husband sent off to slavery in the Anglo-American colonies : and saddest of all, amid such scenes of Puritan barbarity, was the grief of husbands and wives torn from each other's arms and clamouring to be allowed to die together whatever and wherever their lot might be. I have read in trustworthy letters addressed to Rome, that in this year 1654, there did not survive more than a sixth part of the population of Ireland, and from this sixth part are to be deducted 50,000 of our people who in this very year were transported to the American islands or to Belgium and Spain. With all nations and even with barbarians it is the usage to deal leniently with the remnant of a conquered people, but quite the reverse is the conduct of the most cruel Puritans of England, by whose orders the whole island after laying down arms is groaning in chains, the country dotted over with prisons and gallowses, savage inquisitors and heartless judges investigating into everything done by Catholics in the past war, and barbarously sentencing so many to death that a great part of the island is saturated with blood, and all this at the hands of most criminal rebels and regicides; and the whole kingdom is confiscated and partitioned among Cromwell's followers, a vile horde of robbers who are the very scum of society in England."

3. Before entering into particulars connected with this unparalleled slave trade, we may remark that the Island of Barbadoes was first seized on by a small band of English adventurers, in 1625. The richness of its produce soon attracted a large number of colonists, and its population still more rapidly increased, when the Parliament of England, in 1636, passed a law "authorising the sale of negroes and Indians for life. Ten years later, so large was the population of the island,

that its militia amounted to 10,000 infantry and 1,000 cavalry."* During the closing years of Charles's reign some traders, indeed, had stealthily endeavoured to carry on a slave trade in Ireland with English undertakers, but, after the triumph of the Puritan armies, the sale of the Irish as slaves was publicly authorised by the Government. Hence, the Irish bishops, having assembled at Clonmacnoise, on the 4th of December, 1649, published an address to the people of Ireland, warning them against placing any trust in the promises of the Puritans, whose aim, they say, it is "to root out the inhabitants, and plant this land with colonies to be brought hither out of England, as witness the number they have already sent hence for the tobacco islands, and put enemies in their places."†

4. The official documents, published by Mr. Prendergast, fully reveal to us the barbarous manner in which the natives were thus sold into captivity. "While the Government," he thus writes, "were employed in clearing the ground for the adventurers and soldiers, they had agents actively employed through Ireland seizing women, orphans, and the destitute, to be transported to Barbadoes and the English plantations in America. . . . . Just as the King of Spain sent over his agents to treat with the Government for the Irish swordsmen, the merchants of Bristol had agents treating with it for men, women, and girls, to be sent to the sugar plantations in the West Indies. The Commissioners for Ireland gave them orders upon the governors of garrisons to deliver to them prisoners of war;

---

* Poyer's *History of Barbadoes*, in Quarterly Review, i. 262.
† See Wadding MSS., Rome.

the keepers of gaols for offenders in custody; upon masters of workhouses for the destitute in their care, and gave directions to all in authority to seize those who had no visible means of livelihood, and deliver them to those agents of the Bristol sugar merchants, in execution of which latter direction Ireland must have exhibited scenes in every part like the slave hunts in Africa."*

A Government order, published on 4th March, 1655, states that, in the four preceding years, 6,400 Irish (men and women, boys and maidens) had been disposed of to the English slave dealers. It further details the course pursued by the men-catchers, viz., " to delude poor people into by-places, and thence they forced them on board their ships. The persons employed had so much a piece for all they so deluded, and, for the money sake, they were found to have enticed and forced women from their children, and husbands and children from their parents."†

5. A few instances will best illustrate the course thus pursued by the Puritans. On 14th of September, 1653, two English merchants, named Selleck and Leader, signed a contract with the Government Commissioners, by which a supply was granted to them of 250 women and 300 men " of the Irish nation, to be found within twenty miles of Cork, Youghal, Kinsale, Waterford, and Wexford." Roger Boyle, Lord Broghill (afterwards Earl of Orrery), deemed it unnecessary to take such trouble in visiting different parts of the kingdom, and undertook to supply the required number

* *Settlement*, p. 238.
† *Ibid*. p. 240.

from the county of Cork alone. Hence, on 23rd of October, 1653, he received an order, empowering him to search for and seize upon that number, "and no person, being once apprehended, was to be released but by special order, in writing, under the hand of Lord Broghill."*

Again, in January, 1654, the Governors of Carlow, Kilkenny, Clonmel, Wexford, Ross, and Waterford, had orders to arrest and deliver to three English merchants " all wanderers, men and women, and such other Irish within their precincts as should not prove they had such a settled course of industry as yielded them a means of their own to maintain them, all such children as were in hospitals or workhouses, all prisoners (men and women) to be transported to the West Indies."

In the month of November, 1655, all the Irish of the townland of Lackagh, county of Kildare, were seized on by the agents of Government. They were only forty-one in number, and of these four were hanged by sentence of court-martial, the remaining thirty-seven, including two priests, were handed over to Mr. Norton, a Bristol merchant, "to be sold as bond slaves to the sugar planters at the Barbadoes." In this batch of white slaves were Mr. and Mrs. Fitzgerald, of Lackagh, both of the noble house of Kildare, and both over eighty years of age. With them were the widow of their deceased son, and their son Maurice, and their daughters, Margerie, Bridget, and Mary. Again we find, on 8th December, 1655, a letter from the Commissioners to the Governor of Barbadoes, "advising

* *Ibid.*, p. 239.

him of the approach of a ship with a cargo of proprietors deprived of their lands, and seized for not transplanting. . . . . They add that amongst them were *three priests*, and the Commissioners particularly desire that these may be so employed as they may not return again where that sort of people are able to do much mischief, having so great an influence over the Popish Irish."*

As the Tories, from time to time, gave trouble to the new settlers and despoiled them of their ill-gotten goods, it was enacted, as a remedy, that wherever any such crime occurred four persons of the neighbourhood "of the Irish nation and Popish religion" were to be taken, and, after twenty-eight days, transported to the English plantations in America, if the criminals were not, in the meantime, made amenable, and further, all the "Irish inhabitants of the Popish religion" of the barony were to be transplanted, except such as might prove their constant good affection to the oppressors of their country.

It happened that, towards the close of 1655, some of the early Cromwellian adventurers were themselves entrapped and carried away to the Barbadoes. This occasioned a suspension for awhile of the Puritan slave trade. It was only a momentary calm, however, and, as Jamaica had, in that very year, been seized by the English, we find the men-catchers commissioned again, in 1656 and the following years, to pursue the remnant of the Irish Catholics. Thus, on the 3rd of May, 1656, the governors of the various prisons re-

* *Ibid.*, p. 161.

ceived orders to convey their prisoners to Carrickfergus, "to be there put on board such ship as should sail with the first opportunity for the Barbadoes." One aged priest, named Paul Cashin, arrested at his mission in Maryborough, was amongst those thus hurried off towards Carrickfergus. On the way he fell dangerously sick at Philipstown, and, a petition being sent in his name to the Commissioners to be allowed to remain, they replied, by an order of 27th August, 1656, allowing him sixpence per day during his sickness, which munificent sum "was to be continued to him in his travel thence to Carrickfergus, in order to his transportation to the Barbadoes."

In Scobell's *Acts and Ordinances*, there is an Act of Parliament passed in 1656, which, after stating that "the children, grandchildren, brothers, nephews, uncles, and next pretended heirs of the persons attainted, do remain in the provinces of Leinster, Ulster, and Munster, having little or no visible estates or subsistence," adds a command for all such persons "to transplant or be transported to the English plantations in America." We also find a commission, in 1658, to Sir Charles Coote (Lord President of Connaught) and Colonel Sadlier (Governor of Galway) to treat with a certain Stubbers and other merchants, about procuring a ship for 80 or 100 prisoners, "to sail with the first fair wind to the Indian Bridges (the usual landing-place in the Barbadoes), or other English plantations thereabouts in America."* This was only the first batch of those sentenced during the preceding assizes. Morison,

* *Order of Council Chamber, Dublin Castle,* 26th *Oct.*, 1658. Ibid., p. 64-5.

too, gives another instance. In 1657, a gentleman of Clare, named Daniel Connery, was sentenced to banishment by Colonel Henry Ingoldsby for harbouring a priest. The wife of the gentleman fell sick and died; and "three of his daughters, most beautiful girls, were transported to the West Indies, to an island called the Barbadoes; and there, if they are alive, they are in miserable slavery."*

7. The author of the *Description of Ireland in* 1654, observes that it was enmity to our holy faith that impelled the Puritans to this barbarity:—

"The heretics, at length, despairing of being ever able to alienate the Irish from the ancient faith, transport their children in shipsfull, for sale, to the Indian islands, that thus, forsooth, no remnant of the Irish race may survive, and none escape from the utter extermination of the nation."

And the same writer adds an instance of the sufferings to which the Irish slaves were subjected in these distant islands:—

" God alone knows the severe lot that awaits the Irish children in that slavery. We may form some idea of it from what happened to some others of our nation there last year, that is to say, in 1653. The heretics, seeing that matters were prospering with the Irish in the island of St. Christopher, and being excited partly by envy and partly by hatred of the Catholic religion, seized in one night and bound with chains, three hundred of the principal Irish that were there, and carried them off to a desert island, which was wholly destitute of all necessaries of life, that there they might inevit-

* *Threnodia*, printed in 1659, p. 287.

ably perish from cold and starvation. This was, alas! too sadly realised in all, excepting two, who, through despair, cast themselves into the sea, resolving to risk their lives rather on the waves than on the barren rocks. One of these soon perished, and the other reached the mainland, bearing the sad intelligence of the dreadful fate of his companions."

8. As in the preceding articles, so also in this, we may adduce the authority of the learned Archdeacon of Tuam :—

"They banished," he says, "to the remotest depths of India, crowds of old men and youths, great numbers of matrons and virgins, that the former might toil in hard slavery, and the latter support themselves by prostitution. Our enemies are more cruel than Ælius Adrianus himself; for, if he has justly been stigmatised as atrociously cruel for prohibiting, under penalty of death, any citizen of Jerusalem from coming within sight of his native walls, what foul stigma can adequately express the guilt of the monsters who banish men, not from the sight of one city alone, but from every part of their native land." (*Camb. Evers.*, vol. iii., p. 183.)

We have already seen how elsewhere he relates that "many priests were banished to the West Indies, where they were sold as slaves, and condemned to work in twisting tobacco and other slave labours."

A letter from F. Hartigan, S.J., from Paris, on the 30th of March, 1643, makes known to us that even at that date a vast number of Irish Catholics were scattered throughout the West Indian islands, driven thither, probably, by the confiscations and other hardships endured at home during the reigns of James I. and Charles I. "Five days ago," he says, "I received the petition of 25,000 Irish, whom the violence of persecution and the iniquity of the times have forced into exile, and to settle in St. Kitts and the neighbouring islands. Admiral Du Poenry, the French commander of that station, is the bearer and supporter of this petition of the Irish exiles, which prays that two or more Irish Jesuit Fathers may be sent to them, to take charge of their souls, as they are destitute of spiritual help." Fr. Hartegan volunteered his services, being skilled in the French, English, and Irish languages, "which are all used in those parts;" but no record is preserved of his being permitted to proceed thither.

As soon as the Puritans obtained the mastery in any of those remote islands, one of their first cares was to demolish every trace of Spanish or French piety, and to interdict every exercise of the Catholic religion. Thus it was when Jamaica fell into their hands in 1655: "conspicuous evidences were found of the care taken by its Spanish masters to establish in that island the symbols of their faith. Among these were two churches named the Red and White Cross, and an abbey, all of which were erected in the capital St. Jago de la Vega. But that destroying zeal which had made such havoc of our noble sanctuaries at home, and broken down all the carved work thereof with axes and hammers, was not likely to spare, and did not spare, the altars of Popish enemies abroad. These churches were among the first that fell a prey to the fury of Cromwell's army." (Anderson, *History of the Church of England in the Colonies*, ii., 74.) In St. Kitts, however, and several of the other West Indian islands, there were, besides the English settlements, other Catholic settlements or stations belonging to the French or Spaniards, and thus at times the suffering exiles were enabled stealthily to receive some spiritual succour. Fr. John Stritch, a Limerick Jesuit, landed in the French possessions at St. Kitts in the year 1650. He built a chapel at Sandy Point, in the French quarter, but pretty near the English settlement, so that the Irish could proceed thither. They hastened to welcome him as they would an angel from heaven, and they hesitated not to expose themselves to imminent danger of the lash or of death itself that they might sanctify their souls. In his report to the Superior of the Society, he states that his congregation there numbered about 3,000 souls. After a few months he proceeded to Montserrat, then wholly subject to the English, who would not suffer a priest to land. He, however, disguised himself as a merchant, and went thither under pretence of buying timber. When he got into the woods he made known his true character to some of the Irish exiles, and the news soon spread among the rest. In a secluded spot he celebrated Mass and administered the sacraments every morning, and then they cut down timber and carried it for their good Father, the better to confirm the delusion that he was a timber merchant. The natural features of the country favoured them in this, for there are deep gullies at intervals, whilst the mountains are richly clothed to the very summit with towering trees, and green savannahs are constantly met with in the midst of the woods. When he returned to St. Kitts he found that the Puritans had taken alarm, and that strict watch was

IRISH EXPORTED AS SLAVES. 339

kept to prevent the Irish from visiting the French settlements, and to force them to attend the Protestant service. Such difficulties, however, could not damp the ardour of the Irish faith. As sentinels guarded the passes, the exiles travelled by night through the woods and ravines, and, heedless of danger, assisted at the Holy Sacrifice. The French Superior of that mission could not conceal his admiration for their heroism, and he mentions in his letters one notable fact: " Among the Irishmen who usually came to Mass I remarked particularly two good old men, who, after making that difficult journey with incredible inconvenience, never failed to be first in our chapel, where they assisted at Mass, and fulfilled all their devotional exercises from the dawn of day till ten o'clock, with an attention and a fervour of spirit which filled me with rapture." The same writer tells us of some of the cruelties practised by the Puritan masters against those fervent Irish Catholics. Thus he mentions how a poor girl who refused to go to the Protestant church, was dragged thither by the hair and beaten without mercy. Again, on one night no fewer than 125 of the most fervent and influential among the Irish were seized, put on board a vessel and cast upon Crab Island, a desert place wholly unprovided with anything to sustain life. For some days they subsisted on the shell-fish cast upon the shore, till they signalled a Spanish vessel. The vessel, however, could not hold all, and thus some had to remain on the barren rocks without any hope of help. The vessel encountered many perils at sea, but a merciful Providence watched over it, and at length it landed safely its living freight of Irish exiles at Tortuga, or the

Tortoise Island, where they were well received by the French. Those that were left at Crab Island all perished. Fr. Stritch continued for twelve years to labour with apostolic zeal among our exiles in those Indian Islands. Among other things it is recorded of him that, being heartbroken at the tyranny to which his countrymen were subjected at St. Kitts, he contrived, in 1653, to gather together all the then surviving exiles of that island, and transferred them to the French settlement at Guadaloupe, where they were cordially welcomed by M. Houel the governor. The shipment, however, of our Irish people sold into slavery continued throughout the whole time of the Puritan rule; and the letter of Father Grace, already referred to, states that those who yet survived in 1666 were cruelly treated both temporally and spiritually: "The administration of the sacraments, and the giving of instruction, is wholly interdicted, nor can any priest visit them without risking his life."*

10. Another "Relatio" of the same islands made about the same time, reckons the population of Barbadoes at 40,000, of whom 8,000 were Irish; and it adds, regarding these Irish, that "they are sadly deprived of spiritual assistance; nevertheless, their constancy in the faith is wondrous and miraculous (*mira et miraculosa*), for they cling to it despite the oppressive

* A decree of the Provincial Synod of Tuam, held in January, 1660, is as follows:—"Intimetur S. Cong. de Prop. Fide necessitas missionis faciendæ pro exulibus Hibernis qui sunt in insulis Americæ, ex clero nationis nostræ qui sunt in partibus ultramarinis et quod alii ex eodem clero ad nos remittantur ad sustinendum onus curæ animarum, sub quo ultra vires laboramus in summa temporum calamitate."

exactions, and threats, and promises, and innumerable arts employed by the heretics to withdraw them from it." In another small island adjoining St. Kitts, the same narrative says, there were 600 Irish ; these stealthily sought to frequent the sacraments, and assist at the holy sacrifice in some of the French chapels, but "as often as they are discovered they receive the lash, and are fined by their English masters" (*mulctas et verbera patiuntur ab Anglis.*)

After the fall of Limerick, in 1692, an attempt was made to renew this Puritan traffic in Irish slaves. A letter of Fr. Garganet, the French Superior of the Jesuits in Martinique, written in 1699, petitions for some Irish priests for that mission, and the neighbouring islands, for, he adds, "every year shiploads of men, boys, and girls, partly crimped, partly carried off by main force for purposes of slave trade, are conveyed hither by the English from Ireland." In the course of years many of those Irish exiles became proprietors of the estates on which they laboured, and attained great wealth. The Patois still used by the natives in some of those West-Indian Islands is little better than a corrupt form of the Celtic language ; and in the churchyards no names are more frequent than the O'Neills and O'Reillys, and other names familiar in the last resting-places of our faithful people at home.

CHAPTER VIII.

THE OATH OF ABJURATION.

1. Attempt to force Catholics to take the Oath of Abjuration.—2. Form of that oath.—3. Penalties for not taking it.—4. Activity of clergy in opposing oath.—5. Puritans thirsting for confiscation.—6. Noble conduct of Catholics of Cork; all refuse the oath publicly.—7. Other districts equally faithful.

1. Father Richard Shelton, Superior of the Jesuits in Ireland, writing to the Sacred Congregation, on the 29th of April, 1658, conveyed the sad intelligence, that the persecution of Cromwell against the Irish Catholics was carried on with ever-increasing fury; two of the Jesuit fathers had lately been arrested, and were treated with great cruelty; especially, he adds, "every effort is now made to compel the Catholics, by exile, imprisonment, confiscation of goods, and other penalties, to take the sacrilegious oath of abjuration, but all in vain, for as yet there has not been even one to take it, with the exception of a stranger residing in our island, who had acquired large possessions, and being afraid of losing them, and at the same time being ashamed of the other Catholics, undertook a journey of more than 200 miles to present himself to one of Cromwell's commissaries."*

* In a note of the Sacred Congregation at this period, reference is

2. This oath, devised by Cromwell, condensed into a few formulas all the virulence of Puritanism against the Catholic tenets. It was as follows:

" I, *A. B.* abhor, detest, and abjure the authority of the Pope, as well in regard of the Church in general, as in regard of myself in particular. I condemn and anathematize the tenet that any reward is due to good works. I firmly believe and avow that no reverence is due to the Virgin Mary, or to any other saint in heaven; and that no petition or adoration can be addressed to them without idolatry. I assert that no worship or reverence is due to the sacrament of the Lord's Supper, or to the elements of bread and wine after consecration, by whomsoever that consecration may be made. I believe there is no purgatory, but that it is a Popish invention; so is also the tenet that the Pope can grant indulgences. I also firmly believe that neither the Pope, nor any other priest, can remit sins as the Papists rave. And all this I swear," &c.*

A simpler form of this oath of abjuration is given by F. Dominick de Rosario, from a work published in England, by William Berkley in 1653, as follows:

"I, *A. B.* do reject and abjure the supremacy of the Roman Pontiff, and assert that he has no jurisdiction over the Catholic Church in general, or myself in particular. I abjure the doctrine of transubstantiation, pur-

---

made to a Brief sent by the Holy Father to console the Catholics of Ireland, and animate them to endure with constancy the persecution to which they were exposed.

* Morison *Threnodia*, &c., p. 31; Ant. Bruodin, p, 95; De Burgo, p. 708.

gatory, and the worship of the crucifix, or other images. I abjure, moreover, the doctrine which teaches that salvation is to be procured by good works. This I swear without any gloss, equivocation, or mental reservation. So help me God."

This short form, however, was judged insufficient by some of the Independents, and the more detailed and more insulting abjuration of their religious tenets was exacted from the Irish Catholics.

3. It may be well, however, to place before the reader the Act of Parliament which commanded this oath to be taken by all Roman Catholics, and enacted the severest penalties against those who would refuse it:

"It is manifest (thus runs the preamble of the Act), that the number of Popish recusants has of late greatly increased in this republic owing to the negligence with which the laws are carried into execution against them, and that infinite dangers arise hence to disturb the public peace. . . . Wherefore, to check these evils, it is commanded by the authority of Parliament:

"That the grand juries will make a diligent inquiry after all persons who are suspected of Popery, and have attained the age of sixteen years; and all persons so accused will be obliged to present themselves at the next assizes, or at the quarter sessions, to there make, and subscribe to, the oath of abjuration as follows:

"I, *A. B.* do abjure and renounce the primacy of the Pope, and all his pretended authority over the Church in general, and over myself in particular, &c.

"It is commanded that all the justices of peace will send four times every year to each parish clerk to have a list of all persons suspected of being Popish recusants, who have attained their sixteenth year, and are consequently obliged to take the oath of abjuration. And that on the presentation of this list, each justiciary shall send his orders to the bailiffs to summon those whose names are thus presented, to appear personally before the judges at the next sessions. And if such persons do not appear at the next sessions to subscribe the oath, it shall be proclaimed in public sessions that such persons do appear at the following sessions. And if they do not then appear to take and subscribe to the oath of abjuration, they will be judged to be Popish recusants, and subjected to all the penalties that may be incurred as such.

"That on the suspicion which any justice of the peace may have, he may summon the person whom he so suspects to appear at the next sessions and subscribe to the oath of abjuration, under penalty of £100. And should such person refuse to submit to the pecuniary fine thus imposed on him, he may be placed in custody until the time of sessions; and should he then refuse to take and subscribe to the said oath, he shall be judged to be a Popish recusant as above.

"The Lord Protector is empowered to seize by order of the Court of Exchequer, and take possession of, for the necessities of the republic, two-thirds of all the goods, and chattels, and property whatsoever, belonging to persons so convicted each time that they thus refuse to subscribe to the said oath.

"That before the expiration of the next term following on such conviction, it shall be notified to the Court of Exchequer to the effect that the said court may give its order for the seizure of the two-thirds.

"Should a person convicted as above, present himself before either the judges of assize, or the barons of Exchequer to take and subscribe to the oath of abjuration, he shall be exempted from all future penalties: but should such person die and leave an heir of sixteen years of age, said heir will be immediately cited to appear in judgment, and be proceeded with as above.

"Should the said heir not have attained his sixteenth year, his guardians will receive all his property, provided they be such persons as the barons of the Exchequer approve of, for such guardianship, and that they make a return each year of the profits, and surplus they receive, and that they pay such sums to the said heir on his attaining his sixteenth year, should he take and subscribe to the oath of abjuration, and otherwise to the exchequer, which will take care, moreover, to seize on two-thirds of all his remaining property.

"The same order is to hold good in regard of all money or property bequeathed by said persons to their wives or children, or any other person whatsoever.

"Should a person, of whatsoever condition he may be, contract marriage with one whom he knows to be a Popish recusant, said person will himself be held as such, and subject to all the penalties as above, till such time as he shall take and subscribe to the oath of abjuration.

"That no tribunal whatsoever can recall to itself this charge directed against the Popish recusants, or introduce any alteration for any motive whatsoever; but all shall remain in full vigour until such persons will have taken the prescribed oath.

"That should any person receive any real or personal

property from a Popish recusant, to retain it for him by secret compact, and should he neglect to make it known within three months from its being delivered to him, he shall be fined one-third of his own goods or property, of which one-half will be given to the Lord Protector, and the remaining half to him who gave the information on the matter.

"Each justice of the peace, who shall neglect his duty in fully carrying out this order, will be fined £20; each parish clerk will be fined for a like neglect £10; each registrar of assizes, for each person that he omits in the registry, £20; and of all these fines, one-half will be distributed to the poor of the parish, the other half to the accuser.

"Should the property of any Popish recusant pass into the possession of one known to be a Protestant, such Protestant will present an attestation to that effect at the quarter sessions, to be signed by a majority of the judges, to the effect that such a person of such a condition and sex is truly what he professes to be, and he may then hold such property with exemptions from all taxes.

"That no person once condemned as above, be admitted to take the oath without producing two unexceptionable witnesses to swear that within six months he had been often present on Sunday in some approved Christian assembly, and that he heard the word of God as it was preached there.

"That should anyone, after taking the said oath, relapse, he shall be again subjected to all the preceding penalties, till such time as he again subscribes to the oath.

"That no subject of this republic, with the exception of the servants of an ambassador or minister, be allowed to hear Mass at any hour whatsoever, either in their houses or in any other place, under penalty of £100 fine and six months' imprisonment, half of which fine will be given to the Lord Protector, and the other half to the informer."

Thus the penalty enacted against all who should refuse to take this oath was the confiscation of two-thirds of all their goods, which was to be repeated each time that they should prove refractory. It was expected that the Catholic gentry, already reduced to poverty by continued exactions, would be terrified into compliance by the dread of absolute penury and utter ruin which now impended over them. As to the poorer class another penalty remained, forsooth slavery in the Barbadoes. In every town commissaries and officers were specially deputed to receive this oath, and these received instructions from Government to commence with such persons as would probably assent to the oath, and to proceed in the matter with the greatest energy.

4. At this moment of peril for the faith of our people, the Catholic clergy were everywhere to be seen abandoning their hiding-places to encourage their flocks, they fearlessly went around from house to house, admonishing the rich to despise their transitory possessions, when an eternal inheritance was at stake, and reminding the poor that God's providence would not abandon them, and that in his own good time God would repay an hundredfold all their sufferings.*

* MS. Relatio, &c. "Tunc videre erat e clero latebris exeuntes, cursare per Catholicorum domos," &c.

"These exhortations were not made in vain (we quote the words of a contemporary narrative), and the innate constancy of the whole nation in the Catholic faith, shone forth with such splendour, that a like instance of national constancy can nowhere be found in history: all, animated with the spirit of faith, declared that they were ready to endure extreme torture rather than obey the impious edict. Even the most wealthy betrayed no apprehensions, and they avowed that of all the penal enactments, this was the most grateful to them; for in the others some secondary motive was often assigned, but here the only and express motive was hatred to the Catholic faith, for which it would be to them a matter of joy to sacrifice whatsoever they possessed."

5. For once the heretics were found to second the efforts of the Catholic clergy. They yearned for new confiscations, and already had marked out for themselves the lands now possessed in Connaught by the transplanted Irish gentry. The better to secure their prey, they assumed the sheep's clothing, and going round amongst the Catholics, they declared that the act of parliament was most unjust, that no one should interfere with their conscientious convictions, that they admired the steadfastness of the Catholics in adhering to principle, despite every enactment, and this heroic constancy of the nation had won for it an immortal fame throughout the kingdoms of Europe.* The Catholics were not deceived by these vain appearances, but,

Ibid. " Videres lupos vulpes imitantes ut certius prædentur et devorent,"&c.

nevertheless, they clung unflinchingly to their holy resolve.

6. The citizens of Cork had already distinguished themselves by their constancy in the Catholic faith; when summoned to take the impious oath their laurels were multiplied tenfold.

To the city of Cork all the Catholics of the surrounding territory were ordered to repair on a stated day to have the new oath proposed to them; the penalty of imprisonment and confiscation of all their goods was enacted for all above fifteen years of age who should neglect to attend. On the appointed day between five and six thousand Catholics entered the city walls; a few only absented themselves, anxious to await the result. According to the heretical custom of holding the assizes in the cherished sanctuaries of the Catholics, the magistrates took their seats in *Christ's Church*—a happy omen that even the material edifice should be dedicated to Him whose faith was now so nobly to be confessed.

All were arranged in processional order, that the oath might be more easily administered individually to each of them. In the foremost ranks was a young man who entered the church with a light step, and whose looks beamed with joy. The clerk received immediate orders to administer to him for the first the oath, for the magistrates saw in his joyous countenance a readiness, as they imagined, to assent to their desires. The young man requested that the oath should be translated into Irish, for he feared lest some of those around him, not understanding the English language, might inadvertently take the oath. A crier at once read it aloud in

Irish, so that all within the church might hear. "And what is the penalty," he then asked, "for those who refuse the oath?" "The loss of two-thirds of their goods," was the magistrate's reply. "Well, then," added he, smiling, "all that I possess is six pounds: take four of them; with the two that remain, and the blessing of God, myself and my family will subsist; I reject your oath."

An aged husbandman that stood by his side, filled with admiration, cried out aloud, "Brave fellow, reject the oath." The words were caught up from rank to rank till the church and the street without rang with the echo, "*Reject the oath, the impious oath.*" For half an hour these words and the exclamation, "O God, look down on us;" "O Mary, Mother of God, assist us," could alone be heard. The magistrates, as though a thunderclap had rent the heavens, were struck mute with terror; then, rising from their seats, they commanded the assembled multitude to disperse, and every one of them, under pain of death, to depart from the city within an hour. Thus, concludes the contemporary narrative, the glorious confessors of Christ went forth with joy, praising God for the mercy He had shown to them.

7. In other districts similar scenes of Catholic constancy were witnessed, and none could be found to assent to the impious oath, or barter for the momentary enjoyment of their perishable goods the priceless treasure of their faith.

CHAPTER IX.

Constancy of the Irish in the Faith.

1. Misery of Ireland in comparison to other countries; progress, education, trade impeded in Ireland.—2. No penalty could shake the Catholic faith.—3. Prayer and fasting of the people.—4. Only 500,000 Catholics remaining in Ireland.—5. Statistics at various times; Sir William Petty's estimate and Lord Orrery's; Dr. Plunket's.—6. Extract from Jesuit narrative.

1. THE author of *Cambrensis Eversus* well contrasts the condition of the Irish nation with that of other countries at the close of this sad period:—

"The happiness of the other nations of Europe has often excited our envy. They have peace on every side, and dwell every one under his own vine and fig-tree, but we are expelled from our home and country; others overflow with abundance of all things, we are emaciated by want; the foreigner is naturalised amongst us, the natives are made aliens. In foreign cities majestic piles of new buildings are every day towering to the skies, with us the foundations of not a single house are laid, while the old are heaps of crumbling ruins, their roofs open to the rains, and their walls rent, or mere shells and shapeless masses.

"In other countries temples are zealously decorated, with us they are either levelled to the ground or roofless, or desecrated by tribunals which condemn men to death, or by similar sacrilegious uses.

"The children of foreigners receive a learned education, which is contraband and penal in our country. With them the clergy are honoured, with us they are either in dungeons or forests, in bogs or caverns. The universal law of the Christian world has exempted from slavery all who profess the Christian religion; but your Irish subjects are torn from the arms of their wives and children by civic vultures, and transported and sold as slaves in India. Thus are the children of the Irish made a prey, and their wives carried off, and their cities destroyed, and their holy things profaned, and themselves made a reproach to the nations. . . . There is no species of injury which the enemies have not inflicted on the Irish, no virulence which they have not disgorged, no torture which they have not employed."*

2. It would, indeed, be difficult to find in history a parallel for that ever-redoubled cruelty which the Puritans displayed. Yet it was impossible to weaken the innate attachment of the Roman Catholics to their holy religion. Countless was the number of those who perished by the sword of the persecutor or on the scaffold, yet the survivors declared themselves ready to risk the same torments rather than renounce the Catholic faith. When they were offered the enjoyment of their possessions, should they embrace the new creed, all, as in Cork, went forth from their homes, embracing

* Nullæ sunt nocendi artes quas in Hibernos inimici non exercuerunt nullum virus quod non effuderunt; nullum tormentum quod non intentarunt, p. 61.

poverty, and cold, and nakedness, in preference to prosperity with the wicked; when their lives were offered to them if they only delivered up their priests to the mercy of the enemy, they chose to be butchered with the martyrs of God rather than live with the impious; when, as we have just seen, the oath of abjuration was commanded, under penalty of the loss of the little goods that yet remained to them, they, with one accord, resolved to cling to the cross of Christ, and reject the proffered boon. As a true Christian people, they looked upon all their sufferings as chastisements from the hands of God, and their chief care was, by penitential deeds, to avert his indignation.

3. One instance is especially recorded in the "Description of Ireland in 1654:"—*

" Throughout the entire kingdom prayers and fasting were ordered, the priest in each district exhorting the people to appease the anger of God by penitential deeds. With such exactness was this order obeyed that there was not one Catholic throughout the entire kingdom who did not fast for three days on bread and water, and even the little children of four, or perhaps only three years, most rigorously observed that fast; moreover, all that had attained the proper age were consoled with the holy Sacraments of Confession and the Eucharist. No sooner did this piety of the people become known than, like oil cast upon the fire, the fury of the heretics was rekindled threefold, and, like hungry wolves, they now breathe nothing but slaughter, and threaten to pursue, with still more atrocious violence, the children of Christ."

* Status, &c., 1654.

4. Thus, as often in the ways of God, the immediate result of the piety of our people seemed to be only a redoubling of the persecutor's rage, and yet these prayers were not breathed in vain: "a remnant remained in Israel;" all the power and ingenuity of the enemy could not root out the tree of faith, and the 500,000 Catholics that then survived in Ireland were in less than two hundred years swelled to more than eight millions.

Father Read (or Redanus), writing in 1651, even then eulogised their immovable attachment to the faith, and predicted that heresy would rage in vain against the time-honoured Church of our island:—"The Puritans," he says, "have essayed to achieve what Henry the Eighth, and Elizabeth, and James attempted in vain; what neither a hundred years of persecution nor the thousand arts of Protestants could effect. Hence, they destroy our altars, statues, and paintings; our churches are made stables for their horses; our bells are turned into cannon; our baptisteries are made receptacles of filth; the Catholics are expelled from their lands, and homes, and country; unheard-of torments are employed against our martyrs; all this, however, only serves to render more illustrious the unflinching firmness of the Irish in the faith—as the rock remains unmoved amidst the foaming waves." And he adds: "Certain it is that in a hundred years the Irish coast has not been so lashed by the waves of the raging ocean that surrounds it as the faith of its people has been assailed by the storms of persecution and the fury of the English and Scotch heretics."*

* *Comin. Macchab.* (Lyons, 1651), p. 31.

5. Sir William Petty, writing in 1672,* states that the population of Ireland, in 1641, was 1,466,000, the Catholics being to Protestants as *eleven to two*. After the devastation of the country by the Puritans the population could not be accurately determined, yet the same writer (page 29) estimates the proportion of Catholics to Protestants as *eight to one*. Lord Orrery, writing to the Duke of Ormond, February 26th, 1662, says :—" It is high time to purge the towns of the Papists, as, in most of them, there are three Papists to one Protestant."

At the same time, in the rural districts, the Catholics were as fifteen to one. Dr. Plunket, in some of his letters, sets forth the proportion of Catholics to Protestants throughout Ireland as eleven to one, but he subsequently adds that the proportion was smaller in the northern counties. It cannot, of course, be pretended that these calculations were accurate, for, owing to the state of the country, it must have been impossible to learn the precise number of the Catholic inhabitants in the rural districts. One thing, however, they sufficiently prove, that the persecutors had not attained the desired end, and that, with the Irish race, the Catholic religion was still firmly rooted in Ireland. Sir William Petty describes as follows the religion of our country at this period :—" *All the Irish are Catholics; the Scotch colonists are Presbyterians; the English are one-half Protestant, the other half Independents, Anabaptists, Quakers, and other dissenters.*"

6. We have already often had occasion to refer to a

* *Political Anatomy*, &c., p. 13.

manuscript narrative of the Jesuit Mission in Ireland, written about the year 1655. From it we extract the following record of the devotedness of the surviving natives in enduring every suffering rather than abandon the Catholic faith :—

"Although heresy and tyranny, in the fulness of its pride, strove by every sacrifice and cruelty to extirpate this people, and wished that there should be *no smith in Israel*,[*] that thus the natives might be either overwhelmed in ignorance, or compelled to whet their arms in the forges of the Philistines, nevertheless the Irish, despising every danger, choose rather to send their children to distant lands in search of learning, than that they should enjoy at home domestic ease under heretical masters, imperilling their faith. So tenaciously and indomitably has the whole nation clung to the Catholic faith in its full integrity and purity, that, in a thousand Irishmen, scarcely one can be found who is not thoroughly devoted to the Holy See, and even the heretics, who came to Ireland from other countries, when they have lived there for a little while, and become accustomed to the genius of the people, gradually detest heresy and embrace the Catholic religion."

It was the old story of Irish plantations. The planters were absorbed by the natives, and, thirty years later, the sons of many of the Cromwellian settlers were found to be Roman Catholics and to speak nothing but Irish.

---

[*] Cambrensis Eversus writes, in 1662, almost in the same strain. "They have drawn their precedent from the policy of the Philistines, who, *after banishing all smiths* from the land, fell upon the Israelites unarmed," &c. *Edit. Dublin*, p. 23.

CHAPTER X.

DECAY OF THE PURITAN COLONISTS.

1.—Protestant colonies never prosper in Ireland; they pillage and seize on the country, but, visited by the hand of God, they fall away; contemporary testimony; faith deeply rooted in Ireland.— 2. Diseases and afflictions with which the invaders were scourged.

1. THAT Protestant colonists have never been able to secure a permanent hereditary succession in Ireland is a matter of notoriety. As regards the Puritan hordes that rushed over to seize on the devastated country, we shall merely cite an extract from the manuscript narrative just now referred to :—*

"The English Parliamentarians, in the beginning of the war, inflated with their own power and strength, did not hesitate to parcel out Ireland for sale to the London merchants and other heretics throughout England. The whole kingdom was thus divided, as if by agrarian law, into geometrical portions, a certain price being fixed for each farm. Each one purchased for himself some vast territory, subdividing it at a higher price to others.

"New colonists thus flocked to Ireland in countless numbers †—artizans, merchants, soldiers, and others, numbering more than 200,000. To consummate the

* Relatio rerum quarumdam, etc.
† "Ingens colluvies."

insolence of their pride, they already prepared ships, with chains and cords, and more than 30,000 iron manacles are said to have been made, to transfer the Irish slaves (it was thus they designated our free and innocent people) to the Indian Islands to cultivate the tobacco plant, and they were all persuaded that the old inhabitants being expelled, they had nothing to do but to settle down at their ease and enjoy their estates.

"But behold, the hand of the Lord struck these persecutors, I might say, with Egyptian plagues. They were not, as yet, three months in Ireland, when most fœtid vermin crawled forth from their bodies in such swarms that their hair, and beard, and garments, were covered with them, so that they could not appear in public through shame, nor could they anywhere find rest; and, what increased the wonder, though their beds and rooms were filled with this pest, yet the contagion did not spread to the neighbouring Irish, nor did it even touch the Irish servants of those who were infected with it, not one of whom is known to have suffered from this disease. It was confined to the strangers alone, and by that disease, and in other ways, God so humbled their pride that, from 1641 to 1650, more than 180,000 English, in various parts of Ireland, were carried away, not so much slain in war as destroyed by this Herodian disease and other plagues. And though the Puritans have now nearly all Ireland in their own hands, still we are confident that they will not last, nor strike deep roots,* but when our offended

* "Persuasum habemus eos non fore diuturnos, nec radices altas acturos."

God will have, through them, scourged us for our iniquities, the earth shall, in the words of scripture, vomit them forth, and, like their predecessors, they too will fall away.

"For it is observed and confirmed by experience that, since the beginning of the Anglican schism, all the heretics that went from England to inhabit Ireland, though they were, by rapine and exactions, raised on a sudden to immense wealth and the highest titles, yet, like snow at sunrise, they melted gradually away, and, as smoke and vapour, they quickly disappeared. Not that this is to be imputed to the English nation, whose natural disposition and innate uprightness, were they not infected with heresy, would be admired and loved by all, but in these facts we recognise the special punishment of God for heresy, and the special protection of St. Patrick for our island, who, as he expelled all serpents from our shores, so that none can, to the present day subsist there, so did he obtain for us this blessing from God, that the Catholic religion, being once planted in Ireland, it should never be infected by the poisonous breath of heresy. The Catholic religion has certainly continued untainted for twelve hundred years and more in our island, so that, from the blessing already received, through the intercession of our holy Patron, we have reason to hope for the future blessing, and the present firmness of the nation, in the faith of Christ, is a pledge of its future constancy."

2. Whilst the war continued, nothing is more striking in the letters of the Cromwellian officers than their clamour for fresh troops, and complaints at the number of their men who, every day, succumbed to sickness.

Even when the last strongholds had surrendered, the same doleful tale continued. Thus Colonel Jones, one of the Parliamentary Commissioners for Ireland writes, in the year 1653, to Mr. Morgan Lloyd, a sympathising, independent friend:—" God is pleased to hold forth some tokens of His displeasure. The sickness rages in Galway and is spread over all that province. It fearfully broke out at Cashel, a few days since, the people being taken suddenly with madness, whereof they die instantly. Twenty died in that manner in three days in that little town. The sickness is in Dublin and country about, but not so violent as in other places, but few escape that have it. Mr. Richardson, our auditor, sometime a member of All Hallowes Church, came home with us on Monday night, and the next day his wife, his maid, and two of his children were visited. I desire, in behalf of the servants of God here, that our fellow-members with you do earnestly seek the Lord on our behalf, that His mind may be revealed unto us in these His reproofs, and that the Lord may deliver such of his servants as are now cast into the furnace of affliction." (Appendix to *Aphorismical Discovery*, vol. iii., p. 372.)

There are few facts in history more striking than this decay of the Puritan colonists. It is only, indeed, by some such act of Divine vengeance that we could explain how our country was preserved from their poisonous infection. The fact, moreover, is confirmed by the contemporary, the Archdeacon of Tuam, whose numbers, however, are less than those given in the passage cited above, as he speaks only of the *English and Scotch soldiers*. " Charles Coote," he writes, " suffered the just punishment of his most atrocious cruelty. He was mortally wounded by some unknown hand, and thus, like another Julian the apostate, appears to have fallen under a judgment sent down on him by God himself. In their own printed account, the English confess that of the 60,000 English and Scotch soldiers sent over to Ireland, the great majority were carried off by unknown and horrible distempers, in such heaps that the cemeteries of Dublin, Drogheda, and Cork could not contain them, and pits were dug in the fields, outside the walls, to bury them. This was the just punishment for those torrents of innocent blood so savagely shed, when the victims, after surrendering, on the promise of life, were first stripped naked and then treacherously massacred." (Vol. iii., p. 101.)

PART THE THIRD.

INDIVIDUAL INSTANCES OF THE PERSECUTION OF
THE CATHOLICS.

CHAPTER I.

1. Sufferings of D. Delany, P.P. of Arklow.—2. Various instances of cruelty in the North, in Meath, Wicklow, and Kildare; death of Donnchadh O'Conaigh at Wicklow.—3. Roche Mac Geoghegan, Bishop of Kildare.—4. Sufferings and constancy of Peter O'Higgins.—5. Of Albert O'Brien, Bishop of Emly—6. Death of FF. Bernard and Laurence O'Ferall.—7. Of Thaddeus Moriarty and others.—8. Of A. Cahill.—9. Martyrdom of John O'Cullen.— 10. Account of Anselm Ball and his labours in Dublin.—11. Of Bonaventure Carew.

1. WE have already in the preceding pages given instances of the excessive cruelty with which the Puritan persecutors raged against the Irish Catholics. There are, however, many others which deserve a special commemoration. We do not, indeed, propose to ourselves to enumerate all who, by their heroic sufferings, attained the martyr's crown,* but we shall endeavour

* We here have to protest, that when calling any of our countrymen martyrs, we wish to conform most strictly to the decrees of Urban VIII. and Benedict XIV. We do not use the word in its

to cull from contemporary writers sufficient examples to enable the reader to form a more complete idea of the worse than pagan persecution to which our country was subjected at the period of which we treat.

Daniel Delany.—This worthy priest had charge of the parish of Arklow; and Gorey was the theatre of his martyrdom. Dr. John Lynch, writing in 1662, thus describes his heroic death : " The enemy came by surprise on Daniel Delany, parish priest of Arklow, and savagely massacred, before his eyes, his servant named Walsh, who was flying for his life with a packet of the sacred vessels and ornaments; but the priest himself being a powerful man, drew his sword, and defended himself so well against the attack, that he compelled his assailants to promise him his life if he delivered up his sword. So far, however, from keeping their solemn promise, they immediately stripped the venerable man naked, and tied him to a horse's tail ; the rider goaded his horse to full speed along a road covered over with brambles and thickets, and rough with frost and frozen snow, and dragged the priest to the town of Gorey. There the savage commander of those hunters condemned him to death in violation of the solemn promise. He was covered over with blood, his sides torn, and his whole frame exhausted; he was, nevertheless, delivered up to a guard of soldiers who were to watch in turn during the night. While he lay there naked, sleepless, frozen with cold, and livid with bruises, his guards

official sense, as if the Church had spoken in the cases referred to; we leave the final decision of all the cases of sufferings which we mention, or have mentioned, to the infallible judgment of the Church.

amused themselves with twisting and plucking his long beard with a cane, and cruelly beating his sides with cudgels; but these excruciating tortures could extort no other answer than that he would bear his sufferings more patiently as it seemed to afford them some pleasure. Next day he was three different times hanged to the bough of a tree, and three times let down to the ground to protract the agony of his torture; but he was strangled with a rope at last, and thus ended his life of suffering to reign triumphant in heaven." (*Cambr. Evers.*, vol. iii., pp. 182-3.)

2. Before taking leave of the learned Archdeacon of Tuam, we give one more extract from his invaluable work, in which he details some scenes of Puritan barbarity, and especially the martyrdom of the aged Donatus, or Donnchadh O'Conaigh:—

"Before the slightest disturbance had appeared in Ards (a district of Ulster), Hamilton, governor of the district, ordered all his dependents and farmers to retire and shut themselves up in his castle, that they might save themselves from the impending fury of their enemies. The poor victims rapidly flocked thither from all quarters, never suspecting the honour of their master; but when they were all locked up in a barn the brand was flung on the roof, and all perished in the flames.

" Charles Coote, a most blood-thirsty monster, perpetrated horrible massacres in several parts of Meath and Leinster. In the village of Munenasrule, about a mile from the town of Wicklow, he put the muzzle of a horse-pistol into the mouth of a beggar who asked alms, and then ordering the poor creature to blow into the barrel, he fired the bullets into his throat, and murdered him in sport.

"Francis More, son of Viscount Mellifont, committed a similar atrocity in 1641, on one Thomas Philips, in the village of Balrudery.* At Blackhall, in the county of Kildare, he committed a horrible massacre of old men, women, and children, and transfixed the little infants on their mothers' breasts with his swords and lances. Having spent a night with some of his officers in the house of a noble lady whose husband was absent, he was treated with splendid hospitality and costly presents; but when the lady followed him to the door to bid him adieu on his departure, he ordered a rope to be thrown around her neck, and hanged her before her own door.

"Donnchadh O'Conaigh, aged sixty years, had the soles of his feet smeared with grease, and burned at a fire in the camp at Wicklow, by order of Colonel Crawford. The noble old man survived the torture only one day." (*Camb. Evers.* loc. sit., pp. 91-95.)

3. During the first years of the Confederation, Roche Mac Geoghegan, Bishop of Kildare, was privileged to suffer a great deal for the Faith. Born about the year 1580, he at baptism was called Ross, after his father, who was the chief of the sept of the MacGeoghegans of Moycashel or Kinelfiacha. His mother, a lady of great piety and virtue, was daughter of Dempsey, Viscount of Glenmalure, and Lynch remarks that the

---

*An act of the same kind was committed in the chapel of Castlecomer, in 1798, by a yeoman officer, who afterwards died devoured by vermin in the house now occupied by the National Bank, Kilkenny.

birth of the future Bishop of Kildare took place in the ancestral mansion of the Dempseys at Clunagoon, and was accompanied with many presages of future sanctity. Whilst he pursued his studies in the Irish College at Lisbon, his father died, and he was summoned home to administer the paternal estate. He chose, however, to proceed to the University of Coimbra to perfect himself in sacred science, and whilst there enrolled himself in the religious Order of St. Dominick, in which he received the name of *Rocchus de Sancta Cruce*. He made his novitiate in the convent known as La Penna de Francia, and subsequently devoted himself for eight years to study and to the exercises of the religious life at Salamanca. The General of the Dominicans was at this time desirous to revive the spirit of the Order in Ireland, and Roche was selected for that important mission. At the death of Elizabeth, the Order was well-nigh extinct in Ireland, only four religious surviving in that once most flourishing province. Others, indeed, returned from the Continent during the reign of James the First, but they seldom ventured to lead a community life, and they devoted themselves to assist, as best they could, the secular clergy scattered through the various dioceses. The Dominican Father Daniel Credegan appears to have been the only one who throughout all this period kept alive the spark of religious observance which was to be fanned into a flame by Fr. Mac Geoghegan's zeal. He rented a small house in Galway, and leading a retired life kept strictly the rules of his Order. He was subsequently, during the reign of Charles the First, for a time Provincial of the Order, and lived to a great old age. For several years before his death he was quite blind, but nevertheless, continued to administer the sacrament of penance to those who flocked to him from all parts. He died in Sligo during the Cromwellian usurpation. Fr. MacGeoghegan in a short time established several houses of the Order in different parts of the country, and founded a novitiate at Orlare, in the barony of Costellagh, county Mayo. He was a model to all the brethren in the observance of the Rule, being earnest in self-discipline and fasting, and devoting several hours each day to solitary meditation and prayer. These religious exercises gave offence to some individuals who would rather choose to lead a life of dissipation and distraction. The Government was informed that he was an emissary from Rome, and was engaged in introducing usages and observances unknown in Ireland. His name was accordingly set in the *Hue and Cry*, and Captain Lyons was sent to Mayo to ensure his arrest. He contrived to evade pursuit, however, and, under the protection of powerful relatives, continued in Dublin itself to labour assiduously for the salvation of souls. Through his private conferences, Sir Edward Herbert, baronet, and member of the Privy Council in Ireland, and all his family, were converted to the Catholic Faith. Sir Arthur Blundell, vice-treasurer, also wished to confer with him, and declared himself convinced that it was only in the Catholic Church there was hope for salvation, and on his death-bed received at Fr. Mac Geoghegan's hands the last sacraments, and the consolations of religion. When this became known to the Government the writ for his arrest was a second time issued, but he escaped from Dublin in disguise, and sought safety in the West. About this time great crowds began to flock to the religious pilgrimage at the Holy Well of St. Brigid, in the county of Roscommon, and it was said that many miracles were daily performed there.* Fr. Mac Geoghegan also hastened thither, and Judge Gosport happening to be present at one of his instructions, resigned his office, and with it his salary of £400 a year, and was received into the Church. Another of his converts was his own relation, Richard Duinn, or O'Doyne, son of the Lord of Duharegan, who being sent to pursue his studies in England, attained the highest honours in Cambridge, but lost the faith. Returning to Ireland he was promoted to the Provostship of Trinity College, Dublin; but moved by the fervent exhortations of Fr. Mac Geoghegan, renounced that dignity, and was reconciled to the Church. The Protestant Vicar-General of Kildare, Thadeus O'Donellan, was also led by Fr. Mac Geoghegan to the true Church, and many others, among whom was the Lady Elizabeth Glaney, heiress of the Barony of Rosenolch, in the county Leitrim. A third time his arrest was ordered by the Government, and it was declared an act of felony to harbour him, and a reward of £200 was offered for his capture. Fearing the imminent dangers that now threatened his friends, he resigned the office of Provincial, and proceeding to Belgium, laboured with success in the erection of a convent of the Order for Irish students at Louvain. Promoted to the See of Kildare in 1629, he received the episcopal consecration at the hands of the Arch-

* "Maximus utriusque sexus concursus eo fiebat quod creberrim miracula ibi patrata fuerint." Lynch, MS. History.

bishop of Mechlin. It is related that at this time there were in the whole diocese of Kildare only three native priests, so completely had the higher schools been swept away, and so beset with difficulties was the preparation of the youth of Leinster for the sacred ministry. In a few years, however, through his exertions, the schools were revived, and a numerous clergy, second to none in the kingdom for learning and piety, sprung up to minister to that faithful flock. Throughout his episcopate he was repeatedly subjected to persecution at the hands of the heretics, and was forced to fly from place to place, concealing himself from his pursuers. He added many deeds of voluntary self-denial to these hardships, frequently sleeping on the bare ground and otherwise mortifying himself. The author of the *Aphorismical Discovery* reckons Peter Walsh, the notorious promoter of the Remonstrance, among the special enemies of our prelate: "You informed the Protestant State of Dublin, in a time of persecution, against an apostolic prelate, a true child of Dominic's Order, Roche MacGeoghegan, Bishop of Kildare, saying that he was not Kildare's, but Tyrone's Bishop, to exasperate the State against the holy prelate, which cost him many a night's wail" (vol. i., p. 276). Dr. MacGeoghegan sold or pledged everything most precious that he possessed that he might have wherewith to relieve the distress of the poor, and it was his custom in the town of Kildare to distribute food and other alms with his own hands. A choice library which he had collected was burnt by the heretics, and in the conflagration perished the *MS. History of a Hundred Years*, written by Rev. John Copinger, of Cork, in which the sufferings of Ireland for the faith from the beginning of the Reformation period were faithfully recorded. He restored and reconsecrated the ancient cathedral of Kildare, and performed there the sacred ceremonies of religion with solemn pomp. He died at Kilbeggan, after a lingering illness, in 1644, and his remains were, with all due civil and religious honour, interred in his cathedral. Lynch adds that by his will he bequeathed to the poor the price of three horses, all the earthly wealth of which he was possessed.

I have dwelt on these details of this illustrious bishop's life, as he was mainly instrumental in restoring in our country the Order of St. Dominick, which at this period shed lustre on the Irish Church by the heroism of its martyrs.

4. Fr. Peter O'Higgins was one of those martyrs of the Order of St. Dominick, and in 1641 was led to the scaffold, for the Catholic faith, in the court yard of Dublin Castle. We will allow Fr. Dominick O'Daly to describe the scene of his suffering: " This pious and eloquent man," thus writes O'Daly, in 1655, " was arrested and brought before the Lords Justices of Ireland, on a charge of endeavouring to seduce the Protestants from their religion. When his accusers failed to sustain any capital charge against him, the men in power sent to inform him, that if he abandoned his faith he might expect many and great privileges; but all depended on his embracing the Protestant religion. From the first he knew well that they had resolved on his death; but it was on the morning of the day fixed for his execution that the messenger came to him with the above terms.

"O'Higgins, in reply, desired to have those proposals made to him under the signature of the Justices, and requested, moreover, that it should be handed to him in sight of the gibbet. The Lords Justices, hearing this, together with the order for his execution, sent the written document for pardon on the aforesaid condition. Now, when the intrepid martyr had ascended the first step of the ladder leading to the gibbet, the executioner placed the paper in his hand. He bowed courteously on receiving it, and loud was the exultation of the heretical mob, who thought he was about to renounce the Catholic faith; but he, standing on the scaffold, exposed to the view of God and man, exhibited to all about him the document he had received, and commenting with warmth on it, convicted his impious judges of their own avowed iniquity.

"Knowing well that there were Catholics in the crowd, he said, addressing them: 'My brethren, God hath so willed that I should fall into the hands of our relentless persecutors. They have not been able, however, to convict me of any crime against the laws of the realm; but my religion is an abomination in their sight, and I am here to-day to protest, in the sight of God and man, that I am condemned for my faith. For some time I was in doubt as to the charge on which they would ground my condemnation; but, thanks to heaven! it is no longer so, and I am about to suffer for my attachment to the Catholic faith. See you here the condition on which I might save my life. Apostasy is all that they require; but, before high heaven, I spurn their offers, and, with my last breath, will glorify God for the honour He has done me in allowing me thus to suffer for his name.' Then turning to the executioner, after having cast the Justices' autograph to the crowd, he told him to perform his task, and the bystanders heard him returning thanks to God even with his latest breath. Thus did iniquity lie unto itself—thus did the martyr's constancy triumph."

5. *Terence Albert O'Brien, Bishop of Emly.*—The spot where this holy bishop was martyred is yet pointed out and venerated by the Catholics of Limerick :—" When Limerick was besieged," writes O'Daly, only four years after Dr. O'Brien's death, " Ireton sent him word that he would give him forty thousand pounds sterling, and permission to retire whithersoever he should wish out of the kingdom, provided he ceased to exhort the people against surrender; but his heroic soul spurned the offer, as he had resolved to fight the good fight, and win that crown which is the guerdon of the just. When the English commander heard this, he excepted the bishop from amnesty and every other condition that he proposed to the besieged, and swore, moreover, that he would visit the citizens with the most rueful retaliation if they did not bring to his quarters the head of the prelate, together with those of twenty men who voted against giving the city into his hands. Two hundred ecclesiastics assembled in council, and after mature consideration, resolved to interpose between Ireton and the twenty whom he had doomed to die ; but in vain, for *all ecclesiastics, too, were excepted.* The bishop offered to give himself up, provided the lives of the rest were spared, but the ecclesiastics would not hear of his proposal. At length the city was surrendered, and the holy bishop fell into the enemy's hands."

We glean some additional particulars of his glorious death from the Acts of the General Chapter of the Dominican Order, held in 1656 :—He went with joy to the place of execution, and there, with a serene countenance, turning to his Catholic friends, who stood in the crowd inconsolable and weeping, he said to them: "Hold firmly by your faith, and observe its precepts; murmur not against the arrangements of God's providence, and thus you will save your souls. Weep not at all for me, but rather pray that in this last trial of death I may, by firmness and constancy, attain my heavenly reward." He then, filled with a prophetic spirit, reproved the ferocity of the heretics, declaring that divine vengeance would soon await their crimes, and summoned Ireton, the arch-persecutor, to appear before many days at the tribunal of the just Judge, to answer for his deeds of cruelty. This prophecy was verified, and before a month Ireton, stricken with the plague, and crying out that the execution of the innocent bishop was the cause of his death, miserably expired. As to our holy martyr, his head was fixed on a spike and remained long exposed to public view on the tower. O'Daly thus writes, in 1655: "The bishop's head may yet be seen, covered with hair and with flesh quite incorrupt, on the tower which rises in the middle of the city over the great bridge, and drops of blood frequently issue from it."

Lynch, in his *MS. History of the Irish Bishops*, writes of Dr. O'Brien: "That he was of a most noble family, and at an early age was enrolled in the Dominican Order in the city of Limerick. He pursued the higher studies in the convent of St. Peter the Martyr at Toledo, was subsequently Prior in Limerick and at Lorrha, and being chosen Provincial for Ireland proceeded to Rome in 1644, to attend the General Chapter of the Order. It was on his homeward journey, whilst he was engaged in the visitation of the national communities of his Order in Lisbon, that he received the intelligence of his promotion to the See of Emly. Consecrated by the Nuncio Rinuccini, he was assiduous in his spiritual labours; and was, in particular, remarkable for the stainless virtue and simplicity of his life. As Limerick had yielded the first-fruits of his zeal, it was meet it should be the theatre of his martyrdom. Throughout the prolonged siege of more than five months none were more energetic than he in stimulating the courage of the defendants, and urging them to uphold perseveringly the cause of religion and country. When the city fell into the enemy's hands, though he was excepted from all hope of pardon or life, he made no attempt to escape, but proceeded to the hospital of those stricken with the plague to comfort the dying and minister to them the last consolations of religion. He was there arrested, and, with his hands tied, and with fetters on his feet, he was brought before Ireton, who was sitting in court-martial. In reply to the usual query, he fearlessly stated that he was a bishop, and was guilty of no offence but the faithful discharge of his sacred duties, and for this he was ready to meet death with joy ; and he summoned Ireton to appear before many days at the tribunal of God to answer for his cruelty. Next day, amid the loud laments of the people, he was led to the scaffold, and thus, on the 30th of October, 1651, he attained his crown. His body was left hanging at the

gallows for three hours after death, and, during that
time the Puritan soldiers, with fiendish malice, heaped
every dignity on his hallowed remains. With ribald
jest and mockery they whirled the body to and fro, and
made it a target for their muskets. The body being at
length taken down quite covered with wounds, the head
was cut off and set on a stake on the Bridge Tower."
The particulars relating to the martyr's death were attested by Fr. Dionysius Hanrehan, O.S.D., whose privilege it was to administer to him the sacrament of
penance for the last time, in preparation for his martyrdom on the day that the enemy got possession of
Limerick.

6. The family of the O'Feralls (now commonly written
O'Farrell) had for centuries been reckoned among the
patrons of religion throughout the territory of their
ancient sept in the diocese of Ardagh. They were in
particular remarkable for their munificence to the spiritual children of St. Dominick, having erected and endowed at Longford, about the year 1400, the famous
Convent of St. Bridget, for a community of Friars of
that Order. During the period of the Confederation
we meet with several illustrious scions of this old Celtic
race in the senate house and in the camp; but, perhaps,
none reflected such credit on the name as the two
martyrs, Fr. Bernard O'Ferall and Fr. Laurence O'Ferall,
both enrolled in the Order of St. Dominick, in St.
Bridget's Convent, and both privileged to die for the
faith in 1651. The following account of their death is
given in the Rinuccini MS.:

" They both belonged to the illustrious house of the
O'Feralls, and were alike eldest sons born to hereditary

estates and wealth. They were, moreover, alike in that they were masters in S. Theology, and famed as preachers of the truths of religion. They had held honourable posts in the convents of the Order at Longford, Roscommon, Derry, and elsewhere; and throughout the whole period of the Confederate war had proved themselves staunch champions of the Faith. Alike revered by the clergy and people, their names had been presented as most worthy to be promoted to the episcopal rank, and in common with their devoted sept they resolved either to preserve intact and incorrupt the Faith handed down to them for twelve hundred years, or to die gloriously in its defence. Animated with such sentiments, when arrested in the habit of the Order, they could not be induced by threats or promises to embrace the tenets of heresy. Wherefore they were cruelly treated as defenders of Popery, spies of the Roman Pontiff, enemies of the Protestant Church: and the heretics shouted out, 'Away with these champions and leaders of the Papists; kill them, hang them.' Fr. Bernard, struck with swords and spears, was on the spot pierced with eighteen mortal wounds, and was left for dead, being almost suffocated by his own blood. Life remained, however, till the last sacraments were administered to him, and then the crown of martyrdom was added to that of the Doctorate, which a little while before had been deservedly awarded him by Fr. Marinus, the General of the Dominican Order. Fr. Laurence O'Ferall, was made prisoner without receiving any wounds, and being thrown into prison he was ordered to be hanged on the following Wednesday. Led to the scaffold, he displayed the greatest courage and joy, but at the request of some English noblemen and others, who came to the unwonted spectacle, a respite till the following Saturday was granted. When this announcement was made to him nothing could exceed his grief, to the astonishment of all who were present: and when they asked why he thus sorrowed, he replied, because I feel myself at present so well disposed to meet death for God and for the Catholic Faith, that I fear I never again may be equally prepared for so happy a death. In the meantime several English Protestants petitioned and made great efforts to have his life spared. All was in vain. On the following Saturday he was led to the scaffold. From the steps he addressed a most earnest exhortation to those present, so moving that all shed tears, and some were converted to the Faith. His discourse being ended, he was hanged and thus attained the martyr's crown."

It is of Fr. Bernard O'Ferall that the words of O'Daly are to be understood: " On being arrested and examined, some letters from the apostolic nuncio were discovered sowed up in his inner garments. None could have been more active than this zealous man in promoting the Catholic cause during his career. His death was painful as fiendish ingenuity could make it. Beaten with sticks, burned with gunpowder, and finally pierced by the sword; this holy champion committed his soul to God in 1651."

De Burgo gives, from the contemporary acts of the Order, further particulars of the martyrdom of Fr. Laurence O'Ferall: "Through the intercession of some friends, though contrary to his own desire, three days were given him to meditate on the expediency of renouncing his religion. These three days were passed by him in tears and prayers that it might be granted to him to receive the martyr's palm. On being led to the scaffold, he addressed an exhortation to the Catholics with great fervour and unction, then arranged his beads around his neck, and grasping his crucifix in his right hand composed himself in prayer. What was viewed as a great prodigy by all, when he was hanging from the scaffold, and in the agonies of death, he raised aloft his hands holding in them the crucifix, which was thus presented to the gaze of all as the trophy of victory."* This most singular prodigy made a very great impression on the beholders, and the officer in command was so struck and terrified thereat that he ordered the body to be cut down respectfully, and gave it over to the people to be buried without molestation.

7. *Thadeus Moriarty.*—Killarney was the theatre of his martyrdom, in 1653, and the heretics themselves affirmed that his calmness and firmness in death exceeded anything they had ever witnessed. Father O'Daly, writing only two years later, thus sketches his life: "He was the last Prior of the Dominican Convent of Tralee. Well skilled in moral and dogmatic theology, the splendour of his birth was surpassed only by the brilliant effulgence of his virtues. The learning and piety of this holy man soon came to be known by the relentless persecutors of his creed, and they left nothing undone in order to seize him. Never did the bride more joyously go forth to the marriage altar than

* *Hib. Dom.*, p. 569, ex actis general. Romæ, an. 1656. See also the *Irish Eccles. Record* for 1865, vol. i. p., 131.

he did to death, and never did the starvling more eagerly desire food than did this glorious champion the scaffold of martyrdom.

"When the death-warrant was read for him, he clasped the messenger and distributed money to his executioners; from the scaffold he exhorted the spectators not to be dismayed, but to cling with tenacity to their hallowed creed, and to be ever mindful of the vicissitudes and transitoriness of this life; he moreover described martyrdom as the most secure as well as the shortest path to the heavenly crown, and was then immediately executed. It was deemed by many most wonderful and deserving of attention how the body of the martyr, which the gloom and miseries of the prison had emaciated and distorted, became, as it were, transfigured after death, beaming with such splendour and comeliness, and radiating such rays of beauteous light, that the executioners themselves were heard to say that he wore an angelic countenance.

"Throughout life he was a model of humility and mildness, and never known to have lost his temper. During his martyrdom, though beaten with clubs, and lashed with whips, he gave no sign of impatience, but seemed wholly insensible to all these stripes. Interrogated by his judge why he did not obey the laws of the kingdom, he mildly answered that he had to obey God, and His vicegerents who had commissioned him to preach the Gospel of Christ. Truly was this venerable man an apostolic minister, a true disciple of our Lord, walking in the footsteps of Christ, and displaying all the characteristics of a true apostle. He suffered on the 15th of October, 1653, and the heretical soldiery still continue to guard his grave, lest the people should bear away his honoured remains."

The Rinuccini MS. further attests that the father of this heroic martyr was the head of the sept of the Mac Moriartys, whose hereditary possessions lay on the banks of the Mang in the county of Kerry. Thadeus, with one of his brothers proceeded to Spain, and both were there enrolled in the Order of St. Dominick. In the Spanish schools, Fr. Thadeus was remarkable for his philosophical and theological research, and he was no less remarkable in Ireland, by his success in leading back heretics to the true fold of Christ. He was also noted for his meekness, and throughout his whole life he had never been known to lose his temper. Notwithstanding the penal decree issued on the 6th of January, 1653, commanding all the religious and clergy to depart from the kingdom under pain of death, he remained at his post, being Prior of the convent of Tralee, and he laboured throughout the whole of Kerry with the zeal of an apostle. When arrested by the Puritan soldiers he was treated with every indignity, nevertheless he displayed his usual serenity and welcomed with joy the humiliations and sufferings to which he was subjected for Christ's sake. Two years before his martyrdom, one of his brothers named Daniel was slain, when the family castle was besieged by the Puritan troops under Nelson, who was appointed by the Parliamentarians governor of the fort of Ross and of the county of Kerry. The martyr's brother-in-law, Peter Feriter, also suffered death about the same time. He had surrendered with the troops under his command to Nelson, on the condition of their lives being spared.

Notwithstanding this, he was thrown into prison and sentenced to be hanged. Fr. Maurice O'Connell, a Jesuit, who lay concealed in the neighbourhood of Killarney, visited him in prison, disguised as a labourer bringing some material relief, and administered the holy sacraments to him. He was soon after led out and hanged in Killarney at the place known as Sheep-hill.* His loss was deplored throughout all Ireland; for not only was he distinguished by his bravery during the Confederate war, but he was also famed for his liberality and greatness of soul, as well as for eloquence in both the English and the Irish tongues, and for his singular poetic genius particularly in Irish.†

8. *Æneas Ambrose Cahill, O.S.D*, was arrested not far from the city of Cork, and the enemy soon discovered that in him they had captured a valiant soldier of Christ. "Powerful was his eloquence," says the historian of the Dominican Order, "in combating false doctrine, and dauntless his heart in the defence of his country. Furious was the hatred of his enemies, and bitter was the agony to which he was consigned. His body was cut into minute particles, and cast for food to ravens, an. 1651."

9. Indeed, the Order of St. Dominick yielded at this period an abundant harvest of martyrs to our Irish Church. The names of no fewer than fifty members who received the crown of martyrdom may be seen in De Burgo and O'Daly. For the present we need men-

---

* "Killarniæ in *Colliculo Ovium* laqueo sustu!erunt." Rinuccini MS.

† "Poetam utraque lingua et præsertim Hibernica insignem." *Ibid.*

tion but one other distinguished ornament of this Order, Father John O'Cullen of the Convent of Athenry, "A man devoted to observance of his rules, a model of piety, wholly given to prayer and mortification, ever desirous of the poorest apparel, and at the same time endowed with such a penetrating genius that he mastered almost every science. In many public conferences he, with great learning, refuted heresy and animated the Catholics, and more than once risked his life in the defence of the authority of the Holy See. At length being seized by the heretics, and covered with innumerable wounds, he joyfully laid down his life for Christ, in 1652."*

10. *Anselm Ball* was a priest of the Order of Capuchins, a native of Fingall, and for more than twenty years laboured on the Irish mission. Most of the clergy having been expelled from Dublin by the fury of the Puritans, Father Anselm succeeded for awhile in disguising himself, whilst, at the same time, he indefatigably laboured in consoling the afflicted faithful of that city, and administering to them the holy sacraments, "so much so, that he often passed two successive days and nights without having an interval for repose." As the danger increased within the city, seeing it impossible any longer to escape the snares of his heretical pursuers he fled to the country parts. Finding that even there "none were allowed to receive him into their homes under penalty of death and of the confiscation of their

* O'Daly, after commemorating very many of his own Order who thus suffered death for the faith, adds : "But, alas! I am not able to tell you in detail how many of my fellow-countrymen were made to drain the cup of persecution even to the very dregs."

properties, he built for himself a little hut of brambles in a rocky district; thence he went forth at midnight, covered only with rough and tattered garments, and exposed to rain, and wind, and snow, and frost, visiting the surrounding towns, and risking every danger in order to satisfy the ardour of his charity. More than once his hut was discovered by the enemy, and then he was compelled in the depth of night to fly for refuge to the mountains or subterraneous caves, having nothing for his food but a little barley bread and water, which itself was sometimes wanting to him. So great was the devotion of the people in these calamitous times, that whatsoever place he marked for the Holy Sacrifice, and no matter how dark or stormy the night might be, all assembled there."

When it pleased Providence to afflict his children with the scourge of pestilence, a new theatre was opened for the zeal of Anselm. At that time "in the city and adjoining country, no fewer than 2,000 were weekly hurried to the grave." For four months it raged with special violence, and it was three years before it wholly ceased. During all this time Father Anselm devoted himself to the attendance on those that were stricken with the disease "being often obliged to enter, creeping on hands and feet, the fetid huts of the persecuted poor;" to no fewer than 7,000 persons infected with the plague did he administer the consoling sacraments of the Church, and many of the most destitute he was obliged on their decease, to bear on his shoulders to a place of sepulchre.

Seven times he fell into the hands of the heretical troops, and, besides being bruised and beaten, was despoiled of his books and vestments, and all that he possessed; he was, however, each time, either by the interposition of Providence, or by the exertions of some Catholics, enabled to escape. On one occasion he was recognised and assailed by one horse soldier alone; the good father, however, proved more than a match for his assailant, and soon unhorsed and disarmed him, and then obliging him to solemnly promise that he would never more pursue any priest, he restored to him his horse and arms. Once he was brought before the magistrate, and received sentence of transportation to the Tobacco Islands; even then, however, his good fortune did not fail him, and, through the influence of a friendly nobleman, the sentence was remitted, and he was enabled to pursue his ministry of charity.*

11. *Bonaventure Carew*, a native of Killarney, belonged to the same Order. Being arrested and cast into prison, he was thence sent into exile. Returning, however, to his missionary labours, he was again made prisoner, " cast headlong into a subterraneous dungeon, so small that he could neither stand erect nor lie down, and there, without one ray of light, he was detained for eighteen months in a lengthened martyrdom."†

These particulars have been taken verbatim from a paper of Fr. Barnabas Barnewall, written from Dublin, on 4th October, 1669.

† *Ibid.*, Relat. P. Barnab. Barnewall, 1669.

CHAPTER II.

INDIVIDUAL INSTANCES OF THE PERSECUTION (*continued*).

1. F. Dowdall's zeal in Dublin; he dies in prison in London.—
2. Death of B. Egan, Bishop of Ross.—3. David O'Mollony of Killaloe.—4. J. Lynch and R. Nugent, P.P.'s in Meath.—5. Phelim Mac Tuoll.—6. Labours of J. Forde in promoting education.—7. Zeal of S. Gelosse in promoting religion and education.—8. Death of D. O'Brien.—9. Of Ladies Roche and Fitzpatrick, and Esma Plunkett.—10. Of Mrs. A. Read, described by her son.—11. FF. Brien and Barry, of the Congregation of St. Vincent, and Brother Lee; their sufferings.—12. Death of Fr. O'Higgins, P.P. of Naas.—
13. John O'Cullenan, Bishop of Raphoe.

1. *Father John Dowdall* was remarkable for the number of heretics whom he brought back to the bosom of the Catholic Church. One of these was a Presbyterian in Dublin, who was so inflamed with hatred of the Catholic religion that each Sunday he regularly bound his wife (who was a Catholic) with cords, lest she should assist at the Sacrifice of the Mass. By the exhortations of Father Dowdall he first desisted from this cruel practice, and soon after became a fervent convert to our holy faith.

The occasion of another conversion was wholly peculiar. It proceeded from a dream. The heretic dreamt that, advancing to the gate of heaven, and boldly knocking for admission, St. Peter came to the door and sternly reproved him, saying, " No heretic can enter here." Full of courage, however, he knocked and re-knocked, but finding all in vain, he at length asked aloud, "What should he do to obtain admission." St. Peter then, returning to the door, admonished him to go and seek a priest, and to be, through him, received into the true Church, as none but its children could be admitted into the heavenly mansions. Awakening from his sleep, he could find no rest till he sought for a priest, and, being conducted to Father Dowdall, was by him reconciled to holy Church. This good father was frequently arrested by the heretical troops. The last time he fell into their hands he was transferred to London Prison, and there, wasted away by hunger and cold, attained his heavenly reward.*

2. *Boetius Egan*, Bishop of Ross, was a member of the Order of St. Francis. This prelate, whose memory is yet fresh in the traditions of our country, had, in the fulness of his zeal, ventured to make his way to some distant and abandoned parts of his diocese, whilst the country was laid waste by Broghill and his savage bands. On his return towards the lonely retreat in which he had for months lain concealed, being in company with some Catholic soldiers, he was overtaken by a troop of the enemy's cavalry. The renunciation of his faith, he was told, would secure not only his pardon, but even the confidence and patronage of their general; various bribes and promises were also held out to him, but he rejected them with disdain. He was then abandoned to the soldiers' fury, and his arms being first

---

* See Notitia Historica Ord. Cappuc. in Hibernia, printed in Rome in 1859.

severed from his body, he was dragged along the ground to a neighbouring tree, and being hanged from one of its branches with the reins of his own horse, happily consummated his earthly course, A.D. 1650.* Lynch adds that he was a native of Duhallow, in Munster, that he studied in Spain, and that on the 6th of May, on the roadside between Macroom and Carrigadrohid, he attained the crown of martyrdom. His remains were interred at night in the neighbouring old church of Achannach, and during the interment the place was lit up with heavenly splendour. This zealous Franciscan had acted as chaplain to the troops under Owen Roe O'Neill. At Benburb he pronounced absolution over the kneeling army immediately before it advanced to a brilliant victory, and he was deputed by the victorious general to carry the banners taken from Monroe's Scots to the Nuncio Rinuccini, then in Limerick. It is said that Broghill offered him pardon on condition of his ordering the garrison of Carrigadrohid to deliver up the castle. They carried him before the walls, as the Carthaginians carried Regulus to Rome, with the full persuasion that he would recommend his countrymen to surrender; but his words to them were: "Hold out to the last." The Rinuccini MS., commemorating his death, styles him "a veritable seraph of the seraphic Order, and most glorious martyr."

3. *Rev. David O'Mollony*, Archdeacon of Killaloe, was

* Bruodin "Passio Martyr." p. 530. The Louvain record of the order thus briefly notices this great man: "Pater Boetius Egan Momoniensis, Epus. Rossensis orthodoxæ fidei strenuus defensor et assertor; pro qua an. 1650, glorioso martyrio vitæ finem et coronidem imposuit."

arrested in the city of Limerick whilst in the act of offering up the Holy Sacrifice on Christmas Day, in the year 1653. He was carried off in triumph by his captors, and was without delay sentenced to be hanged. On the 1st of January, the day fixed for his execution, he was led to the scaffold with his hands bound behind his back. He showed the whole way along the greatest signs of joy at the privilege granted him of dying for the faith. From the ladder of the scaffold he addressed the assembled crowd, exhorting them to shun heresy, and to prove themselves devoted children of the one true Church. In the meantime, however, some wealthy citizens had succeeded by offering a large sum to obtain a respite for the zealous confessor of Christ, and before he ended his discourse a message from the governor ordered him to be conducted back to prison. This news, which gave joy to the whole city, overwhelmed him with sadness. He shed bitter tears, and he openly lamented that his crown should be thus deferred. He was detained some time longer in prison, and was then shipped with some soldiers for France, where he continued to labour as a zealous missionary till death.

4. *James Lynch* and *Richard Nugent* were parish priests, the former of Kells, the latter of Ratoath, in the county of Meath, and were both put to the torture, and suffered on the same day in defence of the Catholic faith. Father Lynch was a venerable old man, nearly eighty years of age, and was massacred in his bed, to which, through infirmity, he had been a long time confined. Father Nugent was sent under an escort to Drogheda, and a gibbet having being erected within sight of the walls, he ended his course with such

serenity and firmness as confounded his enemies, and drew forth the tears and benedictions of the faithful inhabitants of that ancient city.

5. The death of Colonel Phelim Mac Tuoll also merits particular mention. He held his commission in General Owen Roe O'Neill's own regiment, and was famed throughout the kingdom for his bravery and military skill. After the disastrous defeat of the Ulster army at Carrigholles, he was made prisoner, quarter being given. He was brought before Sir Charles Coote, the younger, to arrange terms for his ransom, and it was agreed that Mac Tuoll on procuring one hundred head of cattle from his friends, to be delivered to Sir Charles, would be set at liberty. The articles were being signed when a sergeant came into the tent with an account of his having brought Colonel Henry Roe O'Neill, Owen Roe's son, prisoner. Without more ado Coote reprimanded the sergeant for making him prisoner and not bringing his head instead, and commanded him to go and despatch him at once. On hearing this, Mac Tuoll let the pen drop from his hand, and began to plead for the life of his kinsman and fellow-prisoner. But all was in vain and the orders were executed; and Coote, turning to Mac Tuoll, told him that if he did not cease his prattle he too would be served in the same way. Whereupon Mac Tuoll, indignant at his brutal cruelty, cried out that "he would rather be served so than to owe his life to such a monstrous villain as he was." Coote at once gave orders to his men to take Mac Tuoll and knock him on the head with tent-poles. Whilst his sentence was being executed one of the Puritan officers seeing the indignities to which the brave officer

was subjected, ran him through the heart. The head of Mac Tuoll was then cut off, and with the heads of Henry Roe O'Neill and other prisoners was set upon the gates of Derry.

6. One of the chief objects of solicitude of the Irish clergy has ever been the promotion of science and the establishment of colleges and schools. The deluge of Puritan persecution laid in ruins the many establishments which, despite preceding oppressive laws, had sprung up in every district of the kingdom. Even whilst this storm raged, however, many zealous priests were not wanting, who, in the depths of the woods, or on the summits of the mountains, sought to keep alive the spark of learning as well as of religion. Amongst those we find, especially recorded, the Rev. James Ford, of the Society of Jesus, who, in the centre of a large bog, chose a little spot of ground of more than ordinary consistency; there he erected a wooden hut, and numbers of children from the surrounding districts flocked to him for instruction; they too erected little huts all around, and that cherished spot soon became a true oasis in the wilderness that surrounded it. The progress of these youths in virtue and learning consoled their zealous master; and they, moreover, vied with him in enduring, not only with fortitude, but even with joy, all the inconveniences to which they were exposed.*

7. *Stephen Gelosse* was another of those worthy fathers who devoted their lives to the instruction of our youth in literature and piety. The following sketch

* Status Soc. Jes. in Hib. an, 1654.

of his life was compiled by Dr. Oliver,* from the original acts of the Society. "No dangers that threatened him from the Cromwellian party, who filled every place with blood and terror, could deter this genuine hero from doing his duty; no weather, no pestilential fevers, no difficulties could hold him back from visiting the sick and the dying in their meanest hovels. His purse, his time, his services were always at the command of the distressed Catholic; it was his food and delight to exercise the works of mercy, corporal and spiritual. Though the tyrant Cromwell had issued a proclamation to his troops, that, should they apprehend a priest in any house, the owner of such house should be hung up before his own door, and all his property be confiscated, and that the captors of the priest should be rewarded at the rate which destroyers of the wolf formerly received; nevertheless, Fr. Gelosse managed every day to offer up the unbloody sacrifice of the altar: his extraordinary escapes from the clutches of his pursuers border on the miraculous. He adopted every kind of disguise; he assumed every shape and character: he personated a dealer of faggots, a servant, a thatcher, a beggar, a gardener, a miller, a carpenter, &c., thus becoming all to all in order to gain all to Christ. However, he was four times apprehended, but his presence of mind never forsook him, and he ingeniously contrived to extricate himself. After the restoration of Charles II. he set up a school at Ross, which took precedence of all others in the country, whether rank, numbers, proficiency, discipline, or piety be taken into

* "Collections towards illustrating the Biography of the Scotch, English, and Irish members of the Society of Jesus," p. 284.

consideration; but this was broken up by the persecution in 1670. He then removed to the vicinity of Dublin, where he taught about forty scholars; and in August, 1673, he returned to Ross to reopen his school; but at the end of three months he was obliged, by the fanatical spirit abroad, to abandon his favourite pursuit." It is further related of this devoted priest that he was remarkable for his skill in horsemanship, and that the better to conceal his sacred ministry he rode races with Cromwell's troopers.

8. *Donatus O'Brien*, as we learn from an eye-witness of the Cromwellian cruelty, was descended of the royal race of the O'Briens, a most generous man, and of surpassing hospitality; after the Protestants had plighted to him their faith, and given him a safe-conduct, he was advancing one day to meet them when a certain Protestant knight shot him through the body. "Dissatisfied with this cruelty, when the venerable old man (then aged about sixty-four years) had entered a hut, half dead, that he might in penitence commend his soul to God, a soldier followed, set fire to the hut, and burned this courageous martyr, in Thomond, A.D. 1651.*

9. We shall conclude our extracts from Morison with his account of the martyrdom of two noble ladies. "The inhuman fury of the Protestants," he writes, " was not satisfied with the slaughter of men, but they also drew their swords against women. Thus the noble Lady Roche, wife of Maurice, Viscount of Fermoy and Roche, a chaste and holy matron, whose mind was

* Morison's *Threnodia*, printed in 1659.

solely occupied with prayer and piety, being falsely accused of murder by a certain ungrateful English maid-servant (whom she had compassionately taken when a desolate orphan, and supported and educated), was hanged in Cork in 1654, although stricken in years and destined in the course of nature soon to die. The noble Lady Bridget, of the house of Darcy, wife of Florence Fitzpatrick, one of the barons of Ossory, was also put to death by the Protestants at Dublin, in 1652, without the form of law or justice. Ludlow adds that this Lady Fitzpatrick was condemned to be burnt, and that this cruel sentence was executed accordingly. From another source we learn, that the witness on whose evidence she was condemned afterwards acknowledged to having been suborned by the Parliamentarian Colonel Axtel, Governor of Kilkenny, who was anxious to secure her property. This perfidious man was one of those who received well-merited punishment, being hanged at London by order of the King, in 1660.

Morison concludes his narrative with the following words: "What shall I yet say? time would fail me to narrate the martyrdoms of chiefs, nobles, prelates, priests, friars, citizens, and others of the Irish Catholics, whose purple gore has stained the scaffolds almost without end; who by faith conquered kingdoms and wrought justice, of whom some had trials in mockeries and stripes, moreover, also of chains and prisons; others were overwhelmed with stones, cut asunder, racked, or put to death with the sword; others have wandered over the world in hunger, thirst, cold, and nakedness, being in want, distress, and afflicted, wandering in deserts, in mountains, and in dens, and in caves of the earth; and all these being approved by the testimony of the faith, without doubt received the promise."*

The supplement to *Alithinologia* states that during the Confederate war *Esma Plunkett*, sister of the Earl of Fingal, and the wife of Lynch of Knock, defended her house, situated about three miles from Trim, with great valour against the Puritan assailants, so much so that whilst the ammunition lasted they were repelled with great loss. When the powder was exhausted, and the assailants applied scaling ladders to the walls, the defenders poured out boiling water on them and compelled them to desist. The place was surrendered only on conditions of life being granted to the inmates. The Puritans, with their usual perfidy, violated the conditions and put them to the sword. The courage o this noble lady became a theme of eulogy throughout all Ireland.

10. *Mrs. Alison Read*, in 1642, sealed the confession of her faith by an heroic death, in the town of Dunshaughlin. The soldiery, rushing in on that defenceless town, seized on fifty old men, women, and little boys, and mercilessly slew them with their swords and spears. Mrs. Read, then in her eightieth year, encouraged these sufferers to endure every torment with constancy for the faith. Fired with rage at her exhortations, the Puritan soldiers, after inflicting many wounds, set her up as a target for their guns; and thus she happily expired. The son of this venerable martyr has preserved to us her memory; and in his commentary on the Book of

* *Threnodia*, p. 72.

Machabees mentions her heroic death to illustrate the fortitude and holy sentiments of the mother of the seven Machabees—the true model of female heroism.*

Some particulars regarding his own family, which he incidentally mentions, illustrate the devoted piety of our people at this trying period. "There was not one of the family," he says, "even among the distant relatives, who renounced the faith. His father daily recited the little office of the Blessed Virgin, and Mrs. Read was especially remarkable for her tender devotion to the Mother of God; she instilled the same into her children, and Father Read gratefully recalls to mind how, when a child, he was every morning before breakfast obliged to recite the 'little office' in her honour. Providence rewarded this piety of the worthy matron, and notwithstanding the poverty of the clergy, and the severe edicts against them, and the watchful vigilance of their persecutors, she was enabled to approach the holy sacraments of Penance and the Eucharist, on the

---

* *Redanus Petrus,* in Machab., p. 257. This learned man died on the 1st August, 1651, the same year in which he published the first volume of his commentary, the only volume that has been published. He thus describes the fury of the Puritan enemy: "Non omnia rapiunt, deprædantur, ferro et flamma devastant, modo, sed et in pueros, fœminas, senes ferinum in morem sanguinolenti sæviunt, pusionesque et infantes Catholicos (ut mihi narravit qui præliis interfuit) decussatos ad formam crucis pugionibus transfodiunt. . . . Pervenit Dunschaghlinum (abest ab urbe Dublino, milliaria duodecim) tertio Idus Junii an. 1642, Calvinistarum immitis et prædabunda caterva, iram immanem in fidem Catholicam et Hiberni sanguinis exsatiatura sitim, quam multa jam, per vicos, agros, et castella Midiæ, patrata cædes accenderat potius quam lenierat." &c.

sixth day, and again on the second day before her martyrdom."

11. We have here to mention Fathers Brien and Barry, and Brother Lee—the two former, Fathers of the Congregation of St. Vincent, and the last a lay brother of the same Order. In a preceding chapter we have described, at great length, the apostolic labours of these holy missionaries in the city of Limerick. It was only after concluding that article that, through the kindness of the learned archivist of the Lazarist Order, we were enabled to ascertain their names, as well as the following additional particulars connected with their missionary career: "Although the three fathers who had laboured in Limerick during the siege escaped the fury of Ireton on its surrender, one of them resolved to remain in the city to assist with his sacred ministry the remnant of its Catholic citizens, and after awhile consummated his holocaust of charity. The two others, Brien and Barry, escaped with about 120 other priests and religious, in various disguises, mixed up with the garrison of the place, who, by the terms of the capitulation, obtained their lives and permission to retire from the city. As there was no toleration for any ecclesiastics, these holy men, sure that death awaited them, passed the night preceding their escape in prayer and preparation for their martyrdom. They were not, however, recognised; and after escaping from the city they separated, Father Brien taking the road towards his native district, in company with the Vicar-General of Cashel; whilst Father Barry went towards the mountains, where a charitable lady received him and concealed him for two months. A bark, freighted

for France, appearing on the coast, he availed himself of the opportunity thus presented, embarked in the vessel, and, happily, landed in Nantes. This caused indescribable joy to St. Vincent, who had already given up these two fathers as lost, believing them to have been involved in the general massacre of Limerick. Although these good priests escaped from that general massacre, the congregation paid its tribute to the persecution, and a lay-brother of the Order, named Lee, being discovered by the heretics, was brutally put to death by them before the eyes of his own mother: his hands and feet were first amputated, and his head was then bruised to atoms."*

12. In addition to the Father O'Higgins whose happy martyrdom we have already commemorated, there was another holy priest of the same name put to death in 1641, by that worse than Gothic persecutor, Sir Charles Coote. Naas had been for many years the scene of Father O'Higgins's evangelical labours; and we are informed by Clarendon and Borlase that, on the first outburst of popular fury in 1641, he had preserved the life of very many English Protestants who were living in the neighbourhood, concealing them in his church, and afterwards sending them safe to Dublin.

We shall give, in the words of Lord Clarendon, the account of his arrest and execution: "In the town of Naas, some of the soldiers (of the Marquis of Ormonde) found Mr. Higgins, who might, 'tis true, have easily fled, if he had apprehended any danger in the stay.

---

* These particulars are taken from the acts of the Order, and a letter of St. Vincent to Lambert, the Superior of Warsaw, on 22nd March, 1651 (styl. vet.).

When he was brought before the marquis he voluntarily acknowledged that he was a Papist, and that his residence was in the town, from which he refused to fly away with those that were guilty, because he not only knew himself very innocent, but believed that he could not be without ample evidence of it, having by his sole charity and power preserved very many of the English Protestants from the rage and fury of the Irish; and, therefore, he only besought the marquis to preserve him from the violence of the soldiers, and put him securely into Dublin to be tried for any crime. Which the marquis promised to do, and performed it, though with so much hazard, that when it was spread among the soldiers that he was a Papist, the officer into whose custody he was entrusted was assaulted by them, and it was as much as the marquis could do to relieve him and compose the mutiny.

"When he came to Dublin he informed the Lords Justices of the prisoner he had brought with him, of the good testimony he had received of his peaceable carriage, and of the pains he had taken to restrain those with whom he had credit from entering into rebellion, and of many charitable offices he had performed, of which there wanted not evidence enough, there being many then in Dublin who owed their lives and whatever of their fortunes was left, purely to him; so that he doubted not he would be worthy of protection. Within a few days after, when the marquis did not suspect the poor man's danger, he heard that Sir Charles Coote had taken him out of prison and caused him to be put to death in the morning before, as soon as it was light; of whose barbarity the marquis complained to the Lords Justices; but so far were they from bringing the other to be questioned, that he found himself to be under some disadvantage for thinking that proceeding to be other than it ought to have been."

Thus far Lord Clarendon, in his *History of the Irish Rebellion*. We learn from De Burgo that the day of his death was the 23rd of March, 1642: his constancy in suffering, and the heavenly joy depicted in his countenance, moved many of the heretics to tears; others, however, redoubled their fury on witnessing his calm composure—nor did they cease their insults even after his death. His mortal remains were denied sepulture within the city, and as the friends of the martyred priest were carrying his corpse to a cemetery outside the walls the partisans of the Lords Justices shattered his lifeless head with their muskets. (*De Burgo ex Actis Capit, Gen.* 1644, p. 561.)

13. **Dr. John O'Cullenan**, Bishop of Raphoe, belonged to a family that had given many illustrious ornaments to the Church. His brother James was Abbot of Asseroe, in the county of Donegal, and died, at the venerable age of ninety-five years, in 1637. His uncle, Gelasius, who was Cistercian Abbot of Boyle, suffered torture, imprisonment, and death for the faith under Queen Elizabeth. Dr. O'Cullenan was appointed Bishop of Raphoe in 1625, but in consequence of the difficulties and dangers which then beset the clergy was unable to receive consecration till 1629. The diocese had suffered a great deal from the English and Scotch sectaries. There were only sixteen priests to minister to the wants of the faithful, and so completely had the inhabitants

been exterminated that scarcely seven hundred Catholics of any note could be found in the whole diocese. At the very outset of his episcopate Dr. O'Cullenan had been arrested and thrown into prison in Dublin for three months for exercising his episcopal functions. In 1643, however, he suffered still greater hardships at the hands of the Puritans. With a number of the Catholics of Donegal he was thrown into prison, and notwithstanding the promise that their lives would be saved, seventy-two of his companions were led out and put to the sword. The soldiers threatened him also with death. In the absence of the officer they led him out to the brink of the river, and told him to choose death by shooting or by drowning. He desired that he should not be thrown into the river, and remonstrated with them on their breach of faith in putting to death those who had done them no injury, and to whom life had been promised. This only excited their rage the more and they resolved to despatch him at once. Kneeling down, and with his arms outstretched in the form of a cross, and with his eyes fixed on heaven, he calmly awaited the death-stroke. Three of the soldiers levelled their loaded matchlocks to shoot him, but all that they could do failed to ignite the powder. They then cried out that he was "a devil, guarded by charms, enchantments, and hellish superstition," and prepared their pikes to despatch him. At that moment, however, Colonel Askin came up and commanded them to desist. The bishop was then conducted to Londonderry, where he was thrown into a foul dungeon, from which the very light of day was excluded, and there he suffered extreme hardship from cold, hunger, and thirst for four years. Repeatedly his liberty and high honours were offered to him if he would apostatise, and when he replied that though they gave him the whole world "he would never forsake God or Holy Church, out of which there is no salvation, and against which all the powers of hell can never prevail," they told him that death would be his reward. He owed his release to the great victory of Owen Roe O'Neill at Benburb in 1647. During the Cromwellian usurpation he lived in exile in the Convent of the Regular Canons of St. Augustine at Brussels, and there closed his days in peace on 24th March, 1661. His remains rest in the Chapel of Our Lady in the Cathedral of SS. Michael and Gudule in that city.

CHAPTER III.

INDIVIDUAL CASES OF THE PERSECUTION *(continued).*

Hugh M'Mahon executed in London in 1643.—2. Death of Fergall Ward.—3. Of Cornelius O'Brien.—4. Of Christopher Ultan.— 5. Of Malachy O'Queely, Archbishop of Tuam, and his chaplain.— 6. Of Denis Nelan.—7. Of T. Carighy.—8. Of Felix O'Neill.—9. Of Heber Mac Mahon, Bishop of Clogher.—10. Of Arthur Magennis, Bishop of Down and Connor.—11. Of Connor Mac Guire, Lord of Enniskillen, tried in London and executed in 1644; his piety and attachment to the Catholic Faith; prayers.—12. Letter of A. Nugent, Capuchin.—13. Richard O'Connell, Bishop of Kerry.— 14. Fr. O'Sullivan.

1. *Hugh M'Mahon*, the head of his most noble family in Ulster, being arrested in Dublin in 1641, was sent to London, and after a close confinement there for two years was led to the scaffold; being first hanged, his body was cut into quarters and affixed on London Bridge. Before execution the Parliamentarians more than once sent to him offering him his life and the restitution of all his property, should he only consent to renounce his spiritual allegiance to the Church of Rome; he heroically disdained this vile offer, and thus passed to a better life in 1643.

2. *Fergall Ward* was a native of Ulster, and a member of the order of the strict observance of St. Francis. He was renowned for his eloquence and for his zeal in the exercise of the sacred ministry. In 1642 he was

seized by a cruel and barbarous pirate, a Scotchman, named Forbes, who kept six vessels in the service of the Puritans, and chiefly infested the banks of the Shannon. In the third month after his arrest he was hanged from the masthead *in odium fidei*, in the very centre of the river Shannon, where the pirate then lay in wait for some prey, about the end of October, 1642.

3. *Cornelius O'Brien*, the Lord of Caringh, in the county of Kerry, a man of great hope to his family and his country, was arrested by the piratical bands of the same Forbes, in the castle of Glanens, which was situated on the banks of the Shannon, and was the property of John Geraldine. Being conducted to their vessels, threats and promises were alike employed in vain to induce him to abandon the Catholic faith. He was therefore led out to execution, and on the same day with Father Ward, and by a similar death, attained the martyr's crown. Both were hanged at the same time, one at each extremity of the masthead, and subsequently, at full tide, the ropes being cut, their bodies were cast into the river.

4. *Christopher Ultan* (or Donlevy).—This father of the Order of St. Francis, after completing his studies in Spain, for many years preached with great fervour the sacred truths of the Gospel in the province of Ulster. He was concealed with Father Ward at the time of his arrest, and shared in his captivity. The Puritan pirate Forbes, anxious to supply a bloody feast to the London mob, sent Father Ultan a prisoner to England; for three years he was detained a captive in Newgate (London), and there subjected to many cruelties; his constitution yielded to the severity of

the prison, and he expired, before being led to the scaffold, in the year 1644.

5. *Malachy O'Queely*, Archbishop of Tuam.—This prelate governed the See of Killaloe for some years as vicar-apostolic, and on the 10th of October, 1630, was consecrated Archbishop of Tuam in a private chapel at Galway by Dr. Thomas Walsh, Archbishop of Cashel.* All contemporary historians agree in extolling the virtues of Dr. Queely. No one was more humble or fervent in the discharge of his sacred duties, whilst at the same time no one was more active and energetic during that period of extreme peril to his religion and country. He was the father, and protector, and advocate of the poor, and the widows, and the oppressed; and he was eminently distinguished for his learning and hospitality. He accompanied the Connaught army when it achieved many brilliant victories in 1645, but at length, being mortally wounded, he fell into the enemies' hands at a place called Clare, near Sligo. The Puritans first cut off his right arm, and then cruelly mangled his body, cutting it up into small pieces.† Fr. Thaddeus Conald or O'Connell, chaplain of the Archbishop, shared his fate. He was an Augustinian being enrolled in the Order in Galway, and had held many posts of high dignity in the Irish province. His hands were cut off and his body lacerated, and thus he attained

---

* His *professio fidei* and the letter of Dr. Walsh announcing his consecration are preserved among the Wadding MSS.

† Hardiman's Hist. of Galway, who gives the letter of the contemporary Dr. John Dowley, also Bruodin and others. For a sketch of his life, see *Collections on Irish Church History*, vol. i, p. 402.

his crown (manibus abscissis, vulneribus confossus, triumphali martyrio coronatur. *Elsius*).

6. *Denis Nelan*, was a priest of the Order of St. Francis, and descended from noble parents in the county Limerick. Before entering the Franciscan Order he was for many years parish priest of Kilragty, and his labours produced an abundant spiritual harvest. From 1642 to 1651 these labours were happily continued by him as a Franciscan father, till at length Limerick became a prey to the Puritan strangers. With many others, Father Denis fell into their hands, being arrested in the house of his relative, Mr. Laurence Ncherenny. With his hands tied behind his back, he was led along like a convicted robber to the island of St. Cunan, where was then the heretical camp. The whole way along he fervently exhorted the heretical soldiery to attend to their eternal salvation; and when interrogated by the commander whether, renouncing the doctrines of Rome, he would subscribe the Puritan tenets, he courageously replied that he had long anxiously sighed for an occasion when he might lay down his life for the Catholic faith, and he not only would never renounce its saving doctrines, but was ready, moreover, to endure a thousand torments in its defence. These words were scarcely uttered when the surrounding soldiers, erecting a temporary gallows, hanged him on the spot.

7. *Thadeus Carighy* made his solemn profession among the religious of the Franciscan convent of *Inish*, and filled the whole district of Thomond with the odour of his virtues. In 1651 he was arrested by the Cromwellians in the neighbourhood of his convent, and was tempted with the promise of riches and dignities should

he renounce the Catholic faith; but neither allurements nor tortures could turn him aside from the path of virtue, and, by order of his captors, he was immediately hanged and his body barbarously mangled.

8. *Felix O'Neill*, an illustrious prince of the noble family of O'Neill, was captured by heretical device and sent to Dublin in 1652; he was first half-hanged, and, whilst yet alive, was quartered. His head was stuck upon a spike at the western gate of the city, and his quarters were sent to different parts of the kingdom to be set on stakes, in order to terrify the Catholics. Before this brave champion of the cross was led to the scaffold, the heretics offered him his life and the restoration of his property should he consent to embrace the Puritan tenets. These offers, however, were made in vain, and the thrice happy Felix chose rather the eternal felicity that awaits the true soldiers of Christ than the fading, deceitful joys of this transitory world.

9. *Heber Mac Mahon* was a scion of the princely family of the native princes of Monaghan. His father had taken an active part and proved himself a brave soldier in all the battles of the northern chieftains against Elizabeth. Heber was born in the year 1600, and, proceeding to the Continent at an early age, pursued his ecclesiastical studies at Douay. He was subsequently for some years superior of the Irish College at Louvain, and was appointed, in 1637, Vicar-Apostolic of his native diocese of Clogher. Soon after his return to Ireland the agents of the English Government reported that he and others of the clergy were carrying on negotiations with Cardinal Richelieu for the French invasion of Ireland. An order was issued for his arrest

but he succeeded in concealing himself for a time till the storm had passed. The Archbishop of Armagh was less fortunate, and was led a prisoner to Dublin, where he was detained till the rumoured treasonable negotiations were found to be groundless. Dr. Mac Mahon was appointed Bishop of Down and Connor in 1642, but before his consecration was in the following year translated to Clogher, for which see he was consecrated with great pomp in the presence of the members of the Supreme Council at Kilkenny. On the death of Owen Roe O'Neill, in 1649, great dissensions prevailed among the Irish officers. At length, in March, 1650, all united in requesting the Bishop of Clogher to assume the supreme command of the Ulster army. In the hope of preserving union he yielded to their request, and was at once confirmed in this command by Ormonde, as representative of the royal authority. For some time success attended the Irish arms. Several castles and strongholds were taken from the enemy; and a great part of Ulster was freed from the Puritan army. Elated with their success, several of the Irish leaders returned to their homes, and only a small select body remained with the Bishop-General in Letterkenny. Coote marched his army to attack them, and, concealing a portion of his troops, led the Irish to underrate his strength. In the battle which ensued, on the 21st of June, 400 Irish soldiers were slain, and many more were killed in the pursuit. Dr. Mac Mahon and his troop of cavalry cut their way through the enemy, but two days after were attacked unawares by the garrison of Enniskillen. Dr. Mac Mahon with his own hand struck down several of his assailants; but being at length wounded, he surrendered on the promise of quarter. Captain King, the Governor of Enniskillen, who was subsequently raised to the peerage with the title of Viscount Kingston, treated his prisoner with great kindness, and expressed the greatest admiration as well for his heroism in the field as for his piety and constancy in prison. Twice he contrived to evade the order which was sent him to have the bishop put to death, and, at Dr. Mac Mahon's request, he permitted an Irish priest to visit him and to administer the last sacraments to him. At length, in the beginning of July, 1650, an imperative order arrived from Coote that the Popish bishop should be forthwith hanged. Dr. Mac Mahon, who was unable to walk, being still suffering from his wound, was drawn on a hurdle to the place of execution. He there with tears asked pardon of any whom he might have offended, and continued for some time in prayer. He then addressed the assembled crowd at considerable length in the Irish tongue, in which he was most eloquent, exhorting them to constancy in their present trials, and, having again prayed for a little while, joyfully died for the faith. Dr. Lynch, whose MS. narrative I have followed, expressly attests that his death was ordered by Coote through hatred of our religion, *in odium fidei*, and contrary to the promise of quarter which had been given. The head of the martyred bishop was spiked on the tower of the castle of Enniskillen, where it remained for many years a trophy of Puritan impiety, but his body was conveyed by the Catholics to Devenish Island, and was there with due honour interred under the shadow of the oratory of St. Molaise.

10. *Arthur Magennis*, Bishop of Down and Connor. —

Few dioceses in Ireland contributed more martyrs from its hierarchy than the ancient see of Down and Connor. Under James I., and again under Charles I., we find its bishops laying down their life for their flock. During the persecution of Cromwell, it not only shared with Clogher the glory won for the Irish Church by the heroism and fortitude of Heber Mac Mahon, but merited, moreover, to have its own chief pastor put to death for his unflinching attachment to the Catholic faith. This was Dr. Arthur Magennis. Dr. French, indeed, in his *Catalogue of the Irish Bishops*, merely states that he died at sea;* and Bruodin only adds that he was advanced in years, that he was, at the time, suffering from a violent fever, and that he was subjected by the heretics to much hardship and persecution. From Lynch's MS. history and a letter of the Bishop of Clonfert, we learn a few particulars regarding his death. As he suffered from a burning fever, and was weighed down by years and his preceding hardships, he was compelled to keep to bed when sailing towards the shores of France.† He was not more than a few days at sea when a parliament cruiser gave chase, and, coming within range, fired into the ship. The shot crashed through the bulwarks and into the cabin where the bishop lay sick, and so severe was the shock to his shattered constitution that he expired a few hours afterwards.

11. *Connor Mac Guire*, Baron of Enniskillen.—This

---

* See De Burgo, Hib. Dom., p. 490.

† Letter, 31st Aug., 1652: "Dunensis, proh dolor! dum hinc transfretaret, tormenti globo non attingente, sed horribili tremendoque cum sonitu sub lectulum, in quo jacebat, transeunte, deterritus expiravit."

nobleman was arrested in Ireland in 1641; and, after the sufferings of a long imprisonment in the Tower of London, was at length brought to trial in that city on the 10th of February, 1644. An account of his trial, written by Wm. Prynne and M Nudigate, who conducted the proceedings against him, was published in Dublin, 1724. He was charged with high treason against King Charles the First, by parties who very soon afterwards brought that unhappy monarch to the scaffold. Tried by men most hostile to everything Catholic and Irish, Lord Connor Mac Guire could expect no justice, and he was found guilty, and sentenced to be hanged, embowelled, beheaded, and quartered.

This sentence was carried into effect on the 20th February, 1644, at Tyburn. Lord Mac Guire's petition, to be allowed the assistance of a priest to hear his confession, was refused. The sheriff and others made several attempts to make him renounce his faith, but their efforts were rejected with scorn. They even endeavoured to prevent him from spending a few minutes before his death in prayer, and repeatedly interrupted his devotions. The sheriff even ordered his pockets to be searched on the scaffold; but nothing was found in them except a crucifix and some beads.

Dr. Sibbald, a Protestant clergyman, attempted to bring him over to heresy, but "he regarded not his discourse" says the report of the trial, and read the following words to the people:—"Since I am here to die, I desire to depart with a quiet mind and with the marks of a good Christian, that is, asking forgiveness first of God, and next of the world. And I do forgive from the bottom of my heart all my enemies and offenders, even those that have a hand in my death. I die a Roman Catholic, and, although I have been a great sinner, yet am I now, by God's grace, heartily sorry for all my sins, and I do most confidently trust to be saved, not by my own works alone, but by the passion, merit, and mercy of my dear Saviour, Jesus Christ, into whose hands I commend my spirit."

The sheriff after this repeatedly interrupted MacGuire in his devotions, " but," adds the narrative, " all this while his eye was mostly upon his papers, *mumbling* over something out of them to himself, whereupon one of the sheriffs, demanding those papers of him, he flung them down."

We copy some of the prayers which were found written on the supposed treasonable papers then seized on by the sheriff:

" Into Thy hands I commend my spirit; Thou hast redeemed me, O Lord God of truth; Thou hast created me, O my God; Thou hast redeemed me, O most holy Father. I am all Thine; let Thy will be done in me; illuminate mine eyes that I may never sleep in death.

" Mary, mother of grace, mother of mercy, do thou protect us from the enemy, and receive us in the hour of death.

" O holy archangels, and my angel guardian, my patrons, and all the saints of heaven, intercede for me, and help me by your prayers and merits.

" O Lord Jesus Christ, I believe that Thou art my God and my Redeemer, and I firmly believe whatsoever Thy holy Catholic Church propounds to be believed, and profess that I will live and die in this faith.

"It grieves me that I have offended so great goodness, and it grieves me that I can grieve no more for my offences committed against Thee, my Creator and Saviour, in thought, word, and deed, and by omission, and I humbly beseech Thee to pardon me by Thy blood, which Thou hast poured out for my salvation, and if I have forgot anything which hath offended Thy Majesty, or do not know it, I desire to know it and repent it.

"And, in the meantime, I ask forgiveness of all, and likewise for Thy sake do, from my heart, pass by all offences whereby others have offended me. Also I pray them to forgive me, and, if I have detained anything from any man, my heirs shall make restitution to them to whom it is due."

When, at length, the sheriff gave the final order for execution, Lord Mac Guire said : " I do beseech all the Catholics that are here to pray for me, and I beseech God to have mercy on my soul." Such is the account of the death of this truly Christian nobleman, which has been handed down to us by his enemies and executioners. His faith, and courage, and patience, render him equal to the martyrs of the first centuries.

12. *Fr. Anthony Nugent*, of the Order of Capuchins, gives some interesting details in the following letter, dated from Waterford, the 23rd of June, 1651 :—

" Since it pleased Divine Providence to give victory to the Puritans on every side, we are scattered, each one seeking, as best he can, to evade the search of our enemies, and, as these have all Ireland now in their hands (with the exception of Limerick—which, however, is closely besieged—and of Galway and Athlone, which will certainly fall during the summer), no ecclesiastic can anywhere appear in public, for neither by reward nor intercession can the Puritans be induced to tolerate any priest in the country.

"On account of this I was compelled to abandon my brother and Westmeath, where all the Franciscans of Multifarnan were scattered, and especially those that had remained in their monastery. I then passed into Meath, where I remained some time. Being recognised, however, I fled to Dublin, where I lived as a gardener, until all the Catholic citizens were expelled from the city. I then went to Kilkenny, where I found our father Fiacre and other priests and religious in prison, for whom our lay-brother John provides by soliciting alms. As my assistance was not needed in Kilkenny, where there were several religious and priests, I hastened to the city of Ross, where there was no priest, but where there is an abundant spiritual harvest.

"Having terminated a mission there I came to Waterford, where the harvest was still more abundant, the city being far more populous, and scourged with the plague. I am here alone for six weeks, attending to the wants of the poor and of the rich, and it is my intention to remain here until the sword or the plague shall terminate my career.

"I had no confessor until God sent an English priest to this city: returning from Spain to England he was forced to enlist by the Parliamentarians, who were ignorant of his being a priest, and being sent into Ireland to join the Puritan army here, he effected his escape, and now lies concealed in the neighbourhood.

"I pass freely through the city, acting as the gardener of the greatest heretic in the place : I work also as a porter in carrying burdens. Should God grant me a continuance of this happy tranquillity I will remain here ; if, however, I am recognised, I shall, if possible, go on to Dungarvan and Youghal, and so make the circuit of Ireland until freed from the toils of this life.

"Father Gregory is at a distance of about fifteen or twenty miles from me ; but as he is well known in the city and weighed down with years, he cannot come to me ; neither can I go to him on account of the great scarcity of priests here, all the clergy having been banished from the city. I pray you to present my love to each of our fathers. I would write to many of them were it not that the letter-carrier is on the point of starting. I beseech you to be mindful of me in your prayers, and when you hear of my death write to Flanders, where the Holy Sacrifice will be offered for me."

13. Richard O'Conald (or, as the name is now written O'Connell) was at this time Bishop of Kerry. Born at Ballicard, near Valentia harbour, about the year 1575, he applied himself with assiduity to the preparatory studies at those Catholic schools which, in the remote parts of the country were kept open, despite the edicts of Elizabeth, and subsequently proceeded to Spain to cultivate the higher branches of sacred science. He completed his studies in Rome, and, being there promoted to the priesthood and invested with the Faculties of Vicar-

Apostolic for his native diocese, he returned to Ireland and laboured with untiring zeal to root out abuses and to promote the practice of virtue. He built for himself a house in a solitary spot in the wood of Mucross, at the foot of Mangerton, bordering on the famed Loch-Leane, and he continued to reside there after his promotion to the episcopate of Kerry in 1643. Many persons flocked thither to approach the sacraments and to receive from him counsel and instruction, and none went away without being edified, instructed, and consoled. In the year 1648 that whole district was ravaged by a body of Puritan troops, and his house was plundered and burned to the ground. On this occasion an Anglo-Irish convert named John Morley gave memorable proof of fidelity and earnest attachment to the Faith. Being led from Protestantism to the Catholic Church by the exhortations of the bishop, he chose for himself a residence in the neighbourhood of Mucross, and married there an Irish lady, although she could not speak a word of English and he could only master a few words of Irish. On the approach of the Puritan soldiers, the bishop consigned all his household goods to his care, which he transferred to a small island in the lakes where he hoped to evade the enemy's pursuit. He was soon discovered, however, but despite threats and promises, persistently refused to surrender the bishop's goods. The heretics then attacked the island, and Morley being wounded by a musket ball, they despatched him with their swords. When the storm subsided, the bishop returned to labour among his flock; and, though worn out with care, and years, and infirmities, he was still at his post when, in 1652, the Castle of Ross, in Kerry, was captured by the Puritan troops. He was arrested by the enemy, and the few cows which were his only support were carried off. Moved to compassion by his extreme misery and many infirmities the Governor of Ross allowed him to live at a friend's house in Killarney, which, for this intent, was made his prison. Full of merits, after a lengthened martyrdom, he expired there in 1653, and his remains were interred amid the ruins of the Franciscan monastery of Loch-Leane. Of two secular brothers of Dr. O'Conald it is recorded that they were remarkable for their piety. One of them named Moruch (Maurice) was accustomed to kneel down frequently every day, even in the fields, to raise his thoughts and affections to heaven; and it was whilst in that attitude of prayer that he was shot by the enemy a short time before the bishop's demise. The other brother named Cornelius was famed for his penitential exercises, whilst at the same time he was unbounded in his hospitality and charity to the poor. He, too, was despoiled of everything by the heretics, and died a confessor for the faith.

14. The Rinuccini MS. from which I have gleaned the preceding facts, records also, under the year 1653, the martyrdom of Fr. Francis O'Sullivan of the Order of St. Francis. He was a native of Kerry, and belonged to that branch of the O'Sullevans whose ancestral property was in the barony of Iveragh. He entered the Franciscan Order in Spain, and spent many years there in the exercises of the religious life. Returning to Ireland about the year 1630, he was assiduous in preaching and administering the sacraments, and in 1650 was appointed to the perilous post of Provincial

of the Order in Ireland. He was not deterred, however, by the dangers that encompassed him, but in season and out of season continued to exercise his sacred ministry, till at length, in the beginning of 1653, he fell into the hands of the heretics, by whom he was at once led out to a cruel death.

CHAPTER IV.

EXAMPLES OF WHOLESALE MASSACRES PERPETRATED BY
THE PURITANS.

1. Pamphlet printed in London in 1662 gives details of massacres in several districts.—2. In Antrim.—3. In Derry.—4. At Newry, in Down.—5. In Donegal.—6. In Monaghan.—7. In Cavan.—8. In Meath.—9. In Westmeath.—10. In Louth.—11. In Dublin.—12. In Kildare.—13. In Wicklow.—14. In Kilkenny.—15. In Tipperary, 16. In Cork.—17. In Waterford.—18-21. In Clare, Galway, Leitrim, and Sligo.

1. IN the year 1662, was published in London a pamphlet, entitled *A Collection of some of the massacres, &c., committed on the Irish in Ireland, since the 23rd of October*, 1641. The author more than once appeals to the testimony of officers yet living, who had been eyewitnesses of the dreadful deeds which he narrates, and no one has ever dared to question his veracity. It will suffice for us to give verbatim those portions of the pamphlet which record the wholesale massacres in some of the various counties of Ireland. It is to be remarked that Lynch, in his *MS. History of the Irish Bishops*, written in 1672, praises this pamphlet as an accurate and most truthful narrative. Curry, also, in his *Historical Review* (p. 409, sec. 9), gives copious extracts from it, and commends " the author's frequent, candid,

and public appeals to things openly transacted, and to enemies themselves, then living."

"*County of Antrim*, A.D. 1641-2.

"2. About the beginning of November the English and Scotch forces in Knockfergus murdered, in one night, all the inhabitants of the Island-Magee, to the number of about 3,000 men, women, and children, all innocent persons, at a time when none of the Catholics of that country were in arms.* Mr. Mac Naughten

---

* Protestant writers have often called in question this massacre of Island-Magee. It is, however, attested in the very "Depositions" of T.C.D., though otherwise so bitterly hostile to the Irish. From this unquestionable authority it appears that the actors in this terrible deed of blood were Scotsmen from beyond the river Bann, and from the neighbourhood of Ballymena. These "Depositions," as was to be expected, lessen very much the number of those who were put to death, but they leave no doubt as to the massacre. Thus, Bryan Magee deposed that about the 8th of January, 1641-2, he was living in his father's house in Island-Magee, when "nine of the family were murdered by twenty persons, reputed Scotchmen;" and he further attests that in the house of the next neighbour, "Daniel Magee and ten other persons were killed on the same day." So also Elizabeth Gormly deposed that she saw Bryan Boye Magee followed by the drummers of the garrison of Carrickfergus, "on the Monday after the great murder." Mr. Skimmin, in his *History of Carrickfergus*, p. 44, states that the massacre took place on the night of Sunday, January 8th, 1642, when some persons, "attached to the garrison of Carrickfergus, sallied out to the neighbouring district of Island-Magee, and cruelly massacred a number of inoffensive Roman Catholic inhabitants." He adds: "The oral history of the parish says, the massacre began at a small rivulet, at the entrance of the parish from Carrickfergus which has ever since from that circumstance been called *Slaughterford*." It is added, on the same authority, "that some of the Catholics were driven over the Gabbon, a dreadful precipice on the S. E. of the island, and that several of them were preserved in a corn kiln by an

built a small fortress in the said county, to preserve himself and his followers from outrages, until he understood what the cause of the then rebellion was; as soon as Colonel Campbell came near with part of his army, he sent to let him know that he would come to him with his party, which he did; and they were next day murdered, to the number of eighty. About the same time, one hundred poor women and children were murdered in one night at a place called Balliaghurn, by direction of the English and Scotch officers, commanding that country.

"About the same time, Captain Fleming, and other officers of the said regiment, commanding a party, smothered to death two hundred and twenty women and children in two caves. And about the same time also, the said Captain Cunningham murdered about sixty-three women and children in the isles of Ross.

" It was likewise in 1641 that the Governor of Letterkenny gathered together, on a Sunday morning, fifty-three poor people, most of them women and children, and caused them to be thrown off the bridge into the river, and drowned them all.

inhabitant of the name of Hill, some of whose descendants still reside in the parish." In the month of May, 1642, a body of Irish troops, who had formed an entrenched camp near Ballymena, surrendered on quarter; but were, nevertheless, all put to death with the exception of three or four, who saved themselves by flight. See *Warr of* 1641, by an English Officer, p. 24. This narrative gives several other instances of such murders after quarter being given. Thus, page 30, when Con Oge O'Neill surrendered on quarter at Clonish, and was being led away by the guard, a minister came behind him and shot him dead. Again, at the battle of Letterkenny, the officers and men of the Irish army that got quarter were, by the Commander Coote's orders, shot or cut to pieces. *Ibid.*, p. 128.

"In November, the same year, one Reading, murdered the wife and three children of Shane O'Morghy, in a place called Ballykenny, of Rameltan, and after her death, cut off her breasts with his sword.

"In 1641 and 1642, the garrisons of Raphoe, Drombo, Lifford, and Castle Ragheen, slaughtered no less than one thousand five hundred of the poor neighbouring inhabitants, never in arms; and three persons were chiefly noted among them for their barbarous cruelty, by name, James Graham, Henry Dungan, and Robert Cunningham, commonly called 'the killer of old women.' About two thousand poor labourers, women, and children of the barony of Tirbu, were massacred by the garrisons of Ballashany and Donegal; and Lieutenant Thomas Poe, an officer among them, coming under colour of friendship to visit a neighbour that lay sick in his bed, and to whom he owed money, carried a dagger under his cloak, which, whilst he seemed to bow towards the sick man in a friendly manner, asking how he did, he thrust it into his body, and told his wife he should be no longer sick."

"*County of Derry.*

" 3. In 1641, some three hundred men, women, and children of the Irish, having freely come under the protection of the garrison of Londonderry, were stripped, plundered, and killed by the said garrison.

"*County of Down* (A.D. 1641).

" 4. The burgesses and inhabitants of the town of Newry, meeting the English army on their march to besiege the castle of the said town, were received into protection, and after quarter given to the garrison of the said castle, the said inhabitants, and the soldiers of the town, to the number of five hundred and upwards, men, women, and children, were brought on the bridge of Newry, and thrown into the river, and such of them as endeavoured to escape by swimming were murdered."*

* The following account of this butchery at Newry, written by Sir James Turner, an English officer who was present, more than justifies the statement in the text: "In the woods of Kilwarning we encountered some hundreds of the rebels, who after a short dispute fled. These who were taken got but bad quarter, being all shot dead. This was too much used by both English and Scots all along in that war. . . . Then we marched straight to Newry, where the Irish had easily seized on his Majesty's castle, wherein they found abundance of ammunition, which gave them confidence to proclaim their rebellion. The fortification of the town being but begun, it came immediately into our hands; but the rebels that were in the castle kept it two days, and then delivered it up upon a very ill-made accord, or a very ill-kept one; for the next day, most of them with many merchants and tradesmen of the town, who had not been in the castle, were carried to the bridge and butchered to death, some by shooting, some by hanging, and some by drowning, without any legal process; and I was verily informed afterwards that several innocent people suffered. Major-General Munroe did not at all excuse himself from being accessory to that carnage nor could he purge himself of it, though my Lord Conway was the principal actor. Our soldiers, who sometimes are cruel, for no other reason but because man's wicked nature leads him to be so, seeing such pranks played by authority at the bridge, thought they might do as much anywhere else; and so ran upon a hundred and fifty women or thereabouts, who had got together in a place below the bridge, whom they resolved to massacre by killing and drowning, which villainy the sea seemed to favour, it being then flood. Just at that time I was speaking with Munroe, but seeing afar off what a game these godless rogues intended to play, I got on horseback and gallopped to them with my pistol in my hand; but before I got to them they had

"*County of Donegal.*

"5. In 1641, about the 20th of November, Sir William Stewart commanded the gentry and inhabitants of that county to join with his forces in opposition to the rebels, and, accordingly, they came to the place appointed, where Captain Cunningham, with a party of the said Sir William's regiment, under pretence of incorporating with them, fell upon the inhabitants with his armed soldiers, and killed very many of them, among whom were Owen Mac Sweeny, Morris O'Farey, and Donagh O'Callan, gentlemen of quality and estate."

"*County of Monaghan.*

"6. In 1641, Captain Townsley, governor of Maghernackle, killed four labourers and a woman, being under protection. Captain Bromwell, Governor of Clones, meeting upon the road with Mark Charles O'Connolly, a gentleman living under his protection, caused him to be shot to death. The soldiers of the garrisons of Dundalk and Trim killed no less than five hundred innocent persons, women and children, in that county. The armies of Munroe and the Lagan, in their several marches through the same county, slaughtered about two thousand poor old men, women, and children.

despatched about a dozen; the rest I saved." (*Memoirs of his own Life and Times*, by Sir James Turner, 1632-1670. Published at Edinburgh 1829, p. 20).

The narrative of the *Irish Warr of* 1641, by an English Officer, p. 27, names as one of the sufferers, "one O'Deery," of whom it relates, that though shots were fired at him on the bridge yet the bullets harmed him not, so that the soldiers wounded him with their swords and then threw him into the river.

"In 1652, Colonel Barrow, of Cromwell's army having taken an island defended by Lieutenant-Colonel Patrick Mac Mahon, after killing the said Lieutenant-Colonel and his soldiers, put all the women and children to the sword, to the number of eighty, among whom a child of six years old being spared by the soldiers, was killed by order of the said Colonel Barrow."

"*County of Cavan.*

"7. In 1642, Mark de la Pool, an English gentleman, having taken lands in that county, some years before the war, invited several of his friends to come out of England and live with him, who were all murdered in their houses by the army, with the exception of the said De la Pool, who was brought into the town of Cavan, and there hanged, for no other reason but their being Roman Catholics, and living among the Irish. Sir Alexander Godven and his lady, both Scotch, but Roman Catholics, each of them above seventy years old, were plundered of their goods, and stripped naked, and their sons, and tenants, and servants murdered. In the same year the English forces in this county drowned six hundred men, women, and children, in and about Butler's-bridge."

"*County of Meath* (A.D. 1642).

"8. In April, Mrs. Eleanor Taaffe, of Tullaghanoge, sixty years old, and six women more, were murdered by the soldiers of the garrison of Trim; and a blind woman, aged eighty years, was encompassed with straw by them, to which they set fire, and burned her. The same day they hanged two women in Kilbride, and two old decrepit men, who begged alms of them. Mr. Walter Dulin, an old man, unable to stir abroad many years before the war, was killed in his own house: and Mr. Walter Evans, a justice of the peace and quorum, an aged man, and bedrid of the palsy, was carried in a cart to Trim, and there hanged by the governor's orders.

"Many ploughmen were killed at Philbertstown. Forty men, women, and children, in protection, reaping their harvest in Bonestown, were killed by a troop of the said garrison; who, upon the same day, killed Mrs. Alison Read, at Dunshaughlin, being eighty-nine years old, and forty persons more, most of them women and children.

"About seventy men, women, and children, tenants to Mr. Francis McEvoy, and under protection, were killed by Greenvill's soldiers; and one hundred and sixty more in the parish of Rathcoare, whereof there was one aged couple, blind for fifteen years before. Captain Sandford and his troop murdered, in and about Mulhussy, upwards of one hundred men, women, and children, under protection; and caused one Connor Breslan to be stuck with a knife into the throat, and so bled to death. Also one Eleanor Cusack, one hundred years old, was tied about with lighted matches, and so tortured to death in Clonmoghon. James Dowlan, about one hundred years old, Donagh Comen, Darby Dennis, Roger Bolan, and several other labourers and women, to the number of one hundred and sixty, making their harvest, were slaughtered by the garrison of Trim.

"About the month of April, the soldiers under the

said Greenvill's command killed in and about Navan eighty men, women, and children, who lived under protection. Captain Wentworth and his company, garrisoned at Dunmo, killed no less than 200 protected persons in the parish of Donamore, Slane, and the adjoining baronies. Forty-two others and eighteen infants were killed at Dormanstown. A woman, under protection, was, by Captain Morroe's soldiers, put into the stock of a tuck-mill, and so tucked to death, in the town of Steedalte. Lieutenant Ponsonby put two aged protected persons to death at Downastone, each of them about eighty years old. Captain Morroe caused about an hundred protected persons, men, and women, and children, to be put to death in the barony of Duleek. Many thousands of the poor inhabitants of this county were destroyed in the furze by fire, and the rest, for the most part, perished by famine."

"*County of Westmeath.*

"9. In 1642, Mrs. Ellis Dillon, of Killenennin, having the Lords Justices' protection for herself and tenants, their wives and children, they were all killed by soldiers under Sir Michael Earnley's command."

"*County of Louth.*

"10. In the month of February, 1641, about three hundred poor people were cruelly slaughtered in the wood of Derrner, by a party of the garrisons of Dundalk and Tredath. In the beginning of March, about three hundred other farmers and labourers, with their wives and children, were massacred by a party of the garrisons of Dundalk and Tredath, in the Redmoore of

Branganstown. About the same time Captain Charles Townsley and Lieutenant Faithful Townsley, with a part of the English army and garrison of Dundalk, slaughtered, at Dunmoghan, two hundred and twenty inhabitants of several villages, commanded by the officers of the said army, who live in that place for their greater security. A party of the said garrison of Tredath and Dundalk killed above two hundred persons in the Castle of Reaghstown, after quarter given. One Anthony Townsley hanged Mr. Dromgole of Dromgolestown, at his own gate. The said Townsley hanged upwards of thirty men and women going to the markets of Dundalk and Tredath, on a tree, commonly called eight mile bush, midway between the said towns.

"In 1642 a party of horse and foot of the garrison of Tredath killed and burned in the furze above one hundred and sixty men, women, and children, of the inhabitants of Termonfeighkin, within three miles of Tredath; no less than one thousand of the poor inhabitants of that county were massacred."

" County of Dublin.

"11. About the beginning of November, 1641, five poor men, coming from the market of Dublin, and lying that night at Santry, were murdered in their beds by Captain Smith, and their heads brought next day in triumph into the city. This occasioned Luke Netterville and others to write to the Lords Justices to know the cause of the said murder; whereupon their lordships issued forth a proclamation that within five days the gentry should come to Dublin to receive satisfaction. Before, however, these five days expired, Sir Charles

Coote came out with a party, plundered and burned the town of Clontarf, killing sixteen of the townsmen and women, and three sucking infants.

"In the same week fifty-six men and women of the village of Belloge, being affrighted at what was done at Clontarf, took boats and went to sea to shun the fury of a party of soldiers gone out of Dublin, under the command of Colonel Crafford, but being pursued by the soldiers in boats, were overtaken and thrown overboard.

"In March a party of horse, of the garrison of Dunsoghlin, murdered seven or eight poor people in protection, tenants of Mr. Dillon, of Huntstown, having quartered in their houses the night before, and receiving such entertainment as the poor people could afford. About the same time a party of English quartered at Malahide, hanged a servant of Mr. Robert Boynes at the plough, and forced a poor labourer to hang his own brother; and soon after they hanged fifteen of the inhabitants of Swords, who never bore arms, in the orchard of Malahyde; they likewise hanged a woman bemoaning her husband, who was hanged amongst them.

"In the same year, after quarter given by Lieutenant-Colonel Gibson to those of the castle of Carrickmain, they were all put to the sword, being about 350, most of them women and children; and Colonel Washington, endeavouring to save a pretty child of seven years old, carried him under his cloak; but the child, against his will, was killed in his arms, which was a principal motive of his quitting that service.

"In April, 1642, one Nicholas Hart, and fourteen

labourers, going with corn to the market of Dublin, and having a pass, were all murdered on the road by a party commanded by Lord Lambert. The same day eighteen villages in protection, the farthest within six miles of Dublin, were plundered and burned, and to the number of 400 men, women, and children were cruelly massacred. About the same time a party of the garrison of Swords, having brought in thirty poor labourers, forced them to dig their own graves, and then killed them; the sheriff, too, of the county, killed sixteen persons coming from the market of Dublin. A party under the command of Colonel Crafford murdered 140 women and children in Newcastle and Coolmain being under protection. Many thousands more of the poor people of that county, shunning the fury of the soldiers, fled into thickets of furze, which the soldiers usually set on fire, killing as many as endeavoured to escape, or forcing them back again to be burned; the rest of the inhabitants, for the most part, died of famine. It is to be remarked that no less than twelve thousand of the poor inhabitants of that county were cruelly massacred the first year of the war."

" County of Kildare.

"12. In 1641, Captain Thomas Hughes, having summoned thirty-three contributors to meet him at Hedgestown, caused them all to be murdered. The soldiers of Clongowes Wood and Rathcoffey, yielding upon quarter, were conveyed to Dublin, and hanged there, and upwards of 150 women and children were found in the said places murdered. It is well known that the common people of that county were, for the most part, destroyed and slaughtered by the English, insomuch that there were not so many left as could gather the twentieth part of the harvest."

"*County of Wicklow.*

"13. In October, 1641, three women and a boy were hanged on the bridge of Newragh, by command of Sir Charles Coote. Mr. Daniel Conyan, of Glenealy, aged, and unable to bear arms, was roasted to death by Captain Gee, of Colonel Crafford's regiment; and in the marches of '41, '42, and '43, the English army killed all they met in this county. In the usurper's time, Captain Barrington, garrisoned at Arklow, murdered Donagh O'Daly, of Kilcarrow, and more than 500 others who had been received into protection by himself; and it is well known that most of the common people were murdered."

"*County of Kilkenny.*

"14. The English soldiers of the garrison of Ballinakil, in 1641, burned an old woman of ninety years of age in her own house in Idough. In the following year the same garrison massacred 180 men, women, and children, who were cutting their corn in that neighbourhood. They also dragged Mr. Thomas Shee out of his own house, with five of his servants, and hanged them all at Ballinakil."

"*County of Tipperary.*

"15. On the 24th of October, 1641, one Browne and Captain Peasely murdered eleven men, women, and children in their own houses at Golden Bridge, before any of the Catholics took up arms in that county. About the same time the said Captain Peasely, going through Clonoulty, Philip Ryan, a peaceable gentleman and owner of the said town, came out of his house to salute the captain, who pulled out his pistol and shot the harmless gentleman dead at his own door. These murders occasioned the rising of the gentry and inhabitants of that county."

"*County of Cork.*

"16. In Condon's country (1641), above 300 labourers, women, and children were murdered by some of the now Earl of Orrery's soldiers. Fifty-six persons, or thereabouts, were subsequently brought prisoners to Castle Lyons and put into a stable; there their beards were burned, as well as the hair of their heads, which so disfigured them that their nearest friends could not know them next day when they were hanging.

"In 1642, in the same county, 355 persons were murdered with clubs and stones, being in protection. Mr. Henly, an English gentleman, dwelling in Roche's county, but a Roman Catholic, had his wife and children barbarously stripped, and most of his tenants inhumanly murdered by adjacent English garrisons, and such cruelty was used that they stabbed young infants and left them so half dead on their mother's dead carcases. In this said Henlystown, and the adjacent villages, at that time there were murdered about 900 labourers, women, and children.

"In 1643, Cloghlegh being garrisoned by the Irish, and surrendered upon quarter of life to Sir Charles

Vavasour, they were all inhumanly murdered, and the hearts of some of them pulled out and put into their mouths; and many other massacres were committed the same time there upon women and children. At Lislee, twenty-four men in protection were murdered by Colonel Mynn's soldiers. At Bellanere eight poor labourers were killed by Captain Bridge's men whilst in protection and engaged in saving the harvest of the English.

"In 1642, at Clonakilty, about 238 persons were murdered, of which number seventeen children were taken by the legs by soldiers, who knocked out their brains against the walls. This was done by Forbes's men and the garrison of Bandon Bridge. At Garanne, near Ross, Connor Kennedy, who had protection for himself and his tenants to save their harvest, were murdered by the garrison of Ross as they were reaping their corn.

"In 1641, the garrison of Bandon Bridge tied eighty-eight Irishmen of that town back to back, and threw them off the bridge into the river, where they were all drowned. Patrick Hackett, master of a ship in Waterford, when the Duchess of Ormonde was desirous to be conveyed to Dublin, left her safe, with her family and goods there, and received from the Lords Justices and Ormonde a pass for his safe return; but being driven by a storm into Dungarvan, he and his men were hanged by direction of the commander-in chief there, notwithstanding that he produced the said pass.

"The English party of this county burned O'Sullevan Beare's house in Bantry, and all the rest of that county, killing man, woman, and child, and turning many into their home, then on fire, to be burned therein, and among others, Thomas de Bucke, a cooper, about eighty years old, and his wife, who was almost as aged."

"*County of Waterford.*

"17. In Decies' country, the neighbouring English garrison of the county Cork, after burning and pillaging all that county, murdered above three thousand persons, men, women, and children, and led one hundred labourers prisoners to Caperquine (Cappoquin) where being tied by couples, they were cast into the river and were made sport of to see them drowned. This was before any rebellion began in Munster."

"*County of Clare.*

"18. In 1644, forty families in protection were murdered by the garrison of Inchicronan; and in 1646, several residing near Bunratty were murdered by the soldiers of that place, who were under command of Lieutenant Adams."

"*County of Galway.*

"19. In 1642, Sergeant Redmund Burke and two more were hanged by the then governor of the fort of Galway. A party of the garrison, too, murdered six people in Rinveel, among whom one Geoffry Fitz-Thibot, aged about seventy years, and in a burning fever.

"1652 and 1653. It was a usual practice with Colonel Stubbers, then Governor of Galway, and others commanding in said county, to take the people out of their beds at night and sell them for slaves to the Indies: and by computation he sold out of said county above 1,000 souls."

"*County of Leitrim.*

"20. 1641. It was commonly known to all sides how cruel the Governor of Mannor Hamilton (Sir Frederick Hamilton) was in that county, and how he usually invited gentlemen to dine with him, and hanged them after dinner, and caused their thighs to be broken with hatchets before execution."

"*County of Sligo.*

"21. There is none at this time who can give an exact account of the murders committed in this county, with the exception of one remarkable instance in Creane's Castle, in the town of Sligo. The Irish had a party numbering about 200 men, commanded by Major Richard Burke, and after obtaining quarter to march away, they were all murdered in cold blood."

CHAPTER V.

THE ACT OF SETTLEMENT.

1. Hopes of the Catholics that Charles II., at the Restoration, would remember their merits to his father.—2. These hopes disappointed.—3. Sufferings of Catholics by Act of Settlement, in 1660.—4. Lord Clare's description of its injustice.—5. Claims for property examined in London where bribery prevailed.—6. The Lords Justices: the Black Act.—7. Compensation to Protestant merchants who had lent money to carry on war against the king.—8. To Cromwell's soldiers.—9. To his officers.—10. Perfidy of the men thus rewarded.—11. New persecutions.—12. Dr. Plunket; Dr. O'Reilly.—13. Remark of M'Geoghegan.

1. In the month of May, 1660, Charles the Second, amid the acclamations of his subjects, returned to the throne of his ancestors. This restoration of the legitimate sovereign, it was hoped, would terminate the misfortunes of Ireland. The whole nation had shared his father's sufferings, and had combated to the last for the royal cause. Even when exiled to France they signalised themselves by their loyalty; and when, through political combinations, the English monarch was compelled to seek an asylum in the Low Countries, thither he was followed by the Irish regiments, though all his other subjects abandoned him. This fidelity won for them the admiration and esteem of the continental nations, and the prince himself after his restoration publicly acknowledged their loyalty and services, and declared

that they were on that account deserving of his special *"protection, favour, and justice."**

2. The hopes, however, that were awakened by these promises were soon blighted, and the sunshine of royal justice never cheered the desolate homes of the Irish. Dr. John Lynch, in 1662, dedicating his *Cambrensis Eversus* to Charles II., exclaims: " Alas! the words of the poet, 'sorrow is mingled with joy,' are not mere poetry; for while your other kingdoms are delirious with joy, Ireland alone grieves and mourns, groaning deeply, and ever reiterating her plaint, 'Lo, in this peace is my bitterness most bitter:' others enjoy security, but we are still oppressed with a load of calamities brought on by that peace. For laws and civil contentions more savage than the sword grind us to the dust; and, after narrowly escaping the sword of our enemies, we are now the victims of their enactments."†

3. On the first announcement of the restoration of the king the Cromwellian settlers were filled with alarm, and agents were at once despatched by them to the monarch to represent the Irish Catholics as rebels, ill affected to the cause of order and royalty. Whilst the royal ears were dinned with these representations, the severest ordinances lately made against the Irish Roman Catholics were strictly executed. " They were not allowed to pass from one province to another on their ordinary business; many of them were imprisoned; their letters were intercepted; their gentry were forbidden to meet, and thus deprived of the opportunity of choosing agents

---

* See the address of Charles II. to both Houses of Parliament on 27th July, 1650, and again on 30th November, the same year.

† *Camb. Evers. Epist.* Dedicat., p. 6.

or representing their grievances. No sooner had the king arrived in London than he was obliged to publish a proclamation for apprehending and prosecuting all Irish rebels, and commanding that adventurers, soldiers, and others who were possessed of their manors, houses, or lands should not be disturbed in their possessions until legally evicted, or his majesty by advice of Parliament should take further order therein."*

It was on the 30th of November, 1660, that the famous Act of Settlement was published at Whitehall. It professed to have for its object the execution of his majesty's gracious declaration for the settlement of Ireland, and for the satisfaction, at the same time, of the several interests of adventurers, soldiers, and others, his subjects there; and after reciting the rebellion, the enormities committed in the progress of it, and the final reduction of the rebels by the king's English and Protestant subjects, proceeded by one general sweeping clause to vest in the king, his heirs, and successors, all estates, real and personal, of every kind whatsoever in the kingdom of Ireland which at any time from the 21st of October, 1641, had in any way been seized by the crown or allotted "to any person or persons for adventures, arrears, reprisals, or otherwise; or whereof any soldier, adventurer, or other person was in possession for or on account of the rebellion."

4. Lord Clare, in his famous speech in Parliament on the Union, after quoting these words of the Act, continues:—

"Having thus in the first instance vested three-

* Leland, *Hist. of Ireland*, vol. iii., p. 410.

fourths of the land and personal property of the inhabitants of the island in the king, commissioners were appointed, with full and exclusive authority, to hear and determine all claims upon the general fund, whether of officers and soldiers for arrears of pay, of adventurers who had advanced money for carrying on the war, or of innocent Papists, as they are called—in other words, of the old inhabitants of the island who had been dispossessed by Cromwell, not for having taken a part in the rebellion against the English crown, but for their attachment to the fortunes of Charles the Second. But with respect to this class of sufferers, who might naturally have expected a preference of claim, a clause is introduced by which they are postponed after a decree of innocence by the Commissioners until previous reprisal shall be made to Cromwell's soldiers and adventurers who had obtained possession of *their* inheritance. I will not detain the House with a minute detail of the provisions of this Act thus passed for the settlement of Ireland; but I wish gentlemen, who call themselves the independent Irish nation, to know that seven millions eight hundred thousand acres of land were set out, under the authority of this Act, to a motley crew of English adventurers, civil and military, nearly to the total exclusion of the old inhabitants of the island. Many of the latter class who were innocent of the rebellion lost their inheritance as well from the difficulties imposed on them by the court of claims in the proofs required of their innocence as from a deficiency in the fund for reprisal to English adventurers."

The Act of Settlement pretended to exclude the

betrayers of the Munster garrisons, but a clause was added allowing them to retain their debenture lands if they should prove that they had rendered some service to the Crown. The only fault that could never be repaired or pardoned was to be an Irish Catholic pretending to some portion of his native land, held in possession or coveted by an Englishman. Hence " Colonel Widnam, the betrayer of Youghal, could securely look down from the towers of Castletown Roche, where Lord Roche's ancestors had for ages fixed themselves, and behold the ancient owner, descended of a long line of loyal forefathers, and his orphan daughters wandering in beggary and slavery below."*

5. Such was the royal "*protection, justice, and favour*," shown to the Catholics of Ireland.† The examination of all claims was, indeed, summoned before the Government in London, and deputations were sent thither from both sides The Protestants, however, took the precaution to send £30,000 with their deputies for immediate distribution, whilst other sums were sent directly to the chief members of the court. Of course the decisions were, almost without exception, in favour of the Puritans. The English judges had, many of them, a special interest in the confiscation of the Irish lands, besides the prejudices they had conceived against the old Irish themselves. " The Irish," writes Leland,

---

* *Prendergast*, p. 194.

† Dr. Lynch, in *Cambrensis Eversus*, vol. iii., p. 135, writes, in 1662 :—" The Irish, though guilty of no crime against the Crown, were, nevertheless, on the solicitation of the English Parliament, branded by him as rebels, and condemned to an unprecedented forfeiture of their property."

THE ACT OF SETTLEMENT. 441

" had neither money nor friends; the English nation regarded them with horror. The council, before whom they were to appear, knew little of the conduct of individuals who deserved favour, and were ready to involve them all in the general guilt of massacre and rebellion."*

6. Among those who were admitted to the king's favour was Lord Broghill, though he had proved himself, under the Commonwealth, a most determined enemy of the Royal cause and a most relentless persecutor of the Irish Catholics. His father, the Earl of Cork, having amassed an immense property, was the first of the Irish Protestant proprietors to insert in leases that no portion of their land should be held by any Papist. Broghill himself, throughout the whole period of the Confederate War, was particularly active in putting the Catholic clergy to death, and made it a rule to give no quarter to the Irish Catholics. Being upbraided with this cruelty, he replied that he did not know what was meant by quarter. After the battle of Knocknaclashy, in which Viscount Muskerry with the Munster army was defeated, in July, 1652, Broghill wrote to the Speaker, giving an official account of the battle :—" We had a very fair execution for above three miles, and indeed it was bloody, for I gave orders to kill all." In England he was known to be one of the most active and prominent supporters of Cromwell, and, as a member of the Select Committee, he, on the 11th of April, 1657, offered the Crown to Cromwell in the Palace of Whitehall. Seeing, however, how the current had changed in favour of the restoration of the

* *History of Ireland*, vol. iii., p. 424.

monarchy, he put himself forward as a champion of that cause, and hence high honours were conferred on him by King Charles. He was created Earl of Orrery, was sworn of the Privy Council of England and Ireland, and appointed Lord President of Munster.

When the Irish Catholics petitioned to be restored to their estates, the king appointed a commission in London to hear their agents and adjudicate upon their claims, and Broghill, now Lord Orrery, was appointed on that commission. Sir Nicholas Plunkett, speaking on the part of the petitioners, referred to the loyalty of the Irish Catholics and the losses they had sustained for the Royal cause, but Broghill asked him had not he signed the declaration of the Supreme Council against Lord Ormonde, and had he not solicited aid from the Duke of Lorraine, and, when an answer was given in the affirmative, he added:—" Are these men, who have offered to give away a kingdom from his Majesty, likely to prove good subjects." . The Commission were only too well disposed to adopt Broghill's sentiments The king, accepting their decision, declared that the petitioners deserved all they had suffered, and that their estates should not be restored to them, and, adding insult to injury, expressed his astonishment at their audacity, appearing before him with so much guilt upon their consciences. Thus the enemies of the Catholics enjoyed an easy triumph. Was there no one to ask who it was that had kept alive the war against the king in Munster and had offered the crown and kingdom to Cromwell?

Lords Justices were appointed to administer the Government in Ireland, and, with the Lord Chancellor,

THE ACT OF SETTLEMENT. 443

were associated, in this office, the two most truculent enemies of the Irish Catholics, Lord Broghill and Sir Charles Coote, now adorned with their new titles of Earl of Orrery and Earl of Mountrath. Such were the men selected by Lord Ormonde and by the king to show fair play to the Catholics of Ireland. No wonder that, guided by these counsellors, the king would deny every favour to the Irish Catholics, whilst he confirmed to the Protestant Church all its former privileges, and bestowed on it, in addition to the 300,000 acres of land, which it held before 1641, a further grant of 20,000 acres, the property of Irish Catholics.

Under the rule of these Lords Justices a Parliament was convened and met in Dublin on the 8th of May, 1661. To the House of Commons there was but one Catholic Member returned: so thoroughly had the Catholic farmers been swept away from the country districts, and so completely had the cities and boroughs passed into the hands of aliens. It was, in fact, a Parliament of Cromwellians, who, as a matter of course, sanctioned the declaration made by the king in favour of the "new interest," and confirmed the enemies of the Catholics in all their pretended rights. Such was the famous Act of Settlement, an Act which, in so far as it rests upon the vote of this Parliament, has not a shred of title of justice, or law, or equity to commend it. It was very much the case of submitting to a party of bandits, the question whether or not the booty they had stolen should be restored to the victims whom they had plundered. In the House of Lords some opposition was given to the measure by the Earl of Kildare and other noblemen, but most of the Catholic Peers were silenced by the intimation that they were outlawed in 1641 and could not vote, as their outlawry had not been reversed. By this rule the Earls of Fingall and Castlehaven, the Viscounts Gormanston, Netterville, Magennis, Fermoy, and Muskerry, with Lords Slane, Trimblestown, Louth, Dunboyne, and others, were obliged to quit the House. The Court, partly with the aid of the Lord Justices and partly through the vote of the Protestant bishops gained an easy triumph, and the law was passed, which practically barred all further investigation into the confiscated estates. This Act the Roman Catholics called the *Black Act*, whilst it was styled by the Cromwellian settlers the *Magna Charta* of Irish Protestants. Thus was the sanction of the legislature and the monarch's approbation given to the confiscation of Ireland and to the ruin of the Irish families.

7. Those to whom the possession of all that was worth cultivating in Ireland was thus secured, were divided into three classes. The first class comprised the adventurers, who had been merchants and citizens of London, and, in the eighteenth year of Charles I. had advanced considerable sums for the reduction of Ireland. This money, however, was applied by the rebellious Parliament to the raising of an army against the king, and this application of the money was subsequently approved of by the adventurers themselves, assembled at Grocers' Hall in London. This was no secret, and it was plain to the world that these adventurers had no title to the lands from which the Catholics had been driven, and yet, notwithstanding their crimes and the invalidity of their titles, they were upheld in their un-

just possessions, and all the adventurers who, at any time, advanced money to forward the Cromwellian cause, were made secure in the lands that belonged to the Irish Catholics.

8. Cromwell's soldiers formed the second class. They were the avowed enemies of the king, and had been the cruel ministers of Cromwell's fury. Twelve counties were, in 1652, distributed among them, and now, as a reward for the murder of Charles I., and for all their butcheries in Ireland, this donation of Irish lands was solemnly confirmed to them.

9. The third class consisted of the officers who had served the king before June 5th, 1649, and whose arrears remained unpaid. To forty-nine of these officers there were given all the confiscated lands in four counties bordering on the Shannon, besides houses and certain privileges in every town and city of the kingdom. These officers had been the chief cause of the defeat of the Royal forces, and many of them had openly deserted the king's standard to join the usurper. Even those were included in this class who had been mainly instrumental in surrendering the Irish towns and fortresses to Cromwell, and thus was the seal of the monarch's approbation publicly given to all their unparalleled iniquitous deeds.*

10. It was thought that, by this course, the new settlers in Ireland would be conciliated to the Royal

* The Cromwellian adventurers, being secured in their estates, the Government sought to create some additional friends, by allowing large tracts of the land that had belonged to the Catholics, to increase the funds of the Protestant University in Dublin, as also for the erection of free Protestant schools through the country. See *Ireland's Case*, also MacGeoghegan's *History of Ireland*, p. 583.

cause, but injustice can never produce fruits of gratitude or honour. When, some years later, another usurper raised the standard of revolt, these Puritan settlers and their children were the first to draw the sword against their lawful monarch, whilst his only faithful followers were the Irish Catholics, whose rights were so unjustly betrayed, and who, by this confiscation, were deprived of the means of defending, with success, the cause which they still conscientiously espoused.

11. The Puritans, knowing well the nature of their claims to the vast properties they had acquired, resolved to perpetuate the deeds of persecution with which they had hitherto pursued the Irish Catholics. "In the present day," writes Dr. Oliver, "we can hardly form an idea of the persecutions and sufferings that the clergy of Ireland had to endure. I have seen a letter of Dr. Anthony Geoghegan, Bishop of Meath, dated 26th of August, 1660, *Ex loco nostri refugii in Hibernia*, in which he says: *Vivo in cavernis adhuc, sicut et cæteri meæ vocationis et status* (I live still in the caverns of the earth, as do also all other members of the clergy). Truly, this exemplary clergy could say: "For thee, O Lord, we are mortified the whole day long." (*Collections, &c.*, p. 246.)

12. It would be foreign to our present purpose to pursue the history of all the sufferings that our clergy and faithful people were compelled to endure during the reign of Charles II. Many particulars connected with that period may be seen in the *Memoirs of the Most Rev. Dr. Plunket*, who died at Tyburn a martyr for the Faith in 1681. The predecessor of that glorious mar-

tyr, Dr. Edmund O'Reilly, as he shared his dignity so did he share his privations and persecutions. In a letter of the 12th July, 1661, he writes to the Holy See that "he was obliged to lie concealed on account of the dangers that threatened the clergy on every side; by night he had to discharge those duties which should be discharged by day, and he had to pass the day as though it were the depth of night. The letters, too, of the Catholics were intercepted, not only in London, but even in Dublin and Paris, by the spies of the English Government." In another letter, about the same time, the same archbishop states that after making the visitation of some districts, an accusation was presented against him "as though he were an incendiary, and engaged in exciting a rebellion ; he, therefore was compelled to take refuge in the caverns, where he still continues."

13. All the persecutions which our Catholic clergy and people were thus compelled to endure, may justly be referred to the iniquitous Act of Settlement which legalised the Cromwellian spoliations, and gave the royal sanction to all the preceding deeds of Puritan barbarity* against the Irish people. We shall conclude our remarks on the iniquitous act, with the words of Mac Geoghegan :—

"It is incredible to think how the king was influenced to act contrary, not only to justice, but even to the interests of his house. Princes have been often

---

* *Priest hunting* continued during the first years of Charles's reign to be a favourite pursuit of the Puritans; they even imported *bloodhounds* from America and trained them to track to the mountain caverns that sacred prey; it is hence at that *word* the heart of the Irish peasant yet thrills with horror.

known, from motives of policy, to pardon rebellious subjects, after returning to their duty and submission, but to heap upon them the rich patrimonies of faithful subjects by which the latter are reduced to the extreme of indigence, is unexampled in history."—(*Hist. of Ireland*, p. 583.)

APPENDIX I.

Letter regarding Monsignore Rinuccini's Mission to Ireland in 1645, and the condition of Ireland at that time.

WE insert here a letter written by one of the Nuncio Rinuccini's *suite* soon after his arrival in Ireland. It gives many interesting details regarding the customs of the Irish in those country districts, which were so soon to be laid waste by Puritan barbarity. From the whole narrative, it appears that there was abundance in the country at that time, and none of that squalid poverty and misery which are now so common, though we are every day told that the country is in a state of great prosperity.

The original letter is in Italian, and was addressed to the brother of the Nuncio in Florence. The only ancient copy extant is preserved in the archives of the Irish College, Rome. In 1845, this letter was communicated by the then Rector, afterwards Cardinal Cullen, to the editors of the *Dublin Review*, who published part of it in the March number, p. 219, seq. :—*

---

*The writer of the article in the *Dublin Review* is inclined to believe that the author of the letter was F. Joseph Arcamoni, the Nuncio's confessor. From the letter itself, however, it is sufficiently evident that its author was the Dean of Fermo, the companion and intimate friend of the Nuncio.

"As soon as, by order of the Nuncio, I had purchased at Nantes the frigate *S. Pietro,* his Excellency, with some necessary attendants, proceeded to Rochelle, where he was awaited by the secretary of the Irish confederation, who had given my Lord Nuncio to understand that he had engaged a fleet of eight good vessels to accompany him into Ireland. I remained at Nantes in the meantime, to prepare some provisions and ammunition which, notwithstanding all the exertions of the different ministers, could not be in readiness for ten days. I then hastened with the frigate and the remainder of the attendants to Rochelle, and throughout I experienced the happy effects of God's protecting providence, owing, perhaps, to the intercession of so many devout persons who, as you more than once assured me, are engaged in offering up prayers for us. We not only escaped when a parliamentary vessel attempted to surprise our frigate as it lay with only a few guards in the port of Painbœuf, but we were also freed from the risk we were exposed to by the same parliamentary vessel in the port of Sanazan; it watched all our movements there, and on our raising the anchor and spreading our sails it acted in like manner and pursued us for a distance of forty miles, expecting that we would be met by two other parliamentary vessels which were expressly cruising for that purpose in those waters, and that thus it would, by following us, be able to secure our capture.

"But God so arranged it that on the preceding day these two parliamentary vessels were drawn off in pursuit of an Irish frigate which, however, escaped between St. Malo and Nantes, and thus we enjoyed an uninterrupted journey. We lost, however, a very favourable prize which presented itself in front of the port of Olon: a corsair Biscayan vessel made preparations there to attack us, sailing towards us with full speed; but when we were just ready to board her she changed her course and fled from us. We could have easily overtaken her, but our captain very prudently deemed it better not to enter on the pursuit, as we had another enemy ever following on our track. During the whole night we sailed along, keeping constant guard, but on the following day we found ourselves not only freed from the hostile vessels, but also close to the island of St. Martin, whence, with a favourable wind, after a few hours' sail we safely anchored in Rochelle. I at once went in the small boat to land, to salute the Nuncio who, at the Jesuits' college, in great anxiety awaited my arrival, for he had heard that we would run greater risks between Nantes and Rochelle than between France and Ireland, and seeing me he raised his hands to heaven giving thanks to God and the Blessed Virgin.

"The eight vessels, of which I spoke above, had been under anchor for four or five days waiting for a favourable wind, and when this at length came (as there was no sign of our frigate), they set sail; another large vessel, which was well armed, and which had promised to await us at all events, started on the very day that we reached Rochelle, and sailed to St. Martin's, and thence towards the Irish coast. We made the best, however, of everything, and the Nuncio, with his usual confidence in the protection of God and in the Apostolic blessing, gave immediate orders to get everything in readiness for our journey; and on the very next day he went on board the frigate (though he was then afflicted with a most annoying cutaneous disease), and accompanied by eighty-three persons, between passengers, soldiers, and mariners, we set sail under happy auspices.

"We sailed with favourable wind during that and the following day; and as we met with no vessel of the enemy, everything went on most prosperously. On the third day, however, at 11 o'clock, we descried eight parliamentary vessels, viz., five ships of war and three frigates, which for four hours pursued us at full speed; but partly through the swiftness of our frigate, and partly because they never imagined that the Nuncio for Ireland could be on board our solitary vessel, they gave up the chase and allowed us to continue our course unmolested. On the following day, being new moon, the weather changed and a storm arose; so dense was the darkness that the captain feared lest we should be driven into the hands of our enemies, and hence kept to the broad sea, steering as best he could not to stray too far from our course.

"At daybreak our troubles increased, for we descried a man-of-war and a war-frigate, which made all sail towards us, and approached so near that we could clearly perceive that they were commanded by a certain Plunket,[*] who was engaged in the parliamentary service, and was a most bitter persecutor of the Irish. He had the advantage over us as the wind was too strong for our

---

[*] Belling, in his Narrative of the Confederate War, styles this piratical Plunket *a noted scourge*. The chase described above is mentioned by Castlehaven and others. From these authorities we learn that a fire broke out in one of Plunket's vessels, which obliged him to give up the chase.

frigate, and the stormy sea was also favourable to his large vessels; he therefore gained ground on us so much that we were obliged to cast overboard boxes, barrels, butts, baskets, and such other articles. The chase commenced between the Scilly Isles and the English Channel steering towards Ireland, and lasted for nine hours, in which we ran more than 115 miles; through the blessing of Providence the enemy never came within range of our frigate, and when we cut away the fore-mast sail, which made her dip too much, they gave up all hope of overtaking us; and when we feared most that we were on the point of being captured, the piratical persecutor gave up the chase and turned to the right towards Capollen; our captain, to whom we are much indebted, displayed surprising courage on that day, animating the soldiers and passengers, and giving the opportune orders to the mariners, who all acted in a masterly manner.

"We sailed, as I have said, about 115 miles from Capollen towards the western coast of Ireland, but so far in the open sea that it afterwards occasioned us new trouble, as I will mention just now. It was surprising that during all this peril neither the Nuncio nor the greater part of his companions experienced any alarm. Whilst his Excellency, with the greatest tranquillity, encouraged all around him, we, without confusion or disorder, got our arms in readiness, and having endeavoured to make an act of contrition for our sins, we prepared to defend ourselves to the last drop of our blood. My Lord Nuncio was always full of confidence that Providence would deliver us from danger, and foretold our escape. It was only when we found ourselves out of peril that our hair stood on an end, and that we fully comprehended the great risk we had run. All, therefore, most humbly returned thanks to God, to the Blessed Virgin, and to St. Anthony of Padua, whose festival was on that day celebrated: the Irish were the more fervent in their thanksgiving, as they had been the more alarmed during the pursuit, knowing well the certain death that awaited them from their most cruel enemy. They therefore raised their hands to heaven and embraced one another, shedding tears of tenderness.

"On the following day, as the bad weather continued, as well as a high sea, we suffered some annoyance; for, owing to the tract of sea we had run when pursued by the enemy, and also to our having strayed about during the night, we had to labour a good deal to make out where we were; and the pilots not agreeing among themselves, we had in the wide expanse of ocean to sail about in search of the kingdom of Ireland, till at length St. Ursula, whose feast it was, consoled us by bringing us in sight of the wished-for Erin.

"Three hours after mid-day we found ourselves on the western coast of the island, opposite the port of Kenmare, at the mouth of the river Maire; but as night was coming on the captain did not wish to enter in, on account of some rocks which were in the harbour, and casting anchor he waited there till the dawn of morning. As a strong land-wind, however, sprung up on the following day, it was not without difficulty that we could enter the port, and as my Lord Nuncio was most anxious to land, it was necessary to lower him into the small boat, and he was conducted to some huts of shepherds or fishermen; and there, his usual bed being prepared for him, he, through the blessing of God, rested very well during the night, which he had not been able to do during the six preceding days of our voyage. On the following day I went from the frigate to salute him, and having found him in a poor hut, I could not refrain from remarking that, as the Irish had looked forward for his arrival with as much anxiety as the Jews for the promised Messias, it was only meet that in imitation of his Divine Master his first abode should be in the huts of shepherds. I there assisted the Monsignor at Mass, which he celebrated for the consolation of an immense concourse of people assembled from the surrounding mountainous districts; subsequently I returned to the frigate with some of the attendants of his Excellency; and on the following day he continued his journey by land towards Ardtully, whilst I sailed along the coast in the same direction.

"The courtesy of the poor people amongst whom my lord the Nuncio took up his quarters was indescribable. A fat bullock, two sheep, and a porker were instantly slaughtered, and an abundant supply of beer, butter, and milk was brought to him; we who were still on board also experienced the kindness of the poor fishermen, who sent us presents of excellent fish and oysters of most exquisite flavour, and nothing was wanting that could possibly be desired. Whilst I went creeping along in the frigate in the track of the Nuncio, I observed a harbour about half a mile in length and a pistol-shot in breadth, so very beautiful that curiosity led me to take the boat and go on shore for the purpose of examining the wonders of the place. In a short time I was surrounded by an immense multitude of men, women, and boys, who had come running down from different places in the mountains to see me; and some of them happening to observe the crucifix which I wore on my breast, they all made a circle round me and kissed it one after another. After this they made signs of the greatest affection and friendship to me, and conducted me almost perforce to one of the nearest huts, where I was seated on a cushion stuffed with feathers; and the mistress of the house, a venerable old dame, sat down beside me along with her daughters, and offered to kiss me, according to the usage of the country; and had I not explained by signs that this would not be becoming in one who bore Christ crucified on his breast, and who, being a priest, accompanied the Nuncio-Apostolic, I am sure they would have been offended. A large quantity of most delicious milk was then brought to me in a wooden vessel by the mistress of the house herself, and she manifested the utmost anxiety that I should drink it. As it was of a most excellent flavour, I drank copiously of it, and was quite revived by the draught. They all endeavoured to stand as close to me as possible, and those who were able to touch me considered themselves happy, so that it was with difficulty I could disengage myself from them in order to return to the frigate; they even determined to escort me to the very water's edge, and some of the young men wished to accompany me altogether. How wonderful it is that in these wild and mountainous places, and among a poor people who are reduced to absolute misery by the devastations of the heretical enemy, I should find, nevertheless, the noble influence of our holy Catholic faith; for there was not one man, woman, or child, however small, who could not repeat the 'Our Father,' the 'Hail Mary,' the 'Creed,' and the commandments of Holy Church.

"My Lord Nuncio, continuing his journey by land, was met by many personages and gentlemen, as well as by numerous detachments of troops; for the Secretary of the Council, who travelled with his Excellency, had despatched messengers to various parts, announcing his arrival. The first night he stopped at the strong castle of Ardtully, and was entertained in a splendid manner by the proprietor of the district. The Nuncio remained there for two days, and then, passing over some very high mountains, he journeyed on towards Macroom, which belongs to Lord Muskerry, one of the chief nobility of the kingdom, being carried in a litter made, as bes he could direct, of planks and cords. On his arrival at that place he was received with all honours by the son of that nobleman, who came out three miles to meet him, accompanied by fifty armed horsemen; nearer the castle a detachment of infantry was drawn up; and farther on was a procession of all the clergy secular and regular, who, preceded by the cross, came to receive the Nuncio; for the last mile he mounted on horseback, and on his arrival was immediately conducted to the church. An immense throng had assembled there, and all fell on their knees to receive his blessing, whilst they at the same time manifested their delight and contentment. From the church his Excellency went to the palace, at the entrance of which he was received by the lady viscountess, in the absence of her husband, who was away at the camp, or perhaps negotiating the peace in Dublin; she prostrated herself, with her children and domestics, and kissed the robe of his Excellency, asking his blessing, which she received with a most marked devotion.

"From Macroom, after four days, we proceeded to Turasengal,* from Turasengal to Colmingh (*Clonmeen*); thence to Kilmallock; and from Kilmallock to Limerick, which is one of the chief cities of the kingdom, situated on the banks of a large river, which is navigable from the western coasts of the kingdom. Everywhere the Nuncio was received with the same demonstrations of affection and courtesy, but in Limerick the Irish resolved to make a grand display of their affection, and I was assured that they could not possibly do more for any prince. Besides detachments of cavalry and infantry, all the gentry of the province came to greet him, and the roads were thronged with immense masses of people who, falling on their knees, with open arms welcomed the arrival of his Excellency and implored the apostolic benediction. The magistrates with the mayor (who governs the city) were assembled at the city gate, where, having received and complimented him, they made way for the clergy, who, in procession, received him under a canopy, and thus conducted him to the cathedral, where he imparted the apostolic blessing.

"The bishop of this city, being eighty-two years old, could not come farther than about half way between the cathedral and the city gate; he was carried in an armchair; prostrating himself before the Nuncio, he could

* This was probably *Dromsacene*, a strong castle on the banks of the Blackwater, about fourteen miles from Macroom, and belonging to the O'Keefe family.

not be prevailed on to rise until he received the apostolic blessing; nay, more, notwithstanding all his years, he had himself carried back by a shorter route to the cathedral, and there presenting the cross to the Nuncio, wished also to offer him the mitre and crosier, saying: *Ab Ecclesia Apostolica hæc recepi, nunc eadem ecclesiæ prompte restituo.* After the usual ceremonies prescribed in the Ritual, his Excellency, as I have said, gave his benediction to the immense multitude that was assembled, whilst I, being authorised by him, announced from the pulpit the indulgence of forty days. The mayor and magistrates and nobility then accompanied him to the house which was prepared as a residence for himself and his attendants.

"It is certainly impossible to describe the manifestations of reverence, affection, and courtesy of all the inhabitants, and their boundless devotion to the Holy Apostolic See; and I solemnly assure you that I often could not restrain my tears in seeing them fall on their knees in the midst of the mire to kiss, or at least touch, the garments of the Nuncio; and when they touched them, they kissed their hands, as if they had touched relics; and when they received the blessing of his Excellency, they returned home with hands upraised to heaven, thus giving us to understand how great was the consolation they experienced.

"For a good part of the road, my Lord Nuncio was accompanied by a large body of cavalry and infantry to protect him from any attack that the Parliamentarian heretical troops might attempt; for they still occupy some strong fortresses* not far from the places through

* These were the head-quarters of Inchiquin.

which we passed; but the all-powerful hand of God was our chief protection, and the heretics never dared to come out from their quarters, fearing that their retreat would be cut off, as indeed would probably have happened.

"Oh! now, indeed, my most illustrious dear sir, your most humble dean,* being at length in Ireland, is joyful and content, especially as my most illustrious master, your brother, escaped so safely and so well from so many dangers. I received as a happy augury what you wrote to me when I was in Paris, and whilst you supposed me to be in Ireland, for which I now render you my most humble thanks, the more so as I know that these auspices were accompanied with your prayers. In a word, we are in Ireland, we are in Ireland! may God be praised!

"The country part through which we passed, though situated in a mountainous district, is agreeable; and being entirely pasture land, is most abundantly stocked with cattle of every kind. Occasionally one meets a long tract of valley, interspersed with groves and woods, which, as they are neither high nor densely planted, partake more of the agreeable than of the gloomy. For seventy miles the country which we met was almost entirely of this character; but having once crossed the mountains we entered upon an immense plain, occasionally diversified with hills and valleys, highly cultivated and enriched with an infinite number of cattle,

---

* This passage sufficiently proves that the writer of the letter was the Dean of Fermo. There are a few mistakes in the Italian text, as printed in the *Dublin Review*, such as Sig. Nunzio for *Sig. mio;* and again, Sigre. for *Padrone*.

especially oxen and sheep; from the latter of which is obtained the very finest of what is known amongst us as *English wool*.

"The men are fine-looking, and of incredible strength; they are stout runners, and bear every sort of hardship with indescribable cheerfulness. They are all devoted to arms, especially now that they are at war. Those who apply themselves to the study of literature are most learned, and such persons are to be found of every profession and in every branch of science.

"The women are remarkably tall and comely, and display a charming union of gracefulness with modesty and devotion. Their manners are marked by extreme simplicity, and they freely mix in conversation everywhere without suspicion or jealousy. Their costume is different from ours, and somewhat resembles the French; they moreover wear a long cloak and profuse locks of hair, and go without any head-dress, contenting themselves with a kind of handkerchief, almost after the Greek fashion, which displays their natural beauty to great advantage. The families are very large; there are some that have as many as thirty children all living, and the number of those who have fifteen to twenty children is immense; and all these children are handsome, tall, and robust, the majority being light-haired, and of clear, white, and red complexion.

"They give most superb entertainments both of flesh and fish, for they have both in the greatest abundance. They are perpetually pledging healths, the usual drink being Spanish wines, French claret, most delicious beer, and most excellent milk. Butter is used on all occasions, and there is no food with which a large quantity of it is not taken. Already we have all accommodated ourselves to the usages of the country (but we give up the language altogether on account of its great difficulty).* There is also plenty of fruit, as apples, pears, plums, artichokes, and all eatables are cheap. A fat ox costs sixteen shillings, a sheep fifteen pence, a pair of capons or fowls, fivepence; eggs a farthing a-piece, and so on for the rest in proportion. You can have a large fish for a penny; and game is so abundant, that they make no account of it at all. Birds may almost be killed with sticks, and especially thrushes, blackbirds, and chaffinches. Both the salt and fresh water fish are most exquisite, and so abundant that for fifteen pence we bought one hundred and fifty pounds of excellent fish, such as pike, salmon, herring, trout, &c., all of exceeding good quality. We got a thousand pilchards and oysters for twenty-five baiocchi (twelve and a-half pence).

" The horses are very plenty, stout, well-built, swift, and cheap; so that for £5 you might buy a nag which in Italy, could not be had for a hundred gold pieces.

" I conclude by repeating that, thanks to God, we are all safe and sound in Ireland, and were it not for the cutaneous disease from which my Lord Nuncio suffers, we would be the happiest people in the whole world. You must, therefore, pray to God for the recovery of his Excellency; for, during the past five

---

* The line in brackets is partially effaced. I have been able with sufficent certainty to trace the words *Per la lingua lasciamola* which are omitted in the printed text. Some of the words which follow, are completely obliterated, the paper itself being corroded away. We merely supply a conjectural sentence.

months, he has continually suffered from it; and now I most reverently kiss your Excellency's hands, &c.

"From Limerick, the 10th November, 1645 (new style)." (The copyist adds*):—

" Die tertia mensis Februarii, 1646,
Fr. Ascanius Malasana scribebat."

---

* The printed copy presents this subscription of the copyist in a most erroneous manner. It is most legibly written as given above.

APPENDIX II.

The Holy See and Ireland.

THE many links that for centuries have united Ireland with the Holy See are familiar to our Irish readers. Even during the persecution of Elizabeth we find our country engaging Rome's special care. Pro-nuncios were despatched to her shores, to guard and defend the interests of the Catholic faith; her children, who rose in arms to assert her rights, received from Rome not only words of encouragement but funds to aid their cause; and when her clergy were persecuted and imprisoned, the Holy Father not only stretched out to them an assisting hand, but by repeated briefs solicited the mediation of foreign princes, that the rigour of the persecution might be relaxed, and the captives be restored to liberty.*

During the period of which we treated in the preceding pages, at the very commencement of the struggle of the Confederates, the saintly Scarampo was sent to encourage them, and guide them by his counsels. Later still, we find the Nuncio Rinuccini sent on a like mission, besides being the bearer of ample subsidies.

---

* Several of these invaluable documents may be seen in the *Spicilegium Ossoriense*, vol. ii.

At every stage of their momentous proceedings, letters were sent from Rome to the French and Spanish monarchs, as well as to the minor princes of Germany and Italy, exhorting them to lend their aid to the Irish nation; whilst other letters were from time to time transmitted to the bishops and the confederate leaders, rejoicing with them in their triumph, condoling in their afflictions, healing their dissensions, and exhorting them to union and constancy in the cause of justice and religion.

It would be easy to give further instances of the solicitude of the Holy See for its faithful children; and to record the many letters of exhortation and encouragement which were addressed to the citizens of Dublin, and others, during their long struggles and sufferings in the cause of religion and their king; but we reserve them for another occasion, not wishing to extend this note to too great a length.

We shall merely state for the present, that, during the interval of Cromwell's triumph, we find the assistance of the Holy See bountifully given to the banished clergy and people; and immediately after the restoration, letters were again addressed to all the Catholic powers, praying them "to commission their respective ambassadors at the English court to defend and protect the interests of the poor Catholics of Ireland, and especially of the priests, who were imprisoned for the faith in many parts of that kingdom."*

* Affinchè vogliano incaricare i loro ambasciadori e ministri nella corte d'Inghilterra di diffendere e proteggere gl'interessi dei poveri Cattolici d'Irlanda, e particolarmente dei sacerdoti carcerati per la féde in diverse parti del regno."—Acts of Sac. Cong., 22 May, 1662.

Thirty years later, when the sword of persecution was again unsheathed against the Irish Catholics, the Pope was still their unflinching advocate. Remittances were yearly sent from Rome to the court of St. Germain for the relief of the Irish exiles, whilst additional aid was bountifully supplied to the banished and persecuted members of the hierarchy. In the Vatican archives we find it registered that 72,000 francs were then annually supplied by Rome for the support of the Irish secular clergy and laity; and on the 15th of July, 1698, we find an additional remittance of 23,655 livres for the religious who were banished from Ireland. Instructions were, moreover, sent to the Nuncios in the foreign courts to give every protection and aid to the Irish Catholics; and even a jubilee was proclaimed in Italy to solicit the prayers and alms of the faithful of that country for our suffering people. In the month of January, 1699, we meet with a list of 27,632 livres received from the Holy Father, and distributed to various Irish ecclesiastics who had lately taken refuge in France and Belgium. In the month of February there is another list of 11,832 livres similarly distributed; and in March, as we learn from a letter of the Nuncio in Paris to Cardinal Spada (dated 9th March, 1699), 58,000 livres were sent by the Pope to St. Germain, and distributed by King James to "the Irish ecclesiastics then sent into exile." There is another list dated from St. Germain, 29th March, 1699, which we give entire. Its details must be peculiarly interesting to our readers :—

"To Mr. Magennis, Superior of the College
  des Lombards 1,200
To do. do. to be distributed amongst the
  Irish Missioners 1,200
To Mr. Nolan, Superior of another Irish Community in Paris for the support of the
  poor students in his community . . 1,000
To Mr. O'Donnell for the Irish nuns in Ipres 1,000
To the almoner of the Queen for the use of
  the community of poor Irish girls at St.
  Germain 500
To Father Nash, an Irish Franciscan, for some
  members of his Order 41
To various other religious 99
To the confessor of the Queen for a young
  ecclesiastical student 150
To Mr. Burke, chaplain to the Queen, for an
  Irish Carmelite 60
Set apart for four missioners coming from Ireland 600
To a poor Irish officer who has a wife and six
  children 150
In all, six thousand scudi."

Again, on the 8th of June, 1699, the secretary of the king, writing from St. Germain, acknowledges the receipt, from the Holy Father, "of 37,500 livres to be distributed amongst his subjects persecuted for their faith."

When, about the middle of the eighteenth century, the enemies of Catholicity had recourse to new arts to assail the time-honoured faith of our nation, and sought to poison the sources of instruction of our Catholic youth, the Holy See was again ready, not only with its exhortations and counsels, but also with its pecuniary aid to support Catholic poor-schools through the country, and from that time to the close of the century, when the Pope was momentarily deprived of his states and driven into exile, 1,000 Roman crowns were annually transmitted to our bishops for that purpose.

Thus were the Roman Pontiffs at every period the fathers of our country, the guardians of our persecuted people, the support of our exiled clergy. "The blessings of faith were transmitted to us by the Popes, not only as the successors of St. Peter, but as sovereigns of Rome; and when an opportunity is given Catholic Ireland of making them some return, it would be strange, indeed, if she did not gratefully remember the services rendered in her hour of distress."*

* Rev. D. M'Carthy's *Collections on Irish Church History*, vol. i., p. 320.

INDEX.

GENERAL PROSCRIPTION OF THE IRISH CATHOLICS BY THE PURITANS.   PAGE.

1. Lord Clarendon and others explain the designs of the Puritans to exterminate the Catholics.—2. Acts of Parliament and Orders of the Lords Justices.—3. Fierce spirit of Puritan Writers.—4. Testimony of various historians.—5. Conduct of Tichbourne, Sir Wm. Cole, Sir Charles Coote, &c.—6. Fate of Sir Simon Harcourt and Sir Charles Coote.—7. Some instances of barbarous cruelty.—8. Dr. John Lynch describes the sufferings of Catholics.—9. Division of this sketch. . 19

Part the First.

PERSECUTION OF THE CATHOLICS IN THE PRINCIPAL DISTRICTS OF IRELAND.

CHAPTER I.
SUFFERINGS OF THE CATHOLICS IN DUBLIN.

1. Proclamation of 1641 prohibiting the Catholic Religion in Dublin; Letter of a Capuchin.—2. Sufferings of Fathers Caghwell and Fitzsimon

and other Jesuits.—3. Doings of Sir Charles Coote.—4. Extracts from Dr. Talbot's Work, "The Politician's Catechism."—5. From Dr. Lynch.—6. Heroism of the Clergy of Dublin.—7. All Catholics banished from Dublin in 1647.—8. The Plague in 1650.—9. Fresh persecutions and constancy of the Catholics in Dublin.—10. Orders repeatedly issued banishing Catholics from the city; number of Catholics according to Dr. Dempsey. 33

CHAPTER II.

SUFFERINGS OF THE CATHOLICS IN CASHEL.

1. Barbarity of Inchiquin at the taking of Cashel.—2. Father Stapleton's death.—3. Of Fr. Barry, O.S.D.—4. Pillage of the Cathedral.—5. Account given by Archdeacon Lynch.—6. Narrative of Fr. Saul, S.J.—7. Sufferings of the citizens in 1654.—8. Most Rev. Thomas Walsh, Archbishop of Cashel. 50

CHAPTER III.

SUFFERINGS OF THE CATHOLICS IN CORK.

1. Cork surrendered to the Puritans: description of the city.—2. Sufferings and constancy of the people.—3. Heroism of the clergy.—4. London pamphlet of 1644.— 5. Lynch's narrative.—6. Colonel Phayre, Governor of Cork.—7. Two devoted bishops. 68

CHAPTER IV.

SUFFERINGS OF THE CATHOLICS IN DROGHEDA.

1. Drogheda remarkable for its piety: besieged in

1642.—2. A price set on the heads of the Irish eaders.—3. The garrison and citizens put to the sword.—4. Massacre in St. Peter's Church.—5. Details of the general massacre.—6. Statement of Froude refuted.—7. Quarter was promised.—8. Hugh O'Reilly and Edmund O'Reilly, Archbishops of Armagh. 80

CHAPTER V.
SUFFERINGS OF THE CATHOLICS IN WEXFORD.

1. Massacre in Wexford in 1649.—2. Several priests and religious killed.—3. Letter of the Bishop, Dr. French, on this massacre.—4. Extracts from his Apology.—5. Massacre of 300 females at the Cross in Wexford.—6. Savage cruelty of George Cooke and Captain Bolton.—7. Sufferings of the Bishop; fate of Cooke.—8. Martyrdom of Rev. Daniel O'Brien, Dean of Ferns, and others. . 98

CHAPTER VI.
SUFFERINGS OF THE CATHOLICS IN KILKENNY.

1. The Mass not to be tolerated.—2. Ravages of the plague; heroism of the Rev. P. Lea, and others.—3. Treason at work: bravery of the Irish soldiers at Callan.—4. The defence of Kilkenny.—5. Barbarity of Axtell and the Puritan troops.—6. The market Cross.—7. David Rothe, Bishop of Ossory.—8. Hardships endured by the clergy.—9. Bernard Fitzpatrick, V.G., John Daton, and others, martyrs.—10. A curious fact.—11. Fr. Fiacre Tobin: all the clergy banished.—12. The decree rigorously enforced.—13. The Catholic citizens driven forth from Kilkenny . . 112

CHAPTER VII.
SUFFERINGS OF THE CATHOLICS IN CLONMEL.

1. First assault on Clonmel, in November, 1649.—2. Cromwell baffled in his attempt to get possession of the town by treachery.—3. Heroism of Hugh O'Neill and the Irish troops during the siege in 1650.—4. The town surrenders on honourable conditions.—5. Cromwell's rage.—6. The citizens plundered; Martyrdom of Fr. Mulcahy.—7. Heroism of Geoffrey Baron.—8. Martyrdom of three Dominican Fathers and others.—9. Hugh O'Neill. 145

CHAPTER VIII.
SUFFERINGS OF THE CATHOLICS IN WATERFORD.

1. Letter of the Bishop of Waterford, Dr. Comerford.—2. Defence of the city against Cromwell.—3. Plague; Ireton occupies the city.—4. Sufferings of the clergy and citizens.—5. Official statements.—6. Fr. Nugent.—7. Patrick Comerford, Bishop of Waterford. 157

CHAPTER IX.
SUFFERINGS OF THE CATHOLICS IN LIMERICK.

1. Ardour of the people of Limerick in the Catholic cause; Letter of the Bishop.—2. Citizens determine not to receive Ormonde; their Letter.—3. Ireton besieges Limerick; is repulsed by Hugh O'Neill.—4. St. Vincent sends Missionaries to Ireland.—5. Their labours in Limerick.—6. Praised by Archbishop of Cashel and Bishop of Limerick.—7. Piety of Limerick.—8. Letter of Dr. O'Dwyer.—9. Limerick taken by Ireton; several put to death.—10. Two facts attested by

Fr. Dominick O'Daly.—11. The articles of surrender violated; Death of the Bishop of Killaloe. —12. Fanning and others put to death.—13. Extracts from the official diary.—14. Execution of Thomas Stritch and Sir Patrick Purcell.— 15. Prophetic words of St. Vincent de Paul.— 16. The Bishop of Limerick.. . . . 171

CHAPTER X.
SUFFERINGS OF THE CATHOLICS IN GALWAY.

1. Clanrickard appointed Lord Deputy; the remedy comes too late.—2. Galway taken after a long siege.—3. Dr. Kirwan, Bishop of Killala's, sufferings in his place of refuge.—4. The enemy enters Galway; military exactions.—5. Plunder of the house of Martin Kirwan.—6. Dr. Kirwan arrested and sent into exile with other ecclesiastics.—7. Calamities that befell the citizens.—8. Extracts from the Annals of Galway.—9. Dr. Fallon, V.G., of Achonry; decree of banishment against the clergy.—10. Violence and brutality of the troops.—11. Some account of the Bishop of Meath and other illustrious sufferers for the Faith. 199

CHAPTER XI.
SUFFERINGS OF THE CATHOLICS DURING THE PLAGUE.

1. The Plague rages in Ireland.—2. Puritans anxious to bring on Famine and Pestilence.—3. Pestilence commences in the West.—4. Heroism of Father Wolf of Limerick.—5. Of Fathers O'Cleary and White in Waterford.—6. Desolation of the Country described by an English Priest-hunter and others.—7. Ireton's Death foretold by Dr. O'Brien, Bishop of Emly. . . . 225

Part the Second.

CHAPTER I.
PENAL LAWS ENACTED AGAINST THE IRISH CATHOLICS—GENERAL STATE OF THE KINGDOM IN 1652.   PAGE

1. Sad State of Ireland in 1652.—2. Its sufferings depicted by a Jesuit Writer.—3. Destruction of Religious Houses; the Franciscans; Testimony of Dominican Chapter.—4. Sufferings of Jesuits and others.—5. Of Nuns.—6. Sufferings of the Irish likened to those of the Jews, or those described by St. Jerome 235

CHAPTER II.
EDICT AGAINST THE CLERGY.

1. Forty Thousand Irish Soldiers leave Ireland.—2. Persecution more violent after their departure: Secular and Regular Clergy Exiled or Condemned to Death.—3. Severity with which this Edict was carried out.—4. Zeal of Clergy: many devote themselves to the mission.—5. Letter of Dr. Burgatt, Archbishop of Cashel.—6. Spies and Informers: the same price on the head of priest and wolf.—7. Several instances of priests in prison and exile.—8. Dr. Lynch's account of the persecutions.   .   .   .   .

CHAPTER III.
OTHER PENAL LAWS.

1.—Confiscation of Catholic Property.—2. Dr. Lynch describes the Cruelty and Perjury of Puritans.—3. Mock Justice of Tribunals.—4. Parliamentary Commissioners in Dublin; Fines on all who do not attend Protestant worship; all children over fourteen years declared the property of the State; any Irishman travelling a mile from his residence liable to be killed.—5. Effects of those persecutions.—6. Degraded strangers occupying Irish soil.—7. Detailed account of Penal Laws by Dr. Lynch; Education Proscribed: Children of Catholics obliged to become Protestants, and to marry Protestants, &c.; thus the Irish nobility destroyed. 268

CHAPTER IV.
PERILS OF THE CLERGY.

1. Heroism of the Clergy of Dublin; *Note.* Many Priests executed.—2. Father Carolan dies of starvation; Father Netterville; Priests carry Holy Sacrament with them.—3. Ludlow's account of Massacre near Castleblaney.—4. Further details of the sufferings of the clergy.—5. Fears that the Irish clergy would become extinct.—6. Edict compelling all Catholics to inform on priests; Number of priests in the country in 1658.—7. Imprisonment in the Islands of Arran and Inisbofin.—8. Father Finaghty. . . 280

CHAPTER V.
TRANSPLANTING TO CONNAUGHT.

1. The cry to Connaught or hell.—2. Lord Clarendon describes this transplanting.—3. Why Connaught was selected.—4. The Commissioners carry out the Transplantation Scheme; exceptions in favour of those who would renounce the Catholic faith.—5. The persecution sanctioned by the Protestant clergy: letter of Peter Talbot.—

6. Other regulations.—7. Particular instances.—8. New trials in Connaught.—9. Catholics obliged to renounce all claim to their former lands; and other severities.—10. Famine and pestilence in Connaught.—11. Seventy stations of Puritan soldiers preying on the natives: constancy of the Catholics. 291

CHAPTER VI.

PURITAN COLONISTS.

1. Ireland confiscated.—2. Protestant settlers from New England; Vaudois from Piedmont.—3. Their character.—4. Manuscript account of the same.—5. Lord Clare's description.—6. Mr. Thomas Wadding.—7. Cambrensis Eversus. . 309

CHAPTER VII.

IRISH EXPORTED AS SLAVES.

1. Irish exported as slaves; Testimony of *Alithinologia*; Sir William Petty and others. *Note:* Rev. J. Grace, in 1666, found 12,000 Irish slaves in Barbadoes, &c.—2. Method of making Irishmen Christians, *i.e.*, selling them as slaves; Cruelty of the Puritans.—3. Slave trade to Barbadoes legalised.—4. Sale of Irish natives.—5. Particular instances.—6. Seizure of Paul Cashin, P.P. of Maryborough, and other priests.—7. Irish children exported; St. Christopher's; Irish there.—8. Dr. James Lynch.—9. Irish treated barbarously, according to Father Grace. *Note:* Letter of Bishops of the province of Tuam to Propaganda.—10. Faith and piety of the Irish during their captivity. 321

CHAPTER VIII.

THE OATH OF ABJURATION.   PAGE

1. Attempt to force Catholics to take the Oath of Abjuration.—2. Form of that oath.—3. Penalties for not taking it.—4. Activity of clergy in opposing oath.—5. Puritans thirsting for confiscation.—6. Noble conduct of Catholics of Cork; all refuse the oath publicly.—7. Other districts equally faithful. 342

CHAPTER IX.

CONSTANCY OF THE IRISH IN THE FAITH.

1. Misery of Ireland in comparison to other countries; progress, education, trade, impeded in Ireland.—2. No penalty could shake the Catholic faith.—3. Prayer and fasting of the people.—4. Only 500,000 Catholics remaining in Ireland.—5. Statistics at various times; Sir William Petty's estimate and Lord Orrery's; Dr. Plunkett's.—6. Extract from Jesuit narrative. . . . 352

CHAPTER X.

DECAY OF THE PURITAN COLONISTS.

1. Protestant colonies never prosper in Ireland; they pillage and seize on the country, but, visited by the hand of God, they fall away; contemporary testimony; faith deeply rooted in Ireland.—2. Diseases and afflictions with which the invaders were scourged. 358

Part the Third.

CHAPTER I.

INDIVIDUAL INSTANCES OF THE PERSECUTION OF CATHOLICS.

1. Sufferings of D. Delany, P.P. of Arklow.— PAGE
2. Various instances of cruelty in the North, in Meath, Wicklow, and Kildare; death of Donnchadh O'Conaigh at Wicklow.—3. Roche MacGeoghegan, Bishop of Kildare.—4. Sufferings and constancy of Peter O'Higgins.—5. Of Albert O'Brien, Bishop of Emly.—6. Death of FF. Bernard and Laurence O'Ferall.—7. Of Thaddeus Moriarty and others.—8. Of A. Cahill.—9. Martyrdom of John O'Cullen.—10. Account of Anselm Ball and his labours in Dublin.—11. Of Bonaventure Carew. 363

CHAPTER II.

INDIVIDUAL INSTANCES OF THE PERSECUTION (*continued*).

1. F. Dowdall's zeal in Dublin; he dies in prison in London.—2. Death of B. Egan, Bishop of Ross.—3. David O'Mollony of Killaloe.—4. J. Lynch and R. Nugent, P.P.'s in Meath.—5. Phelim Mac Tuoll.—6. Labours of J. Forde in promoting education.—7. Zeal of S. Gelosse in promoting religion and education.—8. Death of D. O'Brien. 9. Of Ladies Roche and Fitzpatrick, and Esma Plunkett.—10. Of Mrs. A. Read, described by her son.—11. FF. Brien and Barry, of the Congregation of St. Vincent, and Brother Lee; their sufferings.—12. Death of Fr. O'Higgins, P.P. of Naas.—13. John O'Cullenan, Bishop of Raphoe. 386

CHAPTER III.

INDIVIDUAL CASES OF THE PERSECUTION (*continued*).

1. Hugh M'Mahon executed in London in 1643.—2. Death of Fergall Ward.—3. Of Cornelius O'Brien. —4. Of Christopher Ultan.—5. Of Malachy O'Queely, Archbishop of Tuam, and his chaplain. —6. Of Denis Nelan.—7. Of T. Carighy.—8. Of Felix O'Neill.—9. Of Heber Mac Mahon, Bishop of Clogher.—10. Of Arthur Magennis, Bishop of Down and Connor.—11. Of Connor Mac Guire, Lord of Enniskillen, tried in London and executed in 1644; his piety and attachment to the Catholic Faith; prayers.—12. Letter of A. Nugent, Capuchin. — 13. Richard O'Connell, Bishop of Kerry.—14. F. O'Sullivan. . . 403

CHAPTER IV.

EXAMPLES OF WHOLESALE MASSACRES PERPETRATED BY THE PURITANS.

1. Pamphlet printed in London in 1662 gives details of massacres in several districts.—2. In Antrim. 3. In Derry.—4. At Newry, in Down.—5. In Donegal.—6. In Monaghan.—7. In Cavan.—8. In Meath.—9. In Westmeath.—10. In Louth.— 11. In Dublin.—12. In Kildare.—13. In Wicklow. —14. In Kilkenny.—15. In Tipperary.—16. In Cork.—17. In Waterford.—18-21. In Clare, Galway, Leitrim, and Sligo. . . . 419

CHAPTER V.

THE ACT OF SETTLEMENT.

1. Hopes of the Catholics that Charles II. at the Restoration would remember their merits to his father.—2. These hopes disappointed.—3. Suffer-

ings of Catholics by Act of Settlement, in 1660.
—Lord Clare's description of its injustice.—
5. Claims for property examined in London
where bribery prevailed. — 6. The Lords
Justices: the Black Act.—7. Compensation
to Protestant merchants who had lent money
to carry on war against the king.—8. To Cromwell's soldiers.—9. To his officers.—10. Perfidy
of the men thus rewarded.—11. New persecutions.—12. Dr. Plunkett; Dr. O'Reilly.—14.
Remark of M'Geoghegan. . . . 436

www.ingramcontent.com/pod-product-compliance
Lightning Source LLC
Chambersburg PA
CBHW030321020526
44117CB00030B/321